COMPUTERS IN LITIGATION SUPPORT

Computers in Litigation Support

WILLIAM E. CWIKLO, editor

PBI
a petrocelli
book
new york / princeton

Printed in the United States.
1 2 3 4 5 6 7 8 9 10

Designed by Joan Greenfield

Library of Congress Cataloging in Publication Data
Main entry under title:

Computers in litigation support.

Includes index.
1. Information storage and retrieval systems—Law—United States—Addresses, essays, lectures. 2. Legal research—United States—Data processing—Addresses, essays, lectures. 3. Actions and defenses—United States—Data processing—Addresses, essays, lectures.
I. Cwiklo, William E.
KF242.C637 347'.73'7072 79-13653
ISBN 0-89433-086-1

FOR MY PARENTS

CONTENTS

PREFACE

This collection of articles was gathered out of a personal desire to find and to read all of the important papers which have been published about the use of computers in litigation support. Colleagues frequently mentioned useful articles that they had either read or written, but they were often unsure of when and where the papers were published. A routine bibliographic search in the *Index To Legal Periodicals* produced a long list of potentially interesting citations but it did not describe the depth of treatment nor, of course, provide the text of the article itself. Tracking down the actual articles was both time-consuming and frequently frustrating. During the course of my research, I collected copies of the articles which treated the subject matter credibly. Following many expressions of interest in this collection, I am making it available to the legal community in this book.

Since many of the articles cover a range of topics, it was not possible to organize them by subject area. For this reason, and also because I feel that the articles themselves document the development of the field, they are arranged chronologically by publication date. The first article, "Machine Data Processing Systems for the Trial Lawyer," by Roy N. Freed was published in 1960 in *The Practical Lawyer*. While advances in data processing technology have replaced the data processing tools Mr. Freed discusses, the basic concepts of a systems approach to information processing and its applications to litigation support are as pertinent today as they were 19 years ago.

Although this book brings together the major articles written and published in legal periodicals between 1960 and 1978, it is not meant to be a text on how to design and operate a computerized litigation support system. There are differences in opinion, perspective, and in level of treatment of subject in these articles. Several brief articles, of an introductory nature, have been included because they are useful in explaining the concepts to the uninitiated. A certain amount of redundancy also exists among the articles since they are presented in a complete and unabridged form. To assist the reader in finding discussions of specific topics an index is provided. The topics treated include discussions of the nature of computerized litigation systems, how they work, and what they may cost; criteria for deciding whether or not a system is needed; how to choose a consultant or vendor; the differences between a manual and a computerized litigation support system; and the role of paralegals and nonlawyers in litigation support.

I wish to thank several of my colleagues at Informatics Inc., and elsewhere, for their assistance with this book: First, Robert S. McCormick, for his continued support and encouragement of this project; Jeff D. Emerson and Pat Emerson who were instrumental in bringing this book to publication; Steven E. Rosen, Stephen Gershenson, Patricia Bonner and J. Richard Norton, from whose advice this book has profited; and John D. Rome, a pioneer in the field and co-author of two of the articles contained herein, whose personal interest and infectious enthusiasm were responsible for bringing me into this stimulating and challenging field in the first place. I also wish to thank the authors of the articles selected for putting their thoughts into print, and the publishers of the articles for granting me permission to use their material, in particular, the Section of Science and Technology and the Section of Insurance, Negligence, and Compensation Law of the American Bar Association.

William E. Cwiklo
Arlington, Virginia

INTRODUCTION

It is the purpose of this collection of articles to trace and reflect the origin, evolution, and future of the use of computers in litigation support, and the fascinating new industry that has developed with this application.

The Origin

Litigation support, of course, is as old as the practice of law itself. Classically defined, it refers simply to the process of preparing a case for trial. The techniques and goals are also well known. First, become familiar with the location, content and relevance of every document in the case. Second, do so better than the adversary—and win.

Until the advent of truly large-scale cases, litigation support was accomplished by the lawyer himself diligently perusing the documents and formulating his case. When larger lawsuits became more frequent, litigation support was a phrase known to connote a room full of law students, or even newly admitted lawyers, feverishly annotating 3 x 5 cards. Later, as the computer revolution swept all industries, it was a natural application of the inherent processing speed of computing machinery that the 3 x 5 cards would be "computerized." That word became synonymous with the process of loading all of the contents of the 3 x 5 cards into the computer's memory, and then using information search and retrieval techniques to locate the pertinent documents.

When this technique was first used, it was immediately, utterly and devastatingly effective: causing Clarence Darrow's ploy of reinforcing cigar ashes with a paper clip to pale in comparison. Mr.

Darrow's ash simply held the jury spellbound—causing them to ignore the facts. The computerized advocate forced the opposition to face the facts!

Initially its success was thought of as a fluke or trick. As surely as the initial predictors of computer usage forecasted that "possibly as many as 50 computers might find commerical use in the United States" (this was thought as late as 1949), skeptics in the legal profession regarded the computer as an optional gadget—a luxury which, in any event, would certainly not have an impact upon their practice. The rest is history. Use of electronic data processing techniques is now widespread. Continuing improvements both to computer hardware and software has made this early "courtroom trick" standard operating procedure in today's large or complex case.

The Evolution

The litigation management industry is the result of the convergence of changing political, economic, and social environments, with rapidly developing technology. The trends leading to this development have included: (1) increased government regulation of the private sector, (2) a frenzied pace of mergers, acquisitions and divestitures which have reconfigured the economic landscape, and (3) the phenomenon referred to as the information and paper explosion.

The results in the legal area have been an increase in the number and complexity of lawsuits requiring attorneys to manage huge volumes of documents and information. The parallel technological developments were systems analysis, digital computers, communications networks, and a growing body of theory and practice associated with managing large volumes of records.

The establishment of governmental regulatory agencies such as the Federal Trade Commission, Securities Exchange Commission, and Environmental Protection Agency, among others, has spawned both mass information gathering (based on the requirements for reporting various specifics of business transactions, and their results, both in the marketplace and on the environment) and new types of litigations.

Large-scale data gathering has, in turn, necessitated developments in techniques for handling large volumes of documents and quantities of information. Parallel developments in the military and scientific communities have encouraged the evolution of a systems approach to information handling. Also, the Freedom of Information Act has stimulated the government's contribution to the profusion of information.

As a result of the availability of large (and conveniently accessible) pools of information, new types of complex lawsuits such as those involving employment discrimination and environmental protection first became possible, and then almost commonplace. Class action law has stimulated the number of cases by making it economically feasible for individuals to pursue their legal remedies as a group, where formerly they simply could not afford to do so as individuals. These economic characteristics have increased the number of antitrust and securities actions. The very bigness of everything today has given rise to relatively more frequent Multi-District Litigations.

Two basic tools have evolved to cope with all this data: systems analysis and computer technology. Systems analysis was applied with tremendous success to a number of complex military problems during World War II. After the war, the techniques were applied to a wide variety of problems including how to gather, store, and retrieve large volumes of documents and quantities of information.

Since the mid-1950s, advances in computer technology have put the enormous memory and processing power of these machines within easy reach. Early computers were large, expensive, and limited in their capabilities. These limitations were frequently referred to as "hardware constraints." The first computers were custom-built and wired to perform specific routines or taks. Both the numbers of available machines and qualified personnel were extremely limited. Under these circumstances, whatever the theoretical powers of the early computers, they could not have been of much help in the field of litigation support, where time and cost factors were, and continue to be, critical.

By the early 1970s, this situation had changed dramatically. Advances in the use and character of hardware technology, paralleled by major improvements in computer programs (popularly called "software"), made computerized applications largely independent of the computer. Computers were no longer built to perform specific routines. General applications programs for large-scale document and information retrieval were commercially available from a number of qualified vendors. A large number of sophisticated computers were in general use throughout the country. Advances in communications technology made the power of the computer available nationwide. Whereas early computers could only be used by people in the same room as the computer, by the early 1970s it was possible to access a computer remotely by means of telecommunications networks. Time-sharing techniques allow more than one party to make use of the same computer—at tremendous savings. The combination of increased flexibility of applications, remote accessing, and time-sharing techniques made the large, sophisticated computer into a utility-like resource that was readily available for a variety of uses, at reasonable prices.

The computer is unquestionably a lynchpin in the new science of document and information management. Whereas traditional information systems attempted to physically arrange materials by one preferred parameter (e.g., subject matter), today's new techniques employ similar storage arrangements, but with the significant new benefit of the computer's being used as a tool to index and track the location of specific documents by any element of their content. This, combined with the use of micrographics to store images of documents on films, essentially defines most of the basic components of modern document information retrieval systems.

Although the technological developments in information storage and retrieval were only tangentially related to the problems that were developing in complex litigation, they nevertheless offered certain solutions to them. The possibilities of a systems approach, coupled with digitization of the data, for managing a large document population in a complex lawsuit, were identified as early as 1960 by Roy N. Freed, Esq., in his landmark article "Machine Data Processing Systems for the Trial Lawyer." However, because of the somewhat conservative bias in the legal profession, and real hardware constraints, it was not until a decade later that the theories and techniques proposed by Mr. Freed were used to any great extent. Entrepreneurialism and persistent salesmanship prevailed over resistance to change (facilitated, admittedly, by technology).

The Future

Predicting the future is, at best, an experience conducive to frustration. In the highly technical world of computer science, predictions are even more likely to be wrong. Undaunted, however, the authors will attempt to set forth certain trends which will undoubtedly have a major impact on the evolution of this still-new industry.

By analogy to the almost traumatic changes in, for example, the electronic calculator industry (which witnessed a 90%+ drop in price in less than a decade), it is almost certain that computing hardware considerations will evaporate as any kind of limiting factor: cost, capacity, performance, or otherwise. The other side of the equation, however, just as surely will reflect continuing increases in the costs of labor. The net effect of these two trends will hasten, if not mandate, the use of computerized techniques in legal information management.

The editors also foresee three other important factors giving rise to increased utilization of computers in assisting the practice of law.

First, business records—the stuff of litigation support systems—are increasingly being maintained by clients' computerized data base management systems. Consequently, discovery in the future will more likely consist of retrieving information from opponents' computer systems, rather than from their warehouses. So gathered, the information will naturally be more readily processable by a lawyer's computers rather than his clerks, paralegals or junior associates.

Second, the cost of everything is rising at a rate such as to provoke widespread demands for limits and controls. On the ultimate scale of things, big litigation is economically nonproductive. Corporate executives are not fond of the dent which million dollar legal fees make on the bottom line of their profit and loss statements. Thus, the demand for efficiency will surely contribute to the legal profession's changeover to computer-based techniques.

Third, the era of personalized computing is upon us. People are used to having electronic digital watches. Four-year-old children now announce to their parents that they arose at 8:53—not the "about nine" of similarly aged children only a few years ago. Computers are now becoming commonplace. The personalized computer is finding its way to lawyers' desks, not only for litigation support, but also for word processing, accounting, modelling, estate planning, tax decision analysis, legal research and literally hundreds of other applications. And so go the ramifications of digital technology into the totality of our society.

Finally, increased attorney awareness, through law school courses, pre-law training, industry exposure and other sources, will undoubtedly engender both wider acceptance and use of the computer as an aid to the practice of law. As one noted author in the industry has already observed, "Perhaps lawyers will now confine the use of their adversarial techniques to efforts other than holding forth about advancing technology."

In conclusion, probably all the editors can do to monitor the accuracy of their predictions for the future is simply to promise the release of subsequent editions of this book—possibly more appropriately to chronicle, rather than to forecast, events as they arise.

William E. Cwiklo
John D. Rome

1

Machine Data Processing Systems for the Trial Lawyer

Roy N. Freed

The lawyer who tries a "big case" should observe with envy the rational and efficient manner in which the businessman has harnessed machines for analyzing masses of data. Confronted with a mounting volume of "paper work" incidental to his primary activities, such as manufacturing, selling, or making loans, the businessman has needed little encouragement to replace manual clerical operations with the various types of machine data processing systems available. He does so to minimize labor costs, human errors and operation time and to achieve economies and improve service.

By contrast, the lawyer has failed thus far to utilize in his professional work (as distinguished from office management as such and from statistical analysis of voluminous data) administrative tools from which his business client has benefited economically for many years. The lawyer's lethargy is indeed unfortunate, for it has deprived him of aids to his professional performance and of potential economies.

The lawyer, whose duties predominately concern "paper work," performs many repetitive operations that are ostensibly more amenable to machine management than those of his business client. A significant portion of legal effort entails the accumulation (either directly or through others) of large bodies of information and the searching through those masses for specific items. The two categories of voluminous legal data most readily identified are the vast library of case law and the mountains of trial evidence in certain types of major litigation. Through the law reports, lawyers in all fields constantly search for decisions on particular points. Through each assemblage of evidence, the trial lawyer continuously looks for all facts tending to prove particular contentions. The process of working with such kinds of legal material is, as an administrative technique, one of "data retrieval," or, the location of specific items of information in a mass of stored facts.

CASE MATERIALS

Efforts made thus far to devise a system for performing by machine that aspect of legal research represented by searching the case reports have not materialized. The intriguing prospect of looking up the law merely by pushing buttons, if not achieving the ultimate of writing a brief or a definitive decision in the same manner, will impel continued investigation in this area. However, the technical problems inherent in the subject matter of the law will probably postpone for a substantial time the accomplishment of these wonders. For reasons that will appear below, the primary handicap to harnessing in that fashion the entire body of the law is our inability to establish a universally applicable series of definitions of legal terms, concepts and topic classifications; to find in each decision all of the essential facts; and to agree upon a single, authoritative interpretation of each decision. It is, however, not unreasonable to expect much sooner a less ambitious system of decision searching, such as the simple assembling of superficially relevant authorities in a narrowly circumscribed field of law. Nevertheless, the problem of devising a technique for doing legal research by machines will be left to those who have already devoted considerable effort to it, currently the Electronic Data Retrieval Committee of the American Bar Association, and it will not be considered any further in this article.

EVIDENCE

With respect to trial evidence, however, the utilization of machine data processing is feasible today in major antitrust, patent, tax, minority stockholder, rate, license, and similar litigation before the courts and administrative agencies. Machine management of such data is practical because the volume of information involved is frequently substantial enough to justify the expense, and any system devised would be utilized by a relatively small group of persons who could readily agree on definitions of terms and concepts, factual analyses, and classifications. It would be the acme of legal efficiency to be able to marshall accurately and almost immediately from a trial record comprising thousands of exhibits and pages of testimony all of the evidence supporting particular positions or involving specific witnesses.

A dramatic example of the magnitude of data about which we are talking is the record in *United States v. United Shoe Machinery Corp.*, 110 F. Supp. 295, 299 (D. Mass. 1953). The trial of that case produced a transcript of 14,194 pages, 5,512 exhibits totalling 26,474 pages, about 150,000 card reports of the use by shoe manufacturers of machinery manufactured by others than the defendant (not included in the 5,512 exhibits), at least 6,000 patents, and 47 depositions reported on 2,122 pages of transcript. This is far from an atypical situation.

SCOPE

This article will focus on the function, potential benefits, and mechanics of a data processing system in a single, "gigantic" case. The benefits to be achieved there, although limited primarily to individual law firms and their clients and to legal arms of governmental units rather than to the legal profession as a whole, are significant enough to merit serious consideration. This review will undoubtedly suggest the value of such a system to law offices in other "legal" situations, and ideally might even precipitate the more important ultimate application of researching case law.

THE NATURE OF MACHINE DATA PROCESSING GENERALLY

In general, the use of processing machines for data retrieval represents merely an improvement on traditional administrative procedures rather than a shift in information handling techniques. A data processing system for purposes of this discussion comprises the following basic elements:

A material on which information can be recorded for retention indefinitely

A system of classification in accordance with which the information is recorded

The series of steps by which the recordation is accomplished

The respective machines for recording on such material and for searching through the records selectively

Compared with the familiar West "Key Number" system for uncovering precedents and the current method of organizing trial evidence, the only unique feature of a data processing system, as so defined, is the harnessing of a machine for information searching.

The adoption of data handling machines is probably as significant as the shift from handwriting to the use of a typewriter and is a logical technological progression, facilitating memory to keep pace with our greater ability to create writings and, hence, records. The machines can recall selectively recorded data more accurately and more rapidly than can humans, although presently only within severely circumscribed limits.

Information put in

Information recorded in such a system in any field might be either the entire basic data itself, such as an order for merchandise (including the name and address of the customer, the specific types and quantities of goods, the terms, and the delivery date), or merely an indication of the nature of the basic data, such as a library catalog card subject entry. In determining what data should be recorded, each specific system is a compromise between the ultimate desires of the user and the limitations of the machines.

How information is put in

Data are presently stored in machine processing systems (as defined above) by either of two means, punched holes or magnetized spots. Holes punched in cards according to a prearranged design retain facts either as words and numbers or as symbols for predefined categories of facts or propositions decipherable by reference to a code sheet, or as both. The content entries made are similar to items listed in an index. Punched cards can be "read" from the holes directly, much like Morse code or Braille, or by their operating a printing (typewriting) machine. Some punches simultaneously print along the top margin of the card the letter or number signified by the hole in the column below it (see Figure 2), thus making visual card-reading a simple task. The other means of data recording is by the application of magnetic charges, small in area, in somewhat similar system of arrangement to the surface of such materials as plastic tape or large disks, none of which permits visual translation.

How information is taken out

The stored data are searched by first setting up or instructing the machine to look for and, hence, respond to holes or magnetic charges in particular locations and then passing all of the cards, or the tape or other surface on which records are placed, before the searching portion of the machine. The recorded information matching the search pattern is thereby segregated or selected from the mass by a process of simple physical comparison. This sorting operation is automatic and practically infallible. In sorting punched cards for a combination of subcategories, it may be necessary to do so by successive sorts. Fully electronic machines can sort directly in terms of such a combination.

The mechanical quality of the processing system search demands precision in the feeding of information to it. In retrieving data stored within itself, the human mind can cope, in varying degrees, with many unfamiliar but similar word symbols and concepts by the exercise of judgment based upon experience and reason. The machine, however, has no such facility with new data. It is merely a robot. Deviations from pre-arranged coding either are ignored by a machine or create erroneous responses. Before any information is recorded, a fairly complete plan must be worked out for the ultimate use of the data to be stored. Specifically, the categories or classifications in terms of which the data will be searched ultimately must be established meticulously in advance. The efficiency of a system depends almost exclusively upon the thoroughness with which the classifications in terms of which the data to be searched are set up and defined and the individual items to be recorded are analyzed and classified in accordance therewith.

Although machine data processing systems generally disgorge the requested information by means of a printer (frequently called an "accounting machine") in the form of lists or business forms, the punched card variety has the special advantage of obviating the printing operation where the cards themselves contain all of the desired information in usable form. Being readable visually when printed on as well as punched, such cards are for certain purposes a more convenient source of data than a list. In such cases, reliance on the cards themselves saves operation time and eliminates the expense of acquiring and operating a printing machine.

Illustrations of use

An examination of specific uses of data handling machines in business and other fields will provide clues to their full potential in legal practice. Two examples follow.

A manufacturer places his incoming orders, shipment and inventory records on punched cards and returns the original papers to the files. Thereafter, the cards are the working records which prepare printed production orders to the factory and ultimately shipping and billing papers. At any time, the cards can be sorted to indicate such information as the quantities or dollar value of specific items of merchandise on order or of shipments during a period, the total outstanding orders of a customer, the quantities of specific merchandise available for immediate shipment or sales of particular products. The sorted cards can be used as such or to print automatically the information that is desired.

A publisher continually feeds his subscription records into a fully electronic system that keeps the data current, reflecting expiration dates, extensions and cancellations, and changes of addresses. Periodically the machine prints the mailing labels for the publications. At any time, it will sort out its data to disclose such things as subscriptions expiring in two months or subscribers located in particular areas, and will print the data.

In addition, processing machines are used or are being considered for such purposes as cataloging known chemical compounds and related literature, recording patents issued by the Patent Office, and cataloging library books and recording their current circulation.

For the foreseeable future, the primary value of data processing systems to the lawyer is their ability to absorb large quantities of index-type information (as distinguished from the basic data itself) and to search out from it by categories, accurately and rapidly, references to the locations of the basic data in another file.

THE CONSIDERATIONS FAVORING USE OF A DATA PROCESSING SYSTEM FOR LEGAL EVIDENCE

Since litigation management involves considerable data retrieval, the potential value of assigning the performance of that function to a machine merits especially careful study. Marshalling evidence is a regular operation during litigation, involving a number of extensive searches and innumerable checks for more limited points. Conceivably, all potential evidence is organized first at the very conception of the litigation, as the basis for drafting a complaint. Later, such evidence is assembled for the trial itself to prove the respective pleading or to test the veracity of the witnesses for the opposition by cross-examination. At the close of the case-in-chief, the record as then made is culled broadly to support or attack a motion to dismiss based on failure of proof. Ultimately, the entire record must be analyzed completely for the preparation of proposed findings of fact. In addition, the body of factual data is repeatedly searched for particular items.

The types of major litigation with respect to which this study is directed, namely, antitrust, patent, tax, minority stockholder, rate and license actions, frequently entail administrative elements of such a magnitude that considerations of cost and efficiency compel the investigation of new techniques. They involve prodigious quantities of evidence, both documentary and testimonial. Their preparation and trial extends over many years. (In *United States v. United Shoe Machinery Corp., supra,* the complaint was filed on December 15, 1947, after an extended preliminary preparation by the Government, and the opinion of the court was handed down on February 18, 1953. The hearings took 121 days plus the time devoted to taking depositions. 110 F. Supp. at page 298.) And a veritable army of counsel is required to manage a single case. Such litigation thus earns the label, the "big case."

Because of its sheer bulk, the handling by traditional methods of the evidence in the "big case" suffers from a number of major pitfalls. Reliance upon human memory for the location of particular items of evidence in the preparatory accumulation of data or in the trial record is unsatisfactory. Important items are susceptible of being overlooked. Physical searches through stacks of data are not only very time consuming and costly, but are also subject to the vagaries of human perception and persistence. The inevitable compilation of lists and extensive cross-reference notations are similarly expensive. Finally, it is rare during the course of a large suit that lawyers, in whose minds so much of the essential factual knowledge is retained, do not leave the trial staff. On occasion, the evidence might be so complex that it would be impossible for a new recruit to secure sufficient familiarity with the evidence in a reasonable time to be of any real value. The net result of reliance on usual methods is the simultaneous inflation of litigation costs and depreciation of professional performance.

Advantages of machine system

Consequently, the realities of the "big case" recommend serious consideration of the use of a data processing system. It entails no new steps in the preparation or conduct of the litigation. The establishment of a system of classification of the evidence and the analysis of each item in terms of such classifications are as essential for efficient evidence management without such a system as with one. Although the use of a machine will probably require more thorough classification, such added effort will contribute to better preparation and to a greater likelihood of success.

On the other hand, a data processing system would eliminate costs entailed in the shuffling of papers by professional as well as clerical personnel and would assure the permanent availability of every item of evidence that has been committed to it. It would marshal information by categories with speeds never before imagined by lawyers, a factor especially appreciated during the preparation for cross-examination on short notice. And it would assure a continuity of control over the facts regardless of personnel shifts. It has such additional advantages as the reduction in the volume and, hence, expense of copying items of evidence, and the elimination of the need to maintain overlapping files of documents by subject-matter categories.

Adoption of machine searching of trial evidence in no way sacrifices the remarkable facility of the human mind for uncovering new facets for exploration as the research progresses. The selection from the index of the topics to be examined closely is still a function of the lawyers. They will simply be spared, through the use of the machine, the burdensome task of assembling physically the data relevant to the selected topics. The efficiency of the lawyers will be increased by the delegation of nonprofessional tasks to the new devices.

As will be indicated in the succeeding section, the substantial advantages of a data system are available to the trial lawyer at comparatively nominal expense. However, considerations of sheer cost is not the primary factor for influencing a decision as to its adoption. It is impossible to assign a price tag to enhanced professional competence, an inevitable result.

Although the burdens of a major case would probably influence the adoption of a data processing system because the advantages for that purpose are most dramatic, once established, the system can be used by the law office not only on a number of cases simultaneously, but also for office accounting and statistical analysis as well. The capacity of a system is readily expandible by the addition of machines and operators.

THE MECHANICS OF A DATA PROCESSING SYSTEM FOR LEGAL EVIDENCE

Of the two general types of data processing systems available, the variety based on punched cards exclusively is preferable for handling legal evidence and will, consequently, be the one described in detail. Although electronic data processing systems (which may utilize punched cards as well as magnetic charges) are more versatile, since they operate at very great speeds and search the entire mass of recorded data directly in terms of the most minute combination of sub-categories, they have the dual disadvantages of substantially higher machine acquisition and operation costs and the need to print the information desired (or produce it as a newly created punched card). In addition to less expensive machines and less skilled operators, the punched card approach also uses the handy cards that themselves represent working tools, especially if the recorded data are printed at the top of the cards. Its requirement of occasional multiple or successive sorts to segregate data references common to different categories does not appear to be a serious defect, since at worst the longest sorting time is substantially faster and more accurate than human manipulation.

Procedural checklists

To install and operate a punched card system for trial evidence, the attorney must follow a series of steps outlined in the following checklists and discussed in detail immediately following them:

Adopt a sequential procedure

1. Devise a detailed case strategy.
2. Establish a system for classifying and recording how all items of evidence fit into that strategy.
3. Establish a code system for recording on cards and for searching through them.
4. Prepare an analysis-coding sheet by which the analysis can be signified and conveyed to the card puncher easily.
5. Analyze each item of evidence in terms of the trial strategy data classification.
6. Code the analyzed evidence for recording on punched cards.
7. Digest the item of evidence.
8. Record the analysis data by punching the cards in code.
9. Type the digest of the item on the reverse of its punched card.
10. File the evidence that has been analyzed.
11. File the punched cards.
12. Search through the punched cards.

Select the machines and equipment

1. Select the variety of cards.
2. Secure a card punch.
3. Secure a sorter.
4. Secure equipment in which to file the punched cards.
5. Consider a printing machine.

Assemble the necessary personnel

1. Lawyers to analyze the evidence.
2. Card punch operator to record the data.
3. Sorter operator to search out the data. (In most situations, sorting can be done by a card punch operator or file clerk.)
4. File clerk to handle the punched cards and the evidence.

Since each party has two separate bodies of facts with which to work during a lawsuit, the potential evidence and the trial record, a distinct series of data cards must be set up and maintained for each. The first set of cards will be superseded gradually by the second, as the underlying evidence-to-be either becomes part of the record or is discarded. It might be advisable to use different colored cards for the two sets so that they can be distinguished readily. Hence, creation of data cards is a continuous process that occurs as potential evidence is uncovered, and as evidence is admitted by the court, and that ceases only with the closing of the record. The same procedure, however, governs the making and use of both sets of cards.

PROCEDURE

Classification

After the trial strategy has been devised, in order to decide what information to record on the cards and in what form, it is necessary to determine the various fact categories in terms of which the evidence might be analyzed or organized to carry out that strategy as the litigation progresses. The preparation of a list of such categories is essentially the creation of an index to the evidence for sorting purposes. The bulk of the topics so listed relate to the facts that support the client's case. Although the subjects stem in large measure from the allegations of the party's respective complaint or answer, they will necessarily be much more extensive despite the frequent use of detailed pleading in major litigation.

Because of the importance of the list of subject topics to a data handling system, a sample compilation of fact categories has been created for a fictitious case to illustrate the various approaches. This appears on Figure 1 under the headings "Data Re Industry," "Data Re Defendant," "Extent and Effects of Violation," "Illegal Practices," and "Damages to Plaintiff." Although a workable subject index could be created exclusively of general categories, such as "Refusals to License," "Acquisition of Patents," and "License Negotiations," all of the evidence on any such point might be so voluminous as to require further breakdown. In that case, limiting topics, such as lists of specific products or companies, should be added for finer breakdown of the general groups. It will then be possible, for example, to sort out at least all evidence relating to license negotiations with the "Z" Company and even further limited to plastic molding machinery, if so desired. However, as will be explained, resort to such finer sorting by means of limiting topics may necessitate the use of more than a single basic card for each item. Similarly, where data relating to a particular general point is especially voluminous, the single subtopic should be replaced by two, one for evidence supporting the client's position and another for that negating it.

Record must also be made on the cards of many collateral facts for procedural or tactical purposes. Figure 1 indicates under the headings "Nature of Evidence," "Type of Document," "Data Re Documents and Witnesses," and "Authentication" a few such additional factors. Persons' names are significant to enable the assembling of all papers relating to specific witnesses. Separation by types of documents would be necessary to locate all file memoranda for submission under a "business records" exception to the hearsay rule in the event of an objection to their admission. It might be important to segregate all agreements or patent licenses to which a particular company was a party. The ready identification of unauthenticated documents is essential in all cases.

In selecting the items to be recorded, generosity in quantity and detail contributes to the efficiency of the system. It permits greater flexibility of analysis as the case unfolds and new notions of strategy inevitably evolve, and it minimizes subsequent manual searches of the evidence itself, if it does not avoid them entirely. Determining as it does the effectiveness of the processing system, the selection of the facts to be recorded deserves the most expert and painstaking attention.

Coding

In order to translate the data to be recorded into card punchings, it is necessary to devise a code system. Although professional consultants and representatives of manufacturers of processing machines are available to assist in establishing such codes, an awareness of the elements of the coding process will facilitate the evaluation of the processing system as a tool, as well as any discussions between the lawyer and consultant or machinery salesman on the subject. The lawyer will make a substantial contribution in creating a code, because he will have established the list of topics on which it is based.

Coding, for the purpose of this discussion is essentially the determination of what information will be recorded on the cards as regular words and numbers, and what will be signified as symbols.

ABC CORP. v. XYZ CO.—EVIDENCE COVER SHEET

		NATURE OF EVIDENCE
	1.0	Plaintiff's witness.
	1.1	Defendant's witness.
	1.2	Plaintiff's exhibit admitted.
	1.3	Plaintiff's exhibit excluded.
	1.4	Defendant's exhibit admitted.
	1.5	Defendant's exhibit excluded.
	1.6	Pleading, stip., admiss. or interrog.
	1.7	Plaintiff's deposition.
	1.8	Defendant's deposition.

	2-5.	(For exhibit no., code no. for other item or wit.*-up to 9999.)

		TYPE OF DOCUMENT
	6.0	Letter.
	6.1	Memo to person.
	6.2	Memo to file.
	6.3	Report.
	6.4	Book, pamphlet or press release.
	6.5	Lease.
	6.6	Agreement.
	6.7	License.
	6.8	Chart or table.

DATA RE DOCUMENTS AND WITNESSES

	7-12.	(6)
		(Date of document.)
	13-27.	(15)
		(Author's name or witness' name.)***
	28-32.	(5)
		(Author's company, first party to agrmt., licensor or lessor.)****

		Types of Shoe Machines:
	71.O	Outside rapid lockstitch.
	71.H	Lacing.
	71.I	Rough rounding.
	71.J	Clicking.
	71.K	Eyeletting.
	71.L	Major machines generally.
	71.M	Minor machines generally.

		Types of Shoe Factory Supplies:
	72.A	Nails and tacks.
	72.B	Eyelets.
	72.C	Cements.
	72.D	Lasts.
	72.E	Needles and awls.

		DATA RE DEFENDANT
	73.A	Corporate structure.
	73.B	Subsidiaries, affiliates, etc.
	73.C	Internal lines of authority.
	73.D	Description of plants.
	73.E	Distribution methods.
	73.F	Source of products.**

		EXTENT AND EFFECTS OF VIOLATION
	74.A	Share of the market statistically.**
	74.B	Share of market non-statistically.**
	74.C	Extent of patent coverage.**
	74.D	Non-competitive pricing.**
	74.E	Ability to control supply available.**

	33-41.	(9)

(Author's dept. or other sub-divis.)****

	42-56.	(15)

(Addressee's name.)***

	57-61.	(5)

(Addressee's co., 2nd party to agreement, licensee, or lessee.)****

	62-70.	(9)

(Addressee's department.)****

DATA RE INDUSTRY

	71.A	Description of markets.**
	71.B	Competitors.**

Shoe Manufacturing Processes:

	71.C	Goodyear welts.
	71.D	Cements.
	71.E	Mocassins.
	71.F	Other.

*Witness code number may be omitted if witnesses' names are used in columns 13-27.

**If a specific product is involved, so indicate by also checking that product.

***Two initials and last name.

****Standardized abbreviation.

	75.B	Purch. of compet. mach. for junking.
	75.C	Acquisition of patents.
	75.D	Accumulation of patents by research.
	75.E	Refusal to license patent.**
	75.F	Patent coverage.**
	75.G	Infringement suits or threats.
	76.A	Tying to patent.**
	76.B	Tying to unpatented item.**
	76.C	Compulsory leasing of machines.
	76.D	Long lease term.
	76.E	Return charges in leases.
	76.F	Furnishing service at no extra chg.
	76.G	Belief that use of competitive items will jeopardize service.
	76.H	Fighting machines.
	76.I	Specific exclusion of compet. items.**

DAMAGES TO PLAINTIFF

	77.A	Loss of sales and profits.**
	77.B	Readiness and ability to compete.**
	77.C	Specific addit'l. expenses incurred.
	77.D	Loss from meeting cut prices.

AUTHENTICATION

	78.A	Submitted to defendant.
	78.B	Authenticated by defendant.
	78.C	Authenticity must be proved.

Comments: ____________________

____

Related evidence: ____________________

Figure 1. Blank sample analysis-coding sheet

This step is important because only a limited quantity of information can be entered on a single card of fixed size with standardized punchings. Consequently, the decision between words and symbols represents a compromise between two antithetical goals, the preference for easily readable terms instead of cryptic symbols on the one hand, and maximizing the amount of information per card on the other. Once the choice is made, selection and assignment of symbols, generally considered the very heart of coding, becomes almost automatic because of standard punching practice.

Cards

Although multiple basic cards can be used for each item of evidence, thus achieving an almost unlimited capacity for recording, a single basic card is to be preferred because it is so much easier to handle. If the names of all recipients of copies of documents and participants in reported conferences or meetings are recorded, as they should be, multiple cards will be unavoidable. However, such data can be placed on auxiliary cards that will be searched only for data relating to persons. A similar set of auxiliary cards could be established to record detailed data concerning the experiences of the witnesses, particularly their relationships with the parties, so that the representative qualities of the groups of witnesses produced by the respective parties can be compared for argument to the court.

The volume of data recordable on a card can be characterized as a single line of typing with space for 80 letters. (This is the capacity of the card usable on machinery offered by International Business Machines. The card for Remington-Rand equipment has 90 vertical columns.) The card has 80 vertical columns, each of which has 12 spaces or locations for holes. On the stock cards, 10 of these spaces are numbered "0" through "9," and provision is made for two additional spaces above the numbered section. Under the standard system of punching, it is anticipated that each individual vertical column will be punched to mean either a separate letter of the alphabet or a single digit number from "0" through "9." Figure 2 is an example of a readily available type of punched card with standard printing, in which the punchings have been made for the letters of the alphabet and numerals. Note that the numerals are signified by punching out the number to be recorded. To accommodate 26 letters by the use of only 12 horizontal spaces, multiple punching in the same column is resorted to. Adjoining columns can be grouped for the punching of words or multi-digit numbers. If cards were punched in normal prose, the 80 columns would accommodate about 14 words, including punctuation, a profligate use of precious space. Since words are unnecessarily bulky labels for concepts, the definitions of which can

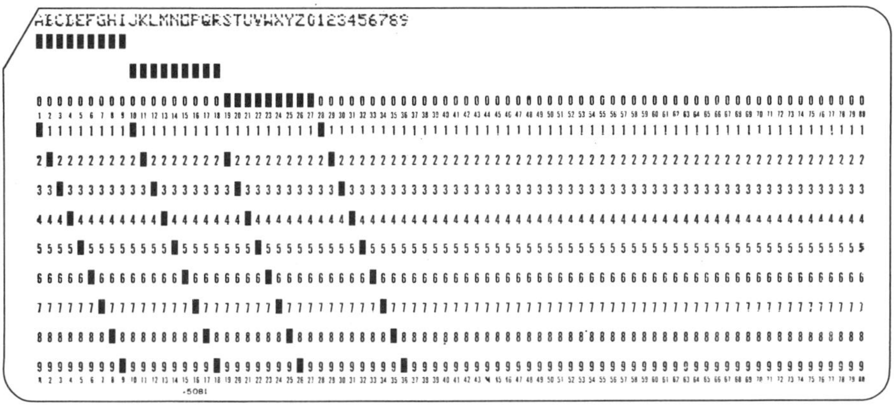

Figure 2. Standard printed card with numerals and letters punched (card size 7⅜ x 3¼)

be agreed upon, their use should be limited to names of persons, and number-letter symbols (e.g., 17.C) should be used primarily. Even names of persons could be assigned numbers, but the probable variety and multiplicity would usually entail such constant reference to a code sheet as to nullify the saving of space. It is recommended that 15 columns be allowed for a person's name. While recording in terms of words consumes at least two adjoining columns for a single fact, by using symbols a single column can provide for any one of as many as 26 sub-topics under a major topic, and a pair of columns allows for any one of a maximum of 676 such sub-items. 676 is the product of two series of the 26 letters of the alphabet each. A double column symbol would be "17.AJ."

In the coding process, the vertical columns of the cards, either individually or in groups of adjoining columns, are assigned to particular general categories of information on the index that has been developed. Each separate column or group so labelled is called a "field." Cards can be purchased specially printed with the titles of the various fields, a step that probably does not merit the effort or expense. All cards in the same series have the same column meanings regardless of the type of evidence covered and of the absence from any item of evidence of information relating to any of the index topics, because the cards are searched as a group and only in terms of the presence or lack of holes in generally assigned locations. As a result, some cards may be substantially perforated while others will have few holes. The omission of punching is as much a record as is the reverse situation.

Once the columns are given meanings, the creation of symbols and their assignment to categories of data entail practically no discretion. As each major category on the index of topics to be recorded symbolically is assigned to a column, it takes that column number as the initial part of its symbol. Then, each subordinate topic receives that column number plus a consecutively higher letter or number as a suffix. Thus, a sub-category symbol would be, for example, "17.C" or "17.3". Figure 1 reveals an extensive system of symbols created in just this fashion. However, since only a single letter or number (and hence sub-topic) may be punched in a column, an effort must be made to avoid the inclusion in any column of multiple sub-topics that might be related to the same item of evidence. To escape such overlapping, the topics of a major category should preferably be divided into a number of columns where necessary. Otherwise, multiple basic cards must be made, as described below.

Analysis-coding sheet

When the details to be recorded by punching and the coding system have been established and committed to paper, an analysis-coding sheet will have been created automatically. Figure 1 is just such a device. It serves the dual purpose of first conveying directions to the card puncher, and later providing a permanent guide to the underlying item of evidence. As the lawyer analyzes a piece of evidence, he signifies its relevance to the case merely be entering check-marks in the boxes to the left of the code symbols for the appropriate sub-topics. He would also write in the proper boxes, preferably with colored pencil, such information as exhibit number, document date or witness' name. This analysis is transposed to a card merely by the operator's punching the items so entered on the form. Thereafter, the sheet should be attached to the face of the item of evidence to which it relates to serve as a ready reminder of the significance of the item. For the most efficient use, the analysis-coding sheet, like the punched card, should be only one page in length.

Evidence analysis and its recordation

Generally, evidence analysis will be a straightforward operation, and only one basic card will be made for each item of evidence. However, if any item contains data relating to two or more limiting index entries that could be punched in the same column, multiple cards must be made up identical in all respects, except for separate punchings on each for each of the conflicting limiting entries and their related basic categories. For example, if a memorandum reports on negotiations with two companies that involve different products, separate cards will record each company and the particular product, but both cards will carry identification of the memorandum and any other facts common to both transactions. Where multiple cards are called for, multiple analysis sheets must be filled out, either completely or by reference, to guide the card puncher. Each such card should bear some written notation to indicate that it is one of a series, as, for example, "1 of 3."

All items of evidentiary nature must be analyzed and recorded on cards. This includes not only documentary exhibits and testimony, but also the pleadings, stipulations, answers to interrogatories, admissions and depositions of all parties.

Being guides through the evidence, the punched cards should contain references to the specific pages of the record transcript or of lengthy documents where the data within the indicated sub-categories are located. However, since it will not be necessary to search the cards to determine the various categories of facts appearing on a particular page of the record or a lengthy document, such page references need not be punched in the cards but may merely be written on them. To this end, the lawyer analyzing the evidence should write the record page on the code sheet next to the checked sub-topic, and a similar page notation should be made by the card puncher on the card, adjoining the punched hole.

To achieve maximum utility from the punched cards and reduce resort to the actual evidence, a digest of each item, made by the lawyer analyzing it, should be typed on the reverse side of the card or at least on the first card if there will be more than one per item. If this is done, page references to the record or lengthy documents might be incorporated in such a digest rather than on the face of the card. The presence of holes in the cards should not interfere with the legibility of such a digest. The card size should be adequate for a brief workable abstract of a document of average size. Since it might be preferable for the digest to appear on the face of the card, consideration might be given to using specially printed cards that will be blank except for the row of column numbers.

Figure 3 is a sample analysis coding sheet marked up to simulate an actual sheet; Figure 4 is a card punched to reflect the entries on the sample sheet; and Figure 5 is a mock digest of the document purportedly so analyzed and recorded. Figure 6 is a segment of an analysis coding sheet with marginal comments on the use of such a form.

Filing

After analysis, the evidence should be filed according to a system that permits ready location of specific items. If a filing system based on other than a purely consecutive numerical, alphabetical or chron-

ABC CORP. v. XYZ CO.—EVIDENCE COVER SHEET

		NATURE OF EVIDENCE
	1.0	Plaintiff's witness.
	1.1	Defendant's witness.
✓	1.2	Plaintiff's exhibit admitted.
	1.3	Plaintiff's exhibit excluded.
	1.4	Defendant's exhibit admitted.
	1.5	Defendant's exhibit excluded.
	1.6	Pleading, stip., admiss. or interrog.
	1.7	Plaintiff's deposition.
	1.8	Defendant's deposition.

	2-5.	(For exhibit no., code no. for other item or wit.*-up to 9999.)

		TYPE OF DOCUMENT
	6.0	Letter.
	6.1	Memo to person.
	6.2	Memo to file.
	6.3	Report.
	6.4	Book, pamphlet or press release.
✓	6.5	Lease.
	6.6	Agreement.
	6.7	License.
	6.8	Chart or table.

DATA RE DOCUMENTS AND WITNESSES

	7-12.	11/20/49	(6)
		(Date of document.)	
	13-27.	L.R. GREENLEY	(15)
		(Author's name or witness' name.)***	
	28-32.	XYZ	(5)
		(Author's company, first party to agrmt., licensor or lessor.)****	

		Types of Shoe Machines:
	71.O	Outside rapid lockstitch.
	71.H	Lacing.
	71.I	Rough rounding.
	71.J	Clicking.
✓	71.K	Eyeletting.
	71.L	Major machines generally.
	71.M	Minor machines generally.

		Types of Shoe Factory Supplies:
	72.A	Nails and tacks.
✓	72.B	Eyelets.
	72.C	Cements.
	72.D	Lasts.
	72.E	Needles and awls.

		DATA RE DEFENDANT
	73.A	Corporate structure.
	73.B	Subsidiaries, affiliates, etc.
	73.C	Internal lines of authority.
	73.D	Description of plants.
	73.E	Distribution methods.
	73.F	Source of products.**

		EXTENT AND EFFECTS OF VIOLATION
	74.A	Share of the market statistically.**
	74.B	Share of market non-statistically.**
	74.C	Extent of patent coverage.**
	74.D	Non-competitive pricing.**
	74.E	Ability to control supply available.**

	33-41.	EYELFT	(9)
		(Author's dept. or other sub-divis.)****	
	42-56.	R. JOHNSON	(15)
		(Addressee's name.)***	
	57-61.	ANDVR	(5)
		(Addressee's co., 2nd party to agreement, licensee, or lessee.)****	
	62-70.	PURCH.	(9)
		(Addressee's department.)****	

DATA RE INDUSTRY

	71.A	Description of markets.**
	71.B	Competitors.**

Shoe Manufacturing Processes:

	71.C	Goodyear welts.
	71.D	Cements.
	71.E	Mocassins.
	71.F	Other.

*Witness code number may be omitted if witnesses' names are used in columns 13-27.

**If a specific product is involved, so indicate by also checking that product.

***Two initials and last name.

****Standardized abbreviation.

	75.A	Acquisition of competitors.**
	75.B	Purch. of compet. mach. for junking.
	75.C	Acquisition of patents.
	75.D	Accumulation of patents by research.
	75.E	Refusal to license patent.**
	75.F	Patent coverage.**
	75.G	Infringement suits or threats.
	76.A	Tying to patent.**
✓	76.B	Tying to unpatented item.** (PG. 5)
	76.C	Compulsory leasing of machines.
	76.D	Long lease term.
	76.E	Return charges in leases.
	76.F	Furnishing service at no extra chg.
	76.G	Belief that use of competitive items will jeopardize service.
	76.H	Fighting machines.
	76.I	Specific exclusion of compet. items.**

DAMAGES TO PLAINTIFF

	77.A	Loss of sales and profits.**
	77.B	Readiness and ability to compete.**
	77.C	Specific addit'l. expenses incurred.
	77.D	Loss from meeting cut prices.

AUTHENTICATION

	78.A	Submitted to defendant.
	78.B	Authenticated by defendant.
	78.C	Authenticity must be proved.

Comments: ____________

Related evidence: ____________

Figure 3 Sample analysis-coding sheet marked up

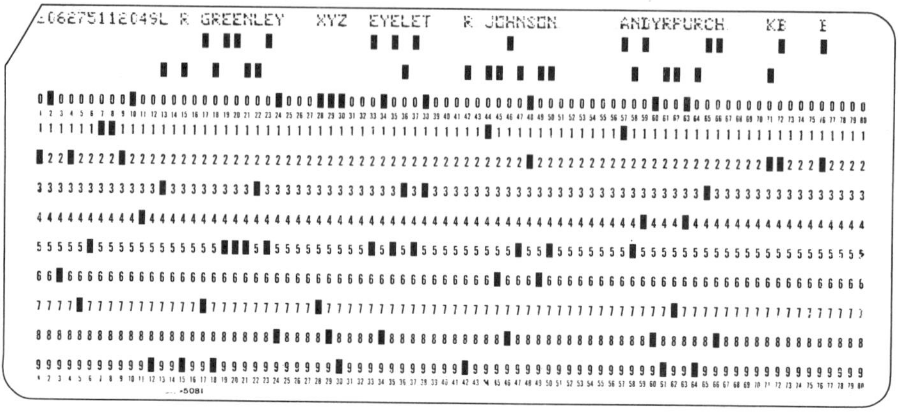

Figure 4. Card punched to reflect Figure 3

PX 627 Adm. Tr 439

Lease, 11/20/49, XYZ Co. (by L. R. Greenley, Mgr., Eyelet Dept.) to Andover Corp. (by R. Johnson, Purch. Dept.)

Leases 4 Eyeletting Machs., Mod. J, for 10-year period commencing 11/15/59, with lessor's option to renew. Requires purchase from XYZ of 70% of eyelets used in machs., at prices specified (Pg. 5).

Note: Cancelled by XYZ 6/30/53. per PX 840, for outside purchs. of eyelets.

Figure 5. Mock digest of document analyzed on Figure 3 and punched on Figure 4, to appear on reverse of Figure 4

ological arrangement is used, the location of each document should be indicated in writing on its punched card.

The punched cards will also be filed in a rational system for ready reference. The set of cards for potential evidence should be segregated from that for evidence submitted in the record. Within each group, cards for witnesses, documents and such other evidentiary sources as stipulations and admissions should probably be filed separately. Cards may be secured in different colors to aid in distinguishing the various types of evidence.

A punched card system has some weaknesses stemming from the use of cards, for which allowances must be made. Since the cards will be used by the lawyers as working tools, their location must be known to the file clerk at all times. The ability to assemble all of the relevant cards for a search is very important, because a search of the

ABC CORP. v. XYZ CO.—EVIDENCE COVER SHEET

1 of 3 — This indicates that other basic cards are used.

CODING SYMBOL
Card Column No. — Sub-Topic No.

NATURE OF EVIDENCE

	1.0	Plaintiff's witness.
	1.1	Defendant's witness.
	1.2	Plaintiff's exhibit admitted.
	1.3	Plaintiff's exhibit excluded.
	1.4	Defendant's exhibit admitted.
	1.5	Defendant's exhibit excluded.
	1.6	Pleading, stip., admiss. or interrog.
	1.7	Plaintiff's deposition.
	1.8	Defendant's deposition.

Various types of data may be number-coded in addition to witnesses, including pleadings, admissions, etc., for example:

Item	No.
Complaint	1
Ans.	2
Stip. 2/17/59	3
Def's Answer to Interrogs.	4

	2-5.	(For exhibit no., code no. for other item or wit.*-up to 9999.)

TYPE OF DOCUMENT

	6.0	Letter.
	6.1	Memo to person.
	6.2	Memo to file.
	6.3	Report.
	6.4	Book, pamphlet or press release.
	6.5	Lease.
	6.6	Agreement.
	6.7	License.
	6.8	Chart or table.

DATA RE DOCUMENTS AND WITNESSES

The lawyer writes in numbers, dates and names.

	7-12.	(6)	(Date of document.)
	13-27.	(15)	(Author's name or witness' name.)***
	28-32.	(5)	(Author's company, first party to agrmt., licensor or lessor.)****
	33-41.	(9)	(Author's dept. or other sub-divis.)****
	42-56.	(15)	(Addressee's name.)***
	57-61.	(5)	(Addressee's co., 2nd party to agreement, licensee, or lessee.)****
	62-70.	(9)	(Addressee's department.)****

These numbers indicate maximum numbers (for date) and letters provided for.

DATA RE INDUSTRY

	71.A	Description of markets.**
	71.B	Competitors.**

Shoe Manufacturing Processes:

	71.C	Goodyear welts.
	71.D	Cements. TR 439
	71.E	Mocassins.
	71.F	Other.

Here write in page of transcript or long document where fact appears.

*Witness code number may be omitted if witnesses' names are used in columns 13-27.
**If a specific product is involved, so indicate by also checking that product.
***Two initials and last name.
****Standardized abbreviation.

These abbreviations will be established separately for each case.

Comments: ________

Related evidence: ________

Figure 6. Segment of blank analysis-coding sheet with marginal comments and suggestions

incomplete file of cards will not indicate the fact of its incompleteness and will run the risk that important data will be overlooked. This deficiency with respect to punched cards is no greater than where the documents themselves are used directly. Since data records are not removed from a system utilizing magnetic charges, that approach substitutes security of the files for the flexibility of punched cards as working tools. Another, but less inconvenient precaution is the need to protect the condition of the cards. They should not be folded or torn lest they not flow through the sorting machine accurately. However, damaged cards can be duplicated easily. Being made of paper, cards tend to absorb moisture and become limp, thus reducing the efficiency of the sorting machines. Consequently, cards give best service in an air conditioned environment. Where they will be stored for any extended period, cards tend to stick together because of moisture absorption. To minimize this problem, specially treated cards with sealed edges should be used.

MACHINES AND EQUIPMENT

Selection of machines and equipment would be determined primarily by the choice of the type and size of cards to be used.

Cards

The offerings of the various card system machinery manufacturers should be compared to locate the type of card that seems to be the most workable device for the particular team of attorneys. In making that choice, such factors as special printing and multiple colors should also be considered. Cards are available from specialized manufacturers as well as from the machinery producers. Running about $1.25 per 1000 with standard printing, card cost is nominal. Once a particular size and style of card has been adopted, machinery of the type designed for that card must be acquired.

Punches

The card punches are key-board type machines about the size of a secretary's desk. They can be acquired by purchase or by lease at a monthly rental of approximately $60 each. It is recommended that punches be selected which simultaneously print the recorded data along the top edge of the card. Such printing makes the cards substantially more useful as working tools. A person with reasonable manual dexterity can become proficient on such machines in about a week, and typists and secretaries on the staff of a law firm are ideal candidates. The punch key board contains only letters and numbers, and the machine automatically punches the equivalent hole or holes in the standard locations within the vertical columns, moving progressively from column to column, from left to right. A punch, like a typewriter, can be used for any case without any special adjustment or adaptation.

Although it may be difficult to determine at the outset how many card punches will be required, the ready availability of machines should obviate any problem. Starting with one machine, others can be added as required. Since on the average an operator can punch 100 cards an hour, the punching operation will be considerably faster than document analysis. Consequently, one operator will be able to handle the work product of a number of lawyers.

Verifiers

Machines for verifying the punchings on the cards are available, but will not be required so long as the punch operators are reasonably careful. Verification is more essential where the cards are used for preparing bills, writing checks and the like. In legal work on trial evidence, the expense for that operation could not be justified.

Sorter

Probably only one sorting machine will be required. Various models are available, the least efficient handling about 250 cards a minute and the fastest, 2,000 a minute. Such rates do not indicate the real speeds with which ultimate sorts are accomplished, because segregating cards related to sub-classes of different major topics requires multiple runs through the machine. A sorter can be leased for as little as $40 a month.

Files

Punched cards are usually filed in shallow trays. Cabinets for such trays might be either large "tubs" on legs at either sitting or standing height, or more familiar and more compact file cabinets with pull-out drawers. Considerations as to available floor space will probably influence the ultimate selection. Although the tubs provide freer access to the cards, they cover a considerable area. A stack of 2,000 cards is 11 inches high.

Printer

The so-called accounting machine for printing on large sheets the data recorded on the cards is probably a sheer luxury for the trial lawyer. Its primary, if not sole, function for him would be the preparation of lists of items of evidence falling within the various categories. Although it would accomplish this substantially more rapidly and accurately than could be done manually from either the cards or the evidence itself, the expense of acquiring such a machine would not be warranted for the sole purpose of printing lists. If an occasional list or mathematical calculation is required, time for that purpose can be rented at reasonable cost from one of the many concerns possessing such machines. However, a law firm, that had such a machine for accounting purposes, could utilize it readily for listing items of evidence.

Use

Obviously, it is more economical to use the machines as intensively as possible up to their full capacity. They can and should be used on more than one case contemporaneously, thus reducing the cost of operating them attributable to any single case and client. The machines can also be used for office bookkeeping, thus achieving greater economy of investment. This is the classic technique of spreading the overhead costs. Being standard machines, this method of utilization is entirely feasible. Only the respective sets of cards have any relationship to specific cases.

PERSONNEL

Lawyers

The lawyers assigned to analyzing the evidence for card punching should be fully aware of the capabilities and limitations of machine data processing. They must take the initiative to adjust their normal methods and to alter the system itself to avoid deficiencies of the method and achieve its full potential. The more complete knowledge they have of the elements of the case, the trial strategy and the evidence available, the more efficient will be their job of creating a valuable file of evidence.

Punch operators

Card punch operators will very likely devote only part of their time to that operation for extended periods. Hence, they should be qualified to perform other functions such as typing, sorting or filing. Their salaries are about the same as those of well-qualified secretaries. Existing office personnel could be readily trained to operate such machines.

Sorters

The only skill required for operating a sorter is the ability to set up the sorting panel by setting buttons. This could be readily acquired by a person with an absolute modicum of mechanical aptitude. Cards are fed to it merely by being placed in stacks in a well and are received from it in similar stacks. During most of the operating time, no attention is required.

File clerks

Filing of punched cards entails no more and probably substantially less skill than other types of filing. Practically no discretion is entailed in determining where to place the cards.

COST CONSIDERATIONS

Considering the relatively low cost of the essential machines, the small specialized staff required to operate them, all of whom could perform other secretarial duties when not needed on the machines, and the elimination of many expenses involved in current manual evidence handling, any net additional cost in using a data processing system would be nominal. It is even a fair likelihood that an actual saving would result.

A DATA PROCESSING SYSTEM MAY EXPEDITE TRIAL OF THE "BIG CASE"

Data processing systems may provide an opportunity for expediting the trial of the notorious "big case" that has been clogging the dockets of many federal district courts and regulatory agencies in recent years. One contribution would be the reduction of the time required by counsel to try their cases by facilitating behind-the-scenes preparation, a major cause of delay. Equally significantly, it might also present an opportunity to reduce the burden on the court or hearing examiner and the time required by them to analyze the evidence and arrive at a decision. The judicial burden in this regard is an immense one. While opposing counsel generally have teams of lawyers and various auxiliary personnel at their disposal, the court is fortunate if it has an experienced law clerk to aid it, and the trial examiner generally has no assistance whatsoever. Any help provided in that direction would be most welcome by the bar as well as by the courts and other tribunals.

Pursuing a suggestion that counsel provide the court with a bare index to the evidence [*Current Indexing of the Record,* Report of Committee on Antitrust Procedure of Section on Antitrust Law of New York State Bar Association, 13 F.R.D. 85 (1952)], a standard set of cards could be prepared for all counsel and the tribunal. These cards would at least identify each witness or exhibit without more. From such a complete set of punched cards, the tribunal could achieve the same advantage of ease of record analysis as would the litigants, thus permitting a prompter decision. If an index system devoid of suggestions of trial strategy could be agreed upon between counsel and the tribunal, each item could be classified in accordance with it on the basic cards distributed among them, and such cards would be more helpful to the tribunal.

Possessing a series of punched cards for all of the evidence, assuming that the necessary card punch and sorter and their operators would also be provided, the trier could put on the cards, as the evidence is introduced, his observations on its respective significance. Of course, this would have to be done pursuant to the same orderly system as described in this article. However, the court could easily adopt as its classification of the evidence the issues as developed in pretrial conferences.

CONCLUSION

The "big case" in the fields of antitrust, tax, patent, minority stockholder, rate, and license suits seems to possess the ideal ingredients for the efficient use of machines for processing the voluminous accumulations of evidence. Greater professional competence will result from the speed and accuracy with which the evidence can be analyzed and assembled categorically. Cost economies can be passed on to the clients, thus minimizing a chronic source of dissatisfaction with resort to litigation.

Benefits of considerably broader significance might be achieved if such a system could be utilized simultaneously by the tribunals upon whom the greatest burden falls in major litigations. Experience gained with such a system in the relatively limited area of litigation evidence might remove the barriers to adopting it for legal research in the case reports.

The enterprising lawyer should explore without further delay the possibility of harnessing for his assistance some of the technological wizardry of our exciting era.

2

General Introduction to Systems Support for Lawyers*

F. Sherwood Lewis

This morning we will talk about litigation support systems for lawyers. This topic is a limited slice of the spectrum of support systems available to the bar. It is not a new one—Roy Freed wrote about litigation support systems as early as 1960[1]—but, to the best of our knowledge, this is the first public discussion of the decision and design process lawyers and systems people must go through in order to create a workable support system.

As general background, let us review some of the major elements of automated support systems for lawyers. While the audience probably has general familiarity with these broad categories, the contrast between these systems and that which we will discuss serves nicely as an introduction.

First, law office and law department administrative systems—computer-based time records, disbursements, client control and the like—are generically automated support systems but not what we have in mind today.

Legislative support systems are coming into vogue. These are of two categories—the vote totalizers and the legislative systems capable of text handling. Vote totalizers are such as in the U.S. House of Representatives and the Minnesota legislature. Legislative systems

*Editor's note: Articles 2 through 7 of this book were published together as papers presented at a joint meeting of the Computer Law Association, and the Standing Committee on Law and Technology of the American Bar Association at the ABA's 1973 annual meeting.

[1]Freed, Roy, "Machine Data Processing Systems for the Trial Lawyer," *The Practical Lawyer*, April 1960.

include projects like LIS, the state of Washington's system for text processing and retrieval, as well as housekeeping, and the Mississippi legislative system, which eventually produces printed text.

There are law enforcement systems available to support criminal prosecutors. To the best of our knowledge, none of these systems are being used as litigation support systems. We will be discussing civil litigation, although I personally believe some of these techniques are applicable to specific criminal proceedings.

Finally, there are the retrieval systems which we classify as legal research systems. Generally, these are full-text systems, designed to retrieve, on a key-word basis, statutory and decision material. Some examples are:

LITE—Legal Information Thru Electronics run by the United States Air Force

QUIC/LAW—Queen's University in Ontario

OBAR—Ohio Bar Automated Research System operated by Mead Data Central which has expanded the system into LEXIS, now under contract to several other state bar associations[2]

While different in approach from litigation systems, these retrieval systems form a basis for understanding what will be described. It may be helpful to focus on similarities and differences initially so that you will have an idea of some particular points to note as the description unfolds.

You will hear much about coding and coded-text systems. We are coded systems advocates; the reasons why will become more apparent as the morning progresses.

It would be possible, and perhaps sometimes desirable, to use a full-text system for discovery and trial support; however, full-text systems are more easily fitted to uniform bodies of text, such as statutory or decisional material. This material is at least uniformly organized in format and as to source. The occurrence of key-words, which the computer can pick out once the full text is loaded, is the fundamental basis of selection.

When faced with a multiplicity of textual forms and contents, codes must be considered. That "conclusion" has been arrived at by the panel in a most empirical fashion, but it is well worth remembering. A coded system is designed to illuminate passages and identify sources. Consider, if you will, the proposition that the more heterogeneous the matter to be assimilated, the more unwieldy it is to use

[2]Many existing legal support systems, especially the research systems, are explained in detail in the 1973 publication *Automated Law Research*, published by the ABA's Standing Committee on Law and Technology, which I recommend to those of you looking for an excellent sampler.

full-text methods. One difference between a coded system and a full-text system is that in the former not all the text is reduced into the system. Also, in the coded system there is discretion in the application of the codes; this bears on what is captured and what is rejected. The amount of material confronting the system also bears heavily on the choice of full text versus coded systems. Sheer numbers may force the use of a coded approach because of data reduction and storage limitations.

This will be a narrative of the trials and tribulations of putting together litigation support systems. They are somewhat specialized, albeit capable of generalization. The basic system is surprisingly simple, although quite flexible. It depends heavily on people—we consider people a primary system component—and human engineering. The data processing system, while indispensable because of the dimensions of the problem undertaken, takes a secondary role, especially in the early stages. There are threshold considerations, time, money and client persistence, for which only your client can set limits. We believe the basic ideas set forth here are applicable to defendants' cases as well as plaintiffs'.

3

Lawyers' Considerations and Requirements for Systems Support during Discovery

Leon R. Goodrich

My purpose this morning is to outline some of the considerations involved in deciding whether to use systems support during the course of representing a client in bringing or defending a lawsuit. At the outset I want to disclaim any high degree of sophisticated technical understanding of how to program computers, how they function from a technical standpoint or how to maintain data files. Rather, my viewpoint will be simply from the standpoint of a lawyer trying to get a job done. The question from this viewpoint is: "Can systems support be used to do the job better than if one had no systems support?"

What do we mean by systems support? Simply the use of computers to assist in handling evidence or other records, which we might refer to as "data," relevant to the lawsuit on which one is working. The issue, then, is under what circumstances should computers be considered as an alternative superior to the time honored and proven method of doing it all "by hand."

WHEN IS SYSTEMS SUPPORT DESIRABLE?

The most obvious reason that the use of the computer should be considered is the quantity of evidence or potential evidence likely to be involved. Will there be large quantities of documents from either the plaintiff's or defendant's files, or both, which must be analyzed as potential evidence, those analyses retained and relocated in preparation for actually going to trial? Is it anticipated that there will be a large number of depositions which must be taken and analyzed?

How many documents or depositions constitute a large quantity? Subsequent speakers will qualify this for you a little more. From the lawyer's standpoint, whenever you find yourself spending a lot of time searching for or trying to locate information of which you were previously aware, you have a signal that you should consider using systems support. For example, is it taking a lot of time to find in whose deposition and at what page certain statements were made? Or to find a particular document that you previously located in a witness's file?

Of course, a good litigator always keeps some hand-prepared record during the course of discovery which enables him to find or return to particular documents or deposition testimony that is likely to be used as evidence at trial. However, there comes a point when the evidence becomes so massive in terms of quantity that it becomes very laborious, if not impossible, to keep handwritten records; at this point potentially relevant evidence may be lost or forgotten. And it is disquieting, as the massive evidence accumulates, if you know your opponent is using a computer to keep track of and relocate evidence, while you rely simply on handwritten notes and memory.

TYPES OF CASES

An obvious type of case where computers or systems support should be considered is securities fraud and Section 10(B) 5 cases. Another obvious type of case is antitrust, and the June 11, 1973 issue of *EDP Weekly* reported that the Senate Select Committee investigating Watergate had begun computerizing its files of names, places and events associated with the case in order to expedite retrieval of the information by members of the committee and its staff.

When you anticipate a large number of related cases, such as in patent or product liability litigation, systems support may be helpful in keeping track not only of the evidence in a particular case, but of what is happening in each case and how they relate to each other.

OBTAINING SYSTEMS SUPPORT

If you suspect you have a case which would benefit from systems support, when should you investigate the availability of it and decide whether to get it? As early as possible—even before filing if you are the plaintiff. An early decision allows maximum time to develop the system, and availability of systems support will heavily influence the procedures you follow during discovery.

Once you decide to utilize systems support, how do you design a system or modify an existing system to fit your needs? Your first task is to select a computer professional to assist you and to describe your needs to him in terms he can understand. He will then be able to determine the nature of the computer system necessary to meet those needs and the software or programs required. Now you face a first class legal challenge; how successfully you meet it will largely determine whether the systems support which you select is, in fact, of assistance to you. The challenge is to forecast how you will wish to use the system throughout discovery, and, indeed, throughout trial of the case.

The primary purpose of the system is to store and relocate later potential evidence items for the lawyer. Thus, during the design period, he must forecast what will be the issues in the case and, in light of those issues, how he will wish to access the evidence which the computer is going to help him keep track of. The lawyer must also forecast procedurally how the case will develop and anticipate his usage of systems support during each procedural phase of discovery.

What the lawyer must do is to "walk through" the various stages of discovery activity and forecast the needs which will arise. Prefiling activities, document discovery, interrogatories and depositions all pose unique data handling problems that can be anticipated. These stages provide the framework within which the system designer operates.

PREFILING ACTIVITIES

If you are a far-sighted plaintiff you may choose to implement your system during the prefiling investigation, i.e., before you file the complaint. You may wish to enter into the system documents from your client's files relating to the subject matter of the lawsuit and summaries of interviews with the client's officers and employees. Even if essentially all of the information available to your client prior to suit is hearsay and not usable as evidence, there may be advantages in placing such information in the computer for retrieval. In evaluating the claims of your client and formulating a final opinion on whether to bring suit, you may wish to use the computer retrieval capabilities for locating and arranging particular subject matter within this information. You may also wish to be able to access this prefiling information to locate specific data, such as lists of customers, that are useful in preparing draft document demands or perhaps even draft interrogatories to serve on the defendant.

In addition to these trial-oriented considerations, early use of the system helps you to become familiar with the system and in locating and correcting deficiencies in design and operation.

DOCUMENT DISCOVERY

Turning to the various phases of discovery first from the standpoint of "offense," that is, discovery of the other party, how can a system help you? If you have decided to use a computer to keep track of the evidence, you have probably concluded that a substantial amount of that evidence will be copies of documents you find from the other party's files. The computer clearly can help you keep track of and relocate the documents you have copied.

You are faced with some real problems of timing and quantity which should be anticipated when you design your support system. The other party might attempt to deluge you with large quantities of documents; you will want to have defined clearly the selection criteria to be used in screening and copying these documents. If, nevertheless, you find yourself copying massive amounts of material, you may want to establish a second set of criteria to enable you to assign priorities for the entry of those documents into the system. For example, when copying documents from the opposing party's files, you might classify them into two categories—those of prime importance and those of lesser importance. If you build into your computer retrieval system a capability of retrieving separately on these two categories, you can retrieve only the most important documents.

There are several reasons why you might want as quickly as possible, during or after document production, the capacity to retrieve at least the documents which you have identified as important. You may need to review the information you have accumulated to date on particular subjects, to see if you need additional discovery relating to those subjects, or you may need such immediate access for purposes of supporting a motion for summary judgment or the like.

INTERROGATORIES

The plaintiff can expect, probably soon after his suit is filed, to be served with a massive set of interrogatories inquiring, perhaps in incredible detail, into every feature of his complaint. In an antitrust case, for example, if you complain that the defendant has engaged in price discrimination in violation of the Robinson-Patman Act, you will be asked to list each such instance, giving the name of the customer, the product involved and date or dates of the sale and any other details that defendant's counsel can think of. If you have made a prefiling investigation, answers to many such questions are in the documents and client interviews you have accumulated. If these documents can be accessed by customer name, your task in relocating the pertinent information and answering the interrogatories should be much easier. Indeed, if the printouts resulting from retrievals on your data file are intelligible without special translation, and if you have recorded sufficient information for retrieval, you may find that you can furnish to your opponent the printouts themselves as answers or partial answers to his interrogatories. A defendant may be served with a similar massive set of interrogatories, requiring review of a substantial number of his client's documents and interviews with many of his client's personnel. Because his implementation of any support system may not have progressed very far, he may find it less feasible to make use of any computerized data file. However, after review of large quantities of data for the purpose of answering interrogatories, he may determine that it is necessary to keep track of such data for future reference, and at that point introduce it into a computerized data file.

If it is necessary for either party to update answers to interrogatories, after there has been a substantial amount of discovery, similar use can be made of a computerized data file—if, but only if, the party has kept reasonably current in adding newly discovered evidence to the data file.

DEPOSITION

How can a data base or computerized data file help in taking depositions? Suppose the other party has fifteen reasonably top level officers and employees whose files you have reviewed and you now wish to depose. Assume further that in their files you found a number of documents relevant to your case upon which these officers and employees should be examined. How do you find those documents again?

If a small number of documents is involved you may have been able to set them aside by hand when you initially made your file review. Assume, however, that for each executive you reviewed two and one-half four-drawer file cabinets full of documents and copied only ten percent of what was produced. For each executive you would then have copied approximately 1,000 documents, or a total of 15,000 documents for all of the executives. You might say that preparation for a deposition of any one executive is not such a difficult task. In a few days you could go through the thousand documents by hand that came from his files and select a much smaller number which you wished to use in deposing him.

But is it 1,000 documents or 15,000 documents you should review as potentially useful for your deposition? You are particularly interested in documents your deponent sent to any of the other fourteen officers or employees, whether or not he kept copies in his files. You are also interested in documents in other people's files that simply mention your deponent, whether or not he received a copy of the documents. If you have entered into a data file the fact that your deponent's name appears in a particular document, and this fact was determined for each of the 15,000 documents which you copied, you can readily locate all documents in which his name appears—in whatever capacity.

You can get more sophisticated information. The computerized retrieval capability can be used to keep track of what has happened to date on depositions you have taken. For example, you may wish to code for later retrieval statements made on prior depositions on a particular subject, so that you can locate such statements to help you prepare for future depositions. You may also wish to keep track of such information on a document by document basis; you can then discover by subsequent search whether a particular document has been used on previous depositions, and, if so, what the previous deponents said about the document.

DEFENSIVE USES

Thus far we have talked about using systems support primarily as an aid to "offensive" aspects of discovery; that is, essentially, the use of evidence made available by the other party to either prove your case, if you are the plaintiff, or defeat the claims made by the plaintiff if you are the defendant. There is, of course, another phase of discovery for each party—"defensive" activities.

Suppose the other party has copied many documents from your client's files for use in taking depositions of your client's officers and employees. One of the less enjoyable tasks in the practice of law is sitting as the defending lawyer while the other party's lawyer interrogates your client. Even less pleasant is preparing for this experience. Therefore, unless the preparation is offered to the defending lawyer on a platter, he may well not take all the steps that would be desirable to prepare himself and his witness.

Going back to the previous example, if the defending lawyer is very diligent, he may review the 1,000 documents which he knows were copied from the prospective deponent's files by the opposing party. However, it is hard to believe that in his preparation he would take the extra step and review the remaining 14,000 documents that were copied from files of other officers and employees of his client. But if these documents had been entered into a data base, you could then request a retrieval for all documents in which the prospective deponent's name is mentioned in any way. The computer would check all 15,000 documents and you likely would be presented with only a small fraction as involving your witness.

From a defensive standpoint, certain "housekeeping" functions should also be considered. If your opponent has demanded that you produce all documents on a particular subject or all documents from a particular individual's files, what records do you maintain to prove that your document production has, in fact, satisfied your opponent's demand? Systems support can help in maintaining and creating such records.

DIFFICULTIES IN DESIGNING AND USING SYSTEMS SUPPORT

We have reviewed the possible uses of systems support in connection with the prefiling, interrogatory, document production and deposition phases of discovery in terms of offensive, defensive and housekeeping needs. What are some of the limitations and problems involved in designing and utilizing systems support in litigation?

First, where do you obtain systems support and information concerning what that support can do for you? Do not assume that it is possible, at present, to go to a computer or data processing firm and find an immediately available system that will exactly meet your needs and that can be purchased and plugged in, up and running the next day. Any available system is going to have to be modified to some extent to fit your particular case. You may find you have to start at the beginning and design a system from scratch because no previous system can be adapted to your needs.

Second, what is the most effective role for a lawyer during the period of systems design? It is a temptation for the lawyer to try to become a systems "buff"—to try to know almost as much about the system as the computer programmer or other expert who will be designing or implementing the system. This temptation should be rejected. The lawyer can't do it, and it may result in the lawyer's spending a lot of time worrying about problems that don't exist and that he can't solve, while he overlooks those problems that he can solve.

The lawyer should spend a lot more time worrying about whether he has imagined every subject or topic that is relevant to his case and by which he wishes to organize the evidence, and whether he has successfully communicated this to the systems designer. This is exclusively the lawyer's province; the systems designer is totally dependent on the lawyer for this. A computerized data file will only be as good as the foresight of the lawyer who specifies his needs and participates in designing it. If the lawyer fails to foresee substantive or procedural subjects by which he wishes to access the data entered on his system, the system will fail to meet his needs.

At the same time the lawyer should not be dazzled by descriptions of what the system will do for him. He should give equal, perhaps even greater, attention to obtaining a very complete understanding of what the system will *not* do for him. In this context, there is no such thing as overattention to detail. A lawyer may be more accustomed to thinking in terms of the "big picture" of the case; however, when it comes to understanding the limitations of any computer system in which he is investing, he should put on his nit-picker's detail hat.

Among the limitations he should keep in mind is system capacity. If the system is only able to contain and retrieve on 10,000 documents or document records, and it ultimately develops that at least 100,000 must be entered as containing potentially relevant evidence, the system needs have been poorly defined.

The lawyer also should understand and see in sample form the format of the printouts from the support system with which he will be working. The printouts should be readily readable and understandable.

It is also important for the lawyer to understand the limitations of the computer system in terms of accuracy. The output is only as accurate as the input. If you are classifying documents by subject matter, for example, and wish to be able to use the computer to retrieve or list all documents on a particular subject, the retrieval will only be as accurate as the subject matter classifications and their application to the documents. The computer will not improve upon the classifications made by the lawyer or his assistant; it simply tells the lawyer how he classified the document. If the document has information on a particular subject that went unnoticed when a coded record relating to the document was input into the computer, the information has, for all practical purposes, been lost.

Computers do not replace people. While computers may be a replacement under some circumstances for some tasks lawyers would otherwise have to do by hand, it takes people, many of whom must be highly trained, to get information into the computer and to get it out of the computer. In deciding whether or not to use systems support during discovery, a lawyer must evaluate how many such people will be required, where they can be obtained, how long it will take to train them, how long it will take them to do whatever jobs the lawyer wants them to do and how expensive they will be. In terms of expense, the people expense in using systems support during discovery usually greatly exceeds the computer expense. Both of these expenses must be carefully estimated by a lawyer considering using systems support in relation to what is involved in his case. The result may be a decision to use much less support than would be ideal.

The time-critical nature of litigation activities also poses a problem. When you are designing your support system, the time required to write or modify the necessary software, prepare and input data into the computer and subsequently to retrieve and analyze that information will be taken into consideration. Designing your system to fit the schedules likely to be imposed on you by the court is essential to successful use of support services during litigation. If the lawyer has too big an appetite and goes for broke, requesting the biggest, best and most sophisticated system he can conceive of, which does everything for him but carry his briefcase to the courtroom, he may end up with a system which breaks his back both financially and functionally. He or his client will spend a great deal of time and money entering into the system information of relatively little importance which will receive no significant use. And it may take so long to input all of the information from each document the lawyer feels should be in the data file that only a fraction of the documents are on the system by the time the case goes to trial.

Principal limiting factors, then, are time and money. You will find yourself, particularly when you are deciding what sort of a system you want, having to make many difficult decisions or trade-offs. The more information you wish to store in a computer, and the more ways in which you decide you will want to access or retrieve that information, the longer it will take to design the system and to get information into the system so that it can be retrieved—and the greater expense you will incur, both in terms of manpower needed to implement the system and the kind of computer capacity you will require.

Even if, in participating in design of the system, you manage to avoid most of these problems, you may find that much relevant documentation or deposition testimony does not readily fit into the system or data file. For example, if you have designed your data file largely to accommodate correspondence and memoranda, what do you do with annual reports or 8-K and 10-K reports submitted to the Securities and Exchange Commission?

Despite these limitations, I believe systems support—specifically the utilization of a computer to keep track of evidence by recording its existence as you initially find it and helping you locate it when you want it again—is an absolute essential when you have a case with a substantial quantity of documentary and other evidence. The human mind is tremendously inventive and imaginative. However, when it comes to rote memory involving the contents of even 15,000 documents, the computer memory is more accurate than the human memory.

In closing, let me pose a practical question. The United Shoe Machinery antitrust case decided by Judge Wyzanski in 1953 had a total of 5,512 documentary exhibits, comprising 26,474 pages. Assume you decide to utilize a system requiring coding or indexing of each document for inputting into the system. Assume that it requires one-half hour to code a document for entry into the system: It would have required 2,256 man-hours or, assuming the average lawyer works 1,500 hours per year, one and one-half lawyer years to code these documents for entry into a system for retrieval. Of course, 5,512 documents is a relatively paltry quantity from today's standpoint and, in any event, those 5,512 documents were probably selected for introduction at trial as evidence from a substantially greater quantity of documents. If the total of documents to be reviewed, coded and entered into the data base were only five times that quantity, coding them under the above assumptions would require *seven man-years.* My question is: How can the lawyer afford to spend seven years—or two lawyers spend three and one-half years—coding documents for entry into the computer system?

4

Systems and Paraprofessional Considerations for Discovery Support

Robert S. Arthur

As a businessman providing information services to the legal profession, the questions directed at me by attorneys are phrased somewhat differently than those they ask themselves. This is only appropriate. They ask me:

How do we get the job done?

How do we get it done right?

How do we get it done right and justify the cost to the client?

Frequently, in civil litigation, an attorney calls upon other professional disciplines such as engineering, market analysis, accounting, and so forth. There should be no novelty in an attorney working with the concepts and techniques of another specialized discipline, such as information systems.

The computer can take a mass of data and store it permanently, so that mass of data remains an authoritative and complete set that cannot easily be corrupted or muddled by the human user. It can select, sort, sequence and retrieve information by complex sets of criteria. It can selectively retrieve by these criteria certain information from among millions of pieces of information at electronic speeds.

There is more novelty in the extensive use of skilled nonlawyers to handle the supporting systems necessary to feed this large mass of critical information into the computer. Like a piece of long-range artillery, the computer requires intensive attention before a single round can be fired at the target.

The use of nonlawyers to handle evidentiary material in terms not just of housekeeping and entering documents into a retrieval system, but in interpreting them for meaning, is the traumatic problem for any thoughtful attorney considering this approach to the pretrial litigation need. The commitment involves delegating a great deal of what you would normally expect to do yourself and still retain control. It is not an easy task.

While the techniques are really not all that novel, the use of significant numbers of nonlawyers in combination with computer systems represents a radical departure. New approaches have to be fully understood by the user—in this case the attorney. This kind of understanding does not come into being overnight as the result of an act of will, but rather through sustained questioning.

SOME CRITERIA

When is the information systems approach relevant to litigation? There are plenty of special situations. There are plenty of gray areas, but there are some key criteria around which you can structure your thinking, with the objective of determining relevance or determining need. The criteria are best set forth as a set of four questions:

1. Do you foresee more than four or five thousand individual documents to control, organize and access by topic?
2. What kinds of information do you need to track for each and every document, and are there more than six specific kinds of information required to describe each document, relative to content, author, recipient, those who received copies, date of document and so forth?
3. Do you foresee the need to access these documents several times during a period of thirty-six months?
4. Do you envision that ten or more users, that is attorneys, accountants and other consultants, will require access to the same master set of documents?

In brief, number of documents, months of planned use, the number of individual users along with the number of specific kinds of relevant information, represent the key set of criteria upon which to base a decision.

If your counts roughly equate with these levels or significantly exceed them, then explore further.

Should you attempt to answer the question of going this route upon the basis of your own judgment? If you are comfortable with basic computer concepts and the generalities of information systems, why not? If you are not comfortable with these methods, then you are well advised to obtain the insurance of an Informed Opinion. If you are, you may be able to produce an adequate feasibility study yourself.

The problem is to qualify the Informed Opinion, and to be sure that he is tuned to your needs as an attorney. If he understands that litigation is a social substitute for physical violence, his attitude is qualified. If he shows no basic understanding of time-critical needs sometimes dictated by others, try somebody who exhibits some gut awareness of what the adversary proceeding is all about.

More importantly, if he cannot talk your language as a user of information services and you gain the impression of talking with somebody at the bottom of a deep pickle barrel, drop it right there. Any Informed Opinion who cannot carry the burden of communicating with you in terms of your needs is not going to provide much service.

The Informed Opinion can be found among attorneys, the serried ranks of the major computer manufacturers, the major management consultants, and the major software houses. At this point in time there are relatively few individuals in number who can prove any extensive experience, but many more who would like the opportunity to gain the experience.

You may have some system capabilities internal to your own organization. However, an outsider is easier to discipline. He is external to management politics which can be gruesome in many situations of this kind, and moreover you can require a finite initial product in the form of a report with concrete recommendations for implementation.

THE FEASIBILITY STUDY

What is required of an Informed Opinion? That he conduct a feasibility study, and that the final written report addresses itself to certain fundamental aspects of your information needs.

First, he must get from you an understanding of the overall strategic considerations of the litigation, be your needs related to single or multiple instances. He must also have a sound knowledge of immediate tactical possibilities, as you see them. If when he writes his report he cannot play back to you a vital and perceptive account of the circumstances of your litigation, you have a problem. It is probably worth a second try, but not a third.

Second, if, as is often the case today, you have some internal capabilities to handle the problem within the client's organization or within your own firm, it is important that he demonstrates awareness of present resources and suggests how these can be incorporated in a larger solution.

Third, the report must give you a budget for these pretrial support systems. What is the entry price and maintenance price in the first year of operation? What is the cost of the total activity in the second year? If you spread the costs over a five-year period, what is the annual budget—$50,000 or $150,000? You can even ask him what the cost is of doing nothing, or whether you can make any saving compared to using a large crew of very junior attorneys. These loaded questions will test his mettle. Incidentally, if the section of the report dealing with dollars is weak, you again have a serious problem because he may be only technically competent as related to handling the computer system but not your client's finite budget.

Fourth, your feasibility study must deal with taxonomy; that is, the kinds and categories of discrete meaning that you must consistently identify in each and every document that you wish to control and access. This taxonomy can only be developed through intensive discussions with you and your fellow attorneys and by actually working with test sets of actual documents or almost identical documents. The problem of meaning is a primary question and must be seen as cutting across all the actual functional legal situations, such as interrogatories, document production and depositions.

On the one hand, while a sound budget is complex enough, unit costing of each function can give you something that well forecasts the level of expenditures over the next five years. On the other hand, the problem of taxonomy is not static and is extremely complex per se. It has nothing to do exclusively with computer retrieval. It is related to the same disciplines by which a specialized glossary or a technical dictionary of terms is developed.

You must be satisfied that your man knows what he is talking about in this area—not in general conceptual terms but very specifically—for example—that he understands the unique terminology applicable to administrative law as applied to the insurance business, or antitrust as related to the utilities industry. It is a noble but expensive experiment to teach an outside consultant the language of your client's business within the constraints of a special legal situation as it relates to information systems in support of litigation.

The whole issue of the input to any retrieval system is governed by the excellence of the logic represented in the taxonomy. As attorneys, your responsibilities to your client are at stake in this instance.

Fifth, the report must describe the retrieval system and show in actual format the end product, or output, that you as an attorney will be working with.

The report should also answer the question as to how much of the proposed system should be organized in-house (within the client's organization or within the law firm) and how much should be bought from outside organizations. The economics of the two approaches are significantly disparate for different reasons in different situations. There are difficult decisions in this area. What about confidentiality? What about the status of the end product as attorney work product? These two critical questions must be answered to your satisfaction and are best answered in this context.

Sixth, your report must relate dollars to levels of manpower by kinds of skills and place key milestone events in terms of the implementation of your systems support in the context of a schedule. For example, if you have 30,000 pages, how long is it going to take to develop the taxonomy? How long does it take to apply this taxonomy to each and every document? When will the information be digitized and loaded into the computer? When will the proposed support system be completely operational and in a maintenance mode?

Seventh, who is needed to create, implement and maintain these support systems? This will impinge on you to a greater or lesser extent depending on how your Informed Opinion answered your other questions, but in every case you will probably face a problem in selecting and training some people. This may not be a major consideration, yet to paraphrase Oscar Wilde, one cannot be too careful in the choice of one's paralegal personnel. Individuals who see information systems in support of litigation as one way of becoming an attorney are contraindicated by motivation and real interest. They tend to second guess. A good nurse is not necessarily somebody who wants to be a doctor. Try to find those individuals who are excited by the semantics of meaning, information systems in general and computerized information systems in particular and who see quite clearly all the pitfalls of even wanting to be identified as an attorney. You want the paralegals to complement your skills, not replicate them.

Let us assume that your Informed Opinion has proven conscientious, thoughtful, communicative in your language, responsive in your terms and meeting all biblical standards of probity as well as proving the possessor of a sharp pencil in budgetary matters. What more can you expect than the report itself?

A great deal more. A number of vital conceptual dividends must become a part of your thinking henceforth as an attorney. These dividends are not an integral part of the report but, to use a contemporary cliche, are a synergistic result of working with an imaginative and fully qualified information systems professional.

These conceptual dividends are critical to your success as an attorney in exploiting these techniques in meeting your goals and objectives. They represent a master set of key concepts with which you must come to feel familiar in terms of the practical consequences of their application. These concepts are useful as a base upon which to build an enlarged understanding of the practical possibilities open to you in gaining control of very large masses of business documents and records.

There are some twelve ideas that I suggest as critical in this area, but I lay no claim to setting forth a Hammurabi-like code.

1. All the lawyers involved must educate themselves in the use of the support system. If time, money and commitment are not found for this priority task, then you must make an expensive farce a real possibility.
2. Eyeball disciplines must prevail for all computer output that the attorney sees and uses. No cryptic codes or abbreviations, no eyeball searing microfilm as end product, but paper laid out to the highest standards of graphic ease and excellence.
3. You need physical control in terms of a place to maintain good order and orderly access—to read, to study, to review and select. If tens of millions of dollars hinge on the ability to access those quarter million documents, spend a few thousand on space.
4. Time on the part of the attorneys has to be committed to planning, and time has to be committed on an on-going basis to functional direction and control of the support systems.
5. Fail safe. Don't approve or accept any system where unauthorized personnel can access critical documents, either through the computer or manually.
6. Documentation, documentation, documentation. If it is not written down, there will not be a system, only a painful dependency on the skills and expertise of one or more individuals.
7. Spend time and effort on all the discovery systems external to the computer which sift out chaff and waste paper. Select and select again for relevancy; everything on the computer costs money.
8. If the adversary has vital information stored on his computer, determine in definitive terms what he has before you let him put you in a warehouse with the input that he used to load his computer from 1960 to the present.
9. Learn all you can about hybrid systems involving computers in combination with high-density microfiche or microfilm. The economics are important.

10. Make your informants explain at every opportunity the difference in meeting your needs between storing the text, or a part of the text, and storing only an index on the computer. Again, the economics are critical.
11. If the human eyeball must scan each relevant document to create an index, be sure that you distinguish between meaning that is obvious upon accurate skilled inspection and that which requires special knowledge and judgment. Don't place yourself in the United Shoe Machinery dilemma of seven man-years of attorney time.
12. Be sure that you know the retrieval criteria that are critical to your information needs—immediate, intermediate and long-term. Be equally certain that you understand the concept of retrieval by sets of criteria and how the set is formed or linked together.

Now you have a set of four questions to relate to in determining the need for support systems. You have a set of seven questions by which to relate to an Informed Opinion working out with you an effective and economical solution to an actual situation. Lastly, you have a set of twelve basic considerations that you are going to have to live and work with whenever you encounter these kinds of situations.

You can certainly improve upon these three sets of questions, but you are going to need something like them to work out these problems as they arise in a systematic and logical way.

One final comment. Any profession has to educate those it works with as well as those it works for. Perhaps vigorous attention to this responsibility will guarantee, more than anything else, your success in the use of support systems for litigation.

5

Lawyers' Considerations and Requirements for Systems Support during Trial Preparation and Conduct

Steven J. Olson

IDENTIFYING "THE NEED"

First, a general question: "Under what circumstance is it desirable to undertake development and implementation of these sorts of techniques?" There are no precise benchmarks; this decision depends principally on the magnitude of the case. My own view is that any time litigation is of sufficient size to require that a multitude of lawyers be involved, it is a prime candidate for implementing some sort of system—to insure internal consistency and avoid overlap. No system can completely replace people; indeed, when it comes to planning for and conducting the trial, people limitations may dictate techniques that fall somewhat short of those I will discuss. And, as in the development of a discovery support system, you must always consider the problems of expense and time.

Assuming that automated trial planning techniques do fit your case, when should they be initiated? The answer is "early." In this connection, it must be stressed at the outset that the systems options available to a lawyer at trial time are substantially dependent upon what has already been done. The automated procedures and inputs developed and utilized during the discovery phase of litigation will determine to a significant degree just what alternatives are available to the trial planner and litigator.

It is assumed that all the pertinent information recorded on the discovery data base will be pulled over into the trial data base and similar capabilities be available in planning for and conducting the trial. This being so, I assume many elements of the discovery support system described by previous speakers will be up and running before trial draws near. I cannot emphasize enough the need for early planning, the constraints of time and budget and so forth. The techniques and systems for litigation support just do not evolve overnight. In addition to assuming that a discovery system is already up and running, I ask you to put yourself in the position of the plaintiff, or at least to imagine that you are the party that has the affirmative burden of going forward. We will touch later on some of the techniques to consider if your concern is more one of defense or rebuttal, although at trial these distinctions blur as each side anticipates and often meets the contentions of an adversary before they are made.

CONVERSION OF DISCOVERY FILE TO TRIAL FILE

Given an up and running discovery system and the necessity of proving something in the affirmative, what is it that you hope to achieve by using automated techniques in preparing for trial? Obviously you want to win the trial. Confronted with a mass of data collected for that purpose, you want to boil it down to manageable proportions without sacrificing anything in terms of proving all contentions necessary to your case, and proving them in such a way as to provide maximum comprehension of your overall case. And the initial problem that you are facing is to take the mass of data which makes up your discovery system and somehow reduce it to manageable proportions.

Prerequisites

Identification of contentions. There are several prerequisites to the development of the trial script, many of which do not have to await the completion of discovery. First of all, you have to know where you stand with respect to *possible* evidence that is available to support your case. To do this, you must first sit down and laboriously break down your case into the *relevant* issues and subissues, and under each issue and subissue specify your position and what it is you need to prove with respect thereto. In other words, you need a comprehensive listing of issues and contentions. It may be that your complaint can be used to develop this, if it is a comprehensive one, but chances are that even a lengthy complaint will not set forth the detail that is required at this point. While you are at it, you should, of course, *arrange* your issues and contentions in the order in which you would like to present them. Once this is done, you will have what could be called a stripped version of a "trial brief," stripped in the sense that it lacks supporting evidence.

Identification of potential evidence. Given this comprehensive arrangement of issues and contentions, the next step is to determine just what evidence is available to support your position on each issue. When I use the word "evidence," I am not using it in the strictly legal sense. At this stage, it would be more accurate to say that the next step is to seek out just what sources of *potential evidence* are available. It is at this point that the computer comes into play and you use the basic tools developed during discovery. If the homework has been done, there should be a fairly close correlation between each factual contention in your trial brief and one or more of the subject matter codes used by the people who entered documents, deposition testimony, interrogatory answers, admissions and so forth, into your discovery support system. You can then run computer retrievals, seeking out references to items of potential evidence which support (or refute) each contention. Unless you have developed a full-text system, however, it behooves you at this point to go back and read each source item designated in the retrievals. From this review, selections can be made of those items you expect to use at trial, weeding out trivial or miscoded items.

Addition of direct evidence. The development of a script for trial includes several other steps, each of which—given the mass of evidence to be referenced—may be susceptible to the utilization of automated techniques. First, an obvious prerequisite to the development and digitization of a complete script is that *all* forms of potential evidence have been entered or reduced to a form that can be automatically manipulated. At this point, however, we are missing—at least in our discussion—the nuts and bolts which will provide the framework for the entire trial—the proposed testimony or direct examination of our own witnesses.

Thus, we need some vehicle to enter into the discovery system, and ultimately the trial support system, the proposed testimony of such witnesses.[1] Several options are available; one possibility is to reduce to writing and enter into the trial support system a summary of the background of the proposed witness and a general outline of his testimony as it relates to those contentions he is evidentially qualified to support—and here I am using "evidence" as a legal term of art. Additionally, any explanatory exhibits specially prepared for

[1]Of course, such witnesses will probably have been deposed by the opposition, and such defensive depositions may have been entered into the discovery support system, depending on how elaborate the support system is. But such depositions by an adverse party will not be structured in the positive manner in which you will wish to present your case. They may also have not covered some of the subjects you will wish the witnesses to cover.

use in connection with a witness's testimony should also be prepared, at least in preliminary form, and entered into the system either verbatim or in summary form. Also, any last minute discovery to fill gaps in your case should have been undertaken and added to your trial support system and its data base.

Selection of evidence for trial

For illustration, it may help to put your present status, at this stage of the litigation, into concrete terms. If you have a really major case in terms of the amount of evidence, your discovery support system may have indexed in its data base the following:

100,000 documents, or in total, perhaps 500,000 pages

50 deposition transcripts totalling 10,000 pages

50 summaries of direct testimony totalling 10,000 pages

Other items such as interrogatory answers and admissions

Reducing the potential evidence in this data base to what will be used at trial is not easy. While the computer can lead you to the materials which support or refute each of your contentions, *you* must read the material, analyze it and make the very difficult decisions as to which items are of sufficient value to leak through this intensive screening and find their way into the trial system. Suppose through this screening you are able to eliminate all but 20 percent of the discovery and other material assembled to date and decide that 80 percent will *not* be used at trial to affirmatively establish your case. You will still have 100,000 pages of documents, 2,000 pages of deposition transcripts and 2,000 pages of direct witness testimony to keep track of as you prepare for trial.

Having identified and boiled down all this potential evidence which is going to win your case, what do you do with it? You could simply make copies of it and file the copies away, perhaps arranged by subject matter in the same arrangement as your trial brief outline. In the case of ordinary size this may well be what you would do. On the other hand, you might begin simply by digitizing all of your contentions in your trial brief and the potential evidence relevant to each. This digitization of evidence likely will consist not only of a listing of evidence to be relied on to prove each point of your case, but a summary of or verbatim extract of key material from each relevant document.

What are the disadvantages of merely working from a hard copy file as opposed to digitizing your trial file of potential evidence?

(1) Evidence can be lost if someone removes a document from the file and fails to bring it back or misfiles it. Although computers make

mistakes, or at least people using them cause them to make mistakes, digitization of the evidence will create a procedure of keeping track of evidence that is much less likely to lose or forget about an item of evidence.

(2) If there is only one hard-copy file and a number of lawyers and paralegals are working to prepare the case for trial, the lawyers may get in each other's way in the attempts to use the file. If, on the other hand, you digitize verbatim extracts from each item of evidence you intend to use, as many lawyers and paralegal assistants as you wish can review this file at the same time—or particular portions of it. They may do so potentially by several means. They may review printouts or microfilm periodically generated from the data base for the trial support system, or they may have a CRT or scope which allows them to sit in their office and call up portions of the trial brief and evidence on a screen. Indeed, the entire trial brief, including summaries of evidence, may be carried around by a lawyer on several reels of microfilm or on a set of microfiche. Note also that when they are done working with the file there is no problem of refiling or avoiding misfiling. Of course, having such a digitized file in no way precludes anyone from actually going to the file cabinets where hard copy of entire documentary or other evidence is maintained and reading those documents in their entirety.

(3) The discussion so far has assumed that the documents and deposition transcripts set aside as evidence are static. This is unrealistic; discovery may continue until just before trial and the documents, etc., selected for trial as the "best" evidence may be constantly changing. If that is the case, the problems of deleting and adding items of evidence by hand with copies of documents in file drawers are greatly magnified. On the other hand, if you have digitized the potential evidence, you would have a convenient means for updating the file of evidence to be used to include new evidence. Further, by use of the retrieval techniques just discussed, a number of lawyers and paralegal personnel can readily review parts of the trial brief to see the latest evidence which has been added. Indeed, if your trial support system is sufficiently sophisticated, it may generate periodic reports showing only newly added evidence that supports your various contentions.

Standing alone, you may not consider these advantages of sufficient importance to justify the expense involved in the digitization of your probable evidence. But there are several enhancements that can be made to the file which are immensely useful but which must be based on the premise that you have digitized the file:

(1) You recall that so far we have only identified *potential* evidence to be used at trial. While it is your responsibility as a lawyer to get

these items into admissible form—through requests for admissions, depositions, or otherwise—your systems man can provide you with the capability of seeing at a glance just which ones have been qualified, together with citations of how and where, and which have not. Of course, objections such as relevancy and materiality will probably have to await the actual conduct of the trial, but basic foundation questions and the very difficult problems involved in the hearsay rule and the various exceptions thereto should be solved in advance of trial, and solutions should be visibly tied to every output from the trial support system data base of the item of evidence itself. If the status in terms of admissibility of each item must be maintained by hand, either in separate listings or notes attached to the documents in the file, each change in status must be laboriously updated by hand in a process likely to be error prone.

(2) The second enhancement is also a practical one, and constitutes an area where automated support can be invaluable. Much of your proposed evidence—portions of documents and so forth—could be introduced in connection with the testimony of several potential witnesses—in other words, at several points in the trial. Your system could be designed to tell you of each possibility so that you can choose the most desirable one, the one where that evidence will have its greatest impact. Thus, you will want some sort of "potential witness" list linked to each item of proposed evidence; that is, a listing for each item of evidence of all names associated with it. Such a listing can be generated readily by a computer but preparing it by hand would be horrendous. Moreover, this enhancement can be easily implemented by merely carrying forward from the discovery system the listings of names associated in one way or another with the document.

(3) There will invariably be particular items of evidence which are relevant to several of your contentions. In addition, these items may have been discussed in many depositions; but not all of these discussions have been pulled over into your trial support system. A computer can readily keep track of such things, whereas a totally manual system would be hopeless. For example, you may find yourself on the eve of trial making final decisions on just what documents to introduce, or which to emphasize. You may select documents as to which foundation for admissibility is established over others lacking foundation. Documents not impeached on depositions will be favored over those which have been questioned. Final selection of documents is facilitated if you can go to one location—a retrieval from your trial support system data base—and see all this information.

THE TRIAL "SCRIPT"

Everything discussed to this point has had as its principal emphasis the boiling down and tracking of potential evidence according to topics or subject matter. *Now,* the emphasis must switch and you must start to think in terms of just what sequence you will use in introducing your evidence at trial. And there are several serious practical problems which will force you to adopt a sequence which may vary from the one you may prefer. The computer can help, however, in the development of the optimum feasible sequence.

Ideally, you would probably like to present your case in the precise subject matter order developed to this point. By digitizing and enhancing your file, you now have the capability to generate a report which will present your contentions in the most desirable sequence. And tied to each such contention is not only an identification of all evidence that you plan to use to support it, but also, in the case of documentary evidence, a list of all witnesses who could theoretically testify as to its contents as well as its evidentiary status.

But this report cannot be used as a script because in providing our case, by introducing each piece of potential evidence, we must make things interesting and hold the attention of judge and jury. Therefore, the items of evidence must be linked to live witnesses. This presents a couple of problems. First, much of your best potential evidence will consist of statements contained in your adversary's documents and the potential testimony of its current or former employees. Presumably the latter will have been deposed.

In large-scale litigation (assuming that you do not have nationwide subpoena power) you will have to read these documents and depositions at some point in the trial. But you must still decide: In connection with whose "live" testimony should these "dead" items be offered?

Second, even as to those witnesses that you know will testify at trial—and whose testimony has been summarized, introduced into the system and somehow linked with each relevant contention you want to prove—no judge is going to tolerate an unlimited number of recalls to the stand paralleling each contention with respect to which the witness can testify. Thus, after you have decided as to which contentions a witness is going to testify and which documentary, deposition or other evidence is going to be introduced with him, you need the capability to list such information for each witness. Such a listing might be attempted by hand. Consider, however, that you may have up to 100 witnesses and up to 10,000 documents and 2,000 pages of deposition testimony to assign among them. Consider further that witness identity, testimony and document assignments may keep changing until the last minute. A computer can keep track of it all. Your systems man cannot solve the actual assignment of topics and documents to particular witnesses, but he can give you the basic tools from which to develop your trial "script"—basic tools in the sense that you will be made aware of all of the alternatives and possibilities available.

Let us summarize what tools the systems man presumably has provided you (leaving up to him just how he did it). (1) From the discovery support system he has linked all items of potential evidence, whether pro or con, to each of your contentions. This has enabled you to boil down from the mass available those items into a digitized trial support system. (2) He has provided a capability of entering into the trial support system summaries of the expected testimony of your own direct witnesses, again linked to your contentions. (3) He has set up a system whereby the evidentiary status of each item of potential evidence can be easily tracked. (4) He has provided you with a vehicle to determine every possible witness that could theoretically testify with respect to each contention or group of contentions and each item of evidence. Conversely, he has provided you with a capability to pull together all contentions that relate to a particular witness or that he can testify to, thus insuring that when a witness is on the stand you won't overlook any particular items. Given these various capabilities, you should now be able to start assembling your "script."

There is no way you can use computerized techniques to actually write the script. What you will have created are key tools that facilitate its preparation. Just as when deciding what evidence to use in the distillation of the discovery data base, so here you will manually have to determine the chronology of the trial; that is, the order of witnesses and just which items of evidence to introduce in connection with the testimony of each. As you then manually put the pieces together, your systems people can digitize and enter this final product into a computer so that the script can be readily updated as you make last minute changes based on late-arriving evidence.

You will have used three basic "reports" to generate your script: (1) a report consisting of all your contentions with the evidence supporting each one catalogued thereunder; (2) a report showing every possible witness that could be used to support a particular contention or provide the proper foundation and background for each item of evidence; and (3) a report made up of a list of witnesses under each of which is catalogued every contention and every potential exhibit he could testify with respect to.

In addition to being useful in developing the script, however, these reports can continue to serve other functions. For example, they will keep track of multiple uses of single documents, thus insuring consistency of use. They will serve as sources of references to backup evidence, available in case your preferred evidence is not admissible, or perhaps useful in rebutting points made by your adversary. For example, if you find that document "A" is not admitted into evidence in connection with your preferred witness, you can turn to the second report noted above to find all other possibilities and modify your trial plan accordingly. And such reports will serve as the common depository for all lawyers working on your side of the case. Not only will this help in avoiding overlap and insuring consistency, but periodic printouts of the entire file will enable all the lawyers to know just where each facet of the case is at any particular point in time. You might even want to have this script on-line to CRT displays located in various lawyers' offices or in the courtroom.

Speaking of the courtroom, let me turn next to a few brief comments concerning automated assistance during trial.

ASSISTANCE DURING TRIAL

There is a myriad of ways in which a professional support group can provide assistance to the trial lawyer. Some are "people" oriented—transporting boxes of documents and depositions, retrieving copies of exhibits to be used, etc. Again, however, there are several needs of the attorney that may lend themselves to automated support. (1) The lawyer will want to have assurance that in working with the large mass of data he has not forgotten to enter into evidence documents or testimony that supports his contentions. Thus, it is necessary that he have some sort of automated tracking procedure tied to the various elements contained in the trial script. (2) The trial lawyer would like to know, when dealing with a particular piece of evidence, whether it has been used before during the trial and, if so, just when and how it was used. It might also be helpful to know whether and how it might be used *later* in the trial. The previously mentioned tracking procedure may also solve this requirement. (3) There is the problem of cross-examining adverse witnesses. Although the so-called "trial brief" contained adverse as well as supporting evidence, the most fruitful sources of impeachment material are documents authored or received by the witness, as well as his deposition, if taken. They are probably not part of the Trial Brief or Trial Script, so the trial lawyer will need some sort of rapid retrieval capability to locate such material in the great mass of documentation obtained during discovery. The discovery support system can be utilized for this. (4) Closely related to this cross-examination point, any documents introduced by the adversary should be introduced into some sort of system providing retrieval capabilities. Some of this may have been accomplished prior to trial based on stipulations. If so, it would allow a search of your file to obtain rebuttal evidence that could be added to your trial plan. (5) There is the trial record itself. The lawyer will want to have ready access to the entire trial record for purposes of final argument and to provide the foundation for the preparation of a post-trial brief for submission to the court. Any identifiers, such as exhibit numbers, will have to be added to the file. You will then have come full circle. From the initial early entry of *possible* evidence linked to your contentions, you will have upgraded the system to an index of *probable* evidence linked to live witnesses, and from this level you will have proceeded to enter *actual* evidence used to support each of your contentions.

There is the practical question concerning what equipment, if any, you should consider having at your disposal in the courtroom. Undoubtedly you will have used various terminals, such as CRTs, during discovery and in preparation for trial. The question of whether to have such equipment actually located in the courtroom is a difficult one. There are valid arguments on either side. To do so would certainly be convenient. On the other hand, it may serve as a distraction to the court or jury. Whichever way you go, at a minimum, an on-line system not too distant from the courtroom is desirable, particularly for retrieval of references to items of possible evidence, the use of which was not anticipated.

6

Software, Human Engineering and Trial Support Systems

Clayton L. Miller

Since discussion of a trial support system to any degree of detail could take several hours, I will present a general overview with enough detail to highlight key points. I will define what I mean by a support system and will place the system elements in perspective. I will review the data requirements and the system requirements. I will discuss what a support system will do and how the system can do it. And I will discuss two aspects of the system's adaptability.

A trial support system is a blend of people and automated data processing. The people are the paralegal staff, all those typists, coders, microfilmers, filers, document reviewers, computer production personnel and analytical experts. Data processing is that combination of computer hardware, operating software and application programs which provides the unfailing memory and the fast recall necessary to keep the mass of trial data organized and available. Data processing cannot effectively support a trial without the paralegal staff. So before we discuss data processing, let me mention a few of the major "people" aspects of trial support.

An obvious paralegal support function is coding or typing data for automated input. During trial this task includes reviewing each day's trial transcript and preparing the appropriate data for overnight file updating.

Another function is analyzing data processing output. By screening reports, the analytical experts can compile only the most relevant and beneficial data for the lawyer to use. The analytical experts also provide backup for the lawyer during trial testimony related to a particular subject. And some of the paralegal staff prepare trial exhibits or other illustrative material. In short, the paralegal staff performs all tasks possible in order to free the lawyer from time-consuming incidentals and to extend his analytical capabilities. Data processing, on the other hand, acts to extend the lawyer's memory and to add speed and flexibility to his recall. Because it's probably least familiar to you, data processing will be the subject of most of my comments.

TRIAL DATA

There must be a clear *statement of the issues* or *contentions*. Likewise, *statements of possible evidence* to support or refute each contention must be developed. These contention and evidence statements are formulated by the lawyer with assistance from analytical experts. Once developed, these statements can be digitized and recorded by a computer.

The *evidence sources* are those documents, depositions and interrogatories which are processed by the discovery system discussed by previous speakers.

Data required for each source includes:

A description in terms of what kind of document it is and when it was written.

All names associated with the document.

All relevant subjects or facts contained in the document.

All usages planned for, or made of, the document.

Indications of authentication and admissibility.

Presumably the evidence sources were already recorded by a computer during the discovery phase. As trial exhibits are developed, they may be recorded as evidence sources.

Witnesses are those individuals around whom evidence may be introduced. Their background may be developed by the paralegal staff or by the lawyer. Their testimony outline is developed by the lawyer. Once developed, the witness data can also be digitized and recorded by a computer.

A simple example will illustrate these types of data.

Assume we are defending Random Machinery Unlimited and are faced with a contention which states "Random Machinery Unlimited has engaged in discussions with its customers and prospects concerning reciprocal buying. "The subject of this contention is rec-

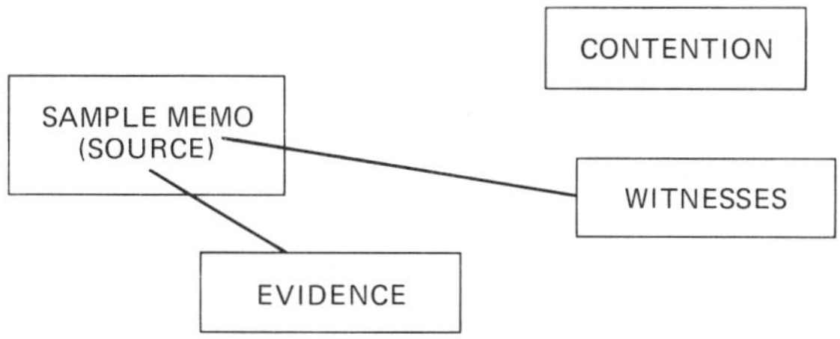

Figure 1

iprocity. If we do a retrieval with our discovery system to find all Random Machinery Unlimited documents dealing with reciprocity, one such document we might find is the "sample memo," or evidence source, from Mr. Myan to Mr. Geary dated July 7, 1970. In the memo is a paragraph which clearly refutes the contention. So an evidence statement can be formulated which references the memo. That is the source, and the evidence is the portion of the memo which refutes the contention. Any names contained in the memo indicate the people who could be used as witnesses to introduce the evidence. The reference numbers C1, S1, E1 and W1 through W5 in Figure 2 will be explained shortly.

SYSTEM REQUIREMENTS

A trial requires data about contentions, evidence, evidence sources and witnesses. While any or all of these data types may be interesting by themselves, something must be done with the data before it can be effectively used. That something is what constitutes the system requirements for trial. The system requires that the data be linked, that it be arranged in the optimum manner and that it be tracked throughout the trial. *Data linkage* is merely tying together those types of data which are related. When you develop a statement of evidence to support a contention, in your mind you have linked that evidence to that contention. The source which documents the evidence statement is also linked in your mind to that evidence statement. And when you decide on a witness to use in introducing that evidence, again in your mind you have linked that witness to the evidence.

Figure 2. Data linkage

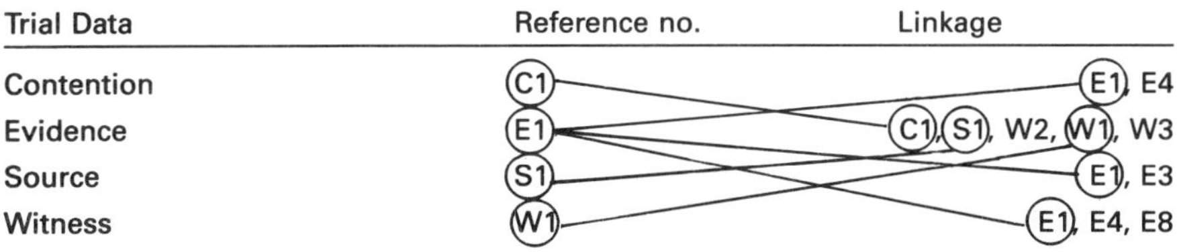

Establishing and retaining the linkage between one contention, one evidence statement, one source and one witness is a snap. But when the case has dimensions such as 30 planned witnesses from a pool of 300 possible witnesses and 1,000 planned sources from 100,000 recorded sources from several million available sources, and when many of the sources can be used for more than one contention and many of the witnesses must treat more than one evidence statement, data linkage becomes extremely complex. These dimension and linkage complexities practically demand a trial support system.

Data arrangement deals with how to present the data to the court in the clearest manner possible. A case involving two dozen issues and nearly 100 subissues, each with several supporting or refuting evidence statements and several possible witnesses, requires delicate and thoughtful arrangement. Direct and contingency planning is highly complex. Once the arrangement is established, any rearrangements must be made quickly and accurately.

Data tracking is knowing at all times which data has been or will be used, where and with what results. In a trial which lasts from six to eighteen months, hand tracking cannot do the job.

So trial data must be organized through data linkage and data arrangement, and it must be kept available through data tracking. Data linkage cannot be established entirely by the computer; the lawyer must supply initial linkage decisions. Then the computer can construct the cross-references. Likewise, the lawyer must make all decisions related to data arrangement. Fortunately the computer can do all of the data tracking by itself.

DATA LINKAGE

When the data is initially recorded, a unique reference number is assigned to each contention, evidence, source and witness by the paralegal staff. Referring to our previous data sample, (Figure 1) let us assign reference numbers to the data (Figure 2). Reference number C1 is our first contention, E1 our first evidence statement, S1 our first source and W1 our first witness. Data linkage is accomplished with these reference numbers. In formulating an evidence statement, the lawyer decides which contention it supports or refutes, which evidence source can be used to back it up and which witnesses can be used to introduce it. He may even designate which witness he plans to use.

Assume that evidence statement E1 refutes contention C1. The lawyer, through the paralegal staff and data processing input, assigns (links) the reference number C1 to evidence statement E1. The computer then assigns the reference number E1 to contention C1; the contention number, C1, is actually recorded as additional data in the evidence statement. Likewise, the evidence number, E1, is recorded as additional data in the related contention statement. The source linkage is established in the same way. The lawyer assigns the appropriate source reference number to the evidence statement and the computer assigns the corresponding evidence reference number to that source.

Witness linkage may be established similarly or entirely by the computer using a fixed set of names from the source. Once the source is linked to the evidence, for example, any name on the source could be used as a possible witness and the source author could be the planned witness. After all evidence statements are assigned cross-reference numbers in this manner, each contention statement has the reference numbers of all evidence statements which support or refute it. Each source has the reference numbers of all evidence statements which use it as backup. And each witness has the reference numbers of all evidence statements to which he can give testimony. In our example, contention C1 is supported by evidence statements E1 and E4. Source S1 documents evidence in statements E1 and E3. Witness W1 could be used for evidence statements E1, E4 and E8.

Suppose you want to know which witnesses are tied to linked to contention C1. Contention C1 refers you to evidence E1 and E4. Evidence E1 indicates that witnesses W1, W2 and W3 are possible for testimony. Evidence E4 might indicate W4 and W5 as possible witnesses. So no matter which data type you examine, the cross-reference numbers stored with it direct you to all the other related data.

At the time the computer assigns evidence reference numbers to a witness, a special indicator can accompany the reference numbers of those evidence statements on which counsel plans the witness to testify. Linkage may be changed or dropped in the same manner it was established. Adjusting the contention, source or witness reference numbers of the appropriate evidence statement causes the computer to adjust the evidence reference numbers in the affected contention, source or witness.

DATA ARRANGEMENT

Numbers are the key to data arrangement just as they are the key to data linkage. Generally, two arrangements of the data are desired. The first arranges data in the sequence it might be presented in a trial brief. The second arranges data in the sequence it might be presented at trial. Since a trial brief is usually structured around contentions, the first arrangement is accomplished by assigning a brief sequence number to each contention according to its desired position. Each related evidence statement is likewise assigned a brief sequence number to position all evidence related to that contention. Trial plans are usually structured around witnesses so the second arrangement is accomplished by assigning one or more plan sequence numbers to each witness. One number is sufficient if the lawyer plans to use the witness only once. But if the lawyer plans the trial around contentions more than around witnesses, and hence will recall a witness several times, multiple plan sequence numbers for each witness are needed. Plan sequence numbers assigned to evidence statements position all evidence related to a witness.

Brief numbers and plan numbers might be assigned in multiples of 100 to facilitate sequencing of evidence related to a contention or witness. In our example, assume the lawyer wants contention C1 to be the fourth contention in the brief. He would assign brief number B400 to contention C1 (Figure 3). Of the two evidence statements related to contention C1, he wants evidence statement E4 to precede evidence statement E1. To accomplish this, he would assign brief number B401 to evidence E4 and he would assign brief number B402 to evidence E1. Our example indicates that according to the plan, witness W1 is the ninth scheduled witness and evidence E1 is the third evidence statement which he will treat. Data arrangement is completely controlled by the lawyer using these brief and plan sequence numbers.

DATA TRACKING

Data tracking is accomplished with computer-generated reports. The Missing Link reports indicate such things as (1) which contentions have no related evidence, (2) which evidence has no related contention, source, planned witness or alternate possible witness, (3) which sources assigned to evidence are not yet admissible or (4) which planned witnesses have no related testimony. These reports alert the lawyer and paralegal staff to weaknesses or oversights in the preparation for trial.

Figure 3. Data arrangement

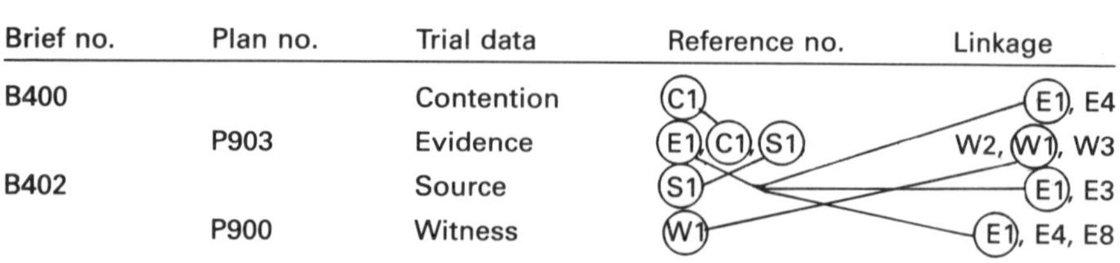

The *Brief Report* (Figure 4) shows contentions and evidence as they will be, or as they have been, presented in the trial brief. The contentions are listed in brief number sequence. Each contention is followed by all supporting or refuting evidence statements. Each evidence statement is followed:

By the plan number which indicates the position of the evidence statement in the plan report.

By data about the source which supports the evidence statement.

By name, background and testimony outline of the witness who will be used to introduce the evidence.

By the plan number which indicates the position of the witness in the plan report.

A version of this report can be produced with appropriate headings and only the contention and evidence statements. This version can serve as the actual trial brief.

The *Plan Report* (Figure 5) shows the data which will be used for trial in the sequence it will be presented at trial. The scheduled witnesses are listed in plan number sequence. Each witness is followed by the contentions, evidence and sources he will treat. Also shown for the contentions and evidence statements are the brief numbers which indicate the position of the respective contention and evidence in the Brief Report.

The *Witness Report* (Figure 6) is very similar to the Plan Report. It shows all contentions, evidence and sources which a witness can treat with appropriate brief and plan report cross-reference numbers. The distinction is that it lists all possible witnesses (not just those scheduled for trial) and it lists them in alphabetic name sequence

Figure 4. Brief report

```
Contention
   Evidence (& Plan No.)
      Source
      Witness (& Plan No.)
   Evidence (& Plan No.)
      Source
      Witness (& Plan No.)

Contention
   Evidence (& Plan No.)
      Source
      Witness (& Plan No.)
```

Figure 5. Plan report

```
Witness
   Contention (& Brief No.)
      Evidence (& Brief No.)
         Source
      Evidence (& Brief No.)
         Source
   Contention (& Brief No.)
      Evidence (& Brief No.)
         Source

Witness
   Contention (& Brief No.)
      Evidence (& Brief No.)
         Source
```

Witness (& Plan No.)
  Contention (& Brief No.)
    Evidence (& Brief & Plan Nos.)
      Source
  Contention (& Brief No.)
    Evidence (& Brief & Plan Nos.)
      Source
    Evidence (& Brief & Plan Nos.)
      Source

Witness (& Plan No.)
  Contention (& Brief No.)
    Evidence (& Brief & Plan Nos.)
      Source

Figure 6. Witness report

(not in trial plan sequence). Another version of this report might list only the planned witnesses in alphabetic name sequence.

The Brief, Plan and Witness Reports are used by the lawyer to optimize the scheduling of witnesses and the presentation of contentions and evidence. During trial, they are also status reports which reflect the usages and admissibility of sources and the witness performance as recorded in the trial transcript. They thereby show which parts of the plan are completed and what degree of success each part has had.

These four types of reports are primarily for planning and monitoring trial activity, but during trial you may suddenly be faced with the crisis for which all the data linkage and data tracking was really established. Your star witness disappears after her second day on the stand and you have six more days of her testimony planned. Or a key piece of evidence has been declared inadmissible. What or whom do you use to achieve the desired results? That is the precise question which can be answered by the *Reflex Reports*. These reports are computer-generated, usually in response to a specific outline request through a CRT.

They show a small percentage of the data on file and their format depends on the nature of the request. They may show additional sources which contain the same subject matter as that of the contention. They may show additional possible witnesses related to the planned testimony. They are designed to point the way to an acceptable alternate approach when the plan cannot be directly followed. They are generated in an on-line environment because time is critical in these unexpected situations.

This spectrum of reports, then, allows the data to be tracked and made available throughout the trial both for planning and for quick adjustments.

SYSTEM ADAPTABILITY

Adaptability of the system during the first trial use is *essential.* Repeated use of the system by the lawyers will always uncover some shortcoming or some new retrieval need or report requirement. The system with flexible files, with spare room in the data records and with reserve power can respond quickly to these new conditions.

Future cases can often make use of the same system with minor adjustments. A plaintiff system can be adapted for defensive use without major redevelopment, because the basic trial needs do not change from case to case. Nor do the needs differ substantially between plaintiff and defendant position. Contentions, supporting or refuting evidence, the sources of that evidence and witnesses must all be linked, optimally arranged and tracked throughout the trial. The trial support system which is structured to meet these basic needs should be able to support a new case with only a minor tune-up.

7

Closing Remarks and Questions

F. Sherwood Lewis

You have been exposed to some of the problems of support systems from the standpoint of lawyers, systems people and the businessman. We have not explored every nook and cranny nor looked at every problem. This is only a small beginning on what we feel will be a growing use of trial support systems. Undoubtedly there is a great deal of refinement to be made and sophistication to be added. That is quite a challenge for this group and the bar in general. This "science" is not as advanced as the retrieval systems and the quantitative analysis techniques often discussed, nor is it as understood, either.

We will now be glad to answer questions.

Q. *What experience level and compensation is necessary for personnel to abstract and code documents for input into the retrieval system?*

A. There are a number of options available in selecting coding personnel, ranging from the use of trained legal paraprofessionals to the hiring and training in-house of individuals with no previous experience in the legal field. Since the particular litigation you are handling will require some specialized training of coding personnel, regardless of their legal background, you can very effectively hire and train your own staff comprised of individuals with analytical capabilities and good reading ability. Salaries for coding personnel would be likely to fall in the area of $500 to $700 per month, depending on their qualifications and the wage scales of your geographic area.

Q. *How do you maintain quality control on classification and coding work to insure completeness and consistency?*

A. Quality control is built into the coding system through the establishment of rigorous training and check-coding procedures, as well as frequent spot checking of the senior coders' work to insure that errors of interpretation do not arise. By using objective rather than subjective code definitions, the problem of conflicting interpretations is minimized.

Q. *Is it appropriate to deliver information in digital form to an adversary?*

A. Sometimes it would be if there was compatibility or some way for the adversary to utilize the data. Certainly presenting human-readable printouts should be acceptable.

Q. *What do you mean by "eye-searing microfilm"?*

A. I was referring to the fact that reading text over long periods of time on a microfilm viewer can bring on severe eyestrain.

Q. *What provisions do you recommend be included in the formal procurement agreement?*

A. The agreement should be with a lawyer involved in the case. This individual could be outside counsel or house counsel, but, in order to protect the work product generated by the system group, it is necessary that work is under the direct supervision of the lawyers.

Q. *How do you adopt changes in criteria (usually additions) as the case unfolds? In particular, are previously handled documents sifted against the new criteria?*

A. While it is hoped that most of the essential coding criteria will be anticipated before entry of any documents onto the data base, additions and alterations will become necessary from time to time. These can be incorporated into the system by rewriting the relevant procedures; the decision on whether or not to go back and resort previously coded documents will depend on a comparison of the significance of the changes and the number of documents previously coded with the time and cost involved in making the indicated changes.

Q. *How do you define "document," particularly as to transcripts or lengthy items?*

A. The term "document" has been used to refer to any item of written material that is to be entered onto the data base. In those rare instances where an extremely lengthy "document," such as a deposition transcript, contains more information than can be fit into the portion of the data file available for each such "document," it can be broken up into two or more segments which become distinct "documents" linked by cross reference numbers.

Q. *Do we have any learning on the extent to which the information generated by or contained on the computer is subject to discovery by the opposing party?*

A. While no decisions have been made regarding this subject, since the data base would be under the control and supervision of the attorneys, it could be reasonably expected to be considered work product.

Q. *To what extent are expenses for systems support recoverable by a successful plaintiff? Does recovery turn on the nature (legal or paralegal) of the support personnel being employed?*

A. The recoverability of such expenses is in doubt, but, assuming a statute authorizes recovery of attorneys' fees, such expenses arguably are recoverable because the paralegal support personnel perform work attorneys would otherwise have to do, and typically have done in the past.

8

Electronic Data Processing as an Aid to Trial Lawyers*

Labron K. Schuman and Philip R. Bagley

Trial lawyers should consider electronic data processing as a tool to help organize groups of documents involved in litigation. The proper application of electronic data processing in appropriate situations provides a more thorough, a more rapid and a less expensive analysis of material than traditional methods.

Unorganized groups of documents can be placed effectively in several significant sequences simultaneously through the use of electronic data processing. Obvious classifications by computer are sequences based on date, document number, document character, recipient, subject, subject access, deposition reference, issue reference and proof procedures. Specialized printouts reflecting unique needs also may be developed. Two brief illustrations of how EDP could be used in litigation as an aid to document analysis may assist the reader; they are merely illustrations of classifications and indexing by computer.

Exhibit 1 illustrates use of electronic data processing for information flow. The problem was to organize, preliminarily, quantities of documents and to gain perspective on litigation. The printouts aid the lawyer in determining key witnesses, sequences of events and the important information contained in the documents.

Each document in Exhibit 1 is summarized in an entry consisting of: (1) file number assigned to the document, (2) document identification number or designation, (3) date [year month day], (4) sender, (5)

*This material was first printed in the committee's publication, *Computers and the Law*, 2nd ed., 1969. The entire book is available from the ABA for $9.50.

Exhibit 1 (see table on page 84 for abbreviations)

A. Citations by initials

PRI	R	SER	T	DOC-NO	YMODA	SDR	ADR	SUBJECT/TITLE
DSD		DONALD S DELMAR						
DSD	S	4204	A	PB4312	31215	DSD	BA	RAINBOW CARWASH-INVITATION VISIT
			X			FJK		
DSD	C	4202	A	PB4106	50401	FJK	BA	CANCEL GAS PUMP FOR NATIONAL OIL CO
			X			AJD		
			C			DSD		
FJK		FELICE J KANE						
FJK	S	4202	A	PB4106	50401	FJK	BA	CANCEL GAS PUMP FOR NATIONAL OIL CO
			X			AJD		
			C			DSD		

B. Short citations by date

SER	DOC-NO	YMODA	SDR	ADR	SUBJECT/TITLE
4235	PB3664	10321	AJD	BA	ANALYSIS OF CALL REPORTS & SERV
4229	PB3849	10817	FJK	DSD	CARBON MONOXIDE WARNING
4203	PB3102	11015	BA	FJK	USE OF ACTIVATED CARBON

C. Short Citations by Document Number

SER	DOC-NO	YMODA	SDR	ADR	SUBJECT/TITLE
4258	PB3049	11122	FJK	DSD	ESTIMATED TANK CAPACITY
4203	PB3102	11015	BA	FJK	USE OF ACTIVATED CARBON
4228	PB3253	40209	DSD	AJD	MARK YOUR CALENDAR

D. Citations by serial number

SER		DOC-NO	YMODA	SDR	ADR	SUBJECT/TITLE
4202	A	PB3720	10202	FJK	BA	CANCEL GAS PUMP FOR NATIONAL OIL CO
4202	X			AJD		
4202	C			DSD		

E. Index by title words (KWIC)

		SER.
MARK YOUR	CALENDAR	4228
GRAND OPENING MARCH	CALENDAR	4205
RE-MARK YOUR	CALENDARS	4211
ANALYSIS OF	CALL REPORTS AND SERVICING	4235
WIN A POLAROID	CAMERA	4206
GRANDS TO HANDLE PROMO	CAMPAIGN FOR TOWN	4255

Exhibit 2 (*see table on page 84 for abbreviations*)

A. Citations by subject, scope and date

SUBJECT/SCOPE	YMODA	ROLE	ORG	NAME	DOCUMENTS	ANNOTATIONS/BID
PRICE CHANGES—MID-ATLANTIC	590403	PRI	ROM	McCARTHY E	GNI-KWC-P-006	NOTE: LETTER FROM
		ADR	GNI			NASSAU CO.
		COP		LOVEN SD		SUPT. OF HWYS
		REF	BRG			
		LOC	GNI			
	590927	ADR	GNI	CHANCE KW	GNI-KWC-P-039	
		COP	GNI	TRILL DA	CITES: GNI-KWC-0271	

B. Citations by organization, person and date

ORG	NAME	ROLE	YMODA	ROLE	ORG	NAME	SUBJECT/SCOPE/ANNOTATION	DOCUMENTS
GNI	CHANCE KW	PRI	580801	SDR	GNI	CHANCE KW	PREPARATION FOR BRANCH OPENINGS	SOURCE: GNI-KWC-P-047
				ADR	GNI	CHANCE KW	SCOPE: MID-WEST	
				ENR	GNI	CHANCE KW		
GNI	CHANCE KW	PRI	581030	SDR	GNI	CHANCE KW	PRICE CHANGES—NEW ENGLAND	SOURCE: GNI-KWC-P-039
				ENR		UNKNOWN	PRICE DEVIATIONS	CITES: GNI-KWC-478
				LOC	GNI		COMMUNICATIONS DIRECTLY FROM COMPETITORS	
							SCOPE: REGIONAL-MID-ATLANTIC	

C. Citations by date, subject and scope

YMODA	SUBJECT/SCOPE	ANNOTATION/BID	DOCUMENTS
590102	PRICE CHANGES—NEW ENGLAND	NOTE: GNI REDUCE $2	
		COMPETITORS MET THAT PRICE	GNI-KWC-1260
		NOTE: GENERALITIES AND POSSIBILITY OF A JOINT VENTURE	GNI-KWC-0162
	PRICE DEVIATIONS—MID-WEST	BID:AZ	GNI-KWC-0595
		NOTE: GNI BID HIGHER THAN COMPETITION	
	DISSEMINATION OF NEW PRICE BULLETINS	NOTE: PRICE BULLETIN MAY BE SENT TO OTHER COMPANIES IF THERE WAS A BUY AND SELL OFFER	GNI-KWC-0970

D. Citations by source

SOURCE	ROLE	ORG	NAME	YMODA	CROSS REFERENCE	SUBJECT/SCOPE/ANNOTATION
GNI-KWC-P-043	PRI	GNI	STANWICK JE	590514	CITES: GNI-KWC-0692	SCOPE: MID-ATLANTIC
	ADR	ROM	CRAWLEY MB	590222		NOTE: PRODUCER-DISTRIBUTOR RELATIONSHIP LETTERS TO OR BACK OUTLINING RELATIONSHIP
	ADR	BRG	FARBER R	590706		
	REF	ROM				
	ENR	GNI	SST			

E. Citations by role, relationships and date

PERSON	ROLE	NAME	ROLE	YMODA	SUBJECT/SCOPE/ANNOTATION/ SOURCE	ROLE	ORG	NAME
CHANCE KW	PRI	AMAN GR	REF	580510	MEETINGS	REF	BRG	MONTI A
					SCOPE: MID-WEST			
					SOURCE: GNI-KWC-P-130			
CHANCE KW	PRI	AMAN GR	ADR	581009	PRICE CHANGES—NEW ENGLAND	COP	GNI	DAVIS EG
					MEET, NOT BEAT, COMPETITION	REF	GNI	CHANCE KW
					SOURCE: GNI-KWC-P-061	LOC	ROM	

Code Descriptions and Abbreviations

Code	Description
A	See Role
ADR	ADDRESSEE
C, COP	COPY TO
DOC	DOCUMENT NUMBER
ENR	ULTIMATE DESTINATION OF DOCUMENT
LOC	LOCATION OF DOCUMENT
PRI	PRINCIPAL
REF	MENTIONED IN DOCUMENT
S, SDR	SENDER
SER	SERIAL NUMBER
T	TYPE OF RELATIONSHIP
YMODA	YEAR MONTH DAY
X	MENTIONED IN DOCUMENT
	Abbreviations
AJD	Andrew J. Drexler
BA	Bonnie Asher
BRG	Brigadier Industries
DSD	Donald S. Delmar
FJK	Felice J. Kane
GNI	General Nostrums, Inc.
KWC	Kenneth W. Chance
ROM	Roman Co.

addressee, (6) recipients of copies, (7) subject headings and topical phrases and (8) parties mentioned in the document text. Computer programs list the entries by file number and generate indices to the entries. Simple indices are made, sequenced by document number and by date. Initials and abbreviations are listed against full names. A permutation or KWIC index (a concordance with context) makes it possible to look up an entry, given any word or phrase recorded as subject matter. The most important output is a list giving for each party all entries in any way associated with that party.

Exhibit 2 represents the use of electronic data processing as an organizing tool after completion of discovery procedure. The primary classifications are much the same as in Exhibit 1. However, because of the status of the case, classifications are amplified. The basic entry for each document consists of: (1) dates, (2) sender, (3) principal, (4) addresses, (5) copies, (6) references in the document to people or companies, (7) locations where the documents were found, (8) author of any writing on the document, (9) identification and (10) description of the document.

The classifying and organizing of the material could be done manually. The expense and time involved in doing the job in large cases or even, under certain circumstances, in less complex litigation would far exceed the time and expense involved in developing the same information by computer. Furthermore, because of the speed and capacity of electronic processing equipment, information can be developed more thoroughly than is feasible through manual methods.

Exhibit 1 represents a primary step. Exhibit 2 is an intermediate step. The final step is to relate the program as developed in Exhibit 1 and Exhibit 2 to the actual trial procedure that the attorneys wish to follow. This means developing programs which will set forth the actual sequences and organization for trial.

9

Coping with the Fruits of Discovery in the Complex Case— The Systems Approach to Litigation Support

James T. Halverson

It is a pleasure for me ... to discuss with you one of the most important problems encountered by the trial lawyer in the preparation of a major piece of litigation. The perspective which I bring to the subject of information management and systems arises from my experience in private practice. As some of you may know, the Bureau of Competition has recently developed an information system to assist trial lawyers in the preparation of several matters being litigated by the Bureau. I do not, however, intend to discuss this system.

To understand how the trial lawyer uses an information system in complex cases, you must isolate the practical problems he will face during preparation for trial and the actual trial of the case.[1] When I use the term "complex action," I am referring to a case which involves not only large numbers of documents but large amounts of data requiring analysis.[2] Because the scope of this subject is so broad ... I have covered in detail in the footnotes ... some issues which I can only touch upon briefly.

PROBLEMS FACING THE TRIAL LAWYER DURING THE PREPARATION OF A COMPLEX CASE

As many of you know, the problem of organization can become the trial lawyer's most severe headache. There are times a lawyer finds himself devoting most of his attention to the organization and

Halverson, *Coping With the Fruits of Discovery in the Complex Case—the Systems Approach to Litigation Support*, 44 *Antitrust L.J.* 39 (1975). Copyright American Bar Association 1975. Reprinted with permission from *Antitrust Law Journal*, the publication of the Section of Antitrust Law.

management problems associated with a case when his valuable time could be better spent thinking about proper strategies for trial preparation and presentation.[3] There are, as you all know, the problems of:

A. Coping with large amounts of evidentiary materials accumulated in the form of interview reports, interrogatory responses, document production, depositions and so on.

B. Preparing for witness interviews and for taking depositions, which includes the problems of exhibit identification and organization and witness preparation if the witness is "friendly," and drafting interrogatories directed to the opposition and subpoenas duces tecum directed to third parties.

C. Answering interrogatories and preparing for witness depositions taken by the other side, which also include the problems of exhibit identification and organization and witness preparation if the witness is "friendly."

D. Maintaining file organization and preparing indexes and subindexes, such as indexes to document files, depositions, interrogatory responses and legal research.

E. Document control and organization, which involve the preparation of document summaries and subject, person involved, issue, source and other catalogs and document retrieval.

F. Deposition control and organization, which include the preparation of deposition summaries, locating and indexing foundation testimony for exhibits, preparation of exhibit lists and cross-references and witness kits for depositions and trial.

G. Data research and organization, which require meaningful and quick retrieval of documents containing data, data analysis and the preparation of charts and exhibits for a meaningful presentation of data at depositions and at trial.

So far I have simply outlined pretrial preparation organizational problems, but the problems of trial preparation are no less awesome than those I have just described, and unless you have organized the pretrial phase properly, your real troubles may be just beginning. Time is of the essence at this stage of the case, and you will want to devote much of your attention to the legal and evidence presentation strategies—not organization and management problems. You must be ready to prepare your economic, statistical and accounting witnesses for their testimony and you must have your economic and statistical models and other evidentiary materials which you will use to support your allegations and conclusions in final form. You will want to prepare evidentiary witness kits for your witnesses and more detailed witness kits which will help you prepare for examination of your own witnesses and cross-examination of opposing witnesses.

Because I am, for purpose of discussion, assuming that we are dealing with a complex case (with tens of thousands of documents, or more, and the need for collection and analysis of a large volume of sophisticated data), there may be all of the organizational problems associated with the use of the *Manual for Complex Litigation.*[4] You may, for example, have to prepare individually numbered event statements in your pretrial brief in which you will indicate in detail what you intend to prove, and, in the process (at this point for your internal purposes only) annotate the exhibits you expect to use, and the deposition and witness testimony you expect to offer in support of each event statement.

You must devise a system for controlling exhibits at the trial and for locating and identifying exhibits, including such information about them as at what transcript page they were offered and received and the transcript location of all relevant "foundation" information. You have to be able to locate relevant testimony in the record and, for internal use for the time being, annotate it to the pretrial brief event statements, and for this purpose, you will want to have prepared summaries of the daily transcripts produced.

There is also the problem of writing a meaningful post-trial brief paralleling the pretrial brief and annotating the received exhibits (with relevant summaries and the pages of the transcript where they were offered and received) and short summaries (with transcript page references) of the transcribed testimony which support the fact allegations contained in the event statements which you believe you have proved. Finally, there are the post-trial problems associated with the appeal of a case, assuming there is an appeal, which require that you select and find the parts of the transcript and exhibits you wish to use on appeal, both for purposes of putting together the appellate "record" and for use in preparing the appellate brief.

This is an enormous range of problems for the lawyer who is busy trying to develop the substantive issues, focus the issues and formulate strategies for the presentation at trial of the case.

COPING WITH THESE PROBLEMS

The best way I know of to cope with the problems you encounter in a complex case is to use the information systems approach to organization and management. I have used this approach in private practice, have found it to be effective and I understand that more and more firms around the country are finding it to be the best way to deal with these types of problems in complex cases.

What is the systems approach to litigation support? It is an integrated, systematic, carefully planned approach to solving the problems associated with complex litigation, using people, automation and physical resources.[5] Within the overall information system, there are a number of subsystems. Because a complex case will involve a vast number of documents,[6] there will not be a sufficient number of lawyers on the litigation team to do all of the document organization, summarization, filing and retrieval necessary and, frankly, lawyers do this less well than highly trained paraprofessionals.[7] For this reason, a paraprofessional subsystem has to be established, trained and supervised by the lawyers; divided into issue or subject-related areas; and assigned such functions as document searching, sorting, screening, summarizing, indexing and retrieval.[8]

The second subsystem involves automation. In a complex case, there is, in my opinion, no other viable alternative to the computer for the control, indexing, and retrieval of documentation of all types, and for the analysis of complex sets of data which is necessary to prepare economic and statistical models and charts and to prepare the experts for their testimony at trial. I would include as part of the computer subsystem the computer professionals and, in particular, the system's manager who should be a person who understands trial lawyers and their objectives and can work closely with them through all stages of the case, and may be responsible for managing the operations of the whole litigation support system.[9]

The problem of handling a massive volume of documents in a complex case can be solved by the microform subsystem. This system reduces the physical paper burden of the case and allows you to maintain a complete set of files in strategic locations throughout the country.[10]

In the antitrust case, there is an additional subsystem which includes the functions of the various expert economists, statisticians, accountants and other professionals and their relationships with the paraprofessionals and lawyers. The key to the effective use of all of these subsystems is the way in which they are coordinated into the legal framework of the case and the degree to which they are responsive to the lawyer's needs.

DEVELOPMENT AND EFFECTIVE USE OF THE INFORMATION SYSTEM

System development

A modern litigation support system must be designed with the informational needs of the litigation team and the anticipated information applications in mind.[11] To determine the system requirements, the lawyers should sit down with the expert consultants and the technical support personnel and analyze these needs and applications at the precomplaint stage of the case, or, for the defendant, shortly after the complaint is served. The lawyers and economists, for example, should at this point be exploring the theories of liability and damage measurement (or defenses thereto) and should be thinking about the types of issues and the types of data and data analysis which may in the future be needed.[12] The lawyers, paraprofessionals and computer system manager should be exploring the types of documentation which will be needed or can be anticipated being produced by the litigation.

Once you have tentatively agreed upon the possible issues in the case and have some idea of the scope of discovery and the complexity of the issues, you are ready to call in the computer experts who can design the software of your system. Several companies now offer standardized software packages which go a long way toward meeting many of the computer control needs which I am discussing today. At this initial stage, the planning and structure of the paraprofessional system, the computer system, and the economic system can be molded and coordinated to develop the issues tentatively identified. The system structure, however, must be flexible and readily adaptable to meet unanticipated issues raised by the opposition or the changes in strategy or approach which you may devise later on in the case.

The next step is to develop training plans, course outlines and training manuals for each member of the litigation team. You may anticipate that all of the system procedures, except library acquisitions, will require associated training manuals.[13] When you are handling vast quantities of documents, the lawyers must, for the most part, rely on others to do the bulk of the organization and summarizing work.[14] This work can be accomplished efficiently by paralegals who are trained by the lawyers to do initial document screening and to extract relevant facts and to prepare document input forms (DIF) from which information concerning each relevant document will be keypunched into the computer.[15] I should emphasize that the paralegal's role in the information system is crucial in helping to organize document files, create indexes, prepare document summaries and categorize data. I have used paraprofessionals to fill out the input forms which are keypunched into the computer, which in turn will be repeatedly used to retrieve the documents, organized by issue, event, type of data, source, subject, person and so on.

Attorneys sometimes express reservations about the ability of nonattorneys to prepare document summaries and extract facts, but it has been my experience that paralegals trained by lawyers can do this type of work effectively and with a high degree of objectivity and reliability. The key to dealing with paraprofessionals is to define your objectives and what it is you are looking for clearly and concisely. Paralegals should be college graduates who have been taught, preferably through a recognized legal paraprofessional course, practical skills in file organization, document control and organization, deposition control and organization, legal research control and organization, fact discovery assistance and trial assistance. Whether you are involved in a large complex case in which you employ a full information system, including automation, or a small case which can be handled by a manual information system, I think you will find that well trained paralegal assistants can save you a substantial amount of valuable time and money.

Effective use of the information system

Once the system is operational, you have an indispensable litigation support mechanism at your disposal. If you have an integrated data base management capability, you can create and maintain one common set of files which can be used to run searches, generate printed directories and indexes and edit or update files as you may direct quickly and efficiently.[16] This means you can update and reorganize the data base to incorporate new or amended documents and can quickly process and analyze changed conditions of fact, such as market shares and pricing patterns, using the perspective of the total searchable data base.

The system gives you the ability to search all information contained in the document input forms. The questions directed to the computer may be single ones or stated in combination. Thus, the attorney may do single or multivariable file searches with ease. He may request all documents containing the name of J. Doe; he may extend his search by stipulating that the abstract and work product positions within document input forms be also searched. In another search, he may request all documents, for example, dated between July 1, 1971, and January 31, 1973, which passed between or mentioned J. Doe and R. Smith and which relate either to issue X or issue Y. The computer will print out an answer to this question immediately and even, at your request, list the documents in chronological order and supply you with a short summary of each.

In general, litigation support uses two types of information search techniques or methods. The first type involves an index search; the second type involves a conditional search. A simplified example of each type of search will illustrate the method and value of each to the attorney.

Index search. An "index" search involves the use of routine or standard types of preprinted indexes or directories to look for a single fact.[17] One example is the maintenance of chronological printouts of document lists by person or issue. Another example of this would be to use a KWIC or "key word in context" index which lists every word, in its proper context, stored in the computer in alphabetical order down the center of a printout page. The document number would appear on the right-hand side of this page. To find out if a word, name or number is in the data base in the computer's memory, you scan down the index to that place in the alphabetical list where the word should appear. If the word does appear, you can, by reading that single line of text to the left and right of the key word, determine whether you want to retrieve the actual document. If the piece of information you seek involves two different words, such as did Mr. Jones mention Mr. Smith, you may have to make two passes through the index, one for each name, to determine whether the same document or page is listed for Jones and Smith, but, of course, in the Jones and Smith case, you could simply put the question to the computer directly on a special run and obtain the answer more quickly.

Conditional search. The second type of search, called a "conditional search," is more complex and much slower to accomplish by the manual search method using your series of regularly updated standard printout indexes. Here we want the answer only if all of certain stated conditions are satisfied in a document. A simultaneous multivariable search of this type can combine several logical requirements for combinations of facts including the requirement that certain things not be in the record sought.[18]

Computer output. In either the "index search" where you look through a list of preprinted information or the "conditional search" where you ask the computer to match all records with a list of conditions of interest to you, you can select one or more out of several outputs.

The most common output is the document accession or file number. This output lets you either read the original document, look up a microfilm image of it or request a copy of the document for your own use. Other types of outputs would include requesting that the computer extract stored information about the selected or identified documents such as listing authors, addressees, dates, abstracts, work product comments, subjects, issues and so on, and printing it out in a structured format according to the attorney's needs.

Another use of the search is to examine and identify a record in order to update it or eliminate it from the data base. This type of action should only be done by a member of the support organization who is thoroughly familiar with the system and authorized to change the stored information.

Using these types of searches, you can prepare for witness interviews and depositions by requesting computer runs against the names of individuals. If you have a large data base, you may find this method gives you many more documents than you need, but you will have the most complete file your data base is capable of providing from which you can cull out the documents you consider most relevant.

Similarly, the paraprofessionals can use the computer to produce document lists of person or issue related documents from which they can prepare fact or issue-related memoranda, chronologically organized to help the lawyer understand the significance of a particular course of events or transactions or the evidentiary significance of facts which are being used to support an allegation or theory.

I should emphasize that these computer runs do not substitute for the attorney's judgment in selecting the particular documents he should retrieve from the master file and read. They merely create a subfile of the master file which the attorney can use in summary fashion to check off the documents he needs. Thus, for example, you can use issue-oriented and witness-oriented computer runs, and each of these outputs will help you to prepare your own witnesses or question the opposition's witnesses.

Data analysis. I think you will really begin to sense the power of the computer in the litigation support system when it comes time to preparing the economic and statistical models which are the evidentiary basis of your economic liability or damage case, or defenses thereto, and in disclosing behavior patterns or a series of transactions which have evidentiary significance. With the aid of the economist, you can prepare different sets of data which can be fed into the computer and retrieved later for data analysis.[19] Working with the statisticians, accountants and/or economists, you can obtain an almost instantaneous update of any data you may have on market shares, unit costs and pricing patterns over time, patterns of distribution or pricing activities in various geographic markets, and do multi-variable analyses on damage measurement. This not only helps to identify the strong points of your case, but allows you to identify and reject weaker alternative approaches to issues of liability, damage measurement, counterclaims and theories of possible settlement. I must emphasize, however, that the computer output is only as good as the data input, and I am, therefore, assuming that all during the complaint preparation and discovery phases, the economist or other expert has been a working partner in selecting the types of data to be sought and monitoring the quality of the data inputted into the computer.[20] This is important because if you find at some point that there are errors in your data base, you may have to undertake the expensive and time-consuming step of going back and recompiling a reliable data base, at a time when it may well be too late.

The trial

The purpose of the information system is to give you complete control of your file in preparation for and during the trial. As required by the *Manual for Complex Litigation*, you have the ability to prepare quickly individually numbered event statements, to annotate to them relevant documents and parts of depositions, and to prepare affirmative annotated responses to the statements submitted by the opposition. You know with reliability which witness or which document will be used to attempt to prove each event statement. Moreover, should emergencies arise at the trial and you need the answer to the question of whether, for example, any document indicates that Mr. Smith communicated with Mr. Jones in New York in 1974, you can request the multi-variable run on this question, and if the document exists, the computer can quickly identify it for you.

By the end of the trial, the system has helped you control your exhibits when they were introduced into evidence and locate the exhibit foundation material and page of receipt in evidence in the transcript and has produced daily summaries of the relevant text of the trial transcript. The documents received in evidence and the summaries of the transcript can then be compared with the original pretrial plan, annotated to event statements for purposes of preparing for a post-trial fact brief and analyzed to determine whether you are proving what you thought you could prove. When the trial is concluded, you are ready to serve on the judge and the other side a post-trial brief with numbered event statements to which are annotated the supporting evidence which proves the allegations or defenses along with, if necessary, some withdrawals of unproved event statements.

By using the microform subsystem which I mentioned earlier, all of this evidentiary material upon which you rely can be reproduced by computer and copied on a few 3″ x 5″ microfiche cards each of which contains at least 144 printout pages. These cards can be placed in a pocket part of your brief and given to the judge, assuming he is the finder of fact, along with a portable microfiche reader, so he can easily read your brief in his office, at his home, or, as in a case in which I was intimately involved, take the cards and reader on a post-trial vacation, without being burdened with the great volumes of paper which the microfiche cards replace. With this type of pretrial and trial preparation, it is, as you might expect, much easier to prepare the case for appeal, if an appeal is necessary.

CONCLUSION

Now what does all of this add up to in terms of benefits to the attorney? Why are we leaving the comfortable world of litigation where the attorney assembles all of the facts in his own mind and branching out into other technologies, using what must seem to be strange procedures to some who are used to completely manual systems? Do we really gain from using litigation support teams and automation?

I think we have reached a point with many of our complex antitrust actions where old manual methods are simply obsolete and too time-consuming, inefficient and costly for adequate case preparation. Time and practical limitations will prevent you from controlling adequately massive amounts of information using manpower alone. The information explosion caused the automation of information management, and this means that the legal profession, if it is to keep pace with technology, will have to automate.

Another dimension to the problem in addition to the need to compress time and save money is that of complexity of data. It requires the power of modern computers and the disciplines of logical analysis to reduce the facts from a vast number of different sources into an easily understood economic or econometric model output. No amount of individual effort can make up for the ability of the computer to scan millions of separate pieces of information and rearrange them in just a few minutes to meet the attorney's needs. No amount of clerks can find the answer to a simultaneous multivariable search in a library of tens or hundreds of thousands of documents and do it in time to help your case preparation.

The use of automated litigation support systems provides you with a reliable method of systematically handling any large volumes of information and quickly finding the required facts. It gives you a way to coordinate the efforts of the large groups of personnel of different disciplines needed to prepare the information for your use and creates a current record of progress which lets you know quickly whether you have the evidence to support your strategy. In addition, there is vital continuity in the system even though key personnel may leave prior to completion of the case.

Finally, I should emphasize that automation and the other support concepts which I have described to you this morning help you cope with the problem of massive discovery, but they can never substitute for the experience and judgment of the trial lawyer. The most sophisticated system can only provide you with the information to develop your strategies; it cannot select the strategies for you, nor can it select the most effective way to approach a judge and jury. These skills are what ultimately make the case, but without the use of the tools I have described, even the most able trial lawyer might, in the complex case, become bogged down in handling matters which should, in the interest of efficiency, be controlled by others, responsive to the trial lawyer's needs and using the most modern and sophisticated techniques.

Footnotes

[1]Costs associated with establishing and maintaining a litigation support system vary widely, depending upon the complexity of the tasks it must perform, the number of documents it must process, and how quickly the attorney needs to receive the answers to his questions or a response to his instructions.

[2]It is pretty well agreed that some form of Information Management System is needed in any case that involves several thousand documents. Let us examine the potential trade-offs in a case that assembles only 10,000 documents and produces only 5,000 pages of transcript, and a significant amount of numerical data.

Using an average of 10 pages per document or per bundle of documents, we have 100,000 pages that would have to be read by the attorney, summarized and manually sorted without an automated system. Based on experience, at a constant pace, manually processing 100 pages a day is a difficult task where all of the documents are potentially relevant. More important, it would take an attorney about 1,000 days to process the documents even if he spent no time at all working on the other aspects of the case. If we equate this to a total cost to the client per attorney of $75,000 per year, we have spent $300,000 just reading and making notes in a manual system. Using our original figure of 10,000 documents, we see a cost of $30.00 per document. However, even if we spent the four man years, we cannot quickly search for any combination of facts without the time-consuming task of going through all of the document lists and abstracts one at a time and again making a new analysis of the data assembled. If the manual process produces 5,000 pages of work products and abstracts, it would cost you an average of $1.50 per page for typing whether it was a draft or a final.

Using paraprofessional personnel to extract data and write factual abstracts, and a computer aided system for building the data base and printing back the indexes, directories, and other information needed, experience shows that the cost would be under $10.00 per document, with about $7.00 per document being the document review and summarizing and/or abstracting cost. Even though this deprives the attorney of reading all of the additional words, it is doubtful that he will capture any more than the factual abstract even with careful note taking. By using a team of 10 document analysts and working at the standard rate of one document every 30 minutes, you can have all of the facts available in a completely organized form in a little over 3 months at one third the cost of the attorney's time to just read and summarize and/or abstract them. As for the insertion of text into the data base, it costs about the same as typing per page, about 6 cents per line, but the difference is that once in the computer system, you can manipulate the words, search for facts, and even print out the results in a different form for under 50 cents per page. Text can also become the search source for indexes such as the KWIC or Key Word in Context index.

A comparison of searches is even more dramatic in terms of time-cost trade-offs. A manual search of the manual index to the 10,000 documents would take at least one man 20 work days assuming that he could remember and match all of the facts needed and review the file at the rate of one document per minute. If he had to remember and evaluate several simultaneous variables it is doubtful that he could sustain that rate. However, the cost would be about 6 to 7 thousand dollars in manpower, and we would have to rely on his memory to judge the result. The computer could do a ten variable search of the entire data base and make an exact record of the result for about $50.00.

This example assumes a complex case with a large number of issues, persons involved, and subjects to be coded and a larger than average number of pages per document, or per bundle, to be analyzed by the document reviewer. Obviously, data input (documentary information coding and document summarization) costs will be reduced if paraprofessionals do most, if not all, of the coding and summarizing, if the average number of pages per document were reduced to a smaller, closer to normal, number (for example, 5 pages per document), and if the number of subjects, issues, persons involved and other items of information to be coded is reduced. Assuming, then, a less complex case involving the same number of documents, input cost per document could be reduced significantly.

One must also understand that one could reduce the cost of the manual review, coding, and summarization if, in the manual system, paraprofessionals were doing the document review work, and the number of issues and/or subjects to be searched for and referenced and the amount of summarizing to be done were less. If that were so, then the cost of data input (document review and summarization and/or abstracting) for a manual system might be brought down to that for the system using automation, but the data output (information retrieval and document search) *costs* of the manual system would still be *many times* that of the automated system; the manual system would probably yield *less complete and accurate* information retrievals; and the manual search *time* for retrievals would be a *large multiple* of that for the equivalent search by an automated system.

[3]At the discovery stage of the case, for example, there may be a need to minimize the cost of acquiring documents, particularly in instances in which the opposing party attempts to overburden you with a large volume of documents and maximize your expenses wherever possible. If the opposition adopts this strategy or if the case involves a large number of documents, you may want to devise a means for providing only relevant documents, or summaries thereof, to the attorneys and expert consultants in order not to overburden them with unnecessary volume while still providing access to all relevant material.

[4]*Manual for Complex Litigation* (West ed., 1973). If you are involved in smaller types of treble damage actions, the costs of implementing the full systems approach probably are prohibitive; but more important, you could still benefit from use of some of the automation and paraprofessional assistance techniques, described hereafter. If, however, you have several cases, each of which alone might not justify the cost of computerization, you will want to explore the possibility of allocating basic software costs among all the cases, thereby reducing substantially the individual case computer cost.

[5]An example of how documents flow through various processing operations and decision points begins with the attorneys and paralegals screening all documents received for relevancy. Only relevant documents should be copied and sorted into those which are to be treated as "separates" and those which are to be grouped into "bundles." The degree of coding and abstracting to be given to each "separate" or "bundle" should be designated at this stage, and each document should be numbered and logged. Nonrelevant documents should also be logged and stored but need not be processed. Each "separate" document and each "bundle" of documents should be checked for processing, analyzed and distributed to the paraprofessionals to be computer processed. You may want the documents screened again when duplicate and nonduplicate "separate" documents are identified by computer. In a case involving a large number of documents you may find that approximately 10–15 percent of the total number of documents received will be duplicates, and this percentage may be expected to increase from the minimum to the maximum as the file grows with time. The culling out of the duplicates will decrease the workload for subjective coding, abstracting, adding work product summaries, microfilming, keyboarding, computer processing, etc. If the actual percentage of duplicates exceeds 15 percent, the savings on processing costs may become substantial.

The senior paralegals should confirm the duplicate check results and proceed to subject code and abstract the nonduplicate "separates," and all of the "bundles," according to the coding instructions designed by attorneys at the time of logging. The completed forms can then be keyboarded, entered into the computer and various indexes and directories produced according to a predetermined schedule, typically, monthly. All of the relevant nonduplicate documents may also be microfilmed on 16mm roll film, and copies of the microfilm can be made and mounted into cassettes for ease of use.

After you have reviewed the summaries, indexes and actual document collections, you may want to pull out a percentage of those documents contained in the bundles and treat them as "separates." This process of "unbundling" will add relevant non-duplicate documents to the total computer file, and these can be treated in exactly the same manner as "separate" documents.

[6]The intense concentration of the lawyer on the legal aspects of a case may lead to a lack of adequate provision for the physical requirements of a large case. Hundreds of thousands of documents, millions of pages of copies, microfilm, computer terminals, and technical staffs mean that you need adequate facility space, furniture, equipment and other types of overhead. For example, 100,000 documents averaging 10 pages each discovered on a case and processed into an automated information system would, if six working copies of each were made, lead to approximately 6 million sheets of paper to be handled and stored. If you had a high-quality automatic plain paper reproduction machine, you would probably be able to reproduce only 1.4 million sheets per year, requiring approximately four years of continuous 8 hours per work day reproduction to reach the total. Obviously in this case you would either have more machines or go to a higher rate method of reproduction, but it illustrates the point that to handle the very large number of pages encountered in complex antitrust cases, you must plan well ahead for the physical capability to just move, reproduce and store the paper. Of course, to reduce both cost and physical paper burdens, one could use microforms for reproducing and storing documents. See note 10, *infra*.

In addition, the storage of these 100,000 documents in normal 4-drawer files would require 50 file cabinets just for the originals. If you were to store only one of the six copies and distribute the other five to various staff locations, you would need 100 file cabinets just for this 100,000-document file. Now add to that special cabinets for computer printouts, tapes, microfilms, etc., and you can see part of the problems of physical facilities required. Incidentally, the paper for that six million pages would be a stack of supplies 2,000 feet high and can fill to capacity a room 20 by 10 by 10 feet. While we are on the subject of planning for facilities, you must remember the budget impact of such supplies where that same six million sheets of reproduction at 3 cents each would total $180,000 and the 100 file cabinets would add another $12,500 to it. Now add the clerical staff to run the reproduction machines and keep the files straight and you see another dimension to the problem.

The special equipment required to fully utilize an automated litigation support system would include computer terminals for access to the remote computer center; microfilm and microfiche reader/printer equipment; safes for storage of classified or sensitive materials; off-site storage for security master files of critical documents; cabinets for documents, film rolls, punched cards, storage disks, computer tapes, photographs, drawings and other odd-sized items; work tables, book shelves and dead bulk storage; magnet or key locks for access control to the facility; and communications for both voice and data transmission to other sites.

[7]See note 2, *supra*.

[8]The paraprofessional's role in the information system is crucial in helping to organize document files, create indexes, prepare summaries and categorize data. I have used paraprofessionals to fill out control sheets which are keypunched into the computer, which in turn creates the capability of retrieval of documents organized by event, data, subject and person.

In complex case involving vast quantities of documents, the lawyer must depend on others to do the bulk of the organization and summarizing work under his direction. Although this work used to be done by junior lawyers, many trial lawyers are now realizing that it can be done equally well, at a lower cost, by trained paraprofessionals. It is for this reason that litigation paraprofessional positions are being used by an increasing number of law firms throughout the United States.

[9]Just as in any highly disciplined field of effort, the management of information using automation requires several types of special skills. The number and types of skills required depends to a great extent on the size and complexity of the data you want to assemble, and on the sophistication of the outputs.

If the litigation support system grows to any appreciable size, it is wise to have a manager for the support system. The hiring, administration, direction and other management functions of these special skills by a system's manager well versed in the technology can save a considerable amount of time for the attorneys.

A few of the other types of system personnel that must be considered include: data processing system analysts to interpret requirements and design the programs for the computer; programmers to convert the design of the analysts into instructions that the computer will understand; document coders to put the facts and data onto the standardized forms required by the system; keystroke operators to put the data into the computer system either by punching cards or directly onto magnetic storage; microfilm and microfiche operators to put selected parts of the records on film for fast access and security storage; and computer terminal operators to provide remote access to the stored data and assist the attorney in searches.

[10]A. *Microform Systems*

Although not essential to the basic information management system, the use of microfilm, microfiche and other forms of storage of the actual image of the document on film can be a valuable type of litigation support.

There are two general uses for microform systems in litigation activity. The first is to be able to read information received in discovery which is on film and to convert it to paper form for copying and processing. The second general use is to record selected series of documents for storage and for fast scanning during research.

B. *Microfiche*

Microfiche is also becoming a popular method of document filming because it offers great flexibility in use. Here the images are usually reduced to a much smaller size than in microfilm and the strip of images are placed on an index-sized card. These can be sorted either by hand or by suitable machines into different sets of information with much greater ease than cutting up several rolls of microfilm.

Reader/printers are used with both types of microforms. The most common types require that you mount the roll or fiche in a projector with its own screen. You advance the images to the one you want to read and after verifying that it is the information you want, you press a button and a self-developing printer ejects a finished copy of that frame in a few seconds.

C. *Computer Output Microforms*

Computer Output Microforms are increasingly being used for large volumes of information. "COM," as it is called in the trade, is a system where the computer electronically transfers the information to another machine which converts the impulses to letters and numbers in thousands per second, puts them into position on an internal screen or tube, photographs them, develops the image and delivers a completed roll or fiche. Here the full information is captured more quickly than handling individual pieces of paper but the information must be in the computer data base, and the actual image of the original document is lost.

Even if you do not decide to use this form of information automation, either to provide a security master for storage, or for fast scanning for information, you must be prepared to receive this form of information in response to your subpoenas in discovery.

[11]At pretrial, for example, it is necessary to keep track of the legal theories of the case and the factual statements of witnesses or in documents to prevent self-contradiction and to identify contradictions or inconsistencies in arguments advanced by the other side or in the statements of the witnesses. The information system should, therefore, include indexes of pleadings, briefs, proposed pretrial orders and similar documents; the full text of transcripts of arguments by both sides at all of the preliminary hearings and related actions; the full text or abstracts (of relevant parts) of all pleadings, depositions, and briefs from the pretrial stages and any related actions; and abstracts of (relevant) documents introduced as exhibits during the taking of depositions or produced in response to document production demands or requests. (See notes 14 and 15, *infra*.)

[12]When you first bring him aboard, the economist is primarily a research advisor. After you give him a brief summary of your case, he will help you compile the elementary industry data, assess the dollar or other economic benefits or risks of the case, and give you a better understanding of industry setting. As the case develops, the economist's role increases in importance when he begins to compile and analyze the data.

One statistical tool for estimating damage, for example, is the regression analysis. This method of damage proof may give you the average of outputs for each level of inputs, or vice versa. The units commonly used in damage measurement are sales, profits, and dollar losses, although other units of mèasurement may show ratios between output units and sales or input units and sales, or they may use lagged variables as, for example, in the case of research and development costs (input) and revenues subsequently derived from the sale of the product (output). Additional damage problems may involve comparability of damage data when proved inflation and interest costs increase steadily over time. Comparability is also a problem if you are trying to compare lease revenues of one company with sales revenues of another in the same industry. The latter problem can be solved by the concepts of "imputed sales revenue" and "imputed lease revenue." Using this method, sales revenue for units of equipment which were sold can be prorated as imputed lease revenue, or vice-versa, over a specific period of time in order to attain comparability of data.

[13]Once the initial document processing procedures have been developed, the respective training plans, course outlines, and training manuals can be designed. You may anticipate that all procedures, control and reference, will require associated training manuals, such as:

Procedure Manual	*Training Manual*	*Category of Personnel To Be Trained*
Screening and logging	Screening and logging	Attorneys Senior Paralegals
Objective coding	Objective coding	Junior Paralegals Senior Paralegals
Descriptive coding and abstracting	Descriptive coding and abstracting	Senior Paralegals
Library acquisition, control and reference	None	Librarian
Keyboarding	Keyboarding	Keyboard Operators
Search framing	Search framing	Librarian Attorneys
Microfilming	Microfilming	Microfilm Operators
Systems users	Systems users	Attorneys Senior Paralegals Librarian

Library procedures are excepted because the librarian should be a trained professional.

Because procedural changes in the information processing system may be deemed desirable during the initial operation of the system, printing of the various manuals should be deferred until the second or third group of individuals have to be trained. In addition, your information system consultant and system's manager should provide continuing technical assistance to assure the smooth start-up and continued operation of the basic information system, and should work closely with your lawyers and paralegals on all document screening, logging, descriptive coding and abstracting functions. The consultant should also provide on-the-job training of the supervisors of these functions, and conduct formal training programs for other paraprofessional personnel. Since these functions are critical to the success of the system, the consultant or system's managers must perform quality control inspections and tests to insure that the procedures are being executed properly.

[14]All documents acquired for input into the system must be screened for relevance. Effective screening procedures are necessary in order to keep the costs and size of the collection within reasonable bounds. During the document screening phase, the attorneys or paralegals should indicate—on a special log sheet—the type of processing each document is to receive and the type of facts and the degree of detail which should be processed into the computer. This can be done by simply making check marks on a preprinted form or list.

Once the documents have been screened, selected documents should be coded and described on document input forms.

[15]This step involves the process of bibliographic representation which consists of entering on the DIF head basic information describing the document or bundle, but not describing its substantive contents.

Bibliographic representation begins with the selection of a document or bundle from a file and determining (by looking up its number in a copy of the log book) the degree of processing it is to receive. Any special instructions in the "comments" column of the log book are, at this point, noted and followed by the paraprofessionals.

Bibliographic representation includes, for example, placing the following items on the DIF: Document Type, Document Date, Document Source, Authors' Names, Authors' Organizations, Number of Pages, Copyees' Names, Document Title, Addressees' Names, Authors' Positions, Cross-Referenced Documents, Log Sheet Number, Remarks or Comments, Subpoena Specification Numbers, Document Treatment to be Provided.

If the instructions in the log book call for more than bibliographic representation processing, document analysis is performed. This analysis can involve any of the following items on the DIF: Relevance Code, Confidentiality Code, Taxonomy Code, Market Area Codes, Organization Names, Document Summary, Subpoena Specifications, Work Product, if required.

The relevance code and work product items should be entered by the attorneys working on the case. A "Full Text" note on the DIF would, for example, indicate that the document is important enough to have all of its text keyboarded and included in its computer record for subsequent search and retrieval. A system's coding scheme, as reflected on the DIF, should provide for all possible items of information of potential interest to you. Flexibility in this area is important because, as the system matures and new needs are discovered, new codes or types of codes may have to be added or the old ones changed. The users of the system should study the DIF carefully because, in a sense, this document constitutes the range of their information retrieval options.

[16]While directories address themselves to specific items of information, context indexes list alphabetically all information containing words or phrases, together with the context in which the words are used in a sentence. For example, the indexed words can be listed in alphabetic sequence down the middle of a computer printout page, each word accompanied to the left and right by all or parts of the sentence in which they occurred, as well as the document's page and/or reference number.

This type of index directory relieves the attorney of the burden of having to determine which subjects might be important within any given document, because the directory can index every word stored in the computer. To simplify the use of the index, however, the computer can be instructed not to index certain commonly occurring words such as "the," "but" and "or" and not to cite duplicate references to specific phrases. These indexes are useful because specific documents can be identified which support a particular theory, involve a particular witness or are otherwise deemed significant. The coded items noted in a particular document can be cross-referenced and indexed for a large number of documents, and can be used to help identify for the attorney important points about which he or a witness should be knowledgeable.

At times you may be more interested in "classes" of documents rather than their overall subject content; and for this purpose computer directories can be extremely valuable. Directories can be produced by author, date, subpoena item number, subject code or any other key characteristic which may be of interest to the attorney.

An author directory, for example, may cite for each author the documents he authored by attorney-assigned document number, file location number, document date, type of document security code (i.e., personal and confidential) if one existed for the document, number of pages in the actual document, subpoena item number and computer document number.

Printed directories represent one of the most effective and inexpensive ways of listing some or all documents according to predetermined criteria. Depending on the system users' needs, the documents may be listed chronologically and/or alphabetically by their titles, names of their originators, taxonomy codes, etc.

[17]You might compare the "Index Search" to the standard way in which the yellow pages of the telephone directory are used. Each company can be listed in more than one

place if that company has more than one product or service. You would have to look under the two separate product or service sections of the yellow pages for the same company name to find the answer. Within the product sections of the yellow page directory, the names are listed alphabetically to speed up your search.

[18]An example of this type of search using the yellow pages of the telephone directory as an example would be to find the name of a company that makes refrigerators and light bulbs but not airplanes. The researcher would have to list manually all of the companies in each part of the yellow pages and compare all of the possible combinations to find the answer to this combination of an "and" condition with a "not" condition. In a manual system this is often done by making multiple index cards or xerox copies and sorting them into piles. You can see that even if it is determined, in this instance, that General Electric meets the multi-variable simultaneous search definition, by simply adding one more condition that it be the only company satisfying the conditional search, the task is compounded many times over. In an automated or computerized system it is possible to string combinations of requirements that include words, relative location of words in the same page or document, limiting dates, geography, organization, titles, and many more facts and the system can find all of the places in the record that the exact search is satisfied, in seconds or less. This type of search employs Boolean logic using "and," "or" and "not" as the primary connectors between the chain of interrelated facts.

[19]There are in addition to the economist's role in analyzing data, several other advantages of having an economist supervise the collection of data. He can, as an outside consultant, sign protective orders covering sensitive competitive data acquired from non-parties and shield it from your client. Subpoenaed parties are likely to interpose fewer objections to this type of arrangement than they would if the data were being turned over to your client for in-house analysis. Second, if you are going to issue a large number of subpoenas you will want to target the right type of information in your specifications on the first round. Having the advice of an economist in drafting specifications can avoid the expense and embarrassment of issuing a series of burdensome dragnet subpoenas. Third, the economist can save the attorney time by advising the attorney in responding to inquiries from the client and third parties concerning the data collection methods, scope, and processes. Fourth, if the economist is to use the output as a basis for testimony or as a basis for statistical analysis, he will have to be thoroughly familiar with the methodology of collection and the rationale for the various data compilation decisions made in the process of gathering the data base.

[20]Clients frequently think they can compile the data you need without the aid of an outside consultant. This, however, is a hazardous undertaking. More often than not, the people assigned to gather the data are inexperienced or are simply not trained to identify data inconsistencies or lack of historical comparability. Production and sales data may not be recorded in the same manner by all units of a multi-division company or sales records for old products and new products may be lumped together for a few years, then separated, or new accounting methods may have been adopted some years back. These are just a few of the innumerable problems which, if not taken into account, can undermine the reliability of your data base. In addition, the economist is skilled at spotting the absence or limitations of important data and in selecting the second best form of data to estimate the variables in which you may be interested, if that is necessary.

10

Computer Aid for the Small Law Office

John D. Rome and Ronald A. Rust

It took Iowa corn farmers at least two decades to switch to the new hybrid seed—and realize an enormous increase in yield per acre. The technology was there. It was cost-justified. There was enough seed. But most farmers still would not use it until long after it had "really been proved." Unfortunately, it was simply another illustration of the Principle of the Diffusion of Innovation: the top 5% are the imaginative ones, the next 15% are early-comers, followed by the middle-American 60%, the 15% who are late-comers, and the 5%, "I'll-be-damned's."

Computerized document and evidence management is the hybrid seed of large-scale lawsuit control. You can justify using this tool in your complex cases more easily than you may think.

True, litigation management can be done without computers, just like corn can be raised using ordinary seed. Today, there are numerous, thorough articles on the merits of automating a large lawsuit, on the many processing options available, and even several helpful ones of the "How I Won My Four Million Dollar Case" variety. So the small firm (and the solo practitioner) is aware of the potential for computer use in managing large-sized cases. But how is the Diffusion progressing?

In terms of the degree of interest now being shown by the legal community as a whole and of the frequency of computer use in the "obvious" cases (the one-million document, one-billion dollar antitrust suit), the answer is: just fine. In fact, for these large lawsuits, the use of computerized techniques is expanding at least as fast as are the new developments in civil procedure for handling large-scale, multi-district litigation. Further, in some circles it would now be regarded as standard legal care to use computers in these kinds of cases. Just like the multi-section farmers. But how about the fellow with 80 acres: 4 attorneys and 2,700 documents? The Diffusion here is not so rapid. Why?

The answer probably lies in several areas: incomplete understanding of how to do it, concern over costs and paying too much attention to the old wives' tales of this still-new industry. As to the latter, in the authors' collective experience in speaking with more than 500 attorneys about computerization and participating in many automated lawsuits, probably every known argument for not doing it has been raised. The war stories are legion. They are the stuff of which good law professor hypotheticals are made; many could even form the basis for a new legal academician's grubstake.

It would far transcend the scope of this article to deal with the many problems potentially involved in computerizing a collection of documents in a law case. They are effectively dealt with in numerous other articles, papers, and treatises, as are the reasons why automation should be used in certain cases. In any event, this latter question simply boils down to this: can you manage your big case without computerized assistance well enough to win it?

The technology to automate virtually any kind and size of case, in a cost-effective way, exists now. Why is it not being more extensively used? The authors would like to answer that question first, with an anecdote, and then propose a solution which will work.

Before the concept of automated litigation management truly emerged, a number of us in the computer/legal industry were first involved in the field of computerized law office management. Nobody was, or is now, hugely successful in that business. With good reason. Generally speaking, most attorneys or law firms regard the management of the business side of their practice as a unique problem—one which no "outside firm" could fully comprehend. The thought of switching to another (standardized) system was abhorrent. A few firms did free the managing partner so he could work with a computer firm to automate those procedures which were already in effect. These procedures, in many cases, were part, if not all, of the problem, because law office accounting in many firms is a tradition and not a science.

However, where the task was successfully accomplished, the results were often not happy for the computer firm. Some computer companies fixed-priced the jobs and lost a bundle. Most of them simply did not realize just how many "minor modifications" would be required to please all the partners. Other companies developed back-office management systems on a time and materials basis. This usually had the effect of surprising the law firm when the bill arrived, which in turn made the age-old technique of reference-selling impossible, thus limiting the computer concern's future law firm business. As a result of these problems and other characteristics of the law firm marketplace, not many small firms use computers to manage their business.

The same is true for smaller law firms using computers to manage their multi-document lawsuits—and for the same reason. The lack of standardization in the computerized lawsuit information management process invokes the antithesis of Henry Ford's principle: the cottage-industry or individualized approach is conducive neither to lower prices nor to wide-scale distribution.

The concept of Information Control has several attributes relevant to the point here: (1) it can never be perfectly achieved, since it is an inexact science; (2) its costs vary proportionately with its quality (for example, the more information you have to control, the greater the requisite paralegal effort); and (3) it does involve certain fixed organizational costs, such as your own time in planning for automation.

The George Orwell of the computer-legal Animal Farm might have said: All Law Firms are Created Equal, except Bigger Law Firms are Created More Equal. To have a reasonable level of information control necessarily presupposes some fixed costs, like a core paralegal staff. To the large law firm, this fixed cost is quite a small percentage of its total revenues. For the very large firm, the fixed costs even include having a computer on-hand, so when the appropriate large case appears, the firm only has to be concerned with the incremental (e.g., cost-per-document) costs in evaluating the economics of whether to automate. Not so for the small firm—or so it has been popularly thought.

CONSIDER SHARING SYSTEMS

There are several workable approaches to automated litigation management for smaller firms. First, as scary as it may sound, consider sharing the system with the other side. If your opponents on a case are big enough to merit your using a computer as a tool to help you fight them, then the chances that they have not thought of using a computer in your suit are a flat zero. Today, the chances are that only you will be surprised by the involvement of a computer. If it is a "full-text" system (defined as the computer's maintaining a complete copy of all the words in the contract, depositions, testimony or whatever), attorney work-product considerations may not even arise. For example, both sides are entitled to full access to the words in a deposition, and the computer is simply the conveying medium. If it is an "index/abstract" system, both sides may nevertheless desire access to the same documents. You need only share their data culling, keying and computerizing costs—not the way in which you analyze and/or retrieve the data. The "sharing," incidentally, need not be voluntary. Your opponent's system, and its use, may be discoverable. Nevertheless, it is recognized here, as the court did in *In Re IBM Peripheral EDP Devices*, an antitrust suit consolidated in the US District Court for the Northern District of California, No. MDL 163RM, that there are certain suits in which the sharing of an information system with your opponent is impractical or otherwise not feasible. In this case, the court felt that it would be too prejudicial if the composition of the system itself were to be revealed.

Then share someone else's system. Why not approach the large, friendly law firm down the street about using its system? Understand that by "system" the authors do not mean to imply only computer hardware. Sharing can also mean using the other firm's document encoding forms (stripped, obviously, of the pertinent identifying data they have put on the form for use in their suits—but retaining the same format, to eliminate any reprogramming costs) and possibly also using their paralegal personnel (they are not likely to be busy all of the time, and the big law firm certainly wants to avoid the morale problems which the hill and valley effect of hiring and laying-off can mean).

Although it may have its own system, that big firm down the street more than likely is not using its own computers, but rather is renting access to someone else's machines or systems. You can approach the remote vendor directly. The vendor will not let you use the big law firm's precise techniques (if he even knows them), but will be thoroughly versed in the information control processes involved. Further, software systems have evolved to the point where the most sophisticated of them can now manage multiple suits and/or multiple indexing or document-encoding forms concurrently within the same vendor's system. Full-text systems, of course, do not need to utilize a format which is unique to any one lawsuit except to the extent you desire to supplement them with certain catalogs or subject indices.

Consequently, system sharing to today's law firm does not equate to what sharing means to a two-year old: giving something up. It simply means taking advantage of an existing capability. In the authors' experience, sharing or repeating a process used by others has additional side benefits: the full system is tested and already refined. Since the path has been blazed, there are not quite so many apparently formidable obstacles to the process of computerizing. To attorneys, after all, sharing is an inherent part of the profession—legal forms and the ATLA information pool being two examples.

What does sharing mean to the small firm with a 2,700 document case going to trial in six months?

It means being able to overcome the inertia and the quandary-type problems of getting started. It also means a major reduction in the fixed costs: no system development or tailoring, no form design costs and lesser paralegal/indexer associated costs due to reduced hiring and training time. In short, it substantially increases the chances that you can justify the cost of computer assistance.

COST CONSIDERATIONS

There remain, however, two significant other kinds of costs to consider. First, using a shared approach, be it in data collection or computer system design, means that you have to fit your information handling requirements into an existing system. Frankly, sometimes a standard document coding form will not permit the contents of the actual documents to be depicted adequately. For example, if the document coding form contains only information about the date, author, subject code and significance, a subsequent computer search may locate 50% of the total number of documents in the data base—no help at all. The authors have found, though, that with a reasonably comprehensive form, and careful thought, a standard form can be made to work for more than one suit, especially if the suits are in the same legal area.

As the sophistication of computer systems increases, this problem will diminish. Even now, a few systems, such as RECON IV, Model 204 and DASH, have an "intelligent front end," allowing them to adapt automatically to the document description form you design (within broad limits). These "standard systems" can give you a great deal of latitude in designing your Information Control forms, so the forms can depict the documents accurately, still with no major up-front investment.

The second kind of cost is usually the one which attorneys mean to cite when they mention cost as the reason why they do not use computers. This is the variable, or cost-per-document, expense in getting the information to the point where it can be used by the computer. The variable costs consist of document control, indexing, keying and loading (into the computer's storage device) expenses. These costs can vary from 75 cents to more than $10.00 per document. This large variance is directly related to the amount of information collected about, and the analysis made of, each document, and consequently the amount of effort involved in indexing and keying it. So, indeed, in a large and complex case the "get ready" costs can be quite high.

In very large cases, the fixed cost portion of using a computer (design, planning, set-up, etc.) is normally a relatively small percent of the total costs, perhaps 2% to 10%. However, in the 2,700-document case, the fixed costs of using a nonstandard (i.e., not-in-existence) total system could easily be half of the total cost. By using an existing or standard total approach to organizing the information in your case, the cost of computerizing can be significantly reduced.

However, the cost-per-document portion is virtually independent of the number of documents involved in the case, save for certain economies of scale (i.e., volume discounts). In our experience, the average cost per document is about $3.00.

CAN YOU AFFORD NOT TO SPEND THE MONEY?

So the question is: can you afford to spend $8,100 to obtain complete, high-quality computer control over the documents in your 2,700-document case? Assuming your time is worth $50.00 per hour, you took notes quickly and you could review documents at the very high rate of 30 per hour, your own information control cost would be $4,500. Doing it manually, you have expended considerable effort and cost to cover the documents once. However, can you sort back through them with enough efficiency to see trends in the sundry memos between Smith and Jones? Can you trace the subtle changes in your opponent's pricing policy to the newspaper ads of your own client?

Finally, the purpose of building an automated litigation support capability is simply to "get ready." The real benefit comes in using the system, and in the confidence in knowing that you have all the information, and the sophisticated analyses of it, literally, at your fingertips. The cost of system usage, incidentally, has not been addressed here since it rarely comprises a significant portion of the total.

As mentioned previously, this article is not intended to remake the case for computerization. Rather its purpose is to illustrate that with the use of a standardized approach, or by sharing an existing system, the true difference between what you would otherwise spend, and the cost of using a computer is not all that great—and is likely well worth it in light of the benefits obtained.

Can you afford, then, not to use computers in those cases where a well-managed collection of documents could make the difference between losing and winning?

11

How the Computer Can Help the Litigator

Roger P. Stokley

Computers are a new and helpful tool for the trial lawyer. Immense amounts of information taken from interviews, interrogatories, depositions, documents, and other sources can be stored in a computer and then retrieved for use in the trial of a case. The trial lawyer and his staff need to know nothing more about computer technology than how to classify the information for storage.

The growth in the volume of major litigation and the increase in its complexity have combined to add to the problems of trial lawyers. Private antitrust actions, suits under the Securities Acts and concern with the environment have all sparked what has been called the "litigation explosion." But the trial lawyer has acquired a new tool to assist him in performing the work required by these developments. This new tool is the computer.

Most lawyers avoid using computers because of a mistaken belief that their use requires a knowledge of mathematics. It does not. Indeed, it requires little more than a willingness to recognize that a modern computer combines an incredible memory (far greater than that of any lawyer) with an equally incredible ability to search through this memory to find material the lawyer wants. To use this tool, however, one must do more than feed documents into it.

The computer is able to store virtually unlimited quantities of information in its memory. When asked about a subject, it goes through all this information in a fraction of a second, selects what is relevant (that is, what is asked for) and supplies it to the questioner.

The memory of a trial lawyer is one of his most valuable assets, and the computer will not take its place when the lawyer cross-examines a witness. It will help him in that task, however, by giving him the material to be remembered. It will always answer the question of "where." Is there anyone who has not said, "I've seen a document on that," or "Somebody testified on that," and then spent hours looking for the material? The computer offers relief from that problem. It tells you not only what but also where.

No upper limit exists on the ability of a computer to cope with the vast quantities of information, whether acquired by way of answers to interrogatories, depositions, documents or otherwise. Indeed, in the next few years the major development in this area will not be application of the computer to larger and larger cases but to smaller and smaller cases. The lawyer who learns how to use the computer in relatively small cases will obtain the greatest benefit from its ability to memorize, screen and locate information.

So far as I know, this use of the computer was initiated by Control Data Corporation in its antitrust case against International Business Machines Corporation. Control Data was confronted with literally millions of documents. It coped with the veritable flood of paper by mobilizing its powerful computers and creating a "data bank" that enabled Control Data to call forth relevant information on any subject or person in the case. The best tribute to the efforts of Control Data's computers (as well as its lawyers) is the settlement obtained from I.B.M.

The starting point in the use of a computer in a particular case will be the question, "What computer?" In most instances the answer should be "The client's computer," because more and more clients these days do have computers. The large computer is easier for the lawyer to use, but even a relatively small computer can do a trial lawyer's work.

Using the client's computer has definite advantages. It reduces expense significantly, and it involves the client in the process. If nothing else, the client is likely to give better service than a computer service bureau.

After arranging for the use of a particular computer, this procedure is followed:

First, information is recorded on data input sheets. Second, the information is transferred to punch cards. Third, the information goes from the punch cards to the computer memory. Fourth, the lawyer asks questions and gets answers if he and the person in charge of the computer have done their jobs.

For example, the trial lawyer preparing to take the deposition of John Doe asks for a list of every document in which the name John Doe appears, every time John Doe has been referred to in a deposition and every reference to John Doe in an answer to an interrogatory. A program for the computer has been prepared so that the lawyer gets a list giving this information. The lawyer also may wish to know everything in the records with respect to certain subjects. For example, he may want to know about a particular meeting on January 18, 1969, which he believes John Doe may have attended or was told about. The lawyer can ask about the meeting and obtain a list of every reference to the meeting.

The computer can be used in the same way when preparing one's own witness for a deposition. Every trial lawyer knows the problem of a witness who has forgotten about a particular document. A lawyer preparing his own witness can act in precisely the same way as a lawyer preparing to take a deposition, anticipating what the other lawyer will do. The witness is given the help of all available information.

These examples make obvious the use of a computer in preparation for trial. The trial lawyer is able to obtain quickly all the information on a particular subject; he can then determine efficiently just what evidence he wants to introduce. He can separate rapidly the essential from the nonessential, locate inconsistencies and work out the best method of proving a point.

The first stage of the process (and the most important) is preparing data input sheets. The lawyer and the computer programmer go through four steps. First, they decide on a method (code) for identifying particular depositions, documents and answers to interrogatories. Second, they agree on a form for a data input sheet. Third, the lawyer prepares a list of topics or names in which he is interested and assigns each a number. This list can be supplemented later. Fourth, the lawyer enters (or has others enter) material on the data input sheets.

The data input sheet is merely a sheet of paper on which information is recorded in the first instance. A separate data input sheet will be filled out for each document, for each answer to an interrogatory and for each section of a deposition. If the lawyer has available a large computer, he can prepare a form of data input sheet that records an almost incredible amount of information. With a smaller computer, the form is less complex. In any event, the form of the data input sheet should be designed by a computer systems analyst familiar with the particular computer.

This article will assume the lawyer is using a relatively small computer. The lawyer's problem is easier with a larger computer, and in that situation he should take full advantage of all the capabilities available.

In its simplest form the data input sheet contains a space for entering an identification number and spaces for entering subject matter numbers. If the computer programmer tells the lawyer he can use a more complicated form than this, the benefits can be enormous.

NUMBERS FORM IDENTIFICATION CODE

An identification code for depositions, documents, etc., is simple. A complete and useful code of identification numbers can be worked out using seven-digit numbers, the first three numbers identifying the source of the information and the last four digits the precise location of the information within that general source. Thus, a number beginning with 0 or 1 shows that the source of the information is a deposition; the three numbers would designate the precise deposition. For example, any number beginning 017 would refer to the deposition of a particular individual—deposition 017. Somewhat similarly, the numbers starting 2 and 3 might refer to your client's answers to interrogatories; numbers starting with 4 and 5 might designate answers by the other side to your interrogatories; a number starting with a 6 might refer to a statement obtained from a witness (the particular witness being identified by the second and third numbers); other numbers would refer to sources of documents; and so on.

Ordinarily, the last four numbers of the seven-digit identifying number would indicate the more precise location of the information. In the case of a deposition, these numbers would identify where the information is found in the transcript. The obvious procedure is to have a separate number for each page of the deposition, but this will greatly increase the number of data input sheets required, and usually it will be easier to operate in ten-page segments.

The lawyer may have the best of both worlds. This is done ordinarily by recording the information from a deposition in ten-page batches. Under this system the number 0170160 refers to the deposition of witness 017 and the 160 refers to pages 160–169 of the deposition transcript. If at any time it becomes desirable to break the identification down further, it is simple enough to use a more precise number, such as 163. In that event, a separate data input sheet is required for that page. Ordinarily, however, it will be sufficient to work with ten-page segments.

The data input sheet, in addition to having a space in which to show by number the source of the information, will have spaces in which subject matters are entered by number for each individual. Numbers 1–299 may all be assigned to persons. Under this system number 13 would refer to a particular individual and the entry of 013 would denote a reference to that person. As additional names come up, they can be added to the code. At the outset only numbers 1–50 may be assigned, but later on, as the names of other individuals come up, they are assigned numbers starting with 51. Similarly, a meeting or a conversation can be assigned a number. The number 453 may refer to a particular meeting or conversation of January 18, 1969. Other numbers can refer to particular subject matters, the names of companies and so on.

It is useful to have more than one number assigned to miscellaneous. Thus, 299 may refer to miscellaneous persons, 499 may refer to miscellaneous meetings, 799 may refer to miscellaneous documents and 999 may refer to miscellaneous miscellaneous. The lawyer may also desire a special number (such as 998) for material that is important but does not come within any particular category.

Having prepared a data input sheet and settled on a code of information sources and a code of subject matters (topics, names, meetings, etc.), the lawyer must then fill out (or have others fill out) the data input sheet. A sheet is filled out for each document, each ten-page segment of a deposition and each part of an answer to an interrogatory. First, the identification number is entered and then the appropriate subject matter numbers. When a computer with a large memory is available, the form may permit entry of other information.

Each time new documents are received, or a new deposition transcript is received or a court hearing transcript is received, new data input sheets must be filled out. Like a human being, the computer can't remember something it is never told. The entire computer program is no better than the input code prepared for entry on the data sheet and no more useful than the care used in filling out the data input sheets. If the person preparing the data input sheet makes a careless mistake, the computer will not have that information and the output from the computer will be deficient. Remember the expression "gigo"—garbage in, garbage out.

Once the data input sheets are prepared, they are delivered to the person operating the computer. That person has each data input sheet converted into a punch card and uses the punch cards to enter the information in the computer memory. A "program" for the computer already has been prepared. The computer is now ready to be used.

For the lawyer, the use is a pleasure. For example, he can ask the computer for all sources of information on 357. This may be a person, a meeting or a topic. The lawyer typically will receive a printout—a list of numbers that refers to depositions, answers to interrogatories, and documents.

The printout is valueless unless the material referred to is readily available. It is essential to keep a single, centralized file of documents, depositions, answers to interrogatories, statements, etc. With this file, it is a relatively simple process (and does not require high-priced legal help) to collect copies of the material listed in the printout. This should be done by copying the material, then returning it to the basic file. Only in this way can the basic file be maintained intact.

Despite the best of efforts, however, from time to time a gap will appear in the basic file. It is desirable to have a back-up source of information so that hours are not spent looking for a missing document. This back-up is best provided by making a copy of everything on microfilm, which is relatively inexpensive, requires little space and is generally invaluable. Indeed, it is almost a necessity. Finally, what if the lawyer's client has a computer with a limited memory that apparently will not accommodate all the information he wishes it to memorize? Remarkably, this problem can be coped with.

The typical computer's memory consists of information stored on magnetic tapes or discs. When a computer analyst speaks of the limits of a computer's memory, he is speaking of the maximum amount of information his computer system can handle within one program. This limitation is usually unimportant to a litigator, who ordinarily will be satisfied if the computer first searches through one disc, that disc is removed, a second disc is put on, the computer then searches through that disc, and so on. The computer cannot operate on a disc not "on" the machine, but the litigator usually does not ask it to do so. By storing some information on certain discs or tapes, and by storing other information on others, apparent limitations of memory can be overcome.

The first time a lawyer uses a computer in major litigation (1) he will be delighted at the jobs it can do for him, (2) he will decide that never again in a big case will he forego the assistance a computer can give him, and (3) like me, he will start thinking about using a computer not in bigger and bigger cases, but in smaller and smaller cases.

12

The Employment of Modern Techniques and Technology in Trial Preparation

Lee Turner

As never before, the legal profession is under attack. We are indicted by the judiciary. Congress proposes extensive regulations. We are regularly flagellated by almost every segment of our society, including our own bar associations. Increasingly, we are named as defendants in malpractice litigation. To prepare for the future, examine the present. To understand the present, study the past. To say the legal profession is in trouble is to state a commonplace fact. Troubled by client resistance to ever higher costs, troubled by the low median income received by the average practitioner, troubled by the vast number of people economically excommunicated from equal protection of laws. To understand the source of our troubles and proceed to elimination, one must consider the role of lawyers in present-day society.

The age of the industrial revolution is past. Historians refer to the present system of mass production, electronic communication and the welfare state as the post industrial society. In the midst of this post industrial society, there yet exists an anachronism. The spectacle of a major service industry tied to concepts of eighteenth century piecework methods. The defense of a products liability case has become an economic horror story to our clients as a result of our cottage craft approach to each individual case. Society, through No-Fault Automobile Insurance has begun to turn away from our professions. Skyrocketing malpractice premiums points to a No-Fault solution for the medical malpractice problems. Early warning indicators are out for products liability litigation. I submit our failure to keep pace in the practice of law lies in the failure to analyze the source and evolution of law. Consider the fact each of the world's twenty-one advanced civilizations, save one, has been based upon the concept of law, according to the historian, Arnold J. Toynbee. Law founded not on verbal transmission but rather on written codes. Hammurabi, the Ten Commandments, Roman Law, the evolution of English Common Law, all have in common their expression in written form; written precedent repealed only by later written laws. Why the emphasis on written law in advanced societies? Simply because written law is not subject to progressive distortion as in the case of verbal transmission. For precisely the same reason, rules of evidence generally prohibit hearsay statements. Filtered through more than one source, verbal transmission becomes distorted and unreliable.

Written codification of law is the indispensable instrument in the development of ecumenical government. It originates in the developing common sense of a society through customs or taboos as prohibition of deviate behavior. Soon reason for taboos is forgotten and lost in the maze of verbal transmissions; thereafter, precedent alone serves as the deterrent. Finally, the specialization of an advanced society gives rise to the orderly collection of law based upon precedent, founded in turn on earlier customs or taboos in the form of written legal codes.

True to its tradition, law expressed either by code or judicial fiat, is invariably expressed in writing. Contrast this expression with the practice of law in the law office. Our relations within are almost entirely verbal, and in reliance on verbal transmission lies our failure to adapt to the requirements of twentieth-century America.

Whenever people work together, whether in miniscule units or nation states, some form of guidance is needed. If we are not to become exhausted through noncumulative verbal transmission, instructions must be reduced to writing. Indeed, this is the framework upon which the scientific method is built. Scientific method consists of five simple steps with the completion of each step expressed in writing so that any may understand the nature and extent of the problem and work towards its solution. *First,* recognize the problem; *second,* collect facts; *third,* analyze facts and set up a hypothesis; *fourth,* test your hypothesis; and *fifth,* prove or disprove the hypothesis.

Put it this way, facts do not explain themselves. It is necessary to arrange facts, relate them one to the other, then to generalize and, where possible, discover cause and effect relationships. In the cumulative effect of science through the scientific method, enormous economic profit accrues. Compare this process with the noncumulative effect of verbal transmission and it becomes evident why the practice of law remains pre-industrial in nature.

Scientists alone could neither build the atomic bomb nor construct the moon rocket. Through the application of the scientific method, the complex was broken down to the simple, written procedures established, with the result that these highly complex products have seen seventy-five percent of their development by relatively unskilled persons. At the beginning of the century, business was already expressing the scientific method through the phrase "Systems Management." Even though law comes to systems management seventy-five years late, I submit through the application of the principles of systems management lies the cure for the deadly illness threatening our profession.

Systems Management means you must first organize, then delegate. Responsibilities are clearly defined and require an accountability for actions taken. In our firm, we first determined where the particular field of law involving the greatest concentration existed. Obviously, it was the field of negligence and trial practice. We then proceeded to collect facts. By facts I mean that information that could tell us how we really had been practicing law in that field. Everyone of us has a superb source and that source is past effort. We conducted a random review of closed legal files. In analyzing our approach, we found amazing similarities between work product from file to file. Collate the pleadings, review correspondence, examine memos, and soon you will find a pattern of repetitious behavior emerging. For years I had been dictating, many times without reference to form books or other visual aids. Always, however, on a piecework basis. What I didn't realize was that I was saying the same thing over and over again, case to case. Without knowing it, I had already established the standard approach to many of the problems with which I was confronted. When a nonlawyer suggested my standard approaches could be codified in the form of written standard procedures which a nonlawyer could be trained to follow, the way was open to break the barrier between eighteenth-century piecework methods and twentieth-century Systems Management. A review of past files soon disclosed any task coming easily to a lawyer without reference to any aid, usually could be broken down into an established procedure. Past efforts, in effect, simply represented establishment of written precedent. Prior to our conversion to Systems Management, most transmission between lawyers and staff was based on verbal transmission. We found we were constantly repeating ourselves. We were constantly plowing the same ground. We concluded if our hypothesis was correct, all verbal transmission had to be replaced by written communication. Concluding whenever people work together within small units, some form of guidance is needed, we began to issue all instructions in the form of written memorandum with one copy to the file and one copy to the person receiving the instruction, who in turn, ticklered the instruction for deadline. The instructions were placed in a permanent file from which selected training instructions are drawn. Whenever mistakes or bottlenecks occurred, a written memorandum was issued to correct the error and assign responsibility.

From this effort evolved written procedures. A procedure is nothing more or less than a written checklist for a particular unit of effort. When the checklist has been established, then a person less skillful than a lawyer can be trained to administer the checklist. As checklists proliferate, it is necessary to clarify areas of responsibility or accountability by a written chart, always avoiding overlapping areas. Checklists must be periodically audited and refined. When refined, procedures lead to uniform, high-quality effort. Remember, when a lawyer attempts to dictate without resort to visual aids, he is doing so because he is simply engaging in repetitious activity. Yet, how many times when interrupted, he may miss some vital point to his later sorrow. The trained, nonlegal assistant, guided by a written checklist, produces the same effort and less error than if done by a lawyer without reference to the checklist.

Bear in mind, clear communication is always essential to success. People will do that which is expected of them only if they know what is expected of them. Does the listener receive the same impression that the teller has in mind? It was said of Napoleon, before any order was issued to his commanders and thence to the troops, he first reviewed it with an orderly of lower than average intelligence who was always stationed outside his door. The reason is obvious—if the orderly could understand the instruction, Napoleon could safely assume the generals, who must execute, would likewise comprehend without confusion. Clear communication in a law office is assured when you do it in writing.

The principle followed is the delegation of routine tasks to the lowest level of skill possible consistent with a uniform, high-quality work product. No lawyer should ever do work a highly skilled nonlawyer can do. Products liability litigation can be an absolute nightmare for the defense. Astute plaintiff's counsel will have thoroughly researched his case. By the time suit is filed, he should know, not only the misrepresentations made in his case, but similar misrepresentations allegedly made by the defendant and other such cases. If negligent design in involved, he should have an expert available who can qualify as an expert. That is to say, someone who designs similar type products. He will know whether failure to provide safety devices and to otherwise keep up with the state of the art and the trade is a factor and in short, be fully acquainted with the basis upon which he intends to proceed, having examined the various repositories of information generally available concerning similar type cases. Under notice of pleading, however, only the barest of allegations need be made in the petition. Most usually, the defense counsel receives a copy of the complaint and summons from his carrier with instructions to protect our interests and the interests of our "assured" with the further request that counsel advise regarding liability as soon as he has had opportunity to review the file. The file most often is nonexistent or contains summarized efforts of two days' work by a general adjuster. Immediately upon receipt of a file in our office, rather than the file going directly to the attorney, it first must go through calendar and docket control. A deadly routine for a busy lawyer is reviewing mail and calendaring for answer dates, trial dates, hearing dates, appointments or any other deadline. For a lawyer to conduct this review and thereafter prepare ticklers to make certain no deadline is missed, is to virtually ask the impossible. We, long ago, concluded this work could not only be performed by a nonlawyer specialist, but a specialist could do it far more efficiently in all respects than could a lawyer. In short, we established a procedure. This procedure requires the mail be opened, examined, calendared, ticklers prepared for answer, hearing or any other deadlines by the calendar specialist before any lawyer or any other person is permitted to review. We no longer wake up in the middle of the night worrying whether the answer date was yesterday or is tomorrow.

As soon as the lawyer receives the file on the desk, he reviews and in the typical products liability case, simply dictates an answer, raising every possible defense, including (1) misuse of the product, either in the nature of contributory negligence or assumption of the risk, (2) unintended use of the product, (3) use with knowledge of the alleged defect or the dangers involved, (4) where applicable, use and disregard of warnings, (5) where involved, use contrary to instructions, (6) abuse of the product, (7) statute of limitations, (8) third-party liability. As soon as the answer is dictated, the case then is assigned to a trial specialist who will be primarily responsible for the case from the time she receives it to the time litigation is terminated. If any of the items on the checklist for the answer have not been dictated in the pleading, she will inquire as to whether there is an oversight on the part of the dictating lawyer.

Ordinarily, we respond immediately after receipt of a petition, with both an answer and outgoing interrogatories. With the great pressure to bring dockets current and assure the right to any litigant to have his case heard within a year from the date of filing, it becomes necessary for files to move forward with dispatch. This cannot be done, however, in the typical products liability case. Both the defense lawyer and the trial specialist must become educated as to the issues involved. Our first order of business is to contact corporate counsel, advising we are assigned defense attorneys and inquiring as to the names of the people in his company who have primary and superior knowledge concerning the issues involved. We will want to know the name of the engineer and scientist who designed the product. A complete packaging of the materials involved from design of the product to its development, assembly and, finally, shipping from the plant. We will routinely require of corporate counsel, concerning the size and nature of the industry involved, its manufacturing and sales practices, and the position of his company's product in such industry. We will want to know from him how the product is marketed. That is, what part wholesalers and dealers play in the distribution, are there any warranties and if so, the nature and scope of any written warranties. If a multidivision company is involved, a clear identification of these divisions and/or corporate entities and the part each of them play in the products design, manufacture and distribution. Corporate counsel will be asked to provide a copy of any and all advertising pamphlets, brochures, operator's manuals or service instructions. He will be asked to assemble copies of any and all records showing the time and place of manufacture, including any quality control records used in the manufacturing process. He will be requested to furnish sales records, showing how plaintiff achieved title of the alleged defective product, including the name of the retail salesman, copy of the customer order and the resultant invoices. We will next request a complete listing of similar complaints made to the company by others where a lawsuit was or was not involved. If litigation was involved, complete information concerning the case, including the names filed, the names of the attorneys involved, particularly defense attorneys and the outcome. Our requested information will conclude with the request that corporate counsel contact us by telephone immediately upon receipt of the letter. Why do we know that all of these items will be requested? Simply because the information is contained in the checklist which is utilized by the trial assistant in drafting the letter. When corporate counsel calls, we will advise from the inception of litigation to its termination, the name of the legal assistant with whom he can communicate at any time. That in addition, the legal assistant will have the same detailed knowledge concerning the status of the case as that of the defending lawyer.

As soon as the information requested from the company is received and reviewed, contact is again made with corporate counsel with the request a meeting be arranged between key design and products engineers, superintendent of the primary manufacturing division, together with that division's chief of quality control. Thereafter, both defense counsel and the trial specialist should have a preliminary discussion with the aforedescribed personnel and thereafter being given a full and complete tour of the manufacturing plant. Special emphasis should be given to inspection of the quality control procedures, including the percentages of "horrible examples" that escape through even the most rigid quality control apparatus. After the tour is complete, the defense lawyer and trial assistant should again meet with the key personnel described above to be further educated concerning the product, the alleged defect and thereafter, discuss and if possible, arrive at a consensus as to the specific questions, through interrogatory, to be submitted to the plaintiff. The defense lawyer will find he can function much better if he can act as an interlocutor rather than scrivener when engaged in discussions with persons involved in the manufacturing process.

Upon return to the office, the trial assistant, based upon the discussions had, will prepare a series of interrogatories concerning the desired information, and thereafter submit the same to the defense attorney for review. The defense attorney will make whatever changes are necessary, make whatever additions are required and conclude by dictating additional interrogatories designed to narrow the issues, i.e., is plaintiff proceeding on the basis of negligence, improper design, breach of warranty, express or implied, failure to warn or otherwise. Through interrogatory, he will attempt to determine the nature and extent of plaintiff's preparation, including the name of any experts consulted, the witnesses available, the location of the alleged defective product, the place where the accident occurred, what changes, if any, have been made in the product, is the product available for inspection and/or testing. These proposed interrogatories thereafter will be returned to corporate counsel for final review with the in-house experts engaged in the manufacturing process. Thereafter, whatever changes or additions required are returned to the defense attorney's office. The defense attorney and the trial assistant will prepare the final outgoing interrogatories and ticklers prepared for answer dates. If the plaintiff attorney has failed to answer when answer is due, the trial assistant will prepare routine request that the interrogatories be answered and automatically extending an additional 20 days' time in which to answer the interrogatories. If no reply has been received by defense attorney upon the termination of the additional twenty days, motions to compel answers are immediately prepared by the trial assistant and submitted to the defense attorney for his approval. The trial assistant has the burden of seeing to it the case moves forward with dispatch, exerting pressure not only upon the adverse attorney but the defense attorney as well.

In-coming interrogatories—Every lawyer plays the game on interrogatories. Provide as little information as possible short of sanctions being invoked, obtaining as much information as possible from the other side. The game can be dangerous, however, for the reason incoming interrogatories are a booby trap for the unwary. If you give only cursory answers, you run the risk of a later production of written material and statements from both your file and the company file that may show great discrepancies. Demonstrated discrepancies cause juries to lose faith in both the lawyer and the client's integrity. When interrogatories are received, our trial assistant immediately forwards a copy to corporate counsel with the request the proposed answers be prepared by the company's experts in both engineering, manufacturing, sales and service. The trial assistant immediately prepares a request for additional thirty days' time in which to answer the interrogatories. The trial assistant then attempts to prepare answers based upon the information we have received to date, which then, after review by the defense attorney, are forwarded to corporate counsel, with the request the corporate counsel forward their proposed answers. When corporate counsel's proposed answers are returned, the trial assistant will attempt to merge the answers into a proposed final set of answers for review with the defense attorney. While the defense attorney may make numerous objections to the interrogatories, they usually can be assured there is no discrepancy between information in the company files and his proposed answers.

Motions for production and inspection—Immediately upon receipt of plaintiff's answers to defense interrogatories, motion for production and inspection of the alleged defective article, if it exists, is made together with motion for production of any and all written materials including statements of witnesses, product information, warranties, sales information in the possession of plaintiff attorney. When this information is received and before depositions are scheduled, defense counsel, trial assistant and company personnel should inspect the product if available. Immediately after inspection of the product, a detailed, technical product briefing should be had between defense counsel, the trial assistant and the company specialist involved with design, engineering, manufacturing, sales and service of the product. At this point, defense counsel must be given an in-depth understanding of the design history of the product as well as engineering factors and functional performance requirements which influenced and controlled the final design and mode of manufacture. He must become intimately acquainted with the product, its performance, characteristics, its size, shape, practical uses and all details of the manufacture of the product, including quality control testing procedures. At this meeting, there should be a general concensus as to the questions to be asked by further interrogatory and/or deposition, and the prospects of a successful defense. After this education is complete, the defense lawyer is ready for scheduling depositions and appointments. The hub around which successful defense of products liability revolves is the discovery deposition. Overwhelmed as we are by minutiae, we oftentimes lose sight of the goal. Unfortunately, most competent defense lawyers have many other demands on their time other than a particular products liability case in question. These demands quite often will find him in trial with key witnesses remaining undeposed. Through procedures, we have solved this problem. The trial assistant, who is intimately acquainted with the particular file in question, lists the names of any and all witnesses to be deposed. These names immediately go to an appointment specialist whose duty it is to maintain a master file of all counties and areas in which litigation is pending, addresses of witnesses to be deposed and locations where other work is to be performed. As investigation of interrogatory reveals further information, the names of witnesses are constantly added to our file, with ticklers prepared as to the depositions to be taken. If witnesses are scattered, in an attempt to hold down the great costs inherent in products liability defense, other depositions on additional cases are scheduled. Obviously if one is to travel to Goodland, Kansas, 240 miles distant from Great Bend, one does not look with favor to retracing the journey a few days later. As soon as the notice to take deposition is received, the deposition specialist immediately reviews her file to determine what witnesses can be deposed in the general direction of travel. She will discuss with the trial assistant what witnesses they have in the area involved who have not been placed on the deposition calendar. All the minutiae involved at depositions, such as contacting the witness, issuing mileage and per diem payments, arranging for the court reporter, for transportation and matters of that kind are done by the calendar specialist. As doctors long ago learned, and lawyers are coming to know, we cannot successfully schedule our own time for maximum use. A lay person, however, can.

Medical appointments—If bodily injury is involved in a products case, the trial assistant will prepare medical authorizations and/or orders designed to elicit not only the current medical condition of the claimant, but also any and all past history. She will examine the medical information as it comes in and where unfamiliar, doctors' names or references to previous medical problems are disclosed, will track down the information that so often discloses a pre-existing history of the complaints of which plaintiff is currently complaining.

All medical appointments are made by the legal assistant rather than the lawyer, even though it may be necessary for the lawyers to review the facts with the doctor prior to the examination itself.

Organization of file—A products liability can be absolutely overwhelming in the paper work involved. In a drug liability case recently concluded, stacks of documents were involved exceeding 100,000 pages. For a lawyer to attempt to organize, collate, index and examine each of the documents in question would lead to absolutely prohibitive costs. Under the direction of the trial assistant, additional nonlawyers were recruited for the purpose of reading, analyzing and indexing the documents involved, identifying those bearing upon the issues in the case for the defense attorney's additional review. Information retrieval in complex products cases can require the computerization of the data available. Presently pending is a case involving repetitive product litigation, giving rise to an assignment of four lawyers with a staff of forty nonlawyers to examine, collate, index and computerize all available information. In cases of this complexity it is absolutely mandatory that nonlawyers be used or the costs could escalate to the point No-Fault products liability insurance will be the answer as it has in the case of automobile litigation.

Pretrial—When the case is set for pretrial, the trial assistant will have prepared, outlined and indexed the entire case file, identifying proposed exhibits and otherwise minimizing the demands on the defense attorney's time.

Trials—When notified of a trial setting, the trial assistant immediately notifies corporate counsel and the insurance client of the trial date, schedules a date for meeting between corporate counsel, in-house experts in design, manufacture, assembly, sales as well as the outside expert retained by the defense, and schedules all key witness interviews. Subpoenas are prepared and issued, subject to the attorney's approval. The trial assistant reviews the jury list with analysis of all prospective jurors. While subpoenas may be issued for all defense witnesses at the inception of trial, the trial assistant will attempt to schedule the actual appearance.

The principle followed is: No lawyer performs work that can be delegated to a person less skilled than himself. The same principle applies to nonlegal assistants. As we established our first rudimentary procedures, we selected a secretary and trained her in the use of the procedures. To free her time for this work, we delegated the routine tasks she ordinarily performed to a less skillful person. She was given minimum instruction, permitting her to perform her work efficiently. As procedures and personnel proliferated, we soon abandoned a direct lawyer-nonlegal assistant relationship and used the record transcription unit. All dictation, save emergency, is by machine to the record transcription unit. If the record transcription unit can complete the work product, it is then sent directly to the lawyer for his approval. If the work product cannot be completed in final form, the instructions are placed in the form of written memo with carbon to the file and then routed to the appropriate trial assistant who prepares the work product for final approval by the attorney. If not possible, the proposed work product is presented to the attorney for his review, additions or corrections, and thereafter placed in final form.

In recruiting personnel for specialist training, remember she is to be trained to perform intellectual functions rather than mechanical functions. Just as the lawyer is bored by deadly routine, a nonlegal assistant must be given the challenge of intellectual stimulation and creative thinking. As her skills grow, continue the principle of delegation of her routine tasks to a less skillful person, freeing up even more additional time until finally your most skilled people are entirely occupied with performing tasks in which written procedures have been established.

Not only lawyers, but also all nonlegal assistants are required to organize their knowledge, training and experience for future use in written form. Written form requires clarification. A nonlegal assistant is required to collate into the form of a checklist and to establish a procedure by putting the bits and pieces of the lawyer's instructions together into a coherent pattern. While the lawyer has the duty to initially train the specialist in any field, it becomes the specialist's duty immediately thereafter to train a backup specialist so that no specialist retraining is required by the lawyer in the event of illness or resignation. Unless a new field of specialization is opened, the training function is thereafter conducted by nonlegal personnel. Perhaps the most important service a written procedure provides is the systematic and careful instruction which it gives the office force. The quickest, easiest and best method of doing each task is adopted as the proper procedure. Obviously, errors are less frequent where the procedure is certain and well known and available in a book of instructions which can quickly be referred to from time to time. The lawyer must have complete control of standards and policy. His is the duty of periodic audit to make certain errors do not creep into the system. The object is to relieve him from the burden of responsibility of daily supervision as to routine. The checklist, together with flow charts, delineates the duties of each member of the office force so no one can say the office task should have been performed by another. Once the standard is established, it becomes the inflexible rule until a new or better method is discovered. Whenever a mistake occurs, arrange the system to prevent its repetition. No mistake should be made twice. When it does, memos should be dictated as to the source of error, analyzing the reasons therefor and who is responsible.

Thereafter the memo is to be inserted in a permanent book and dated. The procedure is then expanded to avoid repetition. In other words, you follow the principle of cumulative knowledge based upon written analysis rather than sporadic and uncertain noncumulative verbal communication which has been the rule in the practice of law to the present time.

Recognizing the need for new answers, the House of Delegates of the American Bar in 1968, declared:

1. That the legal profession recognized there are many tasks in serving a client's needs which can be performed by a trained nonlawyer assistant, working under the direction and supervision of the lawyer.
2. That the profession encouraged the training and employment of such assistants.
3. That there be created a special committee of this Association. Prior to the creation of the Special Committee, the American Bar's Standing Committee on Professional Ethics in Opinion 316 laid to rest the specter of unauthorized practice by employment of these methods. It stated:

   > The lawyer can employ lay secretaries, lay investigators, lay researchers, accountants, lay scriveners, non-lawyer draftsmen or non-lawyer researchers. In fact, he may employ non-lawyers to do any task for him except counsel clients about law matters, engage directly in the practice of law, appear in court, or appear in formal proceedings as a part of the judicial process, so long as it is he who takes the work and vouches for it to the client and becomes responsible for it to the client.

Those who fear the use of specialists as infringing on the practice of law by lawyers can readily see their fears are groundless. The opportunities for expansion within the canons are far greater than attempted in my office.

Recognize the problem—eighteenth-century methods are no longer valid solutions to twentieth-century problems.

Collect facts—learn what is mechanical and repetitious as opposed to intellectual, then organize a solution through written checklists and procedures. Delegate by written memo, leaving the lawyer to perform those unique and productive efforts he and only he can perform. Properly challenged, abilities of the nonlegal assistant knows no bounds. Initiative and motivation increase. Accomplishment carries with it a sense of loyalty to the organization in which they play an integral part. In this manner, instead of contracting the parameters, our profession can once again expand as we adhere to the principle of providing maximum service at the lowest cost consistent with a fair return to the lawyer.

13

The Combination of a Manual and an Automated Approach to Trial Preparation

Ronald A. Rust and John D. Rome

INTRODUCTION

A major consideration confronting law firms involved in complex litigation is the decision of whether or not to utilize a computer for document management. A premature decision to automate may result in substantial costs even if the suit never reaches the trial stage. However, too late a decision to automate may result in extensive duplication of effort as manually indexed material is recoded for the computer. The solution to this dilemma lies in early development of internal management procedures which allow the computer to be used when (but not before) it is timely and cost effective to do so. The purpose of this paper is to outline considerations for the development of such procedures. The techniques will be discussed in the context of large-scale litigation, but the basic management principles are equally applicable to the control of small cases, and, perhaps more importantly, to the small matter which grows to be a complex case.

METHODS OF EVIDENCE MANAGEMENT

Manual systems

Traditionally, litigation materials have been organized by the use of manual indexes. In the small cases, the indexes are usually maintained in the mind of the attorney who has studied all of the related documents. In the larger cases, especially those in which several attorneys have been involved, the indexes are typically physical. Two approaches have normally been used to create physical indexes:

Duplication of file materials
Development of index books

In the first approach, document descriptors are defined. For example, these descriptors may include the names of the individuals who wrote the document, those who received the document and those who were copied or mentioned in the body of the document. Additional conventional descriptors include the date of the document, the major subjects covered in the document and, possibly, the legal issues of the case.

When documents are received, they are placed in a chronological file (date index). But further, additional copies are made for each descriptor file under which the document can be indexed. Therefore, if the document refers to seven individuals, seven copies are made, and one is placed chronologically in each of the respective person files. Additionally, if the document concerns five subjects or legal issues, five more copies are made, and one is placed in each of the proper subject or issue files.

There are few advantages to this approach (unless you happen to be in the paper business) other than the fact that the documents are, indeed, eventually indexed. When perusing the documents in this type of index, the attorneys are not inconvenienced, since the documents are physically contiguous. That is, the fetching and returning of individual documents to and from a filing cabinet are not required.

The disadvantages, however, are obvious: first, local facilities can be taxed by their sheer bulk and the consequent storage space which will be required if a great number of documents are multi-indexed. Next, the attorney who reviews documents will usually have to reread them, thus duplicating the efforts of the person who did the original classification. Further, the files are likely to be rather difficult to transport. Finally, unless a great number of indexing parameters are selected, each index may be a significant subset of the entire file, thus defeating the purpose of indexing.

Using the index book approach, the document is physically filed only once (normally, either chronologically or sequentially, in the order of receipt). Each index book, however, has an entry which shows the actual location of the document. Therefore, in the Smith index book, a posting is made to show that there is a document mentioning Smith located in a certain physical file. The same thing is done for every other descriptor which "fits" the document in question.

In the more sophisticated systems of this type, a small abstract, extract or precis of the document is often included in each index book posting, so that some screening can be done before the physical documents are pulled from the master file.

The advantages of this approach are the relative simplicity of index book construction, the increased manageability of documents and the relatively increased speed with which the file can be perused when the index contains some form of abstract or extract of the information in the original document. The chief disadvantages are the amount of paper shuffling involved in pulling the documents and the fact that usually only one person can effectively utilize the file at any one time, especially in those cases where several indexes overlap.

Nevertheless, for smaller cases involving a minimal number of descriptors defining each document, either of these two approaches works relatively well. However, when the number of documents becomes large, and the number of possible descriptors increases, the problem of making the copies or of posting the index references in the proper books, becomes substantial.

For example, if 5,000 documents are indexed by 20 descriptors and by any combination of up to perhaps 100 names, the scope of the problem becomes apparent. In the above hypothetical case, if each document averages only five subject descriptors and refers to only two individuals, the number of copies or references is still 35,000 (5,000 X 7). Continuing the assumption, if the number of documents is 50,000, the number of references would then be 350,000 (50,000 X 7). Obviously, in the case with 100,000 or more documents, the manual filing/indexing task becomes so difficult that ordinary methods are simply not feasible from any viewpoint.

But even if the materials could be managed manually, what about finding cross-related or multi-indexed documents? For example, it is easy to find the documents involving Mr. Smith, or the documents which originated in May, 1966, or those concerning licensing agreements. But, how does one find those documents sent from Mr. Smith to Mr. Jones, in 1966, which refer to licensing agreements, or which concern patents? The answer, of course, is that in large cases, even though an index has been built or separate files have been created, there is no easy way to select cross-related documents without expending massive amounts of time. Happily, computer technology offers a practical answer.

Automated systems

Basically, there are two methods of retrieving litigation materials using a computer:

1. Full-text recording
2. Document indexing

Full-text recording, as its name implies, involves the converting of all the words in all of the documents or at least major extracts to a computer-readable form. Usually, no manual indexing is done, the idea being to direct the computer to prepare its own index when one is needed. There are some advantages to this approach. In suits where words per se are important, e.g., libel and slander cases, such a system is patently beneficial. Another advantage is that no word can escape attention. That point is, however, one of the largest disadvantages, for one request can unleash an unpredictable cascade of responses. The difficulty is that the attorney who wishes to browse through the file is forced to do his own indexing at document retrieval time. For example, in a 100,000 document product liability case involving autos, an inquiry on the word "autos" may produce 40,000 references and omit those which speak only in terms of "automobiles" or "vehicles" or "units" or "assembly line production" or "Deluxe Specials" or "Model 3000s."

Another difficulty is that documents do not often say what they mean. A memorandum—of potentially devastating impact—might say only: "You should see the dillies we got from our friends in the Motor City today. We can't even unload them."

Another major disadvantage of the full-text approach is the inordinate cost of initially getting the data into the computer. These costs typically range upward of $2.00 per printed page. The use of this approach normally means that the reading of documents by attorneys or trained paraprofessionals familiar with the case is by-passed, thereby forfeiting the opportunity to classify the documents further as to their significance. This classification process also facilitates the identification of documents of singular importance for special handling and review. Finally, although the case law on the subject is still unclear, it would seem logical that evidence organization systems which involve relatively little, if any, input from law firm personnel would have greater difficulty qualifying for attorney work-product protection against discovery.

The document-indexing approach is the second major classification of evidence organization. Briefly, the process is this: first, a manual index form is prepared. This form contains blanks for the logging of certain salient descriptors and may have space to note comments, supply names and record observations. The completed portions of each form are then entered into the computer's memory, where they remain accessible to answer literally any conceivable inquiry, limited only by the extent of the data in the index.

There are a number of significant advantages in employing this method of evidence organization:

An index is available on demand for every descriptor and every combination of descriptors, including any text in abstract form. No longer is it necessary for the staff to prepare all such lists long before they may be needed. If the need does arise, the request is submitted to the computer, and in a matter of minutes, the list is produced.

This approach permits the multiple descriptor cross-match of documents, which is unavailable in either the full-text or manual systems. For example, it is possible to request all documents which meet certain date criteria and which reference certain individuals and which concern specific subjects or combinations of subjects. Also, the output can be sorted in any desired way. The computer then processes the request and prints the desired references. These reference lists are analogous to the index books used in manual systems, except that the computer can create any index book or list when commanded to do so.

The document index system permits the interposition of human judgment between the mass of material and the issues of the case. This eliminates the word dependence which characterizes the full-text approach. This human aspect also makes the transition to the use of computers in litigation a less troublesome undertaking, since the attorney continues to control and manage his own case. He is simply using modern technology as a tool to extend the capability and benefits of manual indexing.

Moreover, staff participation in the evaluation of documents creates the opportunity to rate the material as to its significance and credibility.

Another reason for this approach to the automation of the document index in major litigation is the fact that the duration of major cases is now often measured in years and not in months. Over an extended period of time, there will likely be a substantial turnover in the support staff and possibly even the legal staff. The use of a standardized computer index allows for a degree of continuity, since the computer index need not change during the litigation.

The use of the document index approach means that substantially less material need be entered into the computer, with a concomitant reduction in data preparation costs. Generally, regular indexes require less than ten percent of the data composing a full-text system.

Since a standard data collection form is used to record facts contained in the document, the task of reviewing the documents can be performed easily by paraprofessionals, law students and even skilled office staff members. This means that the cost of capturing this data will be much lower than if the task is performed by attorneys. Naturally, attorneys can participate in this document reading and excerpting process to any extent they feel is necessary.

Another obvious advantage of the document index approach is that it promotes the early organization of the lawsuit; maintaining data in raw word form does not require the same degree of preparation.

Finally, since attorney thought and effort are expended in the creation of an index, a strong argument can be made that the index is protected from discovery under the attorney work-product privilege.

DEVELOPING THE INDEX

The first step in organizing materials in such a way that future automation is easily accomplished is to develop a standard manual index. This is similar to the kind used in most lawsuits today. When developing the index, keep the following rules in mind:

1. The index should be designed by attorneys. Certain items contained in the index are similar from case to case. These include document type (e.g., letter, memo, contract, photograph), date, manual file cross reference (e.g., document number), addressee, persons mentioned in the document and abstract. However, the remainder of the index will refer to specifics of the case and must be developed by attorneys who know the facts, issues and contentions of the suit as well as the defensive posture required vis-à-vis the opposing party.

2. Since the majority of the time expended during the process of indexing is spent in reading the documents, our experience suggests that the index should be fairly detailed. The difference in time to complete a detailed index form, compared with that required to fill out a simple form, is on the order of ten percent. However, substantial later savings are made possible since the index itself becomes a screening vehicle and eliminates the need to re-read most documents. Our suggestion is that since all documents obviously have to be read at least once, the majority of them, hopefully, ought to be read only once.

3. In any case involving thousands of documents, it is essential that much of the initial screening be performed (under close supervision) by nonlawyers. This requires that the index contain objective

information *as to the document* and *not* subjective information as to the case. For example, what is necessary is to identify the document as having a source of Smith, a destination to an existing customer, and a reference to product use. What is not required initially is any concept that this document may be introduced later as an admission by a corporate officer as to potential shortcomings of the product. The subjective analysis will be performed when this document is related to other documents containing similar factual information. In short, the index must be fact, and not issue, oriented.

4. Since the issues, factual situations, witnesses and, in some cases, parties tend to change from the time of the initial complaint until the actual trial, it is necessary that the index be flexible enough to accept additional index items and changes to existing items.

To implement indexing of materials, we have found that the development of an index form is most useful. This form should allow the simple checking of the points which relate to the specific document. Generally, one form is completed for each "information unit." An information unit is a discrete "piece" of information important in the suit. As such, it normally is one document but it may be a manual, a photograph, a paragraph of testimony, a membership list or any other information likely to be reviewed together. In designing the form it is wise to keep in mind the potential for the form's becoming the source document for data entry since this will avoid the necessity of recording the material. Also consider the following suggestions:

1. Define abstracts as to maximum length to reduce coding time and avoid unnecessary data conversion.
2. If search of the abstract for key words is envisaged, develop lists of key words and abbreviations which have uniform meaning throughout the case.
3. Enter names in a standardized manner (normally last name first) and keep lists as to the spellings and key names.
4. Instead of numbering documents as they arrive, develop manual file numbers as to origin of documents. For example, assign page numbers 1.00001 to 1.99999 to adverse party documents from their West Coast Headquarters and 5.00001 to 5.99999 for internal documents from defendant's International Division.

At the risk of sounding simplistic in what is a very complex area, the solution to developing a manual index which may optionally be computerized is to *treat the case from the outset as though it were to be computerized.* If the suit is settled early, it is not necessary to generate a computer system. If the volume of material fails to develop, automation is not required. But for the case which requires use of the computer, the conversion effort will be minimized and costs to the client kept within reasonable limits. And, of course, an additional benefit, whether or not automation is used, will be a better organization of documentary material since an index has been created.

The client

Because most attorneys do not have extensive experience with computers, they are often reluctant to recommend the use of automated litigation support to their clients. They have no problem billing for time or charging for travel, long distance telephone calls, document reproduction and the like, but they do not feel confident listing computer services as a disbursement on behalf of the client. In fact, most major clients use computers in their own businesses and really are not adverse to automation of documentary evidence as long as they know about it in advance. The solution is to initially inform the client of the management approach which the firm is to use in the instant litigation matter. This technique does two things:

1. Avoids the unpleasant surprise to the client which occurs when an attorney says "Oh, by the way, we're going to have to spend $14,000 to automate the record system we've been using."
2. Allows the client to provide such resources if he has them available. If the client uses computer services, he may be able to furnish key-punching or other data entry services and in some situations, may provide the computer itself.

The cost to the client can be determined in advance within an acceptable range. For example, the firm can estimate that the automation of an index will cost in the range of fifty cents to one dollar per information unit. A full-text system will cost upward of two dollars per printed page. Therefore, knowing the approach to be used and estimating the number of documents allows for a planning cost of litigation support before discovery even begins.

The decision to automate

Although the decision to automate document management can be made at any time, there are certain factors which should be considered. They include:

1. *Number of Documents.* Although no concrete rule can be stated, it is probably that automation is not required in most cases where the number of documents does not exceed three thousand. Clearly, when there are more than ten thousand documents, automation becomes a cost-effective tool. For the case

with less than ten thousand documents, other criteria must be analyzed in deciding whether or not to automate.

2. *Complexity of Materials.* There is no question that a matter with a single issue set in a clear factual framework (e.g., a breach of contract case) is more easily managed than, for example, a complex price-fixing issue over an extended period of time involving multiple parties and different jurisdictions. In the former case, even if there are substantial quantities of documents, the decision to automate may be delayed since manual management techniques work fairly well.
3. *Time Frame of the Litigation.* If the parties are committed to a firm schedule of discovery, deposition and trial, use of a computer may be essential simply because it expedites the preparation of deposition outlines, interrogatories, witness lists, motions, answers and the like.
4. *Number of Parties Involved.* In a complex case involving several parties and numerous law firms, automation may be essential since it allows for simultaneous access to information at several remote locations.
5. *The Cost-Benefit Decision.* At some point it simply becomes too expensive in personnel time to perform manual searches. In a representative case with which we were involved, consisting of some 20,000 documents, we made the following observations:

   To search the raw documents for the references to a company not originally a party to the suit took about forty hours. A manual index to the same material could be searched in from four to six hours. When automated, the search could be performed in less than five minutes with, of course, considerably improved accuracy.

The computer system

Although different types of computer software have been successfully used in a variety of litigation circumstances, certain characteristics are essential for the orderly management of documentary materials. The following capability should be demanded of the computer system used:

1. *Cross-Relational Ability.* It is important to be able to select documents based upon any criteria specified. For example, it might be required to select all documents in 1973 which were directed to the marketing division, which were sent by Mr. Smith but which were not copied to Mr. Jones. Single selection systems may be useful but are of an order of magnitude less powerful than those with cross-match capabilities.

2. *Selective Search Capability.* Some systems simply disgorge all of the information contained in a series of periodic computer reports. The better approach is to have the computer selectively generate reports as required.
3. *Sorting or Ordering Capability.* Since information is normally not indexed chronologically, it is important for the computer system to be able to sort the material as required. For example, often documents which appear quite innocuous on their face, are extremely significant in showing a pattern of activity over a period of time. Without the ability to automatically generate document indexes in chronological order, the importance of these documents may be missed.

The ideal use of an automated system for control of documentary materials is shown in Appendix A.

CONCLUSION

The development of manual procedures which allow for future automation of documentary materials is a practical approach for most litigation. Whether the computer system is generated or not, the result is:

1. Better management of all materials
2. Better response by the firm to unexpected changes in the suit
3. Better utilization of law firm personnel
4. Continuity for the extended suit
5. Manageable costs to the client

Appendix A

Case status	Manual activity	Computer activity
Initial Pleading	Develop a data collection form which is fact, not issue, oriented.	Review form for potential computer input.
Early Discovery	Modify and refine data form as case develops.	Review form. Paraprofessionals screen, index and abstract materials.
(At this point, if the case justifies, a computer system is generated.)		
Discovery	Continue refinement of the data collection form, and continue indexing of the documents.	Generate the computer system. Load and edit the information.
Deposition	Paraprofessionals, who select documents for attorney's review, use printouts or prepare outlines of key documents for deposition.	Retrieve information by selection on any combination of names, index items, or keywords within the abstract.
Deposition	Index and abstract the deposition testimony.	Load deposition material into computer.
Pre-trial		Prepare witness lists and abstracts of new material for attorney's review. Produce evidence lists for court.
Trial	Index and abstract the trial testimony.	Organize the information by witness for examination purposes.
Post-trial		Retrieve the materials for motions, etc.
Appeal		Organize the materials referenced in briefs.

14

Litigation File Management: Preparation for Trial

Lewis H. Vovakis

INTRODUCTION

While any discussion of computer-assisted litigation support systems is incomplete without relating the application of such systems to both trial and post-trial activity, this paper addresses systems support as it applies to discovery and other pre-trial preparation.

At the outset it should be noted that automated systems used in conjunction with complex litigations are not intended to serve merely as a substitute storage medium for the massive volume of documentary data involved; rather, such systems are designed to manage the large quantities of information which accumulate during major litigations in such a way that counsel can quickly and exhaustively access the pertinent documents during any phase of the litigation. Although the foregoing may seem self-evident, it is a common misconception that once all documents, deposition transcripts, motions, memoranda, briefs, etc., have been entered into a system, the various computer outputs largely obviate the need for further reference to the actual documents, depositions, etc. This, of course, is not the case, as will become evident in the following paragraphs.

SYSTEM OBJECTIVES

Prior to the implementation of a litigation file management system, it is necessary to define for each case the objectives sought to be derived from the system. Briefly and generally stated, following are some of the common major objectives:

1. To establish a controlled central collection of documents relevant to the case at hand.
2. To provide bibliographic and subject access to the data base in order to support effective witness preparation and/or cross examination.
3. To provide the ability to pull together documents supporting major contentions.
4. To provide support for the drafting and editing of trial briefs and other documents, using the data base as a primary source of preprocessed input.
5. To provide effective tools for the control of all aspects of the management of the case from the filing of the complaint through the appeals process.

INFORMATION REQUIREMENTS BY STAGE OF LITIGATION

The following discussion regarding user requirements has been synthesized from observations by Aspen Systems Corporation of the types of problems experienced by attorneys and client management staffs involved in various litigations. This statement provides the rationale for some of the concepts later suggested in Aspen's approach to litigation file management.

Discovery

In order to minimize the cost of document screening and acquisition for the purpose of responding to discovery requests, it is necessary that a common data base of documents relevant to the case be created with an indication of those documents which have been produced for the opposition.

Moreover, there is frequently a need for a means of routing possibly relevant documents, or summaries thereof, to the appropriate attorneys or client management staff so that they are not burdened with unnecessary volume while at the same time ensuring that they are provided access to all relevant materials.

Regarding accessing documents, experience has indicated a need for retrieving documents through directories or indexes, as well as through a search and retrieval system, by scanning for certain descriptive information contained on the face of the document (e.g., author, addressee, date, document type, and other similar data elements or combinations thereof).

Finally, it has been found most useful during discovery to have the capacity through the use of the computer to group documents related to particular contentions or theories through taxonomic coding—both separately and in combination with other codes, descriptive data and information contained in document summaries.

Pre-trial proceedings

Complex litigations involving voluminous documents and transcripts have shown a clear need for the precise recording of positions taken by the attorney on behalf of his client as to various factual and legal issues, as well as procedures, so as to ensure consistency and to guard against compromise of the case. Some of the functions within a litigation file management system which are employed to achieve these objectives are:

1. Indexing of the full text or abstracts, as appropriate, of all relevant pleadings, briefs, proposed pre-trial orders and similar documents.
2. Indexing of the full text of transcripts of arguments presented at all of the pre-trial hearings.
3. Indexing of the full text of all depositions taken in preparation for trial.
4. Tagging of all documents introduced as exhibits or mentioned during the taking of depositions.
5. Indexing legal memoranda and briefs by reference to the particular points of law which they address.
6. Noting of positive or negative character of documents.
7. Making provision for the updating of the document data base to later include attorney's work product summaries related to each document; contention statements; cross-references to other documents; and taxonomic codes.

Trial support

Although this discussion, as earlier mentioned, is concerned with litigation support prior to trial, it is imperative that design specifications and system objectives be established at the outset with a view to providing systems support during the actual conduct of the trial as well. Among the needs during trial which must be anticipated, therefore, are the following:

1. A means for tracking trial exhibits, including the purposes for which they were introduced and their evidentiary status.
2. A means for extracting relevant document summaries, work product summaries, contention statements and other individ-

ual data elements from the data base for possible use in narrative factual statements, trial briefs and trial arguments.
3. A means for creating separate files of proposed event statements, contentions, legal opinions and other material useful in generating briefs.
4. A means for continuous and rapid text editing and easy retrieval of the statements or subfiles in various sequences as required in the preparation of proposed documents in support of the trial.
5. Automated indexing of the entire trial transcript as an aid in preparing and/or impeaching witnesses.
6. Rapid retrieval of any documents or transcript materials in the file during the trial stage with response times of a few minutes.

RECOMMENDED LITIGATION MANAGEMENT APPROACH

The design philosophy for an effective litigation file management system is to allow for wide flexibility in the treatment accorded each of the hundreds of different types of documents pertaining to a given case. Documents which do not clearly have high significance in the case may receive minimal treatment; indeed, where they are homogeneous in nature they may even be processed collectively initially rather than treated as individual documents. The more important or significant documents will normally receive more detailed processing, such as abstracting; assignment of taxonomic codes; review by attorneys and witnesses; addition of work product statements; and, in some more limited cases, input in full text machine-readable form, wherein each word in the text of the document is accessible for search and retrieval.

The overall system approach is divided into two separate flows, viz., input and request processing, respectively.

Acquisition, input processing, and initial dissemination

The first step in the processing is acquisition and screening of the documents to be included in the data base. Where thousands of documents are involved, this can be a major undertaking which may entail coordination in the gathering of documents from multiple geographic sites, together with the assignment of attorneys, paralegals and clerical staff to accomplish this purpose, depending upon the nature of the case.

Screening and logging forms and manuals must be prepared, the former to record any relevant judgments made by the staff initially screening the documents, and the latter setting forth the applicable procedures. The amount of intellectual effort later required in the analysis of these documents is thereby reduced.

Aspen's experience has clearly established that a coded system alone does not suffice since it cannot in all instances provide the litigator with the optimum benefits which can be made available to assist him in the prosecution of his case. Rather, the combination of bibliographic surrogation; document analysis, including the preparation of abstracts or even full-text data entry in some instances; and the application of taxonomic coding (a classification of concepts), as appropriate, has produced significantly more favorable results to the litigating attorney.

After the documents have been collected at a central repository, the manual effort required in document processing continues in the form of inspection and analysis of each document by teams of coders and abstractors whose functions include the recording of pertinent data from the documents onto a Document Control Form (DCF) tailored to the requirements of the specific litigation in progress. Detailed and precise procedures are established to accomplish these functions efficiently, and it is the data appearing on the DCF which is converted into machine-readable form and entered into a data base.

Among the initial listings in the form of computer outputs which are available to counsel and which have been found to be useful in the early stages of document processing are inventory listings, showing by document number and other pertinent identifying data a complete listing of all documents processed to date; and directories sorted by author, for example, which, together with other relevant data, can be utilized as a means of identifying duplicate documents which have entered the data base and which can be culled therefrom through a separate updating transaction. Since these types of listings have a continuing utility, periodic updated lists can be produced as the data base grows to ensure currency of the file.

Request processing and output services

The attorney seeking documents in the data file—either individually or by class—can access the document data either by reference to the printed indexes noted above or by framing a computer search. If he then wishes to examine the full text of documents so discovered, he has the option of requesting copies of the relevant documents from the document repository, or, if reproduction of such documents becomes too burdensome, they can be maintained on microfilm for easy hard-copy or viewing access.

Retrieval of document information

There are a number of methods employed within the litigation support system to provide the attorney with the needed information from the total data collection. Viewed as a whole, the mass of documents constitutes a data bank whose individual entries or transactions are organized and coded in such a way as to permit their retrieval singly or by classes.

The retrieval strategies and information delivery and display methods set forth in this section are not only geared closely to the strategies of the case and the anticipated needs of legal counsel; they are also tailored to suit the characteristics of collected data with the view of retrieving the maximum information with the least possible cost and effort.

Printed directories

Printed directories represent one of the most effective and inexpensive means of listing some or all documents according to predetermined criteria. Depending upon the lawyer's needs, the documents may be listed alphabetically by their titles, authors, dates, subpoena item numbers, taxonomic codes, etc. (see Figure 1). Earlier reference was made to the production of such directories for the purpose of maintaining an inventory listing of documents and to identify duplicate documents in the data file.

Printed context indexes

Whereas directories address themselves to specific items of information, context indexes list alphabetically all information in the form of words and phrases, together with their immediate contextual environment and source. Stated another way, the indexed words are listed in ascending alphabetic sequence in the middle of a computer printout page, each accompanied to the left and right by all or parts of the sentence in which they occurred, as well as the document's page and/or reference number in the right columns.

Since the full text is indexed and printed as above described (with the exception of common words having no information value, such as articles and prepositions), these indexes are particularly valuable and appropriate for application to those document control forms including abstracts or other extensive textual portions of the documents, as well as to deposition, pre-trial hearing and trial transcripts.

Search and retrieval

Although it will be found that the litigation file management system will respond to many of the attorney's requirements through

Figure 1. Author directory

Author	Doc. no.	Fl. no.	Doc. date	Doc. type	Sec. CD	No. pgs.	Sup. no.	Comp. no.
ABRAMS, A.C.	0621	43	071472	LTR		02	009	21
	5233	71	101768	MMO		16	006	14
	6021	42	082970	LTR	C	02	028	18
	6342	36	010369	LTR	PC	01	027	26
ALLEN, B.R.	0498	72	081672	LTR		12	126	32
	0721	21	032170	RPT	C	04	048	11
	5422	35	101969	LTR	C	02	112	31
	6308	72	090172	LTR		02	027	12
	6311	16	060571	MTG		26	072	19
	7201	72	071472	LTR		01	101	23
BATES, R.S.	0202	16	081468	LTR	C	02	094	27
	0431	84	100670	NTE	C	11	119	22
	0543	29	091472	TGM		01	106	16
	6994	81	071472	LTR		01	006	01
	9721	98	081673	LTR		01	028	09
BUTLER, H.B.	7042	71	111472	TGM		01	004	33
	7211	85	091369	MMO	PC	02	016	54
CHASE, S.A.	0732	18	081168	RPT	C	17	022	38
	0941	20	070269	MMO	PC	03	103	41
	1167	24	061771	MMO		02	097	37
	1894	86	101472	LTR	C	02	114	50
	2463	72	112669	LTR		01	128	51
	2464	26	062368	LTR		01	132	38
	2465	74	042167	MMO	PC	04	009	47

the various directories and context indexes described above, there exists in all major and complex litigations the additional need for the ability to request custom searches of the entire file. Such searches allow counsel to request that the computer locate and print all documents containing a given word, phrase or group of words in the same sentence, paragraph or document. The computer locates and prints those documents meeting the attorney's specifications and highlights the words searched both in the text and in the margin for easy reference (see Figures 2a, 2b, and 2c).

SUMMARY

The foregoing discussion is intended to present an overview of a successful pre-trial computerized support system for major litigations and is based upon specific applications of Aspen Systems Corporation's litigation file management services to a variety of such litigations throughout the nation during the past several years.

Excluded from this paper are the myriad of detailed and complex procedures and manuals—both technical and people-oriented—which are required to channel the requisite expertise to the peculiar requirements of large, intricate lawsuits.

Figure 2a Search—request

```
SEARCH XYZ CASE.
TITLE ALL REFERENCES TO "PRIVATE BRANDS."
*
*
*QUERY REQUESTED BY: P. R. CARLIN.
*QUERY FRAMED BY: B. A. ANDERSON.
*SERVICE REQUEST NO. 2417.
*
*
LIST1      PRIVATE.
LIST2      BRAND (R).
****WORDS ADDED TO SEARCH: BRAND
                           BRANDED
                           BRANDS
LIST3      LIST1 & LIST2 (SEN).
           PRINT.
END.
```

This request instructs the system to locate and print all documents containing the words "private" and "brand" *in the same sentence.*

(The (R) instructs the system to treat the word "Brand" as a root word.)

Figure 2b Search—retrieved results

From the search request in Figure 2a search results are produced and delivered to the attorney in a form which:

Cites type of document, author, volume number, date and page number and

PRIVATE BRAND

Highlights the words searched both in the text and in the margin for easy reference.

"PRIVATE BRANDS"

Deposition, J. P. Lomengo, 0001, 061670 11

Q. Was the product which XYZ supplied to your stores resold as their brand?

A. No, sir.

Q. It was sold as a PRIVATE BRAND. Is that correct?

A. Yes.

Q. Did you ever observe or did anyone ever report to you the type of pricing which other stores utilized in selling the product?

A. I read their advertisements in the newspaper.

Q. Can you describe them for me?

A. Well. They were advertising their products along with some big portion of the ad mentioning this specific product at such and such a price. I don't know what the price was.

Q. Was the price below that generally charged at major stores?

A. Yes.

Q. Did your stores use the product as a loss leader?

MR. JONES: I object to the form of the question.

MR. WILSON: Do we have an understanding that all objections as to form that are made are made on behalf of all defendants?

MR. GREEN: Yes.

Figure 2c Title

PRIVATE BRANDS

"PRIVATE BRANDS"
Memo, Petty, J.H., Carson, D. T., 3533, 112069
1
Our assignment to run down the sources of all PRIVATE BRANDS in Pennsylvania and New Jersey is proving to be an exceedingly difficult one. However, our people are now hard at work with the regions and we are hopeful of being able to report to you about mid-December.

15

Litigation Support Systems—Present Status and Future Use

Steven J. Olson and Leon R. Goodrich

INTRODUCTION

In the past five years, use of a computer to aid lawyers in litigation has evolved from a novelty to a not uncommon practice. Review of the present status of computer use may underline computer capabilities to the practitioner not yet fully aware of them. The review will also indicate the future direction of computer use in litigation support.

Advantages of computer-based "litigation support system"

An initial task facing a practitioner considering use of a computer in litigation support for the first time is to overcome any religious awe of computers while at the same time becoming familiar with their superior capabilities for certain specific tasks. There are ample materials available which describe in understandable terms the functioning of computers, and no effort will be made here to repeat those descriptions.[1]

From the standpoint of a practitioner engaged in litigation, the advantage of a computer is its speed and nearly faultless memory.

[1]For example, Roberts, "A Practitioner's Primer on Computer-Generated Evidence," 41 *U. CHI. L. REV.* 254 (1974); Bigelow, "Chapter 1. The Law and the Computer," 1 *Computer Law Service* §1-1, (Callaghan & Company 1974).

While the several means of preparing information to be input into the computer are relatively slow, once within the computer information is processed at speeds approaching the speed of light. For example, a medium-sized computer can review a file containing 100 million alpha-numeric characters of information, searching for a particular element of information, in five to ten minutes. After the computer has completed this review, the results of the review can be produced on a printout, in a form usable by the lawyer, at the rate of up to 1,000 lines of alpha-numeric characters per minute.

Further, if properly instructed to search a file indexed on a computer, the computer unlike a person will remember to look at all of the documents whose index the computer is reviewing. The computer will not forget to look at certain documents because, while it was once aware of them, they have been moved to a different file cabinet or left in the lawyer's briefcase.

Definition of "litigation support system"

In general terms, what is meant by a "litigation support system" involving the use of a computer? A complete record in one of several forms of all potentially relevant information developed during discovery is maintained on a computer. This computer-maintained record is sometimes referred to as a data base.

To be fully effective, the data base must be designed and utilized to accommodate not only documents exchanged between opposing parties during discovery but also interrogatory answers, deposition transcripts, requests for admissions and any other format in which potential evidence exists. Further, the system must be adaptable to provide continuing support during trial. Trial support includes continuing access to the potential evidence indexed on or by the data base and a capacity to add to the data base, usually on a daily basis, a record of what is taking place at the trial. Thus, the data base is fully up to date at the conclusion of trial and available to assist in preparing motions or briefs.

While the computer is the foundation of the litigation support system, it is not the only important ingredient in terms of whether a litigation support system is effective in accomplishing its objectives. The computer is only as good as the people using it because a computer only does what a person tells it to do. Therefore, the choices which a lawyer makes in the design of the system and the securing of professional or paralegal assistance in the use of the system will determine its success or lack of success.

FACTORS INFLUENCING DECISION TO USE LITIGATION SUPPORT SYSTEM

Changes in past five years

Five years ago a trial lawyer typically would not have considered using a computer based litigation support system to facilitate preparation for and conduct of trial. Only in a case of massive proportions in terms of volume of discovery and amount of damages involved would consideration have been given to attempting to keep track of all the discovery by use of a computer.

Principal reasons for nonuse of a computer were expense and lack of familiarity with the technique. This situation has substantially changed. Use of a computer in litigation support is now viable in a wide range of situations including a variety of cases beyond the classic "blockbuster" antitrust case or other cases where multimillion dollar claims are at issue.

Lowered costs

There are now a number of vendors of litigation support systems offering to make such services available to lawyers. These vendors are in a position to offer the services at much lower costs than would have been experienced five years ago. Lower costs in part are due to a continued lowering of the cost of computer equipment and related accessories measured in terms of performance as a constant. Lower costs are also the result of greater vendor experience which permits some standardization in approach from case to case. In particular, the same basic software or set of instructions to the computer is usable in a variety of cases. Vendor personnel assisting in development and use of a litigation support system have developed procedures which fit many different types of cases.

An additional factor resulting in broader use of computer-based litigation support systems is growing sophistication with such techniques on the part of trial lawyers. The cost of a system can be reduced to the extent that the lawyer proposing to use it opts for a relatively simple, basic system rather than an elaborate, more expensive one.

Type and size of case

In sum, use of a computer should not be rejected simply because a case is a tax or patent liability case rather than an antitrust case or simply because documentary evidence consists of only 6,000 rather than 600,000 documents. A case involving a small volume of documents may justify a relatively simple computer-based litigation support system. The system would still offer capabilities for accessing the documents significantly superior to any manual procedures which might be utilized.

Size of firm, plaintiff v. defendant

Further, a law firm should not reject use of a computer for trial support simply on the basis that it is small and that only the larger law firms have the capacity to effectively use a computer. A smaller firm may find itself making fuller use of the full scope of support services offered by vendors in connection with the use of a computer; but the small firm may find that a relatively simple computer-based litigation support system will put it on equal footing with a much larger law firm on the opposite side of a case having substantially greater manpower resources.

There also is no particular bias favoring or disfavoring use of a computer depending upon whether a party is plaintiff or defendant. A plaintiff may seek the advantage a computer affords in quickly absorbing and permitting effective access to documentary and other evidence made available by the defendant. The defendant having made available substantial discovery to the plaintiff will wish a method to access and analyze the information disclosed by that discovery.

SELECTING A LITIGATION SUPPORT SYSTEM

A concrete example—I.R.C. §531 case

Abstract discussion about the use of a computer in litigation support may be less meaningful than a review of pertinent considerations in the context of a specific (but hypothetical) example. For purposes of illustration for the remainder of this article, therefore, assume you are counsel for a client anticipating trial of a claim asserted by the Internal Revenue Service for collection of accumulated earnings tax under Section 531 of the Internal Revenue Code.

This example is deliberately selected to demonstrate use of litigation support in a *non*-antitrust case, which, nevertheless, is suitable for computer use by reason of its possible monetary significance and extent of discovery. A patent case, product liability case, equal employment opportunities case, construction contract case or any other of a wide variety of cases could equally well be selected. The approach in designing and using a computer-based litigation system is essentially the same without regard to the type of case involved.

This example, in addition, assumes that only a relatively small number of documents are involved. Assume that a review of the client's documents has reduced the relevant ones to approximately 5,000 documents averaging 3 or 4 pages apiece and filling one four-drawer file cabinet. The documents consist of a wide variety of materials ranging from annual reports to correspondence to inter-office memoranda.

It will be necessary to review the file of selected documents on a number of occasions during discovery, including preparation for depositions, answering interrogatories and responding to requests for admission. Prior to trial, it will also be necessary to review the documents again and, in addition, deposition transcripts and other discovery to prepare a pretrial brief and identify potential evidence.

Options available in obtaining litigation support—advantages and disadvantages

Identifying sources. An initial difficult question is identifying the available sources from which litigation support systems can be obtained. The "Yellow Pages" do not yet contain a separate listing of firms offering litigation support services, although the "Yellow Pages" for any major metropolitan area will list a large number of firms offering data processing service generally. Legal periodicals, including almost every issue of the *American Bar Association Journal,* contain advertisements from firms offering litigation support systems or computerized litigation file management.

Most clients of any size also will have a substantial internal data processing capability operated by trained professionals. By research of these various sources an inventory of alternatives available in obtaining litigation support can be created. The options available will range from use of the client's facilities, to use of a law office system, to use of a professional vendor of data processing service—or a combination of these.

Criteria for decision. Expense is an element present in each choice available for equipment to use for the system and people to staff it. The possibilities are so varied that generalization as to which choices are more or less expensive is difficult. The other major criterion in selecting a system is performance. The ultimate choice will be made on the basis of cost-effectiveness as it relates to the case for which the system will be used.

Computer options. In terms of selecting the computer on which the data base is to be maintained, the client's in-house facility may be available at a lesser expense than if the necessary computer time were to be purchased from a data processing service. Unless the case is an important one, use of the client's computer may result in conflicts with other demands for its time.

Many law firms now have small computers generally devoted to office accounting and financial matters. Use of the law office system has the advantage of convenience, but the system may be small in terms of quantity of information it will hold and slow in terms of processing retrievals for information.

Further, the client's in-house data processing facility may not have available the appropriate application program or set of instructions for accessing the information to be maintained on the data base. The application program required is a generalized file management program. The law office may not have such a program available either. However, if one is developed for a particular case, it subsequently may be found applicable for other litigation.

Communications expense is also a factor. If the computer on which the data base is to be maintained is at a location remote from the client or law firm to be using it, the question of any added communications or other expense by reason of use of remote terminals inputting and retrieving information over telephone lines must be considered.

Personnel options. The lawyer will also discover that a number of detailed tasks must be performed manually in the routine preparation of information for entry into the data base maintained on the computer and the retrieval of that information. If the form of indexing or access to the information on the data base is based in part upon a coded index, discussed below, each document to be entered into the data base must be classified according to the codes and in the index.

Processing retrievals from the index may also be time consuming. For all these tasks the lawyer may wish to use paralegal or computer professional personnel. Here, again, choices available include law office personnel, the client's personnel or a professional data processing service.

If law office personnel are utilized, they must initially be trained unless the office has previously used its personnel in the operation of a computer-based litigation support system. Similarly, the client may have no trained personnel, although personnel eligible for training may be readily available in such departments as the client's market or economic research departments or computer facility. Such client personnel may offer advantages if it is necessary in their use of the system that they have some substantive understanding of the issues involved in the case. At the same time, use of the client's personnel or law office personnel may result in creation of a staff having no function once the case is completed.

Options as to professional vendors. If the time by which initial use of the litigation support system is desired is short—for example, the 5,000 documents have been made available to the government and depositions will start within a month—use of a professional vendor in the business of offering litigation support services may be indicated. Such a vendor may have available a solution to all of the above identified issues, including the computer system to be used, personnel to input the necessary information into the computerized data base and personnel to retrieve that information.

A professional vendor could have the capability of creation of a data base and a simple method for accessing it within three or four weeks after being retained. There are numerous firms offering general data processing services on a commercial basis, most of which probably have not previously performed litigation support. In addition, there are up to six firms which specifically offer litigation support systems on a national or regional basis.

Criteria for selection of professional vendors. Comparative expense is a significant factor in selecting among the available professional vendors. However, a judgment must also be made by the lawyer as to the ability of each vendor to accomplish the result desired. A prime consideration is the vendor's past experience.

Where the vendor is also furnishing the computer facility to be utilized, the lawyer must make inquiry of the vendor to determine that the facility has the capacity to accommodate the system desired. Availability of sufficient computer time to furnish retrievals on the vendor's computer system in the time frame needed by the lawyer must also be determined.

In comparing litigation support systems available from professional vendors, the lawyer will also encounter apparent significant differences in the methodology utilized by the vendors to retrieve information stored on the data base. There are two major retrieval techniques, the full text technique and the coded index technique. It is desirable that the vendor selected offer some capabilities for utilizing both techniques.

A lawyer may require litigation support ranging far beyond simply creation and use of a computerized data base for documents, depositions and trial transcripts. Assistance in organizing a client's documents for production to the opposing party may be required. Assistance may be needed in initially screening documents produced by the opposing party. Consultive services of a varied nature, such as statistical analyses of evidentiary matters, may be required. In a situation where such additional services are necessary, selection of a vendor to provide computer-based litigation support may be influenced by the ability of that vendor to also provide additional services. There are, however, no barriers to obtaining support services from several different professional vendors if cost-effectiveness criteria are satisfied.

Working with a professional vendor. While substantial progress has taken place in the providing by professionals of litigation support services, it is still necessary in each case for the lawyer to make a number of specific decisions in the tailoring of a system to meet the unique needs of the case. These decisions include the extent of documentary and other potential evidence to be entered into the computerized data base for retrieval, the nature of the indexing to be used for retrieval, and, where a coded index is used, the complexity or depth of the indexing.

At present, professional vendors of litigation support services approach each case as a unique situation calling for preparation of a bid or quotation for services specially fitting only that situation. At the same time, the professional vendor likely will be flexible in offering services and willing to make available whatever limited services are desired by the client.

If requested, the professional vendor will simply consult with the client's own computer personnel and enable them to establish their own in-house litigation support system. Alternatively, the professional vendor may offer to the law firm training of law firm personnel to perform coding and input and retrieve upon document records in the computerized data base. The vendor can rent necessary equipment to the firm.

OPTIONS AVAILABLE IN RETRIEVING COMPUTER STORED INFORMATION

Coded index

Information available for retrieval. The term "computer retrieval" simply refers to the process of instructing the computer (i) to search the information stored on the computer, i.e., the data base, applying certain criteria, and (ii) to furnish a printout or other output presenting or listing the information or documents on the data base which satisfy the criteria specified in the retrieval. Physically speaking, the information in the data base accessible by the computer typically is stored on a magnetic tape or disk. When a retrieval takes place, the tape or disk is mounted on the computer, loaded into it, and reviewed by the computer.

Obviously, the computer can only search for and locate information which has previously been stored in it. If the full text of a document or transcript has been entered verbatim into the computerized data base, then that full text can be reviewed in any retrieval by the computer. If only a listing (based on a coded index) of information contained in the document has been entered into the data base, only the topics included within that listing may be made the subject of a retrieval. While a vendor may offer a combination of both methodologies[2] the approach comprehended by a coded index will first be described.

In a coded index system the full text of documents or transcripts is not converted to computer- or machine-readable form for input into the computer. Rather, a set of classifications or index topics is developed in advance of any input into the computer. Documents are then reviewed by the lawyer or paralegal personnel and a form, sometimes referred to as a coding sheet, is completed by them which lists the classifications or topics applicable to each separate document. The coding sheet is then converted to machine-readable information with the result that a separate record in machine-readable form for each document is input into and maintained on the computer.

A retrieval performed for information accessible by the computer, for example, a search for all documents in which a particular person's name is mentioned, is accomplished by an appropriate instruction to the computer. In accordance with the instruction, the computer looks at each separate document record in machine-readable form and lists those in which the persons completing coding sheets (coders), by means of the coding sheet, have input into the computer the information that that person's name is referenced in the document.

Need for a "taxonomy" comprising the coded index. An initial step in use of a coded index system is identification of information to be coded, i.e., information about a document to be included in the record of the document to be maintained on the data base. This

[2]A brochure distributed by one firm advertising litigation support services in the American Bar Association Journal describes the handling of documents other than transcripts under its system in part as follows: "Exhibits and other documents such as briefs, interrogatories, memos, letters, and records can be handled in one of several ways. The document can be extracted or abstracted by [CompanyX's] trained staff of editors. Or, [Company X] can assist the client in developing formats for abstracting, extracting, and identifying each document. Where desired, [Company X's] legal information specialists can help create a coding system to supplement the textual identifiers. For important documents, the full text can be captured. [Company X] will then keyboard the information at one of its strategically located input centers."

procedure is sometimes referred to as development of a "taxonomy," the term meaning simply an orderly classification.

In a coded index system it is the function of the lawyer to define the information to be extracted from each document and coded, i.e., to develop the taxonomy. The lawyer's function in developing the taxonomy in a coded index system is the single activity by the lawyer most likely to influence the expense of a litigation support system based on the use of a coded index approach.

Simple, complex, and standardized taxonomies. A complex taxonomy will contribute to an expensive system because coding, input of information, processing of retrievals, and output on retrievals will all be more time consuming or extensive. A taxonomy which is, instead, simple, will reduce costs in all of these areas.

A simple taxonomy by definition omits certain information, thereby precluding retrievals for that information. It also involves broader or more general classifications, making more difficult or impossible retrievals for very specifically defined information.

A complex taxonomy may be indicated in some cases. Factors favoring a more complex taxonomy are ample time available to have a litigation support system up and running, substantial amounts at issue, extensive discovery anticipated and personnel available to code documents in detail. To the knowledge of the authors, there are no standard or common taxonomies for particular kinds of cases in use among vendors of litigation support services. However, if a vendor has previously provided to another client litigation support services on a case having similar subject matter, the vendor may have available for your client, a reasonably satisfactory, and tested, taxonomy from the prior case. Importantly, if the vendor's personnel were utilized for coding in the prior case, they will have already gained some familiarity with the codes or classifications to be applied to documents in your client's case.

Specific example of a "taxonomy"—identifier and content codes. Returning to the concrete example, there appears at the end of this article as Appendix 1 a sample taxonomy for the I.R.C. Section 531 case previously hypothesized. In applying a coded index system to this Section 531 case, a person performing the coding would review each document and record on the coding sheet which of the information specified in the taxonomy in Appendix 1 appears in the document being coded.

The taxonomy is divided into two categories of codes or classifications, identifier codes and content codes. Identifier codes represent elements of objective information readily extracted from the document by even relatively untrained paralegal personnel. For example,

Code 4 would require printing on the coding form the name of the person sending the document. Code 2 would require copying onto the coding form the date of the document. A lawyer retaining a professional vendor of litigation support services may find the vendor has a relatively fixed set of identifier codes which it is accustomed to utilizing.

The codes referred to in Appendix 1 as content codes are the codes numbered 20–72. In applying these codes the coder must read each document and enter on the coding sheet a number corresponding to the information the coder feels is contained in the document. For example, in the Section 531 case, if a memorandum from the president of the client to its treasurer expressed opposition to increasing dividends, the coder should enter the number "51" on the coding sheet. Content codes are an area where the lawyer can particularly be influential in development of the taxonomy and creation of an expensive, complicated computerized data base for retrieval, or a relatively simple, inexpensive one.

At present, a practitioner creating a taxonomy for a coded index system has great flexibility in terms of the identifier and content codes which are selected for inclusion in the taxonomy. In the future as vendors of litigation support services—or personnel operating law office based litigation support systems—develop experience with particular taxonomies in a variety of cases, some resistance might be expected on their part to development or utilization of materially different taxonomies for cases similar to those previously handled. At the same time, their past experience should contribute to greater efficiency in the use of coded index systems.

Options available in taxonomy development. Appendix 1 can be used to illustrate the kinds of options available in development of a taxonomy. These options will be present in any kind of case. For example:

a. The identifier codes require entry onto the coding sheet of the names of all persons copied on each document. Is such information necessary or could it be omitted from the data base of information upon which computerized retrievals will be performed?

b. There are no content codes which would permit indexing and retrieval of documents in which reference is made to amount of salaries to be paid. Will the lawyer representing his client in the Section 531 case wish at some point to retrieve documents containing discussions of salary because a contention will be made by the government that salaries were also deliberately kept low by the client to avoid payment of taxes? Is this possibility so remote as to not justify adding an additional content code which must be applied to each document to be entered into the data base?

c. The content codes in Appendix 1 are essentially objective rather than subjective. For example, any document referring to new construction requires entry on the coding sheet of the number "41" without regard to whether the document will support or refute the defendant-taxpayer's case. Thus, a document in which the taxpayer's president states that he does not foresee the need for accumulating reserves for new construction would be coded and retrieved equally with a document in which the president expresses a need for accumulating $500,000 for new construction.

Considerable complexity in coding, as well as facility for very specific retrievals, would be added if the coder were asked to determine whether a document "supports" or "refutes" contentions to be made by the taxpayer. The content codes would be doubled. Thus, Code 41 might be changed to mean "supports the need for new construction" and Code 42 could become "refutes need for new construction." If this sophistication were added the next issue would be how to deal with a document which both supports *and* refutes the need for new construction—in which the president has perhaps contradicted himself.

d. Attention must further be given to whether in the coding process it is desired to *link for meaning* several different pieces of information extracted from a document. For example, will the lawyer wish to be able to retrieve for all documents in which the president of the company referred to the amount of dividends?

Appendix 1 contemplates coding in such a manner that a retrieval for this information would result in a listing of all documents in which both the president was mentioned by name and, somewhere in the document, reference also was made to dividends. Such a retrieval would include documents in which the president himself made no reference to dividends but simply was mentioned by name for some other reason. All of the documents listed on the retrieval would then be reviewed by hand to select those in which the president actually referred to dividends.

Alternatively, the coding could be restructured so that reference to dividends or other content codes is linked in meaning to the names of individuals. This would result in no loss of retrieval capabilities but instead would add a facility to retrieve for a narrower set of documents more likely to contain the specific information desired. At the same time, coding would be more difficult because the coder must carefully review each document to relate content codes to specific individuals' names.

e. Appendix 1 also suggests as a question how precisely coding should be done from the standpoint of the date of the events (to be distinguished from the date of the document) referenced in each document to be entered into the data base. Coding content separately by each year obviously would add yet another level of complexity. Suppose, however, that the Internal Revenue Service is attempting to collect accumulated earnings taxes for several years. Is it then necessary to code separately for each year so that retrievals limited to a particular year can be performed?

f. There is an opposite consideration to that of the specificity or narrowness with which retrievals can be made. On occasion retrievals may be desired grouping related classifications. Appendix 1 is designed to accommodate this in that it contemplates the possibility of a retrieval on all of the "40s" classifications as a group—40 through 48. Availability of such a capability is likely to be inherent in the design of the system; the taxonomy need only be structured to take advantage of the capability.

Procedure in taxonomy development—testing. In practice, development of the taxonomy will be the result of an interchange between the lawyer responsible for the case and whomever is going to be coding documents to be entered into the data base. Ideally, the interchange proceeds on a trial and error basis. The lawyer and the coder attempt to apply a proposed taxonomy to a representative sampling of the documents to be indexed for computerized retrieval.

During this process certain content codes may be abandoned as ambiguous or overlapping with other content codes. Missing content codes may be identified for inclusion in the taxonomy. The precise meaning of each code is identified and documented in writing for instruction of both persons presently responsible for the coding and persons who subsequently may be added to the coding team.

A particular task in developing the taxonomy is to be certain that the taxonomy and techniques utilized in applying it are sufficiently adaptable to accommodate the total variety of documents and other materials to be indexed by the system. These materials will include not only routine memoranda and correspondence for which the taxonomy is obviously suited but more difficult materials such as annual reports, lengthy financial statements, and possibly, Securities and Exchange Commission filings. Further, the taxonomy and techniques for applying it must be adaptable to inputting into the data base a record relating to deposition and trial transcripts.

Versatility of litigation support—an additional example. The authors hope the above discussion on development of a taxonomy for a coded index in a Section 531 case stimulates practitioners' imaginations to envisage the potential general application of litigation support systems. Such systems afford advantages in many areas of law and types of cases—not merely the relatively narrow categories of cases with which they presently are primarily associated, in particular, antitrust cases.

Briefly, by way of further example, the application of a computer-based litigation support system to a significant construction contract action can readily be conceived. Assume an action brought by a developer-landowner against a general contractor alleging defects and delays in construction, the general contractor then impleading the architects and certain subcontractors.

Documentation relevant to the case could include a substantial volume of correspondence, memoranda and other materials from the files of all of the parties. The documentation likely also would include a substantial number of architectural and engineering drawings in various stages and other technical materials.

A trial lawyer with such a case should consider whether a computer-based litigation support system would be of assistance. If a coded index approach were utilized, the identifier codes likely would be comparable to those specified in Appendix 1. Content codes might require substantial imagination to devise. Essentially, they are simply the subjects by which the trial lawyer anticipates it will be necessary to organize the documentation for discovery and trial. So viewing the documentation, the trial lawyer might decide that the case logically breaks down into identifiable time periods relating to the phases of construction or subparts based on separate claimed defects—suggesting appropriate content codes for the taxonomy.

Text handling systems

Advantages of retrieving on full text. Separate discussion of full text retrieval is necessary to contrast that technique with the coded index technique. Many lawyers have become familiar with computerized retrieval on full text in the context of legal research, most notably the LEXIS Service offered by Mead Data Central, Inc. Several recent articles describe this service.[3]

Advantages of computer retrieval utilizing a full text system for legal research can also be anticipated to be applicable in a litigation support system. In a full text system, the entire contents of a document are introduced into the computer in machine-readable

[3]Rubin, "LEXIS Has Made Computer-assisted Legal Research in the United States a Practical Reality," 7 *Law and Computer Technology* 34 (1974); Singular, "Computers and the Law: The Revolution Is Almost Here," *Juris Doctor* 52 (February 1975).

form, and retrievals may be based upon review of the full text. As stated in one recent article concerning LEXIS:[4]

> ... Based on word and phrase searching, full-text research is distinguished from manual research by the total absence of *a priori* indexing and the concomitant interposition of third-party judgment between the researcher and legal authority he seeks. Full-text research permits the researching lawyer to release his imagination from the confines of conceptual rubrics and to bring his own judgment freely into play. Even if in information theory every word in a book can be called an index term the difference between finding cases in a traditional index, with its limited number of statically-defined pigeonholes and finding them using the living language of the courts is significant on a practical level.... [Footnote omitted.]

The full text retrieval may be interactive, that is, the lawyer making the retrieval on the full text system may obtain an immediate response and can then make additional modified inquires of the data base based on the previous response. Such interactive full text retrieval is viewed as a particularly flexible and resourceful tool.

In the context of litigation support systems an advantage seen in full text retrieval is avoidance of human error which can be encountered in the process of coding for a coded index system. Full text retrieval also has the ability to adapt and still furnish meaningful retrievals if the direction of a case changes. Full text retrieval permits retrieval at any time on any words contained within the full text.

In a coded index retrieval system, retrievals can only be made on information recognized as significant at the time of coding. If concepts are missed in developing the taxonomy for a coded index system, retrieval on these concepts will only be accomplished after documents already input into the data base are recoded for the omitted concepts. Such recoding can be time consuming and expensive.

Limitations of full text retrieval. Limitations of full text retrieval by itself include the following:

a. The text of documents to be entered verbatim into the computer data base for retrieval must be converted to magnetic or machine-readable form. Such conversion ordinarily can be accomplished only by manually keying the documents into machine-readable form. In other words, in effect, the documents must be retyped by hand at a keyboard.

Computer input devices known as optical character readers do exist which will read data from certain printed materials, for exam-

[4]Rubin, *supra* note 3, at 40.

ple, bank checks, and automatically convert it into machine-readable form. However, such devices at present are not sufficiently flexible to accommodate the wide variety of typewriter fonts and formats likely to be encountered in typical documentation involved in discovery.

This limitation need not be present with respect to deposition or trial transcripts. Automatic typewriters do exist whereby court reporters or their typists when transcribing, can generate not only the usual typed copy but, simultaneously, a magnetic tape of the transcript in machine-readable form. Special arrangements may be required if such equipment is to be used in any particular litigation.

(While less extensive, coding and input in a coded index system requires considerable effort. For example, the documentary file in the previously hypothesized Section 531 case consists of 5,000 documents averaging 3 to 4 pages apiece. If the completion of coding sheets for those documents could be accomplished at the rate of 1 document every 15 minutes, approximately 1,200 hours or over ½ man-year would be required. Very simple documents and a very simple taxonomy might permit improvement of that rate. These figures indicate, nevertheless, the compelling need to use paralegal assistants rather than lawyers in the coding where there is a document population of any volume.)

b. The particular advantage of a full text data base may also prove to be a disadvantage. Minimization of selectivity before inputting materials into the data base may result, when retrievals are performed, in very large printouts or listings of potentially pertinent documents, many of which are unimportant.

c. The versatility and variety of the English language is phenomenal. The same concept or element of information may be expressed in a wide variety of ways. Comprehensive retrieval on a full text system presupposes that the lawyer specifying the retrieval has thought of all the ways in which the concept in which he is interested could be expressed in the documents on which he is retrieving. In fact, assumption of such power of imagination may not be realistic.

In practice, this limitation is tempered in that a "thesaurus" of words likely to be used in expressing a particular concept can be developed and used repeatedly for the retrieval on the full text. Referencing again the example of the Section 531 case, a lawyer utilizing a full text system may desire a listing of all documents in which the word "dividends" is used. In initially creating a "thesaurus" for such retrieval, the lawyer would attempt to imagine all synonyms for "dividend" including "dividends," "distributions," "allocations," etc. Once developed, this "thesaurus" for retrieval on the full text system for documents referring to dividends can be utilized for subsequent retrievals for the same information. The "thesaurus" can be enhanced each time additional synonyms are identified.

Nevertheless, no document bearing on the taxpayer's dividend policy will be retrieved from the full text system unless it contains at least one of the words in the "thesaurus" developed for retrieval. If the president of the defendant-taxpayer in the hypothetical Section 531 case has written, "the shareholders do not wish to be paid any more cash from this company," a "thesaurus" limited to the word "dividends" and closely related synonyms for that word, would not identify for review the document containing that statement.

Hybrid systems

Emphasis on coded index or full text. In practice, a computer based litigation support system may utilize both retrieval techniques, that is, a coded index technique and a full text technique or some modification of a full text technique. Such a system might be referred to as a hybrid system. The extent to which one technique or the other is emphasized in the system will be influenced by a number of factors. If voluminous documents from various companies' files are to be accessed by use of the computerized data base, this may point towards emphasis upon a coded index system. If relatively few documents but substantial depositions are anticipated, and equipment is available whereby the court reporters will transcribe the depositions immediately into machine-readable form, greater emphasis might be given to full text retrieval.

Compromises between full text and coded index. Several techniques may also be utilized which, in effect, consist of a compromise between the advantages and disadvantages of the full text and coded index retrieval approaches. If there is concern that the full text approach will require a very expensive input process and result in extensive retrievals, there are two ways in which the bulk can be reduced.

A person performing essentially the function of a coder can review each document and underline only key words in those documents, which key words then constitute the only record concerning the document input into the data base for retrieval. Alternatively, a summary or abstract of each document may be prepared and constitute the only input, or various phrases within the document can be identified and input into the data base verbatim in lieu of inputting the entire document.

These techniques to an extent sacrifice the theoretical advantage of a full text retrieval system. They necessitate the intervention of human judgment in selecting for input only certain information from the document deemed to be significant.

Retrieval, however, can still be performed searching for words actually appearing in the document. Alternatively, if solely a coded index retrieval approach is being utilized, the key words, extract or summary may be separately coded; this affords additional assurance that no significant information has been missed in coding the document.

Summary concerning retrieval. It is necessary to retain some perspective when evaluating the intricacies of any retrieval techniques under consideration for use. Sophisticated or intricate capability possessed by one technique must be evaluated in terms of whether such intricacies will be utilized and are worth whatever additional expense they may involve.

A relatively simple system emphasizing primarily retrievals based upon information referred to in Appendix 1 as identifier codes may accomplish 90 percent of whatever the most imaginative lawyer would expect from a computer-based retrieval system. In addition to being less expensive, the more simple system may be more likely to meet the various time deadlines encountered in preparation for and conduct of trial.

COST

Estimating costs

Now to address the critical question—how much will the system cost? Vendors approach each assignment as unique, and, in any event, there are a wide variety of possible solutions in terms of use of vendor, client or law office equipment and personnel. Therefore, representative prices or price comparisons are difficult to come by.

However, in any particular situation the applicable unit costs are readily determinable, allowing calculation of an estimated total cost. Vendors will generally be willing to quote a cost estimate. In addition, a vendor may be willing to initiate a computer-based litigation support system on a trial basis charging only for time and materials actually used.

Assuming again some utility in a concrete example, an estimate of costs can be attempted for a coded index type of data base permitting computerized access to the 5,000 documents assembled for the previously discussed Section 531 litigation.

Start-up costs

Estimated costs can be segmented into the several stages of creation and use of the computerized data base. Start-up costs represent an initial, minimum necessary investment. These costs may make creation of a computer-based litigation support system uneconomic where the document population is significantly less than 5,000 documents.

The start-up costs for creation of a coded index data base for the 5,000 previously selected documents, utilizing a professional vendor, could range anywhere from $20,000 to $50,000. This cost includes participation by the vendor in development of the taxonomy, creation by the vendor of the document archive, coding of the 5,000 documents by vendor personnel, loading of the documents into the computerized data base and validating the accuracy of the resultant retrieval system.

Of this total cost, only about 20 percent might represent the actual cost of the computer itself and related input and output equipment, including, in addition, the expense of the personnel operating the computer equipment. Eighty percent of the cost is for vendor personnel performing the various other tasks discussed above.

The largest single expense, perhaps ⅓ or more of the total expense, is simply the cost of personnel performing the coding of the documents. This emphasizes again the contribution to minimizing costs of using a simple rather than complex taxonomy.

It further emphasizes the significance of the fundamental question of who should do the coding. However, before assuming it is less expensive for law office paralegal personnel to do the coding, their hourly rates should be compared with those of vendor personnel. In addition, the question whether vendor personnel by reason of greater experience might be more efficient should also be examined.

Continuing costs

If the document population to be input into the data base is static, there will be no further coding or other associated expenses once the initial coding and input of the 5,000 documents has been accomplished. More likely, however, there will be a continuing flow of material to be added to the data base, in particular, deposition and, subsequently, trial transcripts.

A crude estimate of the cost of adding documents to the coded index data base might be expressed on the basis of $1 to $2 per page. Thus, if, on a continuing basis, 1,000 pages of deposition transcripts per month are to be coded for addition to the data base, a continuing expense for this purpose of at least $1,000 to $2,000 per month might be anticipated.

Thus far, the only expense considered has been for inputting material into the data base. But if the data base is to be used, retrievals will be made upon it. An estimate of the cost of retrievals, assuming the data base is stored on a vendor-furnished computer system, is $30 to $40 a retrieval, assuming the Section 531 case document population of 5,000 documents. As the number of document records on the data base to be searched in any retrieval increases, the amount of computer time consumed in each retrieval increases; so does the cost of retrievals.

If ten retrievals per month are made, the retrieval costs per month will be several hundred dollars. A vendor may also establish a minimum charge for retrievals of several hundred dollars per month regardless of how few retrievals are performed. This estimate of retrieval costs assumes that the retrieval requests are prepared by the lawyer or his assistants and not by vendor personnel.

Cost of the system during trial is likely to be considerably higher than during the discovery phase of the case. A coded index for the daily trial transcript will be added to the data base on a continuing basis during trial.

Several retrievals or more per day may be made as the trial progresses for various elements of information. Finally, a rapid response to retrieval requests may be desired. This necessitates maintaining the data base on an on-line basis on the computer, immediately available at any time for retrievals, rather than an off-line basis which would require loading the data base into the computer before retrievals could be accomplished.

Cost comparison with manual system

The bottom line question is whether whatever additional expense is entailed in use of a computerized data base rather than a manual procedure is worth it. This is really a question in two parts. The first part of the question is qualitative: how important is it in terms of damages or other considerations involved to win the case—is the case sufficiently important that the greater facility and accuracy afforded by a computerized retrieval system is worthwhile without regard to any additional expense?

The second part of the question is quantitative—how much additional expense in fact does the computerized data base represent as compared with a manual system for organizing and accessing discovery materials? Such a comparison of costs is highly speculative but will be attempted.

Referencing again the hypothetical Section 531 case, assume, as a crude estimate, a total cost of $34,000 for 12 months for establishing and using a computerized data base. This cost is comprised of $25,000 start-up costs, $6,000 for input of an additional 6,000 pages of material after the initial start-up and $3,000 representing 100 retrievals at $30 apiece.

Contrast the above with 100 manual retrievals through the 4-drawer file cabinet containing 5,000 documents at the beginning of the year and 6,000 by the end of the year. If each document is looked at on each manual search from the standpoint of whether it contains the desired information, an optimistic estimate of the amount of time required to read the entire 4 file drawers of documents each time a search is made is 4 hours. (Assuming 16,000 document pages and 240 minutes per four hours, this is scanning documents at the very rapid rate of 67 pages per minute.)

The 100 retrievals over a 12-month period on a manual basis would thus require 400 man-hours. If the cost per man-hour is $100, the annual cost would be $40,000. If $50 an hour personnel were used, the cost would be $20,000.

This simplified comparison is admittedly contrived to some extent but suggests that the cost of a computerized data base may not greatly exceed the cost of doing the same amount of work manually. The comparison further illustrates that the great cost advantage of the computerized data base as compared with the manual approach is in the cost of retrievals or search.

However, the computerized data base involves start-up costs which are not present with the manual system. Thus, to the extent that a large number of retrievals are anticipated on a relatively small and static number of documents, the cost of the computerized data base begins to approach the lower cost of solely manual procedures.

CONSIDERATIONS OF PRIVILEGE

Designing system to minimize discoverability

A frequently expressed reluctance of trial counsel to establish and utilize a computer-based litigation support system is its possible discoverability by opposing counsel. The authors are aware of no situation in which such discovery has been allowed. Indeed, there appear to be no reported decisions in which the discoverability of the opponent's computer-based litigation support system was at issue. However, the authors are advised that in an unreported decision, *In re IBM Peripheral EDP Devices,* M.D.L. 163-RM (N.D. Cal. 1975), the plaintiffs were denied a motion to compel the defendant, IBM, to respond to interrogatories by use of the defendant's data base.

Discovery by the opposing side of a litigation support system is likely to continue to be a matter of serious concern until definitively resolved. Rule 26(b)(3) of the Federal Rules of Civil Procedure provides no definitive solution, instead, providing in relevant part as follows:

> (3) *Trial Preparation: Materials.* Subject to the provisions of subdivision (b)(4) of this rule, a party may obtain discovery of *documents and tangible things* otherwise discoverable under subdivision (b)(1) of this rule and prepared in anticipation of litigation or for trial by or for another party or by or for that other party's representative (including his attorney, consultant, surety, indemnitor, insurer, or agent) only upon a showing that the party seeking discovery *has substantial need of the materials in the preparation of his case and that he is unable without undue hardship to obtain the substantial equivalent* of the materials by other means. In ordering discovery of such materials when the required showing has been made, the court shall *protect against disclosure of the mental impressions, conclusions, opinions, or legal theories of an attorney* or other representative of a party concerning the litigation. [Emphasis added.]

A superficial resolution of the issue of discoverability of the opponent's computerized data base is to focus on the limitation of Rule 26(b)(3) to discovery of "documents and tangible things." Certainly, while stored or being processed within the computer, the data base is not a document or tangible thing. However, retrievals from the data base in the form of computer printouts are documents or tangible.

Referencing again the example of a Section 531 case, utilizing a coded index such as Appendix 1, the federal government seeking discovery of that index likely could demonstrate a "substantial need" for the materials in the preparation of its case. The defendant, of course, would respond that the government has in its possession all of the defendant's documents indexed on the data base, and therefore has no need for discovery of the data base. The government's response is that possession of the documents in no way is equivalent to the capability of accessing and manipulating the documents by computer.

Rule 26(b)(3) also precludes discovery of the opponent's computerized litigation support system if such discovery would involve disclosure of the mental impressions, conclusions, opinions or legal theories of the opposing party's attorney or other representative concerning the litigation. The more sophisticated and subjective are the content codes utilized in the taxonomy in a coded index system, the more such codes are likely to involve disclosure of mental impressions or conclusions of the attorney.

Further, it should not be significant that the actual coding of documents is performed by a paralegal staff rather than the attorney. The coding is nevertheless conducted pursuant to the attorney's design and instructions. In any event, nonattorney coders should be considered an "other representative of a party" under Rule 26(b)(3).

Adding complexity and subjectivity to the taxonomy for a coded index system may make the system both expensive and unwieldy. Futher, many desired uses of the system may necessitate a capability of retrieving solely on identifier codes such as those set forth in Appendix 1, rather than content codes. A retrieval printout showing only identifier codes could not be considered to contain mental impressions, conclusions, opinions or legal theories of an attorney.

If a retrieval system based upon inputting the full text of documents into the computer is utilized, the discovering party can specify his own criteria for the retrieval. This avoids use of work product of the attorney who had established the data base. For these reasons, the prohibition in Rule 26(b)(3) against discovery of the opposing attorney's mental impressions, etc., does not provide a satisfactory or reliable preclusion to discovery of the opposing attorney's computerized data base.

Rule 26(b)(3) "hardship" test

Under Rule 16(b)(3) a party seeking discovery of the opposing party's computerized data base must clear one additional hurdle. Inability to obtain the substantial equivalent "without undue hardship" must be demonstrated. The most frequently expressed claim of undue hardship to justify access to the opposing party's computerized data base is likely to be financial burden.

For example, in the Section 531 case, the government will argue a need to utilize the defendant's computerized data base to access its documents rather than expend substantial sums of taxpayers' money to duplicate something the defendant already has done. A small, allegedly injured plaintiff in an antitrust or securities case will attempt a similar showing with respect to a huge defendant corporation.

The provisions relating to discovery of trial preparation materials were added to Rule 26 in 1970. The Advisory Committee's Note of 1970 concerning Rule 26(b)(3) does not indicate to what extent financial hardship by itself is sufficient to satisfy the "undue hardship" requirement nor does it specify standards for determining financial hardship. In the somewhat different context of obtaining a witness's statement embodying work product, Wright and Miller suggest that in some situations expense or financial burden can constitute undue hardship:

> Thus it will still be true that discovery of work product material will be denied if the party seeking discovery can obtain the information he desires by taking the depositions of witnesses. The fact that depositions are expensive is not a sufficient showing unless the expense would amount, in the particular case, to "undue hardship." Wright & Miller, 8 *Federal Practice and Procedure: Civil* §2025, at 215-16 (1970). [Footnotes omitted.]

If avoidance of expense amounting to financial burden is adequate in itself to satisfy the "undue hardship" requirement, discovery of the opposing party's computerized data base could be permitted under Rule 26(b)(3). Such a result would be a considerable factor in discouraging use of computer-based litigation support. The benefits to the judicial system from use of computers for litigation support strongly favor avoidance of any interpretation of Rule 26(b)(3) which would permit discovery of the opposing party's computerized litigation support data base. Use of computers for more efficient and effective preparation for and conduct of trials should be encouraged.

Permitting discovery of the opposing party's data base on grounds solely of financial hardship would be a misguided effort to equalize resources which the opposing parties are able to devote to their case. Such equalization is not possible. Forcing a party to produce its litigation support data base for the other party, viewed in these terms, may not be much different than forcing that party, if it is being represented by five lawyers, to make available to the poorer opposing party sufficient funds to enable him to hire the same number or equivalent capability in lawyers.

Consideration should be given to an appropriate amendment to Rule 26(b)(3) to make clear that a computerized litigation support system is not discoverable. In the meantime, a party concerned that a system it creates will be discoverable has several unsatisfactory options available. He can design the system to embody his attorney's mental impressions and opinions in every retrieval with the accompanying disadvantages discussed above. Or, if the litigation has commenced, he may, before substantial effort and expense is invested in his system, seek a determination from the court that the system he proposes to create and utilize will not be discoverable.

EXPECTED PERFORMANCE OF A COMPUTER BASED LITIGATION SUPPORT SYSTEM DURING DISCOVERY AND TRIAL

Preliminary considerations

Documents—selection and capacity. A concern addressed at the time of creation of a computerized data base, as well as during expansion of it through discovery and trial is its capacity, i.e., how many documents or document records can it contain. A practical limit of storage in machine-readable form for a litigation support system might be considered to be the capacity of a single disk drive inputting data into the central processing unit of a computer. While there is no computer equipment limitation preventing accessing of a data base on more than one disk,[5] the additional computer time required for the retrieval will add significant expense to retrieval costs.

The capacity of disk drives in general use is up to 100 million alpha-numeric characters. Assuming documents of 2 or 3 pages each, such disk drive capacity should be sufficient to accommodate a coded index data base of 100,000 documents.

Capacity limitations as well as maximizing effectiveness of a computerized data base, require careful attention to the selection of documents to be indexed or input in full text into the data base. Referencing the Section 531 example, the client's entire document population of potentially relevant documents may have consisted of 100,000 documents. From the 100,000 documents, 5,000 were selected as significant enough to be input into the data base.

The selection process can be performed by counsel or by paralegals or personnel trained as coders under the direction of counsel. In important litigation there will be a tendency to be more, rather than less, inclusive in identifying documents to be input into the data base. The result by time of trial may be a very large data base and a need to single out for special attention at trial a much more limited number of particularly significant documents.

This eventuality can be anticipated to some extent by employment of a variety of techniques in the design and use of the system during the discovery phase. A simple method is to rank documents in levels of significance at the time of the coding and input process. Retrieval techniques should then include a capacity to retrieve, for example, only upon that portion of the data base referencing documents ranked as "most significant."

Form of output—options. As the lawyer utilizes the computerized data base, his attention is directed to choices available concerning the form of output. These choices are of two kinds—equipment and appearance of the output.

Several forms of equipment may be utilized to access the same data base. For example, a lawyer may maintain in his office a video display similar to a television screen permitting him to call up onto

[5]The legal research system LEXIS reportedly presently contains 3.5 billion characters of information stored on-line in 88 disk drives of a capacity of 100 million characters each. *Computerworld,* April 30, 1975, p. 27.

the screen information stored on the data base. If a coded index data base is utilized, the information appearing on the screen will be simply listings of documents matching the retrieval criteria keyed by the lawyer into the video display keyboard.

The lawyer may also maintain at his office a set of microfilm or microfiche containing in full text all of the documents indexed on the data base. The video display will identify the documents desired by the lawyer by number; he can then locate those documents by a reference number on the microfilm or microfiche. If a permanent record of the listing of documents is desired it must be obtained through a computer printout, which facility can also be made a part of the terminal maintained by the lawyer at his office. Portable equipment with which the lawyer can access the data base from any location served by telephone and obtain a printout of the desired information is also available. The limiting factor as to the kind and variety of equipment utilized by the lawyer in obtaining retrievals from the data base is expense.

Of particular concern to the lawyer working with the computerized data base is the appearance and format of the output—regardless of whether it is on a video display or in printout form. The lawyer should insist that the system be designed so that the output is readily intelligible. For example, names of senders, receivers and copyees of documents indexed on the data base should be reproduced as fully as possible rather than identified simply by cryptic initials.

Referencing Exhibit 1, content codes should appear on the printout not simply as numbers but with the appropriate meaning appearing in words. If a document deals with loans to shareholders and with dividends, the printout referencing that document should contain not simply "31" and "51"; it also should translate those numbers to "loans to shareholders" and "amount of dividends."

Use of actual documents. While the appearance of the retrieval must be readily intelligible, a lawyer may well find that in most tasks for which retrievals are being used it will be necessary to reference the actual documents identified by the retrieval. Even in the case of a full text system a lawyer preparing, for example, to take a deposition likely will want to review the actual document being considered for use as an exhibit in the deposition.

Such review is required if a coded index system is utilized. The lawyer must determine that the document does in fact contain the information for which it was identified on retrieval and also that it does not contain other information making it undesirable for use in the deposition.

A full text system containing the document verbatim theoretically could be used for purposes of reading the entire document rather than referencing it in hard copy, microfilm or microfiche form. However, the original of the document must in any event be marked as an exhibit at the deposition. Retrieval of the full text through the computer system also may be more time consuming and expensive than simply referencing the files where originals or copies of documents on the data base are maintained.

Depositions

Preparation for depositions—search. The capabilities of computerized data base retrieval are particularly apparent in the discovery phase in preparation for depositions. In a very few minutes the computer can generate a listing of potentially relevant documents for the deposition.

Criteria for relevant documents requested by computer retrieval can be complex by comparison with criteria which could be utilized in a manual review of the 5,000 potentially relevant documents in the Section 531 case. For example, assume the president of the defendant-taxpayer is to be deposed. Assume also that he will be particularly examined concerning loans to shareholders and amount of dividends.

A retrieval request to the computer thus might specify a listing of all documents sent by the president, Code 4, *or* received by the president, Code 6, *or* in which the president was a copyee, Code 8, *or* in which the president was mentioned, Code 9, *or* referring to loans to shareholders, Code 31, *or* referring to amount of dividends, Code 51. Unlike a manual search of the document files, the computer will not forget to apply each of these criteria to each of the 5,000 document records maintained on the data base.

Preparation for depositions—organization. An additional capability of the computer facilitating preparation for the deposition should not be overlooked. The computer has a sorting or sequencing capacity which could not be duplicated in a manual search of the 5,000 documents. The retrieval obtained by computer will list documents in the sequence and subsequence specified by the lawyer.

For example, all the documents requested in the above described retrieval can be sorted by date in the computer printout listing those documents. Thus, when the lawyer reviews the documents in preparation for the deposition, he is able to review them chronologically.

More sophisticated sorting is possible. For example, the retrieval can list all documents (i) referring to amount of dividends in one grouping, (ii) subdividing that grouping into segments classified alphabetically on the basis of the last name of the author of the document, and further, (iii) organizing each segment for each author by date of document from earliest to latest date.

Activities following deposition. The transcript of the deposition is another document to be input into the data base either by coding or in full text. A retrieval in preparation for subsequent depositions will include a listing of any previous depositions in which the content specified by the retrieval was referenced.

For example, assume the vice president of the defendant is deposed following deposition of the president, and the president has been examined on amount of dividends. The president's deposition will be listed in response to a retrieval made in preparation for the vice president's deposition which specifies as a content code #51, amount of dividends.

A capability can be included in the computerized data base to track usage of documents on the data base. For example, a document referencing amount of dividends may have been utilized as an exhibit during the deposition of the president of the taxpayer. A retrieval subsequently made to prepare for the deposition of the vice president may also seek documents referring to amount of dividends. The subsequent retrieval will list not only that same document but the fact that it has been used during the deposition of the president. Appendix 1 includes an identifier code, #11, document usage, providing a capacity to identify the particular deposition in which a document is referenced and the page of the deposition where the reference is made. If a deposition transcript is entered into the data base as an additional document, a record of its subsequent usage in other depositions, pretrial briefs or otherwise may be similarly maintained.

Other applications during discovery

The retrieval capabilities of the computer of value for depositions are similarly applicable in answering interrogatories and pulling a case together for trial, including preparation of a pretrial brief. Of course, interrogatory answers, admissions and pretrial briefs received from an opponent should be handled as additional documents for input into the data base.

Preparation for trial

Selecting potential evidence. As trial approaches, additional features may be desired in the computer-based litigation support system. Early identification during the discovery period of the need for these features will facilitate incorporating them into the system.

Preparation for commencement of trial will involve review of all materials input into the data base to date, including documents, deposition transcripts, and interrogatory answers. Retrievals will be employed similar to those used to prepare for depositions. The initial data base of 5,000 documents or 16,000 pages may have grown during the course of discovery to 30,000 pages. Preparation for trial may result in reduction of those materials to 10,000 pages to be used or kept track of for trial.

The process of selection involves not only setting aside favorable documents which counsel plans to introduce into evidence but also those documents which counsel believes to be adverse but fears his adversary may use. Computer retrievals will provide organized listings of documents according to pertinent categories. However, the process of selecting the pertinent 10,000 pages, favorable and unfavorable, from the larger body of 30,000 pages is essentially a process of hand review of documents by counsel.

Organizing potential evidence. When counsel has selected the 10,000 pages, typically, copies of them are organized in hand-prepared files or notebooks—by witness, by topic or both. Having arrived at this stage the question arises whether there is any capability afforded by the computer which would be of assistance in maintaining these notebooks or otherwise organizing materials counsel intends to rely upon at trial.

If discovery is continuing until shortly before trial, additions and changes in materials to be used at trial may be frequent. The fact of contemplated usage at trial of a document can be entered into the data base as a part of the record concerning that document through usage codes such as contemplated by Code 11 in Appendix 1. The computerized data base will be able then to present a listing of all materials proposed for use at trial and, possibly, some identification of the topic or witness for which such use is contemplated. Through use of the computer this information can readily be updated as plans change.

A very large volume of potential evidence may be contemplated. Creation of a substantially more elaborate support system—in effect, a second data base, limited to materials to be used at trial may be indicated. This trial support system would not only track planned usage of materials but permit manipulation of the materials by various sorting capabilities.[6]

[6]The authors have previously discussed in some detail functions which can be performed with a computerized data base during the course of discovery and in preparation for and conduct of a trial, including creation of a second data base for trial support. "Litigation Support Systems," *Jurimetrics Journal* (Special issue 1974, 5-13, 20-28).

Litigation support system during trial

Additions to data base. Once trial starts, the trial transcript is treated like any other document, i.e., it is entered into the data base either in full text, if that technique is being employed, or by coding. To facilitate retrieval, the transcript may be arbitrarily segmented into separate "documents." A retrieval on a particular content code, such as Code 51, amount of dividends, would report not simply that the topic appeared at some point in the trial transcript, but the page or pages of the transcript or the day of trial and the witness at which such topic appeared.

There also should be a facility to separately search by retrieval the trial transcript by itself. Such a retrieval would use as one of the retrieval criteria the document identification code assigned exclusively to the trial transcript.

Any new exhibits introduced which have not previously been incorporated into the data base are added during trial. Also, the usage codes are utilized to update for each document on the data base the fact of its usage during trial and the place during the trial at which such usage occurred. The exhibit number assigned to the document at trial may also be entered into the document record on the data base.

Specialized printouts for trial use. Various specialized reports or printouts may be developed for use at trial and in preparation of post trial briefs. For example, a report may be generated which is sorted or organized first by trial date or witness and then by either the exhibit in use or the topic (content code) under discussion.

A further sophistication is to retrieve and display on the same report all information maintained on the data base concerning the exhibit under discussion at that point in the trial. The computer also might be instructed to prepare a listing by document number of all exhibits used at the trial.

Other computer capabilities

The above discussion has offered only a glimpse of the capabilities of a computer-based litigation support system. The tremendous speed of the computer and its capability to manipulate, sort or list in various logical sequences materials stored within it permit generation of a variety of reports useful during many stages of litigation.

For example, the computer can generate at any point in time a listing of all document records maintained on the data base, presenting the listing chronologically by document date. It may also generate a listing organized alphabetically for each person recorded as having sent or received a document, listing for that person each such document organized chronologically by date.

A LOOK AHEAD

Growth in need for use of computers

A look ahead to the next five or so years is also useful. A number of factors are at work which may converge to make even more attractive or necessary than at present the use of computers in litigation support in the future.

One factor is the accelerating growth of litigation both in terms of number of cases and volume of materials involved as potentially relevant in those cases. This may be the "computer age," recognizing the increasing impact that instrument will have on our society. Lawyers engaged in defense or pursuit of corporations in litigation may rightly feel that this also is the "paper age" as well, acknowledging the capacity of corporations to generate large volumes of documentation. The computer may become an indispensable tool for dealing with such volumes.

Variety of options; cost expectations

The number of professional vendors of computer-based litigation support services should increase. The variety of hardware and software options offered by vendors will also increase. In addition, as vendors gain more experience, more standardized solutions for providing computer-based litigation support in a variety of cases should develop, including use of standardized taxonomies. More routinized approaches by vendors should afford greater predictability of support needs throughout a case and greater predictability of costs.

Computer equipment or hardware costs measured on the basis of performance should continue to decline dramatically. However, this may not result in a lowering of the overall cost of computer-based litigation support systems because of the heavy labor element in such systems. Greater experience and more standardized solutions may enable vendors to lower overall costs—particularly by means of streamlining services to avoid "extras" that in fact receive little use. Input and retrieval techniques are not likely to change significantly in the next five years. With the exception of machine-readable transcripts which may increasingly be used, input will continue to be keyed by hand into machine-readable form. Retrieval techniques will continue to be coded index, full text or a hybrid combination.

Law office based systems

Lowering of equipment costs and greater familiarity with application of computers to litigation support may encourage many law firms to establish an in-house computer system and litigation support capability. This would presume a commitment by the firm to more routine use of computer-based litigation support rather than employment of it simply for the occasional special case. The variety of computer equipment available and of techniques which can be used for indexing and accessing information by computer suggests that no single approach will predominate.

A particularly viable approach for many law firms may be to perform input and retrieval activities on equipment installed within the firm, using firm personnel, but maintaining the data base and performing the processing involved in retrievals at a data processing center. For example, for in the area of $500 to $1,000 per month the firm may rent a computer terminal permitting input by keyboard of data into a remote computer system through use of telephone lines. The terminal would have a capacity to perform retrievals through instructions keyed into the terminal. Retrievals would appear either on a video screen or in computer printout form on the terminal. Portable terminals with slower printer speeds and no video display can be rented for $100 to $150 per month.

Maintenance of the data base on a remote computer system rather than a system installed at the law firm may afford use of a computer having considerably greater speed and capacity than any computer likely to be installed at the firm. A computer dedicated solely to a particular firm's needs would be much smaller than that maintained at a data processing center.

In the case of a coded index approach, law firm paralegal or other personnel would perform coding as well. Such a system would be designed and administered to emphasize its application and utility to a variety of cases being handled by the firm. In coding, emphasis would be given to identifier codes and a uniform approach would be applied from case to case. Content codes, if any, would be very simplified.

CONCLUSION

In sum, there presently exists both computer equipment and technical capability in utilizing it which would permit widespread use of computer-based litigation support systems. Continued rapid improvement in equipment and techniques will take place. The legal profession, in the interests of efficiency and more effective performance, must make the effort to become familiar with the capabilities of computers in litigation support and give continuing consideration to whether cases presently underway would benefit from the use of computers.

APPENDIX

A simplified "taxonomy" for an I.R.C. §531 case:

[Identifier Codes]

1. Document I.D.
2. Document Date
3. Document Type
4. Sender
5. Sender's Company
6. Receiver
7. Receiver's Company
8. Copyees
9. Names Mentioned
10. Document Source
11. Document Usage
    —Briefs—Page
    —Trial—Page
    —Other—Page

[Content Codes]

20. Date of events?
30. Avoidance of tax [By year?]
31 Loans to Shareholders
32. Payments for Shareholders
33. Loans to Others
34. Payments to Others
35. Investments
40. Needs of Business [By Year?]
41. New Construction
42. Replacement Construction
43. Equipment
44. Product Development
45. Acquisitions
46. Debt Retirement
47. Inventories
48. Loans to Customers
50. Financial Information
51. Amount of Dividends
52. Charitable Contributions
53. Earnings
54. Draft Financial Statements
60. Holding Company
61. Operations
70. Subsidiaries
71. A Company
72. B Company

[Supports/Refutes?]

A Trial Lawyer's Solution to an Age-Old Problem Using a High-Speed Idiot with a Long Memory

Ross H. Sidney

How many times in the past few years, as major litigation has increased, have you encountered that combination of feelings which involve concern, tenseness, helplessness and, ultimately, pure fright or outright panic as you began to realize that the mass of evidence that was piling up by reason of the pretrial procedures had reached the point where not only your personal ability to recall was exhausted, but the systems you had devised were either hopelessly inadequate or had reached a point where they also were out of control? The feeling comes when you project yourself into the actual trial of the case and wonder how to have the benefit of your extensive pretrial discovery at your fingertips when needed.

More and more frequently conversations between trial lawyers involved in major litigation, seminars, articles and other forms of teaching are being directed toward the use of modern technology in the preparation for and trial of lawsuits. One of the age-old problems with which the trial lawyer has struggled, each in his own way, is how to compensate for that fallibility of the human mind that makes it impossible in the courtroom with but seconds or minutes only to recall the evidence that you need right then. The lesser problem is, while in trial, how to prepare for the next day with a minimum of time lost searching for the evidence that will constitute tomorrow's record. Many systems have been devised and those that work the best create the greatest success. It is axiomatic that successful results and successful trial lawyers are the end-products of careful preparation.

The systems that each of us have devised for the cataloging of evidence were structured by the demands of the particular litigation. We all started with a client, a pencil and a legal pad. Remember how much writing we did, and still do for that matter, but these hand methods were later supplemented by dictating equipment and those blessed copying machines. However, these and other technical advancements commenced to compound the indexing and recall problem in arithmetic progression because more material could be assembled more rapidly and the process of cataloging became more complex. But whatever the devices or procedures that have been and are presently being used, they are all designed with but one goal in mind and that is to get evidence back when you need it the most—to put it at your fingertips in that courtroom or while preparing witnesses for direct or cross-examination. No system was perfect and no system ever will be.

The problem was difficult enough when the trial system was one of secrecy and surprise; when 95 percent of our time was spent in the preparation of our own case and 5 percent to exploring the adversary. However, even under this system of nondisclosure, major litigation could rapidly carry us past the limits of human memory and require the institution of some system of cataloging and indexing to retrieve the collected material.

More recently, the problems of how to handle and catalog evidence and exhibits have increased in geometric proportions. This results from a number of reasons but the major ones are (1) more major lawsuits are being filed by the increasing ingenuity of counsel; (2) the ascending popularity of class actions; (3) products liability cases with attendant highly technical aspects; (4) increased litigation by the government, and the last, but which should probably be the first—the liberalization of pretrial discovery rules. This field has expanded and is continuing to expand at an astounding rate.

Wouldn't it be nice if expanded discovery did nothing more than create an *option* on the part of either counsel to probe the adversary's case? It is true that the rules do create rights which one need not utilize, but this is a decision that only the uninitiated trial lawyer would make—there is no option left to the capable one. He has to discover—it is his duty to his client. Someday, malpractice actions may be based in part on the lack of discovery to uncover the information which had a vital impact on your client's results. To put it very bluntly, depending upon the result obtained, the failure to adequately utilize the discovery processes could subject one to the claim of gross negligence.

Discovery and pretrial procedures have, therefore, created masses of documents, transcripts, photos, expert opinions, medical, X-rays and what-have-you before we ever reach the courtroom. The genealogy of an exhibit oftentimes becomes an extremely perplexing one, for as discovery proceeds, any single exhibit may be the subject matter with any number of witnesses and properly cross-referencing them is only one small problem. The evidence accumulates, the transcripts start rolling in, the files get bulky, drawers fill and transfer boxes start to multiply.

For years I had been mounting a continual attack on the problem of sorting, indexing, cataloging and abstracting to bring some sense of order out of chaos with varying degrees of success. What follows is how modern technology was used to solve one such monumental problem.

A better understanding of the solution will require a more thorough knowledge of the problem. Here's how it developed.

Several years ago I was asked to represent a plaintiff, although I'm an Ivory Soap defense lawyer, 99 and 99/100% pure, involving a case which, if it were to be pursued, would most certainly qualify as major litigation both from the standpoint of time and expense.

The case involved Life-Time Industries, Inc. as plaintiff and Winnebago Industries, Inc., and its officers and some of its directors, as defendants. Briefly, Life-Time Industries was wholly owned by a husband and wife who claimed that they had developed the concept for a low-cost motor home and had entered into a five-year exclusive manufacturing contract with Winnebago Industries to build the unit on a cost-plus basis with the understanding that Winnebago would not market or attempt to build the unit as its own. Plaintiff also claimed that after the completion of the pilot model and the start of production of the unit, its success was instantaneous and, recognizing that fact, the defendants cancelled the contract, during the first year the relationship was terminated, and Winnebago then recommended production of substantially the same unit but with a Winnebago label. This, in turn, led to the phenomenal rise of Winnebago who, within a very short space of time, became the number one motor home manufacturer in the United States.

The case involved a number of stages. The first was a four- or five-day interview with the clients which was taped. These tapes were abstracted to form a memorandum of about 150 pages with approximately 100 critical exhibits spelling out generally the clients' cause of action. The next stage was investigation to test the validity of the clients' claims to determine whether we should accept the representation. This took the form of extensive travel, interviewing numerous people, recorded statements, photographs and documents, all done in an effort to determine the strength and weaknesses of what they claimed. Following three months of investigation, we agreed to pursue the matter. Legal research disclosed four possible causes of action which were (1) breach of contract; (2) tortious interference with the performance of a contract; (3) conspiracy to defraud; and (4) theft of a trade secret. Action was then filed by Life-Time Industries, Inc. against Winnebago Industries, Inc. in the United States District Court for the Northern District of Iowa.

Once the action was filed, discovery followed almost immediately for we served with the original notices motions to produce documents and to immediately depose the principal officers. That was only the first shot of a war of discovery that lasted more than a year and a half and involved literally hundreds of depositions, thousands of exhibits and hundreds of thousands of documents of all kinds—records, plans, memoranda, photos, financial statements and other information—you name it, we had it.

The time period involved turned out to be about 365 days. At least 95 percent of all significant facts occurred within this period. The initial investigation, before we commenced the action, involved more material than you would have in 90 percent of most other litigation as of the time of trial. This was only the beginning.

Once the action was commenced we developed three other large masses of evidence: depositions, marked exhibits and literally hundreds of legal filing boxes crammed with documents of every description furnished by both sides in response to motions to produce.

As matters progressed there were several systems that suggested themselves for cataloging and indexing and the first of these was suggested by the fact that we were dealing with a day-by-day set of facts confined to approximately one year. This pointed to an obvious framework to start with—365 file folders each with a date. As the material was produced, we dated everything and put it in the proper folder. If we had an exhibit such as an airplane log, it was duplicated for as many dates as it contained and each was appropriately filed. This we called our *chronology*. It soon expanded into several full file drawers. The system worked pretty well but it didn't begin to serve our overall needs.

The second system we instituted related to witnesses and subject matter. We attempted to file all matters accordingly but before long it was—now where in the world did I put that?

As the accumulated evidence under each of these systems began to expand, at some point part way through discovery that nagging feeling started that I referred to earlier. The mass of evidence was getting out of hand, and projecting ourselves ahead to months of trial and trying to visualize our ability to recall what we knew we would need started to produce panic. It was something like the pioneers must have felt as they crossed the plains and saw what first appeared to be a low obstacle turn out to be a mighty mountain that had to be surmounted. What we desperately needed was some system to index the witnesses' statements, depositions, exhibits, documents produced and so forth, and to try and categorize the major elements of the whole case—to work out a cross-indexing system and to do it all in such a way that we could recall it with a reasonable degree of promptness and accuracy. We evaluated our present system, reviewed the past systems that had been used, and discussed other possibilities. None of them seemed to fit the bill.

The answer we came up with—computerize. Why not? Why not try to adapt its capabilities to the lawsuit? We did this. What follows is what we learned and how we proceeded, coupled with what experience taught us and what additional improvements we'll make next time.

We use the term "computer" throughout this discussion because that is the industry's descriptive word for the machine. The American Heritage Dictionary defines *computer* as "a device that computes; especially an electronic machine that performs high speed mathematical or logical calculations or that assembles, stores, correlates, or otherwise processes and prints information derived from coded data in accordance with a predetermined program." "Computerize" is defined as, "to process or store (information) with or in an electronic computer or system of computers." We will be using the words as defined in the underlined portions of the definitions, namely, as a means by which we can store, in a random fashion, any material we want, knowing that we can get it back in printed form in as many different ways as we previously determine, plus some ways that will be available whether we have preselected them or not. Let's disspell one potential misunderstanding right now. Remember, the computer will be used to store and return to you that which you give it. It doesn't think. It will not answer a question for you unless you have given it the answer. Computers, when used to solve problems, do so only because they have been programmed with the steps needed to arrive at the result. I was surprised to find that when I first made mention of the fact that we used the computer to assist us in the trial, some envisioned what we did was to feed in the testimony of the witness on the stand and the computer spewed out the cross-examination or gave us the critical exhibits needed to respond. No such luck, for if it could, we all would be looking for another specialty. It won't do your thinking for you but its ability to hold, sort out and return to you in an orderly and usable fashion your total input over a period of months, or years, is an invaluable tool in future trial practice.

The use of the computer is probably confined to major litigation because of the cost factors, albeit that there is nothing in the process that would preclude you from applying it to a subrogation claim. When I speak of cost, I mean both the time of counsel, of secretaries, of third parties and of equipment. However, as we will later find, much of what you will have to do to computerize you would be doing in some other form in any event, so much of the cost is involved either way. Computerization can be adapted to any type of litigation once you understand the basics of how to set it up. There are certain cases where its need will be obvious from the beginning. The earlier you decide to use it, the better. I can't place too much emphasis on that suggestion. We waited too long. The final product will be so much better if you can start your input in a more planned and leisurely way as it permits you to start your numbering system and general outline so that the witnesses, evidence, exhibits and so forth can be put in proper order and, as discovery progresses, your input will be orderly and thorough.

When you first realize computerization might help, it is well to estimate the magnitude of your task and to get some reliable cost figures for the entire job. You will know more about how to approach this after you have completed the balance of this text. You might even be lucky enough to be representing a company that has its own equipment and programmers which could be a real plus.

Once you conclude that your litigation will justify computerization, you will want to consult with a programmer and become knowledgeable about what the computer can do for you. There are two ways to go, either to gain the knowledge and do your own programming, or present your needs to a programmer and let him set it up. You constantly update and refine it as the pretrial work dictates. Don't let the thought of doing your own programming scare you; you have already done something similar in all your cases except you haven't reduced it to writing for use with the computer. Every trial lawyer does programming, a form of orderly approach to all forms of evidence and its recall, use and presentation, we just never think in terms of programming for a computer.

Your first foray into the world of the computer will immediately acquaint you with the need to count from one to eighty. One computer line consists of eighty spaces and in each space you can print any letter of the alphabet, any number from zero through nine or any special symbol. You will be using keypunch cards such as you have seen on television. For each line of your ultimate printout you will have to punch one card. One major change, however, is that the manual sorter which you became familiar with on TV that dropped out the single card is now all done electronically by putting the information from each card on a magnetic tape and sorting is now done with lightning speed. You will need a keypunch operator and a verifier to produce the cards.

The most important thing to understand is the number of different ways you can recapture the same information on a printout. To make it simple, the two most obvious ways would be by witness and by subject matter. These two would be pertinent to almost all litigation. Additional printouts will be dictated by the litigation—you might want one by deposition or, if it is a products case and a particular part has failed, you might want a printout of everything anyone has ever said about that part plus any and all exhibits that pertain thereto. The number of different printouts you obtain will be governed primarily by your own ingenuity and funds.

The computer expert will tell you that the number of ways that he can print out your information depends upon the thoroughness of your coding. The ability to retrieve is based on the selection of certain numbers or symbols. Therefore, if you will identify by number or letter as many different aspects of your case as possible then you multiply the number of different ways you can selectively print out the material. Give a number or letter to witnesses, potential witnesses, depositions, statements, exhibits, offerings, pleadings, interrogatories, et cetera. Later you will see how this coding both determines the type of printout and accurately identifies the source of the material.

Therefore, before you can commence your input you will have to set up an identification system by number or letter or both and a framework which, for convenience sake, we will call a category outline.

The first step is to consider all of your sources and potential sources of input. These will include every significant individual, potential witness or not, investigation generally, statements, pleadings, interrogatories, depositions, exhibits, unmarked documents, documents produced and may include any number of other sources dictated by the type of case. One will readily produce certain major sources of input and others can be plugged in as they reveal themselves.

Once you have listed your sources of input you must now estimate quantity, for in order to give them all a number or letter designation we will need to know how many spaces to set aside of the eighty we have available for each of your input sources. As an example: if the witnesses or potential witnesses will be more than one and less than one hundred, we will leave two spaces to identify witnesses. If the exhibits will consist of more than one and less than one thousand, you will need three spaces, et cetera. Thus, your initial source outline would look something like this:

Witnesses—1 to 99

Depositions—1 to 99

page numbers—1 to 999

Statements—1 to 10

Pleadings—A through Z

Exhibits—1 to 999

Other Documents—1 to 999

Dates—1 to 6

Category Outline—1 to 99

Next you should prepare a list of the potential witnesses and assign them all a number or letter. Since most witnesses will be involved with either a deposition or statement or some offering, you should attempt to give the witness, his statement and his deposition all the same number for convenient reference. What is attached as "A" was a partial list of our witnesses and the numbers and letters that were assigned. Follow this same procedure with the rest of your areas of input, pleadings, interrogatories, et cetera.

The category outline is next. You should list the major categories of your litigation and as many subcategories as you can think of. The category outline we put together is attached and marked "B." Since we started late, we were able to put together a much more complete outline than one might be able to put together in the earlier stages of litigation. However, in setting up your outline leave vacant spaces and fill in later as discovery develops new titles.

What you have done so far is put together a working framework for coding identification. We now come to the need for some way to impart the information that you want to put into the computer to your secretary so that a keypunch operator can take her work-product and convert it into a punched card. Thus, what you need is a form that will make your input a simple matter for both you and your secretary. This can be done by yourself or your programmer. It is a matter of allocating eighty spaces on a line to first code and then to set out the evidence.

Let's start with the sources of input and allocate spaces. We need two for witnesses, for the numbers from 1 to 99; two for depositions for the numbers 1 to 99; three for page numbers for the numbers 1 to 999; one for statements; one for pleadings; two for exhibits; three for other documents; six for dates; six for category outline and one more space to put the quotes in proper sequence as we will explain later. Thus, starting from the left, we have used 27 spaces and have 53 spaces left for evidentiary material. Thus you would have 10 columns to accommodate the above and the last a large column for material evidence.

Because our chronology was such a distinct type of cataloging we decided to set up two separate systems for our computer printouts. The first we referred to as our chronology and the second as our category outline.

"C" attached is the bare form designed for use by the secretary for our chronology input. "D" is the bare form designed for secretarial use for our category input. "C1," "C2" and "C3" are completed forms of "C" and "D1," "D2" and "D3" are completed forms of "D."

Briefly, by way of explanation, on form "C" the first column contained six spaces for the date, the second column contained three spaces for witnesses, the third column contained five spaces for purposes of identifying the source of the information, the fourth column contained four spaces for page numbers from sources of information, the fifth column was a one-digit column to be used as a quotation sequence column for if you had more than a one-line quotation or statement in order to print it out in sequence you had to number the lines from one to nine and if it exceeded nine lines you had to begin over again with one. In this way the computer was so programmed that what you set out by way of comment or quote was printed out in proper order. The sixth column was a two-digit column for a second witness designation. Thus, if the material related to more than one witness, we could designate one witness in the second column and a second witness in the sixth column. The balance of the form could be used for whatever comments, quotations or excerpts counsel wanted to preserve.

Turning now to "D," the category form, the first column contained eight spaces. If you will now glance at the category outline, you will see that we had 99 major and minor categories. Therefore, any single piece of information could be placed in four separate categories for subsequent recall since this first column permitted you to designate four one- or two-digit numbers. The second column contained three spaces and was designated a witness column but was actually used as a column to define the source of the input whether it be witness, a response, a pleading or statement. The third column was a source material column and allowed four digits. Thus, in this column we could describe by either letter or number the deposition, document or other source material from which the comment was derived. The fourth column was for page numbers and contained four digits. This became necessary because some depositions exceeded a thousand pages. The last column was a one-digit column and, again, was needed in order to put the comments or quotations in proper sequence. The remaining portion of the form was utilized for comments or quotations. For further clarification, let's take a look at "C1" and on the first line of the form, in the first column, we note the number "050165" which, of course is May 1, 1965. The witness is number "1"—James Baker. The source material or document number was also number "1," being a preliminary recap of their activities done by the clients. The "SEQ" column was to number the first line of the comment and the second line is number "2" which thus printed them out in proper order. The last column referred to a second witness to whom the material was relevant; in this case "4" or Don Johnson. Referring now to "C3," we find in the first column "021566" which is February 15, 1966. The witness was "70" or Larry Dunn. The document involved, "LDO," was a Larry Dunn offering and it was document "12." The other witness involved with the offering was witness "1" or James Baker.

Taking "D1" the explanation is as follows; in the first column we show the figures "349394." That meant that this particular piece of material would be pertinent to three categories; "34"—the tape; "93"—witness Cooper; and "94"—witness Peterson. The second column indicated that the witness providing the information was "63" or Elliott E. Cooper, and the third column indicated that the source material was also "63," which meant his deposition. The next column indicated the information was found on page 14 and the next column was simply our sequence column for proper order. The material is a comment rather than a quotation summarizing the testimony on that page. "D2" contains on the first line and in the first column "30385093." That meant that the comment pertained to category "30-post-contract activity"— "38—January stock-piling"— "50—Cooper memorandum of February 11, 1966" and "93—the witness Cooper." The witness was Larry Dunn, number "70" and the source material was his deposition, also "70." The information for the comment came from page 245. The balance of the forms can be interpreted accordingly.

These secretarial forms then go to the keypunch operator and what is marked "E" are samples of cards after they were punched. Each card carries at the top in printed form what the punched marks mean. You should have no occasion to work with the cards except in rare instances of corrections.

How are "C" and "D" compiled? They are the work product of counsel. However, there is very little additional effort needed over what you would be doing if you were abstracting and assembling the meaningful evidence for pretrial and trial preparation. "C1," "C2" and "C3" are examples of the chronology. The abstractor started with a date file, recited the date and then systematically went through the file identifying each of the documents, the witnesses that it might be applicable to and then gave his appropriate comments, whatever they might be.

"D1," "D2" and "D3" are examples of an abstract of depositions. Here the abstractor first identified the category or categories by number in which he desired to place the particular piece of information; then the witness and deposition by number, then the source material by page and followed that with instructions as to what he desired in the comment section whether by way of quotation, excerpt or whatever.

Both of the forms we devised proved extremely valuable but the chronology printout proved to be invaluable and its ultimate use exceeded our fondest expectations.

This may seem like a lot to remember at this stage but in reality the entire process will develop very logically and as new areas of evidence are disclosed you can easily expand your source of input and category outlines to accommodate them. Again, let me say that what will be required of you in this regard will not be that much different from what you would normally be faced with in your other trial preparations and, in this case, your end-product will be something far superior. Keep in mind, also, that you will only be working with certain segments of input at any given time. Once you get the hang of it the abstracting of a deposition becomes a very simple and speedy process.

When you have identified the witness by number and the deposition by number, each time you reach a significant piece of testimony, you glance at the category outline and recite the numbers on the outlines where you want the testimony to be placed and then your comments or further instructions. The same is true of any other source material. Just identify it, recite the category or categories in which you want it placed and your comments. You will wind up with completed forms such as "C1" and "D1."

I encourage you to start early and to dictate your input as discovery moves along. We started late and our input suffered. Another bit of advice—it is the numbers or letters that precede your comments that are all-controlling. You need not concern yourself with any orderly fashion of input—you can jump all over the map, from one source to another and back again, from the beginning of a deposition to the back to the middle. You can proceed in any fashion that time or availability dictates. Why? Because the punched cards will be put on magnetic tape in random fashion and totally unsorted.

The computer itself will do the sorting according to its programming with lightning speed.

After closing your input, you will select and get proof copies of your various printouts. At this point your sins may catch up with you. Let's hope the accuracy of counsel, his secretary and the keypunch operator are such that corrections are at a minimum. It is inevitable that there will be some. A mistake in any of the numbers preceding the comment will place the information in the wrong spot. Obtain a thorough briefing from your programmer as to how costly, troublesome and time-consuming mistakes can be, since this will have a tendency to promote greater effort toward accuracy during the period of input. Use your smartest and ablest secretary. Commence her learning process with yours so that she understands what it is you are doing. This can cut your mechanical work in half and also provide you with tremendous assistance in the matter of error-correction.

"F1," "F2," "F3" and "F4" are examples of the printout under what we call our chronology; and "G1," "G2" and "G3" are examples of our category printout. We selected four different ways to print out the chronology; first by date, second by the first listed witness, third, the second listed witness, and fourth by exhibit by date. The category printout we did in two ways; the first by category, and the second by witness by category.

Unless you have an opportunity to examine a larger segment of the printout it is extremely difficult to visualize the orderliness with which all of your material will be returned to you. In the category printout it will print out each category from one to 99 and, under each category it will start with witness one and under each witness it will start with the earliest source material and within that source material it will start with page one. In the witness printout it will start with a given witness and thereafter print out each category in numerical order which that witness had any relationship to and under each category will print out all of the material starting with the earliest source information and then the earliest pages from the source. At some point prior to the commencement of trial, you will have your final printouts of all of your pretrial work and discovery. At this point I feel I could probably quit since the last thing you should need is any suggestions as to how to use such a work-product. However, let me simply relate a few of our experiences in connection with it in order to enhance your enthusiasm to both consider and use this new technology in your trial practice.

Since we were plaintiffs, we were faced with the initial task of starting to prepare our own witnesses. Some witnesses had been deposed and others were critical witnesses who had not been. Many were from long distances and we had no opportunity to interview them in depth. When we commenced working with them to prepare their testimony and to project possible cross-examination, the printouts proved to be of inestimable value. A witness who had been deposed was given the abstracted printout to read rather than his deposition to review in its entirety. On a matter of recall as to what had happened during any particular period of time, the chronology was used. If a witness had difficulty remembering details, a review of the date and the events as they had taken place quickly brought back the bygone memory or, in the alternative, if they remembered doing a specific thing but could not think of the date, we could help them by working the system in reverse. It also served to resolve a number of arguments that might have arisen by reason of the dates or the order in which certain matters took place. They also proved to be of the utmost assistance when, as an example, some witness participated in the purchasing of chassis for the motor homes, which activity also involved another witness who had been deposed. We turned to the subject matter in the printout, i.e., 21 or 70 and located the name of the deposed witness and let the prospective witness review the abstract of all of the pertinent testimony which that individual had testified to in his deposition concerning such chassis purchases. This procedure saved untold hours of trying to skim depositions or having the witness review it, looking for certain specific pieces of information. When a witness asked, "What did Mr. Jones claim about that particular matter?" we merely turned to either the witness or to the category involved and there before us was a summary of all that witness had to say with respect to that particular situation.

We prepared for cross-examination in much the same way. We needed only to turn to the particular category or the witness involved and review everything he had testified to in his deposition or statement. It also gave us ready access to what everyone else had said concerning that particular matter. It reached the point where we almost looked forward to cross-examination, for not only could we do an excellent job of preparing our own witnesses but the cross of the opposition was almost fun.

How was it used in the courtroom? The chronology printout was almost in constant use, for whenever a witness referred to a day or a particular activity, or gave some indication about when the event had occurred, we could immediately find it in the chronology, test its accuracy, and review what other events had occurred on that date or close thereto for purposes of further direct or cross-examination. The chronology not only gave us some indication of what was occurring on that particular date, but it also had reference to the various exhibits or documents that supported it. If a witness were in doubt as to where he had been or what he had done, or became confused on the witness stand, we were in a position to quickly remedy it by referring to the chronology, obtaining the correct date, and then pulling the necessary exhibits whether they be the airplane logs, a bill for a motel, or a memorandum made at the time that would support the actual fact.

It would serve no useful purpose here to relate all of the various incidents that occurred where we made use of the printouts. I can honestly state I had never been involved in any litigation where the witnesses on direct examination were as well prepared, where the cross-examination was as thorough, and where we virtually reduced to an infinitesimal fraction the elements of surprise which we encountered, particularly in connection with the cross-examination of our witnesses.

We gave serious consideration to attempting the continuation of the input into the computer during the course of the trial by simply summarizing the testimony of the witnesses as we would in deposition (since there were daily transcripts available), but had to abandon the idea because the press of preparation for trial day by day was all we could handle.

The final use of the printouts related to final arguments. So closely had our case adhered to the information and exhibits that were contained in the category and chronology printouts that they served as a refresher for us for final argument. I neglected to mention that this was a jury trial and we were at it for seven solid months. The jury spent two and a half weeks in deliberation before returning their verdicts.

The total cost of the computerization was between $5,000 and $6,000, exclusive of attorney and secretarial time, and with us doing our own programming.

In closing let me say that as I look back on it now it took me far less time to set up this whole matter than it has taken me to try to tell you about it in printed form. I can't impress upon you strongly enough that what looks like a highly technical and complicated procedure is really not that at all. Look at it this way, how would you feel if you learned that your opponent, in a major piece of litigation, had systematically reduced all of the pretrial material to the computer for instant recall, while you sit there and stare at your pencil and legal pad?

Figure A

Name	Witness letter	Witness no.	Depo. no.	State-ment no.
ARNOLD, Robert W.	RA	84	84	—
AZEVEDO, Robert L.	AZ	07	—	206
BABA, Joe	BJ	29	29	—
BABLIN, Edward	EB	17	—	214
BAINTER, Keith	KB	86	86	—
BAKER, Bettye	BB	02	02	—
BAKER, James G. M.	JB	01	01	—
BALDWIN, Betty	BE	69	69	—
BANK OF AMERICA (ROGERS)	RO	47	47	—
BANKERS TRUST (STERLING)	BT	46	46	—
BASHAM, Paul	PB	75	75	—
BEARDSLEY, Adele	AB	22	—	219
BLUME, Marshall	MB	36	—	—
BOMAN, G.	GB	66	66	—
BUNCH, Fred	FB	41	—	—
CARTER, Ben	BC	82	82	—
COLE, Harold	HC	20	—	217
COOPER, Elliott E.	EC	63	63	—
CORNELIUS, Ben	CO	15	—	212
CORNELIUS, Ned	NC	13	—	210
CORNELIUS, Gladys	GB	14	—	211
CROSS, Art	AC	30	—	—
DAHL, Gary	GB	81	81	—
DEYO, L. A.	DE	28	28	—
DICK'S FORD	DF	74	—	—
DUNN, Larry	LD	70	70	227
ELRICK & LAVIDGE	EL	39	39	—
EVERTON, Harold	HE	91	—	—
FLORENCE, Larry	LF	71	71	—
FRANK, Raymond	RF	11	—	—
FRIEND, Irwin	IF	35	—	—
GALLOWAY, Dewey	DG	65	65	—
GEORGE, Carroll	CG	42	—	223
GIFFORD, James	JG	93	—	229
GROEN, M. C.	MG	83	83	—
HANSON, John K.	JK	60	60	—
HANSON, John V.	JV	61	—	—
HANSON, Luise	LH	62	62	—
HARRIS, Robert	RH	44	—	225
HAUAN, Gary	GH	33	33	221
HILER, EARL	EH	78	78	—
INGRAHAM & KENNEDY	IK	52	52	—
ISENSEE, R.H.	RI	51	51	—
JACKSON, Paul	PJ	10	—	208
JOHNSON, Don	DJ	04	04	203

Figure B

01 MOTOR HOME CONCEPT
02 J. & B. Baker—Baker Trailer Sales
03 Don Johnson—Drawings
04 Sandwich Construction
05 Price
06 Interior Design
07 Japanese Motor Home
08 Squier Motor Home
09 Frank, Ray
10 PRECONTRACT ACTIVITIES
11 Initial Trips—Disclosure of Concept
12 Winnebago Stops
13 September 9/10 meetings
14 Ford-Wells-Pooling
15 Dealer Days—Sept. 20, 1965
16 Prototype—"Big Red"—LT's Help
17 November 12, 1965 Signing
18 Baker/Hanson Relationships
20 PRECONTRACT REPRESENTATIONS
21 Chassis—Winnebago to Supply
22 Time to Pay for Units—10/15 Days
23 Variable Production
24 Modifications and Changes
25 THE CONTRACT
26 Pre-drafts & Communications
27 Variances—Oral Promises/ Contract
30 POST-CONTRACT ACTIVITY—Dec.-Jan.
31 Dunn Drawings—Dec. 7/8, 1965
32 Typewritten Plan—Units Frozen
33 December 9, 1965, Meeting
34 The Tape
35 Baker Finances/Beardsley
36 LA-Louisville Shows—Big Red Trip
37 Price Change Optional Equipment
38 Jan. Stockpiling—Keep out of Plant
39 Contractions Problems
40 FEBRUARY FIFTH MEETING
41 Jan. 30 Planning Meeting
42 Demand for Open Account
43 Demand Immediate Pymt 51 Units
44 Quick Resignation Letter
45 Talcott—Renegotiate $250,000
46 Pickup 5 a/time—Pay before Inspect
47 Resume Production before Price Adj.
48 Riverside Cafe Meeting
50 COOPER MEMORANDUM, Feb. 11, 1966
51 Document—Interpretation—Commentary
52 Compliance with Format
53 17′ Town & Country
54 Short Supply WI Pdts.—Reps Mtg at FCity
55 May Shutdown—150 Chassis on Hand
56 Ford Pooling for Life-Time
57 Keith Sanborn—Morris Laird
58 Factory Reps—Lake MilleLac
59 Model Changes—Engineering
60 CANCELLATION
61 The Notice—Reasons
62 Dunn's Additional Drawings
63 LT Rejection of Cancellation
64 WI Activity to Build WI Motor Home
65 Post-Contract Efforts Destroy LT Mfg.
66 Obtaining Chassis from LT Pool
70 FORD MOTOR COMPANY
71 Wells-Winnebago Pooling Agreement
72 Rands
73 McFall
74 Mullan
75 Dick's Ford
76 Kamish Ford
77 Life-Time Pooling Agreement
78 Post-Contract Dealings—Winnebago + Ford
80 DAMAGES—IRWIN FRIEND/ M. BLUME
81 R.V.I.
90 MISCELLANEOUS
91 Fac. Reps-Bablin-Moore-Kapengst-Cole
92 John K. Hanson
93 Elliott E. Cooper
94 G. Wallace Peterson
95 Attys: Joyce-Weible-Laird-Everton
96 Park Investment, Carl Matherly
97 John Martin
98 Larry Dunn
99 DEFENSE & COUNTERCLAIM

Date	Witness	Docu. no.	Page no.	Seq.	Witness	Commentary
(6)	(3)	(5)	(4)	(1)	(2)	(59)

Figure C. Chronology

Date	Witness	Docu. no.	Page no.	Seq.	Witness	Commentary
050165	1	1		1	4	Jim first calls Johnson about a conference to retain him to make
		•		2		drawings. Johnson in between jobs with Perch & Lockheed
051565	1	1		1	4	About this date Johnson has meeting with Baker Quick etc to
				2		confer with Johnson about concept low cost motor home
080465	1			1	60	Hanson lukewarm to any idea involving motor home talks about
				2		production ability & need for something to build suggests stop
				3		back, knows Bakers are touring other factories
083065	1	DJE		1	4	First motor home sketched bearing notation motor home design
				2		no. 1 date 8/30/65 this is the 19 ft unit
090465	1	DJE		1	4	Johnson drawing no 2 dated this date shows variations in wheel
				2		base & floor plan
090565	1			1	60	Hanson has meeting with Quick Baker Peterson Galloway Dunn
				2		Boman & possibly Cooper meeting continues on 9/10
091065	1	LDO		1	60	This is a typewritten memo with notations of JKH relative to
				2		discussions he had with Baker as to what the contract would
				3		contain It is undated but was probably done following the 9/10
		LDO		4		meeting It is found in Dunns first offering the 9 page or document
				5		of the first group
091465	1	JBO	4	1	60	Hansons letter to Baker enclosing work sheets states we are
				2		continuing work on your project & all looks favorable the work
				3		sheets are probably the features of housecar & the Wells
				4		quotations on chassis
091565	1	JBO		1	91	Life-Time Industries Inc. Articles of Incorp. filed
091665	1	LDE	6	1	70	Dunn talks with Baker discusses coming out to meet Carter & do
				2		art work will bring items requested by Dunn in his letter & talks
				3		about the name & staying over for Dealer Days
092365	1	JKE	2	1	60	This letter to Baker states we will push along on the concept
				2		Hanson writes Baker referring to their meeting of 9/10 & 11 & that
				3		they will exchange notes. The memo previously referred to with
				4		Hansons notations under date of 9/10 or 11 is attached to this
				5		exhibit
103065	1			1	60	Hanson would always say to employees stay with them Baker &
				2		Quick pick their brains in order to get California zing

Figure C1. Chronology

Figure C2. Chronology

Date	Witness	Docu. no.	Page no.	Seq.	Witness	Commentary
021566	1	LDE	106	1	60	Dunn memo of Hanson conversation w/Baker re arranging 5 PM
				2		meeting to review Jim's letter of 12th concerning proposed contract
				3		alterations
021566	1	LDE	109	1	60	Dunn's memo indicating must have been meeting w/Baker Hanson
				2		& Dunn this date because Baker does not appreciate demands of
				3		Misc. Purchases Acct.
021566	3			1		Quick terminates employment with LT & goes commercial to
				2		San Jose
021566	40	LDO	002	1	70	List of Chassis numbers & missing or defective parts
				2		correlate this w/51 units to see how many were not complete
				3		D2-14
021566	60	JKE	007	1	1	Hanson letter to Jim refusing all requests in his letter of 2/12 about
				2		any contract changes
021566	60	LDE	116	1	1	Hanson letter to Baker concerning startup after 106
				2		obviously not written by Hanson. We should find author of this
				3		document.
021566	60			1		Compare Hanson's letter on prices for startup w/Petersons 2/11
				2		memo concerning past costs to see if they are using those price
				3		increases
021566	63	DLO	113	1	1	Dunn memo of telephone call from Cooper advising what steps are
				2		to be taken with LT re Baker's letter of 2/12
021566	63	LDE	108	1	23	Phone call from Cooper suggesting inspection slip be signed by WI
				2		inspector & included in every LT unit hardly a piece of legal
				3		business
021566	67	LDO	011	1	70	Starkey memo asking how replacement parts for motor homes
				2		should be handled such procedure making it difficult for
				3		customer to get replacement see proposed form attached to
				4		D-11-3
021566	70	LDE	111	1	1	Dunn letter to Baker including Misc Purchases Acct
				2		note credits to this acct designed to keep pressure on
				3		financially
021566	70	LDO	000	1	7	Dunn memo of call from Azevedo re blower shortages on
				2		units WI is out & customers will have to take them as is
				3		since it will be 2 wk delay if these are on the 51 sheet.
				4		Further evidence that units were not complete when
				5		demand made

Date	Witness	Docu. no.	Page no.	Seq.	Witness	Commentary
021566	70	LDO	12	1	1	Memo from Dunn's file re changes requested by LT. D12-13
021666	1	LDE	53	1	60	Baker letter to Hanson in response to Hanson letter of 2/15 on
				2		prices stating not to resume production until these are
				3		straightened out.
021666	1	LDE	115	1	60	5 PM meeting with Baker, Azevedo, JHK, Luise, Peterson,
				2		Cooper, Bowman, JVH & Dunn rescheduled from 15th to 16th
				3		Memo indicates almost all items were refused but it is made
				4		clear that WI is continuing and will continue to produce
				5		motor homes. This is consistent with Cooper's memo of 2/11
				6		to "Build like hell until LT defaults & then we get it all,
				7		no sweat."
021666	24	MUE	016	1	40	Ford memo involving addn refund to Kamish for 60 day floor
				2		planning. Refer to note in handwriting probably McFall.
021666	60	LDE	122	1	1	Hanson letter to Baker stating we are already back in production
				2		with notation that it was handed to Baker on 16th in front of JVH,
				3		Peterson, Luise & Elliott who were all at plant in conference
				4		at time.
021666	70	LDE	114	1	72	Phone conversation w/Powell re changes in units 70 concerning
				2		California coding & other matters
021666	70	LDE	003	1	1	Dunn memo re Misc. Pur. Acct which Baker critical of on 2/15.
				2		Credit of $383 on demand previously made by Dunn
021766				1	7	Baker remains in FC Azevedo returns to San Jose
021766	70	LDE	118	1	1	Phone call Baker to Dunn concerning more driver comfort General
				2		discussion re how to move pedals to solve problem
021866	70	LDE	119	1	1	Memo says Jim & Azevedo in Dunn office to review cost figures on
				2		motor home. Not sure Azevedo is in town.
021866	70	LDO	12	1	1	Dunn memo re new extrusions for windshield which they intend to
				2		bill LT for but will get money back if they use certain amount of
				3		aluminum
022166	70	LDE	127	1	64	Note Peterson's memo suggests windshield wipers continue as
				2		option with 50% markup albeit they are a vital piece of
				3		equipment.
022166	70	LDO	12	1	1	Dunn memo indicating that markup on optional items should be
				2		50%.

Figure C3. Chronology

Figure D

Witness name ______		Witness no. ____		Deposition no. ____	Source no. ____
Subject	Witness	SM #	Page	Seq.	Comment
(8)	(3)	(4)	(4)	(1)	(60)

Figure D1

Witness name Elliott E. Cooper Witness no. 63 Deposition no. 63 Source no. ____

Subject	Witness	SM #	Page	Seq.	Comment
349394	63	63	14	1	I asked the defendants about the tape. It was thought there was a tape
				2	of a particular meeting but it had escaped specific memory of any of
				3	them. The whereabouts of the tape was unknown. It was in old records
				4	or storage area. Peterson finally located it. Tape carton contains word
				5	"master". Copies were made of it at time or immediately following
				6	location of the tape.
349394	63	63	18	1	To best of my recollection Baker, Quick, Azevedo, Dunn, Peterson, JKH,
				2	Starkey & myself were present at the meeting of 12/9/65. Mr. Hanson
				3	returned, inquired as to whether or not the matter had been straight-
				4	ened out & repeated his position as announced at beginning of meeting
469093	63	63	27	1	Cooper denies participation in Carter requiring LT to take 5 units at a time.
559093	63	63	31	1	Cooper denies recall on the 150 chassis being provided before WI would
				2	start production after May 66 shutdown.
303893	63	63	34	1	Cooper denies that he insisted Baker pay cash or by certified check on
				2	Forest City bank for delivery of units.
305293	63	63	48	1	Details about the Dunn sale of 16,000 shares of WI stock are uncovered
				2	from pp. 48-54. Here Cooper denies specific knowledge about the
				3	transfer of the stock except his participation as transfer agent of WI.
20307093	63	63	72	1	Cooper attempts to differentiate between first 6 units & the contract.
18337193	63	63	100	1	Cooper admits there is a difference of opinion as to who promised to
				2	supply the chassis, Baker or Hanson.
71929394	63	63	102	1	Termination of Ford pooling agreement, 2/24/66
606193	63	63	192	1	Cooper's participation in cancellation of contract. My participation was
				2	as counsel for WI. I have no idea how many persons it was discussed
				3	with. It would include Mr. Hanson & Mr. Peterson as chief executive
				4	officers of the co. & perhaps would have required consultation with Mr.
				5	Dunn and various people in accounting.

Witness name Larry Dunn   Witness no. 70   Deposition no. 70   Source no. ______

Subject	Witness	SM #	Page	Seq.	Comment
30385093	70	70	245	1	This Ex of Dunn 41 he states was Cooper advising him to make sure he
				2	kept a daily diary of all contracts with LT & to be sure he included all
				3	amounts of overtime in the figures for the next accounting period.
3038	70	70	368	1	LDE 62 memo of Dunn conversation with Baker who wants unit 43 for
				2	dealer in Alaska who is there waiting. Dunn advises unit is ready but
				3	before he will deliver it he wants payment for unit 58 & balance of 10
				4	units of which 6 have been accepted and 4 remain. Also demands
				5	payment for units 63 so he wants payment for 5 or 6 units before
				6	releasing the unit to the Alaska dealer.
30384041	70	70	378	1	LDE 64 is Dunn memo of conversation with Quick on 1/31 which is first
				2	knowledge LT has that payment will have to be certified check, cash or
				3	check on Forest City funds.
30384041	70	70	397	1	LDE 65 Dunn discusses where they have unit 95 ready for delivery &
				2	advises that LT will have to pick up a number of units starting with 55
				3	before they are entitled to unit 95
40419398	70	70	399	1	Q. Why did you tell Mr. Quick that in order to obtain unit 95 he would
				2	have to pay for & accept all units prior to that number that had been
				3	completed. A: I was following instructions. Q. Whose Instructions? A.
				4	From Elliott Cooper. This occurs on 2/1/66.
40419298	70	70	417	1	LDE 51 Dunn's memo with suggested design revisions for LT motor
				2	home. This was after the 1/30 meeting when Dunn had feeling LT was
				3	all done & he was talking about what WI would be building & the
				4	changes that should be incorporated
4044	70	70	461	1	Dunn admits demand letter for Quick's signature prepared by Cooper.
				2	Quick refused to sign this. 2/5/66
4043	70	70	462	1	Dunn states that when Quick told him he could not pay the bill of
				2	$155,349 that LT was therefore in default
404344	70	70	468	1	Ex 90a Dunn informs Quick he considers all 51 units ready for salvage
				2	by WI which is probably why he had receipt for salvage prepared by
				3	Cooper.

Figure D2

Witness name John K. Hanson   Witness no. 60   Deposition no. 60   Source no. ____

Subject	Witness	SM #	Page	Seq.	Comment
9270	60	60	63	1	I met Larry Dunn in 64 at the Testing Lab of Alcoa in New Kensington,
				2	Pa. He was employed as our Chief Engineer
9270	60	60	75	1	Hanson denies that he had Dunn inventory and diagram every piece of
				2	equipment in the old factory
9270	60	60	76	1	Hanson admits he had Dunn plan new building before the fire and that
				2	Allen Anderson helped him
9293	60	60	82	1	I was host to Baker & Quick I picked them up at the airport personally
				2	and introduced them to Wally Peterson
927121	60	60	99	1	Hanson writes Baker 9/23 I feel certain that the written contract can be
				2	waiting for you upon your return to your office in 2 wks or so if your
				3	summary reaches me within the next few days
159192	60	60	103	1	I introduced Quick on Dealer Days 9/21/65. He showed the artist's sketch
				2	or perspective of motor home. He gave the approximate price as about
				3	$5,000 as I remember it on a Ford Chassis
182692	60	60	126	1	Hanson has no recollection of any conversation with Quick on 10/4
				2	about Ford Pooling Agreement Hanson admits signing orders for Ford
				3	chassis in Sept but doesn't know if he signed any in Oct He doesn't
				4	deny that he did, he says he doesn't recall
182692	60	60	134	1	Hanson remembers being with Bruce Wells and a former dealer's wife
				2	in tavern at night. Everybody was drinking.
21717392	60	60	135	1	Hanson does not have any recall about meeting with Wells & McFall on
				2	11/23/65 at Forest City. He does not deny such a meeting took place.
21717392	60	60	138	1	Q. Did you try to work some of Ford business through Dicks Ford
				2	because of Carter relationship? A. No.
02182092	60	60	139	1	Hanson agrees he met with Baker & Quick early Dec. & discussed
				2	problems, where were chassis, who was going to pay for them, is he
				3	going to get his money, where were the chassis, what was order
				4	system, problems re contract.

Figure D3

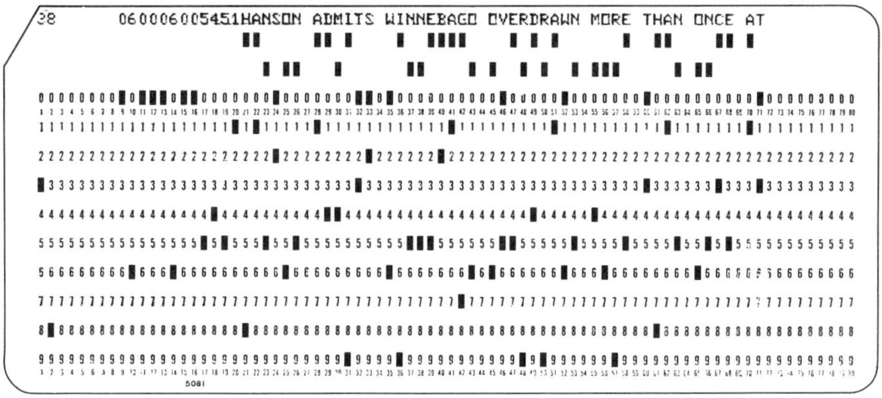
38 060006005451HANSON ADMITS WINNEBAGO OVERDRAWN MORE THAN ONCE AT
5081

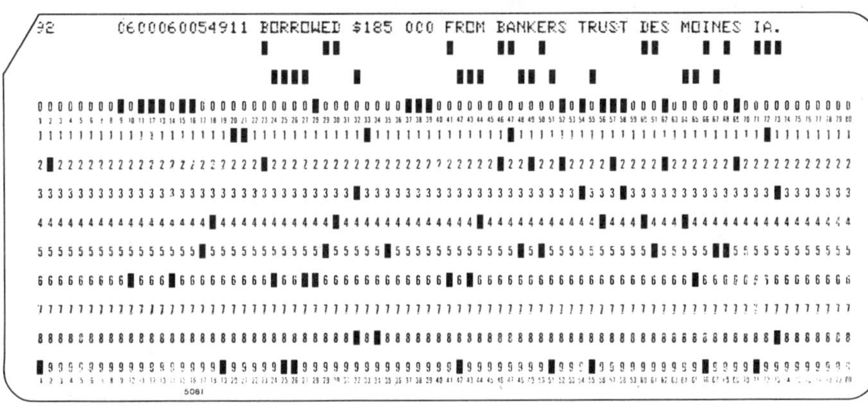
92 0600060054911 BORROWED $185 000 FROM BANKERS TRUST DES MOINES IA.
5081

Figure E

Figure F1

Date	No.	Name / Code	Ref.	Code	Entry	Initials
3/08/66	94	WEIBLE, DUDLEY				DW
9/09/66	31	LAIRD, MORRIS E.				ML
		00000	0000	01	CONF BAKER BURINGTON HEINY	
3/09/66	40	KAMISH, FRANK				FK
		FMD	0000	27	DEMAND FOR PAYMENT 03/09/66 FIVE UNITS	
3/09/66	70	DUNN, LARRY				LD
		LDO	0004	01	D4-38 IS DUNNS MEMO OF THIS DATE CONCERNING REFRIGERATOR	
				01	OPTIONS & HE INCREASES THE PRICE FROM 44.7 TO 50% TO LT	
		LDO	0014	63	D14-8 IS MEMO OF PHONE CALL FROM COOPER ADVISING THAT DUNN	
				63	IS TO MAKE SURE LT IS NOTIFIED THAT UNITS ARE READY FOR	
				63	DELIVERY	
		LDO	0015	65	D15-6 DUNN MEMO OF PHONE FROM GALLOWAY THAT 10 UNITS ON THE	
				65	LINE ARE MISSING FLASHERS EVIDENCE THAT COMPLETION OF UNITS	
				65	HAS ALWAYS BEEN A PROBLEM	
3/10/66	40	WAMISH, FRANK				FK
		FMO	0000	27	DEMAND FOR PAYMENT 03/10/66 TWO UNIT	
3/10/66	60	HANSON, JOHN K.				JK
		W17	0000	01	BATTLE MEMORIAL INSTITUTE REPORT ON THE USE OF SANDWICH TYP	
				01	CONSTRUCTION IN THE RECREATIONAL VEHICLE INDUSTRY SHOULD	
				01	BE READ IN ITS ENTIRETY GIVES PROJECTIONS FOR FUTURE USE OF	
				01	SANDWICH CONSTRUCTION & TOTAL SALES POTENTIAL SHOULD BE	
				01	COMPARED WITH WHAT WI HAS DONE IN THIS AREA AS OPPOSED TO	
				01	THEIR EXPANSION WITH THE MOTOR HOME	
3/10/66	63	COOPER, ELLIOTT E.				EC
		LDE	A142	00	THIS IS A MULTIPLE MEMO & THE MOST SIGNIFICANT ONE IS THE	
				00	NUMBER OF UNITS THEY HAVE COMPLETED & ADVISED US ARE READY	
				00	TO BE PICKED UP THIS MEMO FALLS INTO LINE WITH COOPERS MEMO	
				00	OF THE 11TH BUILD LIKE HELL & WAIT FOR THEM TO DEFAULT	
		LDE	B142	01	COOPERS CALL TO DUNN ADVISING THAT HE SHOULD NOTIFY OF	

Figure F2

1/07/66		LONG, PAUL				PL
10/11/65	86	BAINTER, KEITH				TV
		LDO	0005	00	SEE MEMO OF TREVAILLE LDO 5C-9 IN RE 114 EXT COST	
3/15/66	86	BAINTER, KEITH				TV
		LDO	0001	70	D1-27 IS MEMO OF TREVAILLE ADVISING OF SOME MINOR COST	
				70	CHANGES IT INCLUDES AN 8% FACTOR INVOLVING COPPER & ALUMINUM	
				70	WIRE FOR WASTE AS WELL AS ADDING .47172 TO THE TOTAL COST	
				70	AS A MARKUP FOR LABOR	
9/15/65	91	EVERTON, HAROLD				HE
		JBO	0000	01	LIFE TIME INDUSTRIES INC ART OF INC FILED	
10/26/65	91	EVERTON, HAROLD				HE
		00000	0000	01	BETTYES CHRONOLOGY SHOWS TALKING WITH SAN JOSE ATTORNEYS ON	
				01	THIS DATE & TRYING TO GET CONTRACT	
1/05/66	91	EVERTON, HAROLD				HE
		JBO	0030	60	EVERTON PROPOSED LETTER TO WINNEBAGO DEALING WITH CONTRACT	
				60	PROBLEM NEVER SENT	
11/03/65	92	VASIL, JOHN G.				VA
		VAO	0000	01	NO COMMENT TOOK PLACE ACTUALLY AFTER FINAL AGREEMENT WAS	
				01	DRAFTED—LITTLE CHANCE FOR ANY CHANGE IN HANSON OR COOPER	
				01	THINKING AT THIS POINT	
2/10/66	94	WEIBLE, DUDLEY				DW
		00000	0000	01	WEIBLE STARTS STUDY OF CONTRACT & SEARCH OF LAW ON	
				01	CONTRACT GENERALLY	
2/20/66	94	WEIBLE, DUDLEY				DW
		00000	0000	01	SEARCH OF LAW ON MEANING OF PROVISION PAYMENTS IN CASH	
2/22/66	94	WEIBLE, DUDLEY				DW
		00000	0000	01	CONF WITH BAKER & GOING OVER & APPROVING FORMS TO BE SIGNED	

Figure F3

2/10/66	1	BAKER, JAMES			JB
2/11/66	1	BAKER, JAMES			JB
		ECO	0143	064	THIS PARTICULAR OFFERING CONTAINS 2 ADDN PAGES WHICH DO NOT
				064	APPEAR ON THE PETERSON EX & SHOULD BE VIEWED IN CONNECTION
				064	WITH THE MATERIAL COST & LABOR SUMMARY THE LABOR COST FIGU
				064	RES PREVIOUSLY REFERRED TO
		WPE	A002	064	PETERSONS COMPUTATIONS OF MATERIAL & LABOR COSTS AS OF
				064	THIS DATE FOR THE 1ST 106 UNITS CHECK LABOR COSTS HE IS
		WPE	B002	064	THIS EX ALSO INCLUDES THE LABOR COST & PURPORTS TO BREAK
				064	OUT THE PILOT MODEL AS WELL AS THE DEMONSTRATORS NOTE
				064	FLUCTUATIONS IN LABOR COST BY WEEK REVIEW EXHIBIT IN DETAIL
2/14/66	1	BAKER, JAMES			JB
		LDE	0104	064	THIS IS PETERSONS CREDIT MEMO ADJUSTING PRICE ON FIRST 100
				064	UNITS BY 3.83. GIVES CREDIT FOR 383.00
		LDE	0110	070	DUNN NOTATION RE PROPOSED MEETING OF 15TH WITH BAKER & JKH
				070	AZEVEDO IS IN TOWN
		00000	0000	050	BAKERS AZEVIDO & MR & MRS JOHN MARTIN GO OUT ON THE TOWN
				050	BETTYES BIRTHDAY
2/15/66	1	BAKER, JAMES			JB
		DLE	0113	063	DUNN MEMO OF TELEPHONE CALL FROM COOPER ADVISING WHAT STEPS
				063	ARE TO BE TAKEN WITH LT CONCERNING BAKERS LETTER OF 12TH
		JKE	0007	060	HANSON LETTER TO JIM REFUSING ALL REQUESTS IN HIS LETTER OF
				060	2/12 ABOUT ANY CONTRACT CHANGES
		LDE	0111	070	DUNN LETTER TO BAKER INCLUDING MISC PURCHASE ACCT NOTE
				070	CREDITS TO THIS ACCOUNT DESIGNED TO KEEP PRESSURE ON FINAN
				070	CIALLY
		LDE	0116	060	HANSON LETTER TO BAKER CONCERNING STARTUP AFTER 106 OBVIOUS
				060	LY NOT WRITTEN BY HANSON WE SHOULD FIND AUTHOR OF THIS DOC
				060	UMENT
		LDO	0012	070	MEMO FROM DUNNS FILE CONCERNING THE CHANGES REQUESTED BY LT
				070	D12-13
		00000	0000	003	QUICK TERMINATES EMPLOYMENT WITH LT & GOES COMMERCIAL TO

Figure F4

2/12/66	1	BAKER, JAMES			JB
				70	TO THE UNIT WHICH BAKER WANTS DONE WHEN PRODUCTION RESUMES
				70	SEE ALSO JBO 40 WHICH IS OUR COPY OF THIS EXHIBIT & CONTAIN
				70	S NOTATIONS NOT ON THE DUNN EX
2/14/66	64	PETERSON, G. WALLACE			WP
		LDE	0104	01	THS IS PETERSONS CREDIT MEMO ADJUSTING PRICE ON FIRST 100
				01	UNITS BY 3.83. GIVES CREDIT FOR 383.00
2/14/66	70	DUNN, LARRY			LD
		LDE	0105	33	DUNN MEMO OF DIRTY UNITS THAT WERE DELIVERED TO LT & HIS IN
				33	STRUCTIONS TO BOMAN TO GET SOME PROTECTION ON THE CARPETEIN
				33	G THESE UNITS WERE PROBABLY PART OF THE 51 WHICH ARE BEING
				33	PICKED UP
		LDE	0110	01	DUNN NOTATION RE PROPOSED MEETING OF 15TH WITH BAKER & JKH
				01	AZEVEDO IS IN TOWN
2/15/66	1	BAKER, JAMES			JB
		LDE	0106	60	DUNN MEMO OF HANSON CONVERSATION WITH BAKER CONCERNING ARRA
				60	NGING FOR 5 O CLOCK MEETING TO REVIEW JIMS LETTER OF 12TH
				60	CONCERNING PROPOSED CONTRACT ALTERATIONS
		LDE	109	60	DUNNS MEMO INDICATING THERE MUST HAVE BEEN MEETING WITH
				60	BAKER HANSON & DUNN ON THIS DATE BECAUSE BAKER DOES NOT AP
				60	PRECIATE THE DEMANDS ON THE MISC PURCHASE ACCT
2/15/66	60	HANSON, JOHN K.			JK
		LDE	0116	01	HANSON LETTER TO BAKER CONCERNING STARTUP AFTER 106 OBVIOUS
				01	LY NOT WRITTEN BY HANSON WE SHOULD FIND AUTHOR OF THIS DOC
				01	UMENT
2/15/66	63	COOPER, ELLIOTT E.			EC
		LDE	0108	23	PHONE CALL FROM COOPER SUGGESTING INSPECTION SLIP BE SIGNED
				23	BY WI INSPECTOR & INCLUDED IN EVERY LT UNIT HARDLY A
				23	PIECE OF LEGAL BUSINESS
2/15/66	70	DUNN, LARRY			LD
		LDE	0111	01	DUNN LETTER TO BAKER INCLUDING MISC PURCHASES ACCT NOTE

Figure G1

```
10  PRECONTRACT ACTIVITIES
    11  INITIAL TRIPS AND DISCLOSURE OF CONCEPT
      003  QUICK, MAYNARD                                   MQ
           0003  0237      QUICK SAYS THAT THERE WERE MANY DISCUSSIONS ABOUT
                           DRAWINGS & FLOOR PLANS & THAT WE DIDNT WANT TO
                           REVEAL THEM WITHOUT SOME PROMISE ON HIS PART THAT HE
                           WOULDNT SHOW THEM TO ANYBODY ELSE & I THINK WE
                           LEFT OTHER DRAWINGS QUICK DOES NOT REMEMBER WHETHER
                           HE WAS PRESENT BECAUSE THE PROMISE WAS BETWEEN BAKER
                           AND HANSON HE THINKS HE WAS THERE P 238 AND THE
                           PROMISE CONCERNED QUICK EXH AND 5 AND OTHER
                           DOCUMENTS HE THINKS

           0003  0302      HANSON WAS NOT ENTHUSED ABOUT THE MOTOR HOME ON THE
                           FIRST TRIP BUT HE WAS ON THE SECOND TRIP TO FOREST
                           CITY

10  PRECONTRACT ACTIVITIES
    12  WINNEBAGO STOPS
      001  BAKER, JAMES                                     JB
           0001  0189      JIM STATES HE HAD MET JOHN K HANSON FOR A SHORT PERIOD
                           OF TIME AT HIS OFFICE IN CALIFORNIA

           0001  0363      BAKERS & QUICKS STOP AT FOREST CITY ON AUG 4 1965 MR
                           HANSON MET THEM AT THE AIRPORT WHEN THEY LANDED BAKER
                           HAD MET HIM PREVIOUSLY

           0001  0364      BAKER ADVISED HANSON THAT THEY WANTED TO SEE HIS FACILITIES
                           & TO SEE HIS SYSTEM OF CONSTRUCTION & FIND OUT WHAT
                           SUCCESSES HE HAD HAD WITH SANDWICH TYPE CONSTRUCTION
```

Figure G2

```
30  POST-CONTRACT ACTIVITY—DECEMBER-JANUARY
    30  POST-CONTRACT ACTIVITY—DECEMBER-JANUARY
      060  HANSON, JOHN K.                              JK
           0060  2385        HANSON SAYS I WOULD SAY I WOULDNT KNOW IF HE DUNN
                             HAD DISCUSSED OR NOT

           0060  2453        WE KNEW ALL THE TIME WE COULD BUILD THE TWENTY-FIVE NOT ALL
                             THE TIME BUT FROM THIS TIME ON WE COULD BUILD TWENTY-FIVE A
                             WEEK IF HE COULD JUST PAY FOR THEM FINE WE WERE BUILDING
                             TWELVE FIFTEEN A WEEK SOMETHING LIKE THAT WHATEVER WE COULD
                             WE WERE READY TO GO WE KNEW THAT WE COULD DO IT WE NOTIFIED
                             THAT WE COULD PAGE 454

30  POST-CONTRACT ACTIVITY—DECEMBER-JANUARY
    31  DUNN DRAWINGS—DECEMBER 7 AND 8, 1965
      060  HANSON, JOHN K.                              JK
           0060  2336        QUESTION ON WHICH DAY DID YOU INSTRUCT LARRY DUNN TO START
                             DRAWING PLANS & SPECS FOR THE WINN MOTOR HOME ANSWER
                             BOY I HAVE NO IDEA THE DATE WOULD PROBABLY BE ARE
                             YOU CALLING HOUSE CARS MOTOR HOMES QUESTION IM CALLING MOT
                             OR HOMES MOTOR HOMES HOUSE CARS ARE SOME ODDBALL TERM
                             THAT YOU USE QUESTION WELL OUR CONTRACT CALLED FOR MOTORIZE
                             MOBILE UNITS & YOU ARE GOING TO HAVE TO DESCRIBE YOUR
                             ANSWER I WONT ANSWER THAT UNTIL YOU DESCRIBE WHAT A MOTOR
                             HOME IS ANY LANGUAGE YOU WANT BECAUSE ANSWER WELL LET

           0060  2337        ME SAY THAT ACCORDING TO OUR INFORMATION IT WAS AFTER
                             YOU HAD STARTED THE SECOND MOTOR HOME FOR LT IND INC
                             SO DOES THAT HELP YOU ANSWER YOUR INFORMATION WITH LARRY
                             DUNN I INSTRUCTED AFTER TO BUILD THE MOTOR HOME TO DESIGN
                             A MOTOR HOME I WOULD SAY THAT WOULD BE ERRONEOUS
                             THAT WOULD BE MY THOUGHTS IF I INSTRUCTED HIM IT WOULD
                             BE BACK BEFORE WE EVER SAW JIM BAKER DRAW THESE THINGS
                             I THINK PART OF IT IS RIGHT HERE IN THE FILE SOME OF
                             HIS WORK I BELIEVE IN OUR LITERATURE I HAVE NO MEMORY
```

Figure G3

```
40  FEBRUARY FIFTH MEETING
    46   PICKUP 5 AT A TIME—UNFINISHED—PAY BEFORE INSPECT, ETC.
      060  HANSON, JOHN K.                                  JK
           0060   2469      DUNNS MEMORANDUM OF 2-15-1966 SAYS THAT ELLIOTT COOPER
                            SUGGESTS AN INSPECTORS SLIP 2E SIGNED BY A WINNEBAGO
                            INSPECTOR AND INCLUDED IN EVERY LIFE-TIME UNIT HANSON DENIES
                            THAT HE DIRECTED COOPER TO DO THIS AT 469 HANSON SAYS COOPER
                            WAS AVAILABLE FOR MR DUNN AND MR STARKEY FOR RECOMMENDATIONS
                            OR SUGGESTIONS THEY WOULD CALL HIM BECAUSE HIS OFFICE WAS
                            DOWNTOWN OUR STAFF WOULD BE THE MOST ACTIVE OF THE NON-FULL
                            TIME EMPLOYEES I SUPPOSE THE STAFF WOULD INCLUDE THE
                            AUDITORS AND THOSE WHO CAME TO ASSIST US
40  FEBRUARY FIFTH MEETING
    47   RESUMPTION OF PRODUCTION BEFORE PRICE ADJUSTMENT
      060  HANSON, JOHN K.                                  JK
           0060   0500      PAGES 500 THROUGH 512 HAVE TO DO WITH WINNEBAGOS LETTER
                            TO JIM BAKER DATES 2-24-66 ANSWERING JIM BAKERS UNSIGNED
                            LETTER TO WINNEBAGO OF FEBRUARY 12 ITEM ONE WIRE ALL
                            UNITS FOR AIR-CONDITIONING WE TOLD HIM WE WOULD GIVE
                            HIM THE COST THIS WAS AT A MEETING ON SATURDAY FEB 28
                            AT OUR OFFICE BETWEEN BAKER DUNN AND ME AT PAGE 502
                            HANSON SAID THIS ISNT MY DECISION I ASKED ARE YOU
                            POSITIVE ABOUT IT Q. YOURE SO POSITIVE YOURE BEATING
                            THE TABLE ABOUT IT A. YES SIR BUT DUNNS LETTER OF
           0060   0503      2-24-66 SAYS THAT HANSON JOHN K AND DUNN REVIEWED
                            EACH ITEM ON THE LETTER PAGE 503. PAGE 505. WE WORKED
                            ON A RATTLE-FREE STOVE PAGE 506. THE RECORD SHOWS
                            WHAT ABOUT THE REAR BUMPER THIS SHOULD BE WHAT ABOUT
                            THE REAR BUNK A. LOWER FOR MORE ROOM HANSON DENIES
                            MAKING THE DECISION SAME PAGE, WHAT ABOUT THE WINDOW
                            IN THE DOOR I DONT KNOW WHAT HAPPENED SAYS BAKER
                            SAME PAGE WHAT ABOUT ASH TRAYS THESE ARE PROPOSED
                            CHANGES AND I KNOW WE DESPERATELY TRIED TO MAKE THE
```

17

Employment of Litigation Support Systems in Preparation of a Products Liability Case

William H. Sanders

A computer doesn't think. It's dumb. It doesn't investigate. It doesn't even know the laws of evidence. It merely, simply and purely serves the lawyer as a data retrieval system for his file. It does *not* eliminate any of the lawyer's work but, if properly used, it captures, stores, indexes and, upon command, can instantly retrieve all of the lawyer's work product. This is the genius of the computer.

Don't be misled by the spectacular speed and efficiency of the computer. If you are going to use the computer to prepare your case, you're not going to be able to use the computer unless your law firm goes through all of the documents and indexes them. And do you realize how much time that takes? If I work hard, real hard, I can read and index 30 pages of deposition testimony an hour. How long would it take you to read—and index—100,000 pages contained in 15,000 documents?

Why do you have to use lawyers? If you can buy a computer litigation support system, why can't you hire someone to do the job for you? The answer is the computer man's expression of "GIGO." GIGO means "Garbage In-Garbage Out."

If you don't have the lawyers and their paralegals index your file and decide what goes in the computer, then you are putting garbage into the computer and probably mis-indexing the garbage at that. Even if garbage doesn't go in, you still have the problem of the "hiders" and the "seekers." How many times has your file clerk (the hider) surprised you by the place she chooses to put a particular document in but you (the seeker) can't find it? Only by constantly monitoring the hiders can you as the seeker be assured that you'll know how to retrieve a particular document when needed.

Whether you do or do not use a computer, no lawyer should ever believe he can successfully hire some outside lay organization to study, analyze, index and tell him (the lawyer) what is contained in a large volume of documents.

You may be dreamily floating along a fluffy white cloud in the belief that you will never have to face the problem of grappling with large-scale document production. But with the advent of today's copying machines, like Xerox, and with today's liberalized discovery rules, don't tell me that you can necessarily stop the other side from copying most of your client's records.

When I speak about a party having to produce 15,000 or 30,000 or 60,000 documents, don't tell me "That's preposterous." Too many lawyers who are now sadder but wiser have found that judges are getting consistently deafer and that a hearing aid doesn't seem to help the judge when the lawyer cries out, "Harassment" or "Privileged" or "Burdensome."

Tell me, what *are* you going to do when the court compels your client to allow the other side to copy 50,000 documents of your client?

Are you going to hide your head in the sand?

Are you going to try to skim and vaguely sort together your copy of 50,000 documents?

Are you going to try to study and carefully index 50,000 documents?

Anyway you go, you're in trouble.

Only good taste prevents me from telling you what your adversary is going to do with the documents while you're bent over with your head buried in the sand.

If you undertake to merely skim and vaguely index the 50,000 documents you're as ill prepared to take on your adversary as I am to do three rounds with Mohammed Ali.

And if you study and carefully index 50,000 documents, it's going to take one lawyer years and a team of lawyers months to study and index the documents. Even if this is done, however, no manual index can begin to compete with the capacity of the computer to index your files.

That's what is so deceptive about the computer. The computer looks like Superman himself when with dazzling speed the computer prints out a list of documents in response to a given question. It's dazzling to see. But don't forget that behind the dazzle are months of work of lawyers pouring over documents, summarizing and indexing documents before the computer is loaded.

So you're back to General Custer's problem of what are you going to do about all of those Indians. All General Custer needed was more men. In your office, if you're suddenly faced with the 50,000 document production, where are you going to get the men?

As far as your client is concerned, lawyer manpower is your problem. The client's problem is how can he afford you.

But on the other hand, if your client has serious product liability litigation, with a big—real big—exposure, can your client afford not to adequately prepare when the other side has studied, indexed and computerized the records?

Bear in mind, the plaintiff's lawyer can often make better use of the computer than the defendant. The plaintiff has three big advantages in using the computer.

Plaintiff's Advantage No. 1. Before the plaintiff even files suit—probably before your client even knows it's going to have a claim—the plaintiff can implement and perfect his computer system. Once the plaintiff has his computer running, after it is loaded with the lawyer's work product, before filing suit, the plaintiff can strike an unsuspecting defendant like a poised cobra can hit a rabbit. Plaintiff files his petition or complaint, and immediately moves for the production of your client's records. The naive defendant recoils with amazement when a ten-man team of plaintiff's lawyers and paralegals invade his client. "What are you going to do with all those lawyers?" the defendant's lawyer asks. He rapidly gets his answer when the plaintiff's team of lawyers gets out numbering stamping machines, and starts to number, study and index thousands of defendant's records.

Plaintiff's Advantage No. 2. Plaintiff may go through 100,000 records—but select only those documents which plaintiff deems important enough to put on the computer. That selected group might be only 3% or 3,000 of the documents. But if the defendant does not know which documents plaintiff selects as significant enough to closely study, summarize and index, then defendant is going to have to prepare for any use plaintiff might make of any of the 100,000 records defendant has produced. To put it otherwise, defendant will probably have to study, summarize and index *most* of the 100,000 records.

Plaintiff's Advantage No. 3. It's ZAP!!! when the defendant is hit with new litigation, taken by surprise on production of its records and finds it is facing a well organized, well prepared, well informed plaintiff's law firm whose computer has just swallowed up and digested defendant's records. With his computer feeding him the lists and summaries of the records he needs, the plaintiff's lawyer is in an unparalled position. He will take your client's deposition and keeps saying, "Let me refresh your recollection with another one of your documents." After four or five days of a deposition where the computerized lawyer refreshes your client with a lifetime of his letters, speeches or notes jotted on a memo, it takes a good defense lawyer not to quit on the spot and tell his client to buy out at any cost.

While the computer gets the credit, the computer itself is merely a mechanical means of data retrieval for the lawyer's file.

Nonetheless, when it comes to data retrieval nothing can parallel or even compare to the computer. If the lawyer had done a good job of indexing his file and if he has put the right information in the computer, his computer is invaluable.

You can use the computer to assemble your facts on just about any point.

You can use the computer to answer interrogatories or tell you whether you've answered that interrogatory before.

You can use the computer to prepare you for any witness' deposition. You can ask the computer for any record you have of what the witness knows on almost any given subject.

You can use the computer to put together a Statement of Facts of all you know on almost any set of issues.

You can use the computer to tell you if any case citation has ever appeared before in any brief or pleading—and, if so, where the case was cited.

You can use the computer to tell if you have a record of a certain question having been asked a witness before.

You can use a computer to tell you what to ask for on a subpoena duces tecum.

You can use a computer to keep track of when a particular exhibit has been referred to.

You can use a computer to tell you if you have any records pertaining to a given person—and, if so, what information you have on that person.

You can use a computer to sort out your information chronologically.

You can use the computer to keep updating your file, so that the computer is kept up to the minute as new records, new pleadings and new transcribed testimony pours in.

In fact, it appears to the uninitiated that the computer can do anything. But the computer still remains the electronic data retriever of the lawyer's work product: his file.

If you want to spend a little more money, you can make your system portable. You can get a portable terminal to take along on the road. Then when you are on the road, all you do to get information is call the computer on any long distance telephone, set the phone receiver down on the portable terminal, and the terminal will send and receive messages from the computer no matter where you are.

If you want to make your records portable, or if you want to save space in storing your copy of the records, you can put them on either microfilm or microfiche. Microfilm, as you know, puts the records on a roll of film. Microfiche, as you may know, puts the records on a card.

To demonstrate how easy it is to make all your records portable, you could transport one million documents in two steamer trunks, if you use microfiche. For seven cents you can put 70 pages (that's 1/10th of a cent a page) on a microfiche card—if you supply the microfiche copier and labor.

A microfiche card measures about 3 inches by 4 inches. You can number the pictures on the card for easy reference. You can also number the card.

A portable microfiche reader, which fits in your briefcase, costs about $25.00. You can buy a microfiche reader-printer for $940.00. With the reader-printer, you look at the microfiche card on an enlarged reader or viewer. If you want a copy of what you see, press a button and you have a full-size printed copy of what you see in three seconds. With microfiche, if you want record G9 on card 9076, you pull card 9076, put it in a special portable reader, set the reader to show page G9 on the microfiche card, and you immediately see that record enlarged to full size on the screen of the portable reader. If you want a copy of that record, enlarged to its original size, push a button, and the copier will immediately make you a copy in 3 or 4 seconds.

If you decide to use the computer, you have to use special computer programming. Your client's computer isn't programmed for a litigation support system. Translated, that means you have to go to a software company which has over the years developed special programs to be installed on a computer. These special programs are designed to serve lawyers in data retrieval. The software firms refer to these programs as "litigation support systems."

You can use the software firm's computer which is already programmed for the litigation support system or if your client has its own computer, you may be able to get the software house to license your client to install the program on your client's computer. If you go the latter route, it takes several days to install the litigation support system program on your client's computer.

There are advantages in using your client's computer. Using your client's computer gives security to your client's trade secrets or, for that matter, any confidential information. Further, with your client's computer, you are not depending on any outside litigation support system for either keypunching the information to put into the computer nor dependent on an outsider for the operation of the computer.

If you decide to consider a "litigation support" or computer system, your client will insist his computer can do it—if he has a computer.

But when your client's computer man studies the programs developed by the software services, your client will rapidly back off.

The best way to find a computer service is to ask the lawyers who have used such a service. Most lawyers will not only explain how they have used a system, but will usually know what other litigation support systems are available.

To find the lawyer who has used a litigation support system, you can turn to the American Bar, or Practicing Law Institute or any similar organization for seminar speakers they have had on computer use in litigation. Then, when you have visited one or more lawyers who have used such a system, invite the software services to come see you and demonstrate their system with their portable terminal.

Here is a checklist of what to ask the software service:

1. What is their experience? What law firms have used them?
2. How sophisticated is their programming? Is it just a simple system that identifies and lists computer entries that have the same index number? Or is it a comprehensive, intricate system that can perform much more? *(Beware:* there is a vast difference in what each company's system can do.)
3. Does the software service offer you both the option of putting your file on their computer or, in the alternative, using their program to put your file on your client's computer? If so, what is the difference in cost?
4. Will the software service send experts to your office to teach you how to prepare indexes and how to use the computer?
5. With their programming, what does it cost for the computer to run a search for information when you ask for information?
6. With their programming, what does it cost, with their system, to update or modify information on the computer?
7. What does the software service charge for its computer time (if you use its computer)?
8. Perhaps most important of all, does it offer *experienced* consultants to assist you through your first effort using a computer. Let's face it, no law school prepares you in the use of a computer and rare, indeed, is the lawyer who has a knowledge of a computer system.

If you go computer, here is a checklist of what you need to do:

A. Staff your project with enough lawyers (for a guide of how many lawyers you need, ask a firm which has used the system).
B. Arrange the best method to copy the records—photocopy, microfilm or microfiche.

C. Get space in your office for a computer terminal, storage space for the documents, and work space.
D. With the help of the computer software service, develop a good numbering system for each document you handle.
E. Keep good records of where you got each document.
F. Don't let anyone convince you that outsiders can select, summarize and index the documents you put in the computer—it takes lawyers or lawyers and their paralegals to do it.
G. Have the software service help you work out the problems as they arise in your project.
H. Get a good index when you start—because once you start with one index, its hard to change. You can't very well index part of your information one way and another part another way.
I. Be selective of what you index and put in the computer. The more documents you computerize, the more it costs.

The project sounds formidable, but any time lawyers have to study, know and use the contents of thousands of documents, there is invariably expense—big expense.

Figure out the hours of a lawyer's time necessary to examine and summarize all the documents. Figure out the time it will take the lawyers to index or classify the documents. Then you've got your big cost.

But if that lawyer or law firm gets lost in a White Blizzard of papers, where there is so much paper around the lawyer, he can't tell where he is at, much of the lawyers' time in studying the records is down the drain.

That's why the computer saves money. It saves money not because it does the lawyers' work for him, but because it receives and preserves the lawyers' work product, the computer keeps the lawyers' work product instantaneously available, and the computer retrieves the lawyers' work product exactly the way he wants it.

The computer is the perfect file clerk. The computer comes to work every day, it never gets tired, it politely speaks back to you, it gives you what you want without excuses, it doesn't flirt with the young men in your office. But the computer is a Dracula that is fed by the blood, sweat and tears of the lawyers who handle the 100,000 documents.

But if you don't like consorting with Dracula, you'll find that you are going to have to try to build your own home-made Frankenstein index system to keep track of and know what is in all those records. I prefer giving blood to Dracula rather than trying to build Frankenstein.

18

The Application of Full-Text Retrieval to Litigation Support

Jerome S. Rubin

To a large extent, the litigation support role of computers is closely related to their more general legal research applications, and a discussion of the development of computer-aided legal research in general will help put litigation support in the proper perspective.

Historically, two basic approaches have been taken toward preparing legal information for research with the aid of a computer. The earliest attempts to adapt computer technology to legal research used the computer to search previously compiled indices and abstracts of legal reference materials. These experiments were conducted largely under the auspices of universities or government agencies and usually produced some variation of an alphabetical listing of index terms. Whether the system was based on descriptors, concepts of decisions, points of law or some other organizing principle, legal reference materials were indexed under one or more terms, and were sometimes manually abstracted. The index (and the abstracts) were then loaded into a computer's data bank.

The user of such a system requested information on a particular subject by entering the appropriate index terms at a computer terminal. A printer then typed out a list of citations (and abstracts) in the data bank indexed under those terms.

Systems of this type have proved useful for quickly locating certain kinds of legal materials. They retain, however, the flaw inherent in manual research methods, i.e., the interposition between a lawyer and his legal sources of an indexer's decision about the classification of a case or statute within the hierarchy of subject headings, and about the appropriateness of index categories or terms. If the lawyer cannot anticipate the indexer's interpretation, he may well fail to locate relevant material.

The second approach to computer-assisted legal research was originally developed under the direction of Professor John F. Horty at the Health Law Center of the University of Pittsburgh in 1956. He used a "full-text" approach—different from previous applications of the computer to research of law in that the entire text of a set of documents is stored word for word, precisely as reported, in a computer's data bank. Rather than interpreting a manually prepared index, the lawyer determines which words and phrases are likely to appear in relevant material and submits them to the computer. The computer collects and delivers to the lawyer those documents which satisfy his research request.

The full-text approach to information storage and retrieval has been widely accepted as the optimum method for computerized access to legal research materials. With the full-text method, a computer can, for example, in less time than it takes to read this paragraph, search a file of the texts of 50,000 documents and report the number of documents in which the term "trust" appears within four words of the term "education," and in which the term "spendthrift" also appears. It is important to recognize that the full value of full-text searching can only be realized with an interactive system, however. While Professor Horty's system pioneered full-text information storage and retrieval, it was a "batch processing" system. The lawyer makes contact with such a system by telephoning or mailing his request to the computer center, and hours or days may pass before he sees the results. He has no direct interaction with the system.

With an interactive system, the user instantly sees (either on a cathode-ray tube [CRT] [much like a TV screen] or as paper copy) the citations of the documents located as a result of his search request, the context surrounding his search terms, or the entire text of those documents—depending on the lawyer's choice. He can engage in a dialogue with the computer, can modify his initial request on the basis of the documents retrieved and continue this interaction until he is satisfied with his results.

An interactive system is also an on-line system—one in which terminals in various locations are connected to the computer by telephone or other communications lines. Communication between the computer and the user is direct and continuous, so that the computer's messages are responsive to users' queries and instructions. Since a number of terminals can be on-line simultaneously, such systems are also called time-shared systems.

How can a full-text, on-line, computer-assisted legal research service be applied to a litigation environment? In any litigation or administrative proceeding of significant size, a flood of paper inundates the lawyers involved. Full-text retrieval can be applied to manage this flood—the lawyer can use the system to help summarize and correlate the vast amounts of data with which he may have to deal and to retrieve specific information.

There are certain problems common to any large litigation. Traditional methods of indexing and retrieval have never been wholly effective and, because of their labor-intensive nature, are becoming increasingly costly in any matter where more than a few thousand pages of documents are involved. An example of one aspect of the problem with manual systems for control of materials in a litigation is the management and retrieval of documents produced in discovery.

Typically, a master file of copies of the documents is maintained, either in the sequence in which they were produced (identified by a "production number") or in chronological order. Where the total number of documents is relatively small and when a few categories (or index entries) will suffice, individual documents may be duplicated in full on office copiers, and placed in subfiles which are also usually in chronological order. For example, there may be a subfile of officers' correspondence, a subfile of technical department memoranda, and a subfile of documents dealing with pricing policies. Copies of documents may be made for more than one subfile—a technical department memorandum estimating production costs of a product as part of a pricing decision may appear in the technical department subfile and in the pricing policy subfile.

When more than a few index categories are involved, subfiles containing copies of documents are impractical. Surrogates, more or less lengthy, are substituted for the documents themselves. In some manual filing systems only enough information to permit the identification and location of the original document in the master file is posted under the index category. In other systems documents are abstracted and copies of the abstracts are filed under each of the appropriate index categories so that the researcher can get some idea of the contents of documents without reference to the full text in the master file.

The problems inherent in the manual management and retrieval of documents are all too obvious to any lawyer who has relied on them. First, as a practical matter, there is a rather low limit on the number of index categories that can be set up and on the number of categories under which a given document can be indexed. If, for example, there are 10,000 documents and if each document is indexed under an average of five categories, then 50,000 postings to the index will be required—postings either of the locations of the documents or of their abstracts.

Because of this limit on the number of index categories, concepts or facts which relate to needed documents may not have been indexed. This is especially frequent in a lengthy proceeding where the issues are not well defined when the index categories are set up, and where new issues emerge in the course of discovery. Even when the index categories are useful as a coarse filter, the researcher must rely on the adequacy of prior abstracting, which may not reflect all the issues which have become important since the documents were abstracted, or he must undertake the tedious and time-consuming job of having the documents themselves pulled from the master file and of reviewing them himself.

In addition, there is no easy way to identify documents which are indexed under two or more categories as in our example—technical department memoranda dealing with corporate pricing policies. Either the text of each of the documents (or abstracts thereof) under one category must be scanned to see if they contain references to the other category, or the document identification posted under each of the index categories must be compared by hand in order to pick out documents posted to both index categories.

These problems are compounded if more than one individual wishes access to documents at the same time or if the individuals are working at separate locations. Documents are often not available when needed, and some disappear permanently.

If one's client's own documents, as well as lengthy transcripts, answer to interrogatories and memoranda are added to the documents produced by the other side, the management and location of relevant material can become a nearly impossible task. That the manual task has been performed poorly may become evident only if the other side has access to superior computer-assisted tools. This is increasingly the case today.

The principles of full-text computer-assisted storage and retrieval can be successfully applied to litigation documents. Such a system permits a lawyer or paralegal at his own terminal to perform interactive research on any words or combinations thereof in the original materials or in abstracts of these materials. He can review rapidly on a CRT materials satisfying his search, sort materials or portions thereof into sequences different from that in which they are stored in the computer, and make a printed copy at his terminal of all or part of the retrieved materials.

A computer system can be applied to litigation documents in much the same way as it is applied to case law—searches are formulated using very simple logical principles.

But while a typical search request in a file of cases will have search terms reflecting both legal and factual aspects of the issue, a search request in litigation documents will probably be almost entirely fact-based.

In preparing for the deposition of a witness, for example, if the full text of documents is available in the computer's files, the computer may be queried to retrieve in seconds all correspondence and internal memoranda which were written by the witness, were sent to the witness or mention the witness, and the computer can be instructed to put these documents in chronological order. Logically, much more complex searches are also possible; for example, one might search for documents of a certain type written by the technical department or by any corporate officer other than the Treasurer. The researcher can require that the documents be dated between January 1969 and February 1972 and that they talk about Company A's patent position with respect to electrographic reproduction so long as the Model 4200 is not mentioned.

I am convinced that the most effective use of the power of the computer is made if the full original text is available on-line in machine-readable form. The human abstractor inevitably distorts and omits by the very act of compressing. This is particularly true if, as circumstances so often dictate, the abstracting is done by someone other than the lawyers handling the case. Issues may shift in the course of a litigation, and no one can foresee at the outset all the abstracting guidelines which may at some point be needed for retrieval. A lawyer may want to find a document when all he can remember are facts which would not be abstracted under any conceivable set of guidelines—such as a statement by a witness that he remembers having three martinis while waiting for his flight to Chicago. If the full original text of all materials is available for computer-assisted searching, such problems do not arise. Moreover, the full text of any document of interest can be printed out at any LEXIS terminal without interfering with the retrieval or printing of that same document simultaneously by any other user.

As a practical matter, for a variety of reasons, the full text of all materials may not be available for searching. Even when only abstracts, extracts or descriptors are stored, however, a full-text system can search for any words, phrases or combinations contained in these documents. Full-text searching in something less than the original full source text is infinitely more powerful than manual searches. The number of indexing categories on which searches can be made is limitless, extending to every word and phrase in every abstract, extract or set of descriptors. A document locator, such as its production number, is displayed with each document surrogate retrieved so that the full text may be duplicated from the paper master file if desired.

The decision whether to store machine-readable full text on-line for a certain class of source materials or to store only abstracts or extracts depends on a number of factors: primarily, the availability of source materials already in some machine-readable form, the relative costs of abstracting and of converting the full text of typed, handwritten or printed materials to machine-readable form, the costs of on-line storage and the availability of competent abstractors. These factors differ in importance from one litigation to the next and also according to the types of material involved. Careful planning at the outset of each litigation is needed to determine the proper mix of full text and less-than-full`text and the best method for capturing each in machine-readable form.

One of the most interesting possibilities is the feasibility of converting to machine-readable form various documents such as transcripts of court proceedings and depositions by way of a specially designed stenotype machine. With this device, when the court reporter prepares his document, a machine-readable version will automatically be generated on a paper or magnetic tape. This tape would then be run through special computer programs which would formulate the stenotype symbols and permit human resolution of ambiguities. While such a technique would be extremely helpful, it is not crucial to the application of a computer system to these documents.

A number of peripheral features of a full-text litigation support service can be useful, but are of little value compared to the benefits of the on-line system itself. Two examples of these are computer-generated indices and computer-generated KWIC—Key-Word-In-Context—abstracts. A computer-generated index would, for example, indicate each document and the location within each document of every occurrence of, say, the word "prototype." A computer-generated KWIC abstract would be similar, but in addition to indicating the location of the word the computer would print out the window of text containing each occurrence of the word. So one might ask for a computer-generated KWIC abstract of every situation in which the word "prototype" appeared within ten words of the word "third." The computer would generate a printout indicating every document in which the word "prototype" in fact was within ten words of the word "third" and would also print out a window of text consisting of, say, 25 words on either side of each occurrence of this combination of words.

A full-text, on-line, computer-assisted litigation support service is not only more efficient and effective than traditional manual systems, but it can also lead to substantial cost savings in a major litigation. With such a system, the lawyer can better and less expensively manage the flood of litigation information and locate the facts he needs.

19

Employment of Para-Legals in Trial Preparation

Dudley Hughes

Lawyers have always had nonlawyers to assist them in the preparation of their cases for trial. For example, investigators have helped to develop the case; messengers or "leg men" have helped to round up or subpoena witnesses, and intelligent and experienced secretaries have helped to organize and index files for efficient use during the trial. Undoubtedly, in the day in which they still existed in large numbers, lawyers' clerks or preceptees assisted in the preparation of cases for trial.

However, with the increase in the complexity of lawsuits and the accompanying growth in the use of modern discovery methods, there is an obvious need for assistants to the lawyer specially trained in trial preparation and working in the law office in a formalized special status.

Lawyers handling large complex cases in recent years have tended to rely on junior lawyers in the office to help them with the preparation and trial of the cases. Such lawyers, sometimes rather scornfully referred to as "bag men," since they often arrived in the courtroom weighed down by one or more large satchels while the lawyer whom they served rather ostentatiously walked in ahead of them completely unincumbered, have been largely priced out of the market with the large increases in the salaries of junior associates. At the same time to meet the growing need in law offices for specially trained well-educated assistants to lawyers in various fields, there has developed the para-legal. In February of 1972, a special committee of the American Bar Association having studied the possible use of nonlawyer assistants, reported that the practice of law was getting too cumbersome, inefficient and expensive. The Committee suggested that "the use of legal assistants must be and is an integral part of our solution to these problems. The use of legal assistants is possible when lawyers have analyzed what every legal task actually involves by reducing each activity to its simplest and most basic components." The Committee went on to the happy thought that "experience has shown a definite correlation between increased net income and the extensive use of legal assistants."[1]

The legal profession's reluctance to make available and use the services of specially trained lay technicians in the practice of law, can perhaps fairly be attributed in part to the professional conservatism of the Bar. For a variety of reasons, not all of them the economics of modern law practice, lawyers are changing their attitudes towards legal para-professionals. The often cited surveys of the Missouri Bar in 1963 and 1968 indicate a change from 37 percent in the earlier year to 60 percent in the later year of lawyers who felt there was a need for a legal technician possessing general and specialized skills acquired through a college program.[2]

Virtually all of the literature on the need for the training of and the use of para-legals has been written in the last ten years, and the literature almost entirely reflects the opinion that the need for para-legals is growing and will continue to grow rapidly.

If the legal profession generally has been conservative in its attitude towards legal para-professionals, the trial bar in particular has been reluctant to accept specially trained lay assistants for use in the preparation of cases for trial. The trial of a case is uniquely a lawyer's job, and it is an easy conclusion to reach that trial lawyers generally have not seen the possibilities of turning over many of the tasks of trial preparation to a nonlawyer. The purpose of this paper is to discuss some of these possibilities in the preparation of civil litigation.

As used in this paper, the term "para-legal" or "legal para-professional" means a specially trained layman with a basic college or at least junior college education. The special training needed for a para-legal should come from a college or a special para-legal training school. It may be possible for lawyers to train their own para-legals. Having never tried to do such a thing, I can only guess that the law

[1]ABA, *Report to the House of Delegates of the Special Committee on Legal Assistants* (Feb. 1972).

[2]Survey cited in L. Brickman, "Expansion of the Lawyering Process Through a New Delivery System: The Emergence and State of Legal Paraprofessionalism," 71 *Columbia Law Review* 1153 (1971); and W. Statsky, *Introduction to Paralegalism: Perspectives, Problems and Skills* (1974) at p. 24.

firm which needs the services of a para-legal does not have sufficient lawyer time available to spend on para-legal training, even if the lawyer involved has the necessary experience, teaching skill and temperament to perform such a task.

SETTLEMENT

Any lawyer regularly engaged in litigation knows that he settles more cases than he tries to a verdict. Although this paper is primarily concerned with trial preparation, it does seem appropriate to make a few suggestions on how para-legals can be used to assist in the settlement of cases. Obviously, all information concerning damages should be assembled into as brief a form as possible. This probably will have to be done in connection with the preparation of a pre-trial memorandum or a trial notebook, which will be discussed later, but a simple outline of damages in appropriate order including dollar amounts and a brief explanation of what they represent should be readily available as a trial approaches.

Probably more good settlement opportunities are missed than lawyers realize simply because an apparently casual telephone call ostensibly for some other purpose from one's opposing counsel finally gets around to its originally intended purpose of discussing settlement of a case that looms large on the horizon of the trial list, only to have both parties not prepared to talk in cold-hard terms about the dollars involved. An up-to-date settlement evaluation sheet listing the damages should be prepared by the para-legal early in the handling of the case and then kept up to date.

Also, during the later stages of the case when trial is near it is sometimes helpful, particularly in protracted litigation where there may have been frequent discussions of settlement, to have assembled a negotiation history giving in chronological form the amounts of all demands and settlement offers. Settlement letters or policy limit demand letters can be prepared in rough form by a para-legal, who would also accumulate copies of any materials to be enclosed with the letter. If a settlement brochure is to be used, the para-legal should be assigned the job of preparing a rough draft, and it probably would be helpful to have in the office an outline for preparation or a sample settlement brochure as a guide in the preparation of other brochures.

Last, but certainly not least, should the case be settled there are many onerous tasks accompanying the settlement, such as preparation of a settlement distribution sheet, a rough draft preparation of Petitions for Approval, if the settlement needs court approval and the various letters distributing the settlement proceeds which can be handled by the para-legal.

SORTING OUT THE TASKS OF THE LAWYER AND NONLAWYER

Para-legals exist because it is inefficient for a lawyer to do work which a nonlawyer can do just as well. While it is desirable that lawyers not do the work of a para-legal, it is absolutely essential that para-legals never do the work which only a lawyer can do. Anyone who has read the publications in recent years from committees on professional guidance concerning the line of demarcation between a para-legal's job and the practice of law, knows that a clear definition of the line is elusive. My comments on the ethical problems involved are considered later in this paper, and at present I will set forth only suggestions of what a para-legal can do, with the opening comment that whether used alone or in conjunction with lawyer associates or other para-legals, the trial lawyer and para-legal relationship is based on team work with the lawyer being the captain of the team.

Prior to the time when trial is actually imminent, the para-legal will find his greatest usefulness in the preparation, collection, collation, evaluation and indexing of discovery. The attorney, of course, must make the decision as to what discovery is to be pursued, although it certainly is not inappropriate for the para-legal to make suggestions for discovery. The para-legal prepares interrogatories and Requests for Admissions in rough form to be edited by the attorney. Any interrogatories or Requests for Admissions received from other parties must be read through by the attorney who decides which ones are objectionable and also makes all decisions as to the scope of the answers under the pertinent rules of discovery. The work of collecting the information to answer the discovery and preparing rough draft answers should be assigned to the para-legal with the final editing being done by the attorney. When other parties submit their answers to interrogatories or to Requests for Admissions, these also must be read through by the attorney who has to make any decisions concerning objections to the discovery which may be raised in the answers, as well as decisions concerning the adequacy and thoroughness of the answers, but the para-legal does the work of seeing that the answers are placed in the proper portion of the file with proper entries made on the file index, and further that information is extracted from them to be placed in other parts of the file, such as a settlement evaluation sheet, Pre-trial Memorandum or settlement brochure.

The para-legal can assist in a similar way in the taking of depositions by making the arrangements for the presentation of such witnesses as you are called upon to produce and later extracting information from the deposition to be placed in other parts of the file.

The indexing of a deposition, however, requires some special comment. An excessively inclusive index is not particularly useful and the correct proper indexing of a deposition depends upon an intelligent choice of what is to go into the index. While depositions can be indexed by nonlawyers, this is one area in which particularly close supervision of the para-legal's work should be maintained.

Once discovery is completed, the para-legal can prepare whatever Praecipes, Petitions or Orders are necessary to place the case on the trial list. At that time, the para-legal should accumulate all information necessary to prepare a Pre-trial Memorandum and should arrange all medical records and reports, bills, photographs and other such items in an appropriate order with a list of them so they can be supplied to the Court or other counsel quickly and easily when called for. It is also appropriate at such a time to check with the client or special witnesses, such as experts, to see if the data in the file is accurate and up-to-date, and this work can be done by the para-legal. The final preparation of any Pre-trial Motions or of the Pre-trial Memorandum must, of course, be handled by the lawyer.

At an appropriate period before trial, the para-legal assistant should also update the witness and discuss with the attorney what witnesses should be contacted at that time to make sure of their availability, as well as to simply reaffirm their understanding of the part they will play in the case and the cooperation that you hope they will give. Letters should be sent by the para-legal assistant to all witnesses at that time. Many, if not most of them, should be called on the telephone, and in a few cases, you may even wish to have them called on personally. Who makes any such telephone calls or personal calls should be left up to the attorney. If any depositions have not yet been indexed it should be done at this time. At some later time as trial becomes imminent, the para-legal should arrange interviews with such witnesses that the attorney feels he wishes to interview. At about the same time or later, upon instructions from the attorney, the para-legal can arrange for the subpoenaing of witnesses and the preparation of any subpoenas duces tecum which are necessary.

Throughout the period of trial preparation, depending upon the schedule set by the lawyer, the para-legal can give considerable assistance in the preparation of a trial notebook. There are probably as many different forms of these notebooks as there are trial attorneys, although it certainly would be helpful to para-legals if their office has available to them a sample or form trial notebook. The para-legal can do all of the work of assembling and placing the notebook in a proper form, which would be much easier if he has some guide to follow. The pleadings in a file may have to be reorganized and reindexed, depending upon the desires of the lawyer involved, and also the interrogatories and Requests for Admissions and Answers to them may have to be reorganized and reindexed. This tedious job is best left to the para-legal.

During trial, the para-legal can do some, although obviously not all, of the tasks usually associated with the previously mentioned "bag men." Although some firms use nonlawyer legal researchers in their offices, this practice cannot be recommended during trial when the close supervision of such work which is necessary to its proper performance is not available because the lawyer is too busy trying the case. It is probably best to use other lawyers in the office for this work. However, the custody of exhibits and arranging them in their proper form for presentation in the courtroom can be left to the para-legal as can the escorting of witnesses to and from the courtroom. As any trial lawyer knows, there are innumerable tasks which can be performed during trial by a nonlawyer, and a thoroughly experienced para-legal may even become helpful in making observations of the jury, witnesses and other counsel which can help the attorney in assessing the atmosphere in the courtroom.

ETHICS

Paralegalism is new territory and anyone advancing into new land in the practice of law must take with him an understanding of the ethical problems he may find therein. Nonlawyers cannot practice law. Nonlawyers who assist lawyers in the practice of law must be properly supervised. What constitutes the practice of law and proper supervision, however, are subjects that seem to invite, if not indeed compel, endless dispute, circular arguments and imprecise conclusions. The Law Economics Committee of the State Bar of California concluded, "It is easier to define what supervision cannot mean than to define it affirmatively,"[3] The ABA Code of Professional Responsibility requires that a lawyer should represent his client competently and also that the lawyer should preserve the confidences and secrets of his clients. However, the lawyer is also required to assist in improving the legal system, and a more efficient use of the lawyer's time and para-legal assistance will undoubtedly improve the system. "A lawyer often delegates tasks to clerks, secretaries and other lay persons. Such delegation is proper if the lawyer maintains a direct relationship with his clients, supervises delegated work and has complete professional responsibility for work product."[4] One writer, in discussing the problem, has stated, "The cardinal principle man-

[3]13 State Bar of California Reports 2 (No. 7, July 1973).
[4]ABA Code of Professional Responsibility (EC 3-6 effec. Jan. 1, 1970).

aging the lawyer-lay person relationship is that the dynamics of delegation flows from demonstrated ability rather than from ethical codes or statutory practice norms."[5] If I read that quotation correctly, I think he means that the more competent para-legal will not need as much supervision as the less competent one and the supervising lawyer must exercise ethical judgment in deciding how much supervision is needed for each individual para-legal and each separate task. Perhaps another way of putting it is that the lawyer should ask himself at all times the question "Is the end product one for which I am willing to take professional responsibility?" At the same time, the lawyer-supervisor must keep in mind that the purpose of a para-legal is to free the lawyer from tasks which do not require his immediate attention. "Close supervision, case-by-case, step-by-step of a lay person is not only impractical but is in contradiction to the economy and efficiency motives that originally led the lawyer to hire the legal paraprofessional."[6]

MANAGEMENT OF A PARA-LEGAL SYSTEM

The proper management of para-legals in a law office requires a proper balance between the recognition that para-legals are performing work which many lawyers consider part of the "drudgery" of law practice and an understanding that para-legals are highly trained persons of superior intelligence whose jobs should provide an opportunity for growing creative opportunity to contribute to the lawyer's work. It is considered beyond the scope of this paper to give any suggestions or standards for the particular procedures and practices which should be used in any law office to establish the position of para-legals in that office. Obviously para-legals are more than clerks but something less than full professional lawyers. They should be treated accordingly.

A few remarks should be made about the general relationship between the para-legal and the supervising attorney. A para-legal coming into a law office for the first time, like the young attorney fresh out of law school, has no exposure to or experience with the trial process or litigation generally. I suspect that most trial attorneys in the past have been taught to try cases the way some children used to be taught to swim. They were picked up and thrown in with only a minimum amount of prior warning and explanation of the basic principles. Like some children so treated not a few lawyers have emerged shaken and shivering, running away never to return to the

[5]W. Statsky, *Introduction to Paralegalism: Perspectives, Problems and Skills* (1974).
[6]Ibid.

scene again. A surprisingly large number survived and went on to become fairly competent swimmers and trial lawyers, respectively. It is not a very good system and would not work with the para-legal litigation assistant in any event, since no matter what else they can do, it is quite clear that para-legals cannot try cases.

Para-legals, by definition, always work with a lawyer. The relationship between the trial attorney and the assistant para-legal is one of continual learning and growth. The education of a para-legal in the actual work of litigation must start by example. The law office that has reached the happy state of having experienced para-legals of the highest competence can use them to assist in the educating of the new para-legal, but the litigation lawyer should always play a direct part in showing the new para-legal how things are done. The preparation of a comprehensive set of interrogatories addressed to the particular discovery needs of a lawsuit, is an ability that the litigation lawyer should never lose, no matter how many para-legals he may have assisting him. Certain basic forms for interrogatories will, of course, always be available, but using them judiciously and tailoring them to the particular case involved is a process which the para-legal should learn from the legally trained professional rather than a fellow para-professional. So is an ability to take an overall approach to the discovery in a case, which would of course include an ability to fit the appropriate discovery tools together to best suit the needs of the individual case. Not only will the para-legal gain a sense of pride in his job from learning these skills from the lawyer himself, but like all good teachers, the lawyer may learn as much from the process as does his student.

This same process, of course, would apply not only to discovery but to the preparation of Motions, Pre-trial Memoranda, Trial Notebooks and all the other tasks already discussed in the preceding section of this paper.

While the education of a para-legal starts by example, it continues and grows through experience. Not only do the professional ethics require supervision of the para-legal, but so do the needs of the educational process. Supervising the para-legal is the only way the lawyer can tell accurately just how much the para-legal has learned and is the only way to form an opinion as to when the para-legal can be given different and more difficult tasks. A para-legal assistant who remains always at the beginning level will soon become bored with the job, as would any lawyer, and is being used inefficiently. If a para-legal has demonstrated the ability without close supervision to outline and prepare the discovery in a simple automobile accident case, then let him try his hand at drafting a set of interrogatories in some aspect of a more complicated casualty lawsuit.

Finally, it should be said that throughout the entire process of training a para-professional in the litigation law office, there should be some attempt to let the para-professional get an overall understanding of what the litigation process is all about. The trial system developed historically. An understanding of the evolution is a necessary part of every lawyer's background, but most of us probably don't think of it in historical terms. The answer to the question "is this particular interrogatory one that the court will compel a party to answer?" requires an understanding of how discovery evolved to its present state and a feel for the direction in which the courts are tending in discovery matters. The para-legal who assists in the planning for and preparation of discovery will need to learn about the development process of the law of discovery if he is to develop as fully as possible as a useful assistant to the trial attorney.

The para-legal also must learn why the discovery tasks and the other jobs which he performs for the trial attorney are useful.

> There is a paramount need for the para-legal to "feel" the inner connections among events in the litigation process.
>
> It is one thing for the para-legal to be told or to read about [the connections]; it is quite another to see the connections in operation at time of trial, to experience the way in which the pieces fall together or apart.[7]

Essential to the ultimate education of the para-legal is attendance during a trial. Obviously, not every para-legal can sit through the entirety of every trial for which he has assisted in the preparation, but the para-legal like the lawyer can learn to sharpen his discovery skills if he can see during the use of discovery in the courtroom itself how discovery could have been done better, and probably nothing is better for the para-legal's sense of accomplishment, pride in his job, and morale than seeing discovery in which he has assisted being beneficially used during trial.

The para-legal should also be given the opportunity to learn the actual mechanics of how a lawsuit starts and reaches trial by visiting the Clerk or Prothonotary's Office and seeing Complaints, Answers and other pleadings filed, by seeing what arrangements are made with the Sheriff's or Marshall's Office for service of Complaints and other pleadings, by attending arguments on Motions, and even, if the opportunity presents itself, to accompany subpoena servers in the often frustrating and sometimes entertaining job of trying to serve a subpoena on a reluctant witness.

There are also innumerable other tasks to which the trial preparation para-legal can be exposed to give him a more complete sense of

[7]W. Statsky, *supra* note 5.

the trial process. Title searches, searches of court records, indictment records and other such jobs which may arise only on rare occasions should be experienced by the para-legal. Not only will the para-legal's understanding of the trial process become more complete, but he may even learn enough of these processes to engage in them independently and thus become of wider use to the trial attorney.

Throughout the in-office training and development of a legal para-professional, the attorney must keep in mind who and what he is dealing with. "Students must not come into programs without adequate motivation. If education is done well, there is strong support for the argument that the acquisition and execution of the content of the worker's job will take care of itself. This argument is particularly persuasive in the case of the legal para-professional because of the difficulty in defining for him the precise nature of the content of the job."[8] "Enrich the job of the para-legal by delegating tasks that call for initiative and responsibility. Try to provide dignity and challenge, to reward and encourage, to respect capabilities and contributions. Each person must feel that he is a necessary contributing element to the overall welfare of the organization."[9]

There is no question that the use of legal para-professionals in trial preparation work as well as in many other areas of the law will and probably should work a substantial change in the practice of law. In no small part this will be because the modern specially trained legal para-professional with a background of a liberal college education will bring into the law office a point of view different from, although equally intelligent as, that of the standard law school graduate.

And the change in the practice of law of which I speak is bound to change the life of the lawyer. He will be freed from the repetition of small tasks which most lawyers consider drudgery, and by working with the para-legal assistant the lawyer may learn to see his position in the system of justice somewhat differently; he may see himself on a more elevated plane where he spends more time in work which, as a lawyer, is his alone to perform. Used properly, the para-legal professional will increase the efficiency and the income of a law office. If he is particularly lucky, the trial lawyer, working with a para-legal, will find that in representing, explaining and upholding the system of justice within which we work to the assistant, he, the lawyer, will increase his own understanding of and respect and appreciation for his profession.

[8]W. Statsky, "The Education of Paraprofessionals: Myths, Realities, Opportunities," 24 *Vanderbilt Law Review* 1090 (Nov. 1971).

[9]Fairbanks, "Assistants in the Personal Injury Case," 10 *Trial* 38 (Sept.-Oct. 1974).

20

The Use of Data Processing in Litigation

James D. Prendergast

INTRODUCTION

"Byte my baud." This quote probably means absolutely nothing to the average reader of this article. And well it should not. The quote uses terms that are part of the language of a group of people who work in air-conditioned rooms with raised floors, occupied by spinning tapes, discs and blinking lights. A computer programmer or systems analyst would know that the word "byte" is a generic term used to indicate an identifiable grouping of consecutive binary digits ("bits"), e.g., an eight-bit or six-bit byte. "Baud" is a term used to signify a unit of data transmission speed equal to the number of information bits transmitted per second.

This article purposely begins with a play on words. The world of automatic data processing, comprised of esoteric academic studies such as cybernetics and mundane functions such as programming a payroll, has a language all its own. The language not only represents an integrated and comprehensive body of thought, but also reflects mental processes which are foreign to most lawyers. The lawyer and the systems analyst live in different worlds, think differently, speak different languages and react differently to the same sets of stimuli.

What makes the lack of communication between the world of law and the world of data processing so disturbing is that the legal profession and the practice of law in twentieth-century America

The author wishes to thank Robert Argyle Keller, Esq., who provided extremely important editorial assistance in the preparation of this article.

desperately need the assistance of data processing to remain economically viable. The practice of law is one of the last cottage industries in the United States. By history and practice, almost every legal function must be custom tailored to fit the client's specific needs. Economies of scale and effective production management are alien to the legal profession, a profession that has not advanced too far from the quill pen and legal briefs bound by red ribbon. Whether it is because the legal profession has virtually priced itself out of the reach of the middle class or because of the nearly impossible human task of getting one's arms around an exceptionally complex litigation case, the legal profession is waking up to the fact that data processing and the use of modern technology may make the difference between a profession that can cope with the twentieth century and a profession that will be run over by it.

One thing which will surely cause a lawyer to take note of data processing and its crucial importance to the effective practice of his art is to encounter another attorney assisted by data processing. This could occur at a deposition when opposing counsel drags one's client kicking and screaming through the facts of a given case aided by a computer printout, which chronologically lists all of the relevant documents in the lawsuit with a supporting narrative of the contents of the documents and their relevance to the case. While one rummages through boxes of manila envelopes with paper-clipped documents, opposing counsel is merely glancing at a concise printout and asking penetrating questions. Perhaps it takes such a sock in the jaw to convince a lawyer that the technology which enables men to walk on the moon might be of assistance to the practitioner of the legal arts.

BASIC CONCEPTS

The purpose of this article is not to berate the legal profession for its aversion to data processing. Rather, this article presumes that the reader wants to learn about data processing and how it can assist him in the conduct of litigation, and that he is willing to wade through a minimum of technical jargon to understand automatic data processing. This understanding is crucial. To apply data processing effectively to litigation, the lawyer, as decisionmaker in the lawsuit, must understand the capabilities and limitations of data processing. It is the lawyer who must understand what computers can do in order to envision how the technology that is available can assist him in proving his case. The programmer and systems analyst can provide assistance toward a specific goal, but the definition of goals must be left to the lawyer. It is that lawyer who must understand the technology available in order to formulate goals which must combine what is legally necessary with what is technically possible through data processing.

Once the decision is made to employ data processing, the lawyer must face the computer salesman and choose from the available technology the best mix of hardware and software to do the job. With only a vague understanding of what one wants to accomplish with data processing, coupled perhaps with an irrational reverence for the new and modern, and with no understanding of what product mix might best fit one's needs, the attorney is an easy mark for the data processing salesman. With a fancy soft-shoe routine, aided by slide shows and tours of customer installations, the salesman can take advantage of ignorance, confusion and desire. The attorney ends up with hardware and software capable of putting a man on the moon, with a corresponding price tag, when all he wanted to do was keep track of documents in a lawsuit. The converse might also happen. The attorney, because of ignorance and a tight purse, might buy technology that cannot do the required job, with resulting wasted effort, expense and futile results. It will therefore be the further purpose of this article to convey enough technical competence so that the attorney can ask the right questions of computer vendors, understand the answers, and acquire hardware and software suitable for the attorney's corresponding needs.

Insofar as the majority of the functions the computer will be called upon to perform for the legal community, data processing merely takes a human function that can be defined in human terms and performs that function at phenomenal rates of speed. Operations within a computer are measured in terms of nanoseconds—one thousandth of a millionth of a second—within which to perform a function. However, one should not confuse speed with accuracy or omniscience. When the lawyer puts the computer to work, he is not putting a man on the moon, controlling mass transit, an oil refinery or an early warning missile system. Rather, in most cases, when the attorney resorts to data processing to serve a need, he generally uses the computer to perform a clerical function. The computer is merely doing in an incredibly short period of time what it would take hundreds of individuals to do in a much longer time. The only difference is that, as the magnitude of a lawsuit increases and the documentation expands to thousands or hundreds of thousands of documents, the computer, performing a clerical function such as document storage and retrieval, can handle the job within the time frame required for litigation.

Even though the computer functions at incredible speed, it is still merely a machine which cannot think. A computer might be able to play chess, but only because a human being has programmed every conceivable move into the system. The computer, receiving a given move from an opponent, can scan its memory banks and select the optimum response. The computer, however, cannot invent moves, and it is certainly not intuitive. Therefore, even though the computer does things at incredible rates of speed, it can only do what it has been told to do, no less, and certainly no more. As a result, one cannot be vague with the computer, incomplete with instructions, or provide it with only part of the information. It requires precise and complete instructions and information. Accordingly, before bringing in a computer to assist in litigation, the lawyer must understand his case and what he hopes to prove so that clear instructions and sufficient information may be given to the computer system.

The burden on the lawyer is twofold. First, he must have a basic understanding of the capabilities of data processing so he can correlate those capabilities with what he hopes to accomplish in his legal context. Second, he must know what he wants to accomplish in that legal context. Once he has adequately defined what he wants in the context of the law, he can then apply data processing to reach that goal. This is probably the most difficult obstacle to the effective use of data processing because most lawyers wait until the last minute to effectively grapple with the legal and factual contentions in a case.

This brings to mind the term *GIGO*. This term does not stand for "gospel in, gospel out," which some people enamored by data processing might consider it to mean. On the contrary, the term "GIGO" means "garbage in, garbage out." The computer will do exactly what it is told to do. Unless great care is taken at the outset in defining goals, in formulating the systems design, and in controlling the input to a data processing system, the output of such a system, provided at 2200 lines of print per minute, can be voluminous and absolutely useless. If this is the result, the attorney can only blame himself. Because of its speed, the computer can provide accurate information at incredible rates of speed and in great volume, or, conversely, it can provide garbage at incredible rates of speed and in great volume.

The *systems design* correlates what the attorney wants to do with the capabilities of data processing. The first step in systems design is to state in precise terms what the attorney hopes to accomplish through the use of data processing. Once the goals are defined, the attorney, with the assistance of data processing personnel, can work backwards from those goals and define, step by step and in minute detail, exactly how the computer is to use the information to reach those goals. This process results in the systems design.

Input refers to the information that the computer will process within the systems design. This information, or data, could consist of correspondence germane to a lawsuit which an attorney might want stored in the computer and then returned to him in a chronological, document number sequence, or grouped according to addressee. However, the computer will only return what has been provided. If the initial information is not reliable, or erroneous, the computer will merely reformat the information or put it in a desired sequence. Unfortunately, the computer cannot make unreliable information reliable or wrong information correct.

Regardless of the type of information that constitutes the "input" to a systems design, the attorney alone knows why each item of information is significant to the lawsuit and to the systems design. The attorney must make the initial decisions as to significance and relevance. The computer can correlate or order information according to predetermined parameters, but the computer cannot formulate its own guidelines as to importance. This designation of significance and relevance is the function of the *coding scheme* used to describe an item of input in the systems design.

Once the coding scheme has been developed, the next step is to transfer the information to the computer itself. The computer can ingest information only in machine-readable form, i.e., magnetic encoding on tapes or discs, holes in punched cards, holes in paper tape and so on. One of the jobs incumbent upon the attorney is to translate the documents and other information to be put into the system into a machine-readable form. Normally this is done by having clerical personnel code the documents according to the coding scheme. The information so coded is punched into cards or recorded via a typewriter onto magnetic tapes or other machine-readable media to be fed into the computer.

Now, if we tie the above comments together, it becomes obvious that the linchpin of an effective computer system is an intelligent and thoughtful systems design which describes in detail the use to which the computer is to put the information it is given, the desired output from the computer and the purpose for which that output is to be used. Only be carefully designing the system to accomplish the end result, prior to taking the first step towards coding a document, may an attorney obtain from date processing the maximum benefits of this new technology. An incomplete, haphazard or build-as-you-go system design will only create headaches down the road and perhaps result in a system that, after much expense, is useless to the attorney.

USES FOR THE COMPUTER IN THE LEGAL ENVIRONMENT

Although this article directs itself primarily to the use of data processing in litigation, it is perhaps useful to mention other areas of legal practice where the computer can be of use. The use of data processing for more than one application in the legal environment can be crucial to the decision of whether to acquire in-house computer capability, to use a service bureau, or to forget data processing. Obviously, if more than one application can be found, the fixed costs of hardware and software can be spread.

Within the legal environment, the application of data processing can be broken down into six functional areas:

(1) *Accounting and office management functions,* which would include accounting for attorney time, generating accounts receivable monthly statements, and creating profit and loss statements and balance sheets for the law firm, and other functions generally associated with office management and accounting. The legal profession has started to use data processing in accounting and related functions, but data processing has not been fully applied in this area. The concepts of cost accounting are as applicable to a law firm as they are to a manufacturing firm. It might be useful, for example, to designate each client as a profit center with its separate profit and loss statement. The revenues received from each client would then be balanced against the amount of time charged to that client to determine whether or not the client, over a period of time, is generating a profit.

(2) *Document generation,* where the computer is used to store complete form documents, e.g., joint venture agreements, wills, deeds of trust and standard form interrogatories. The attorney can then take the form document and customize it to fit specific needs. The computer prints out a final, completed document through its ability to rapidly make changes, reform paragraphs and correct typographical errors. This is an exceptionally useful function for the computer, because, as mentioned above, the legal profession must lower the cost of its product. A couple of points probably should be mentioned in this regard. The first is to consider the cost effectiveness of equipment. A document has to be of a certain length, over five to seven pages, before computer document generation is economically justified. There are other types of equipment, such as mag-card typewriters, which are probably more cost efficient for the rapid production of small documents. The second point is the necessity for library management and control of documents stored in a data processing system. Documents must be constantly updated, the design of the form document must be related to the ease of the operators using the computer, an index of available documents must be established and attorneys made aware of how to properly annotate a form document for ease of processing. Once the procedural steps are established a data processing system can be of great benefit in the generation of documents.

(3) *Legal research*, where the computer is used for the storage and retrieval of statutory and case law. Although publishing companies and others have entered the field of legal research utilizing data processing, such application is still in its infancy. Current technology speaks in terms of trillion bit memories. With that amount of on-line storage, it is perfectly conceivable to store the entire statutory and case law of the United States, all services, and all secondary sources directly on-line to a computer system for access by the attorney. In the future, as the cost of hardware is reduced, an attorney could have a cathode ray tube (CRT) on his desk, with a hard output copying device, thereby conducting legal research without leaving his desk. The biggest stumbling blocks today are not hardware or technology, but designing the software for legal research and encoding the statutory and case law in machine-readable form.

(4) *Document storage and retrieval in litigation*, which is the subject of this article.

(5) The most interesting and imaginative use of data processing in the legal environment is as an *expert witness*. Here a data processing system, assuming the evidentiary foundation for its programming, data and output formats has been established, provides the attorney at trial with statistical and other reports as an analytical expert. An example of the computer as an expert is discussed in the last section of this article.

(6) Finally, the computer can be used for the development of *client relations* and the *marketing of legal services*. Because the computer has the capability of storing and handling vast amounts of information in incredibly short periods of time, it is possible to use the computer as a client contact mechanism. For example, a law firm might store all of its wills in a data processing system. Programming could then be set up to divide the wills into functional areas of the law which change from time to time. As a legal change occurs, e.g., in estate and gift taxation, the computer can be called upon to search all of the wills and determine which ones will be affected by the change in the law. The computer can not only provide a listing of all of the wills so affected, but can also type out letters, using law firm stationary, addressed to each client involved, advising of the change in the law and suggesting that it would be appropriate for them to contact their attorney to discuss this change. Thus, in the area of client relations, the computer can not only assist by lowering the cost of legal services, but can also aid the attorney in monitoring client needs and providing continuously updated legal services. Imagination alone limits the use of the computer in client relations, within the confines of the ethics of the profession.

TECHNICAL TERMS

A modicum of technical awareness is useful to the attorney not only in relating his legal needs to available technology, but also in avoiding expensive mistakes in acquiring the technical support required. The computer salesman, like the lawyer, uses his own language to his advantage, capitalizing on the ignorance of the opposition to fill with his product line bigger needs than may exist. For these reasons, the following lexicon will help to assist the attorney.

Hardware and software

The world of data processing is divided into two parts: hardware and software. Hardware is the physical equipment, including a computer and peripheral devices. Software is the totality of programs used to extend the capabilities of the hardware.

Conceptually, hardware can be divided into two units. The first is the central processing unit (CPU) of the computer which is the area where the action takes place. The second unit consists of peripheral input/output (I/O) devices, which, in simple terms, provide the link between the person and the computer.

The CPU contains the main storage of the computer, the arithmetic and logic unit (ALU) and other internal circuitry which gives the computer the capability of performing its function. The ALU performs arithmetic and decisional operations. Conceptually, it is the hardwired brain of the computer. Main storage, or "core," is the blackboard upon which the ALU, as instructed by a program, performs desired functions using variable data which has been fed into main storage.

Software operates within the confines of the hardware. For example, one can view the main storage of the computer as a blackboard, conceptually divided into horizontal sections. On the first section is written the operating system, an integrated collection of programs, which is the umpire and coach of a computer, enabling it to act, both as to hardware and software, as a computer.

The next horizontal gradation of main storage is committed to operational or "user" designed programs (sometimes called "application programs"). These programs are written to direct the computer to perform specific user-oriented functions, such as the preparation of client monthly statements.

The last horizontal gradation of main storage is allocated to variable input data that is used by an operational program to provide a desired result. As an example, consider an operational program designed to provide monthly statements to customers. The operational program would tell the computer the accounting steps to be followed in generating a monthly statement. Once the operational program is fed into the computer, the next procedure is to input the variable data, such as transaction items for a given customer showing the quantity of goods purchased and their price. This variable information is then processed by the operational program, and the computer prints out the monthly statements on the line printer.

Software can be divided into two conceptual groups: The operating system of the computer and user-written operational programs. In general terms, an operating system is a collection of programs written by the computer vendor that provides for the preparation and execution of the user's operational programs (jobs). Most operating systems are stored on an input/output device such as a tape or disc drive and called into main storage as needed by a portion of the operating system which is always core resident, that is, internal to the computer.

The operating system consists primarily of a control program, which is the umpire of the computer, directing and supervising all functions of the computer, and processing programs which can be divided into three categories:

1. Language translators, called "compilers," that take a user's operational program, written in a specific program language, and translate this program into the language of bits and bytes, the internal language of the computer. If one were required to write a program in that internal language, and to know the exact configuration of bits and bytes necessary to impulse the ALU to perform a specific function or to represent a specific alpha-numeric character, programming would be exceedingly tedious. To overcome this problem, programming languages were developed which are, to varying degree, somewhat similar to English and/or customary mathematics. For example, the Fortran compiler is a program which accepts a program written in the quasi-algebraic Fortran "source" language and produces a machine language "object" program in the internal language of the machine.
2. Utility or service programs provided by the vendor to perform basic data processing tasks such as sorting and merging alphabetical lists of data.
3. User-designed operational programs, that become part of the operating system library.

As an example of the relationship between the operating system and user-written programs, consider writing a program to print out

.ccounts receivable monthly statements. A programmer would sit down with a programming language that is business oriented, such as Cobol, and write a program that describes the functions that the computer must accomplish, in terms similar to English, which the programmer can understand. This user-written operational program will define the format of the variable information, and client transactions, which will be processed by the program. It will describe in precise detail all of the functions that the computer must go through, such as adding up the item purchases for each transaction and multiplying by a standard percent to obtain sales tax, in order to arrive at an accounts receivable monthly statement. Once this program is written on coding sheets, the programmer will keypunch the program, normally into cards, and feed these cards into the computer. The computer will first have been told by the operating system, keyed by "job control" cards preceding the accounts receivable program, that there is a user-written problem program, written in Cobol, coming in. The operating system will then call upon the Cobol language translator to read the user-written problem program and translate it into the format that the computer must internally use. The translated user-written problem program can either be put out on a random access device such as a disc for recall by name only when needed, or punched into cards by an output device, a card punch, and stored external to the computer until use.

In summary, software can be divided into two sections. The first is the operating system which includes all of those items listed above, including, in sophisticated data processing systems, translated user-written problem programs that have been stored internal to the system for retrieval by name only and have become part of the operating system. The other section of software are those user-written problem programs, as written in, for example, Cobol, or as translated, which are stored external to the system to be used when needed.

Internal storage

Most computers store information in binary format. This means that information is stored internally in the computer in the form of groupings of electronic on-off switches or "bits," a given sequence of bits signifying a given alphabetic or numeric character. In most computers, data is stored and transmitted between main storage and the CPU for mathematical and decisional operations in multiples of eight bits. As noted at the beginning of this article, these eight-bit multiples are called "bytes." In this regard, when we talk of a "256 KB" computer storage capability, we mean that the computer has roughly 256,000 bytes (kilobytes) of main storage or storage for 256,000 letters or numbers.

Thus, one can look at the innards of a computer as an ordered series of eight-bit bytes, whose contents and locations are managed by the operating system. When a program is loaded into the computer, every instruction of the program is assigned a specific byte or string of bytes. Variable data coming into the computer is similarly placed in specified locations so that the computer knows where all items of data can be found. This allows the computer to have immediate, random access to all information, stored internally in the computer, whether operational programs or variable data.

Input/output devices

Any device which sends information to or receives information from a computer is an input/output device. In simple terms, an input device is a mechanical unit designed to put data into a computer for processing, for example, a card reader, a tape reader, or a keyboard. An output device translates the electrical impulses representing data processed by the machine into a more permanent form (such as magnetic writing on tape), or into humanly readable form, (such as printed forms or words on a display screen). Certain devices, such as magnetic tapes and discs, can be both input and output devices. Other peripheral equipment, such as line printers, serve only as output devices. As the industry advanced, the sophistication and complexity of input/output devices have advanced correspondingly. They now include keyboard terminals that may be carried in a briefcase.

Batch processing, interactive processing and teleprocessing

The attorney considering employment of computer assistance should be aware of the distinctions between batch processing, interactive processing and teleprocessing. Batch processing is a technique whereby items to be processed and variable data to be used by an operational program are coded and collected into groups prior to processing. In the example of generating monthly statements, batch processing would require that all customer transaction cards be collected, coded and fed into the computer at the same time. The computer would respond to all inquiries or all variable data at once. Batch processing is normally done at the physical location of the computer.

To be distinguished from batch processing is interactive processing where an operator sits at a console typewriter, or other form of terminal such as a display tube, and queries the computer question by question, receiving a response to each specific question, before the next inquiry or item of variable data is addressed.

Teleprocessing is basically using the computer as the hub of a network of terminals where, over normal telephone lines or private lines, information from the terminal is sent to the computer for processing.

Data format

To understand the arrangement of variable data, which is used by an operational program to perform a specific function, terminology is important. Three terms are frequently used: *field, record* and *file*. A field is an assigned area in a record to be marked with information, such as a field to be used for the name of an employee in the employee's payroll record. A record is a group of related facts or fields of information treated as a unit, such as a given employee's entire payroll record including the fields of name, social security number, year-to-date pay and the like. A file is an organized collection of information directed toward some purpose, such as all employee payroll records of a given business.

Records, and in turn fields, can be of fixed or variable length. Consider a standard eighty column punch card, very akin to your telephone bill. There are eighty columns on this card running horizontally. Into each given column a number or a letter can be encoded by punching. A number is termed numeric, and a letter is termed alpha. If letters and numbers are combined, the encoding is termed alpha-numeric. In simple computers, in order to work upon the information punched in the card, the computer must be told exactly where to look for certain information. For example, a document number might be punched into columns one through eight of each eighty column card, with each card representing a distinct document. Within the first eight columns, any eight-digit number can be used to signify a specific document. This is a fixed-length field, eight columns for a document number, in a fixed-length record, eighty columns for all information encoded concerning a specific record.

More advanced data processing equipment can handle variable-length fields and records as distinguished from fixed-length fields and records. With a variable-length record, the computer is instructed where the specific field or record begins and ends but not its length. The computer must be keyed by a certain symbol to indicate that this is the beginning of a specific variable-length field or variable-length record and there must be, at some point in a given data stream, other keys to signify the end and the beginning of the next known variable-length field within a given variable-length record, or signifying the next variable-length record. Once the computer in scanning data comes upon such a key, the computer knows that this is a variable-length field or record and will use the information between the beginning key and the ending key in a desired way. Variable records have the unique advantage of not limiting the user to a predetermined number of columns.

A sophisticated computer can "select" information contained in a variable field or record. For example, a record, with fixed fields for date and document number, might have a variable-length narrative section describing the contents of the document. This narrative will describe what the attorney believes to be significant about a given document. Within this variable-length narrative, the attorney can put, in English, anything he desires. Once this information is stored in the computer, the attorney can ask it to read through the variable-length narrative fields searching for records which contain, for example, the word "misrepresentation" and print out all such records.

Once the computer extracts from the data file all of the records containing the key word "misrepresentation" in the narrative variable field, the records can be rearranged or sorted according to fixed fields such as date or document number. However, the computer cannot sort these records in a sequence based upon information contained in the variable field. For example, if significant dates have been included in a variable field, the computer can pull out any narrative that contains a date by using its select capability, but it cannot then sort these dates into a chronological sequence. To do this, the records would have to be rewritten creating a new fixed field for the date selected from the narrative variable field.

On-line and off-line

All information that is to be used by a litigation data processing system, such as narrative summaries of depositions, must be encoded into machine-readable form. This may be done either on-line or off-line. On-line describes the operation of a computer system in which the input/output devices are under the control of the CPU, and in which information reflecting current activity is introduced into the data processing system as soon as it occurs. Teleprocessing and the use of terminals connected directly to the CPU are examples of on-line processing. Off-line refers to peripheral equipment or devices, or the storage of data not in direct communication with the CPU.

The distinction between on-line and off-line includes not only the manner in which information is stored for later retrieval and the manner in which this information is processed, but also the manner in which information is encoded in machine-readable form. On-line encoding of information is the translation of data from hard copy to machine-readable form directly into the computer by use of a terminal without an intervening step such as punch cards. Instead of ending up with a box of cards, the data is transcribed onto a magnetic tape or a magnetic disc by the computer directly from the terminal. The typical off-line encoding of information involves key-punching information which has been summarized according to a desired coding format, into the computer cards. Once the information has been encoded, a box of cards will represent a program or the variable information to be used by the computer. When processing is to occur, the computer reads the holes punched in the cards and the data is fed into the system.

Once the information has been encoded, the next step is to store this information for later retrieval. In an off-line system the variable data will probably be retained in boxes of cards to be used when necessary. If it becomes necessary to store the information in a more accessible form for speedy access, the punched cards can be fed into a computer, and recorded on a magnetic tape or magnetic disc. The tape or disc can then be removed from the computer and stored for later use by the system. Whether in cards or in some other storage medium, if stored data is not directly and immediately accessible by the CPU of the computer, the data is said to be stored off-line.

On-line storage, on the other hand, is the storage of data directly accessible by the CPU and immediately usable by the system. As discussed above, main storage is the blackboard of the computer on which the computer handles information it is currently processing. However, main storage is generally limited to two to three hundred thousand bytes and is very expensive. Therefore, entire data files are not generally stored in main storage; rather, records are fed into main storage from on-line storage devices, such as magnetic tape or disc drives, when needed.

If data files are to be used by the computer frequently or in the regular course of business, on-line storage of the files, coupled with on-line storage of operational programs, allows for immediate processing. The trade-off to this immediate access is the inherent cost in committing a peripheral device, such as a disc drive, to the on-line storage of the particular data file. If immediate access is not necessary, for example, if inquiries to the file are batched and processed against the file on a periodic basis, the file can be stored off-line until needed. This cuts the cost of data storage because the peripheral device is released for other jobs.

THE NEED FOR A GENERALIZED SYSTEMS DESIGN IN LITIGATION

It cannot be overstressed that the computer can only do what it is told to do, and it must be told what to do in extreme detail. Every step the attorney wants the computer to take, every use of information, every output format must be specifically described to the programmer and systems analyst so that they can design the operational required programs. The effective use of data processing is jeopardized when an attorney believes that a computer is intuitive, and assumes that, if he merely codes information, dumps it into the system, pushes a button and asks the appropriate question, the computer will provide the appropriate response. Nothing could be further from the truth. One has to know exactly what output one wants from the computer, exactly what the output is going to look like, exactly what information is available to the computer to generate the output and, in extreme detail, exactly how the computer is to work with this data to generate that output.

This necessity for painstaking detail is probably the greatest stumbling block to the effective use of data processing in litigation. It is, of course, detrimental to the effective use of data processing if the attorney does not take sufficient time to understand data processing so that he can think in terms of the regimen of processing, and design accordingly. A much more fundamental concern, however, is posed by factors inherent in the process of litigation itself. Each case takes on a life of its own as it progresses. It is very difficult to prognosticate all constituent elements of a case. As the process of discovery evolves, the whole complexion of a case may change. However, if the attorney takes the time, at the outset, to understand the case and the application of data processing to litigation, the initial design of a litigation computer system can be sufficiently broad in scope as well as sufficiently detailed for use so that the changes which do occur in a given case can be accommodated. The goal is to broadly design a system, suitable for that first case in the office that is going to use data processing, but flexible enough to fit the needs of subsequent cases.

Therefore, the first step is for the attorney to sit down and learn something about data processing and how other litigation cases have been handled in the past using this technology. The next step is for the attorney to decide exactly what he wants to do with data processing in the context of a particular case. This must be in as much detail as is possible, considering the point in the life cycle of a case where the attorney finds himself. He must analyze his lawsuit carefully and decide upon the relevant information he wants from a data processing system and how he intends to use it. If he wants the system to organize his evidence for trial, he may have to decide, perhaps at the inception of the lawsuit, how he intends to try a case in which he has yet to depose a witness. The goal is to design a generalized systems approach to litigation and then customize it to fit the needs and requirements of the particular case as it develops.

Systems design

The first step in the development of a systems design involves the identification of conceptually distinct categories of information that will be relevant to the lawsuit and their interrelationships. For example, if the attorney wants the lawsuit to be tried on the basis of factual contentions, and wants the computer to list all of the witnesses, documents and depositions that support a specific factual contention, he need not, at the systems design stage, itemize all of the factual contentions that he intends to use. This is probably impossible without some progress in the case. The attorney must, however, decide whether he intends to use the category "factual contention" and store and retrieve information on that basis. Once this is decided, a field within a record will be allocated to "factual contention." As discovery progresses, separate codes can then be assigned to each specific contention.

After defining the categories of information, one must define the interrelationships among categories of information. For example, the attorney may want to store documents according to date in order to develop a chronology of the documents in the lawsuit. This raises the question of what date is going to be used for the purpose of chronology, and whether the system must allow for multiple dates. A letter normally bears the date the letter was sent. However, a specific letter may speak internally of one or more dates that may be, in fact, more significant to the lawsuit chronology than the date the letter was sent. Therefore, in designing the system, the decision has to be made as to whether to allow only for the document date for the purpose of chronology, or to allow additional fields within a record for what might be called pertinent dates, which reflect specific factual points raised in the body of the letter.

Once the lawsuit is understood and the application of data processing to it is defined, the attorney will be in a position to sit down with computer experts and design the system. This step in the formulation of a systems design can be a time-consuming and expensive undertaking, at least the first time through. However, it is the foundation for everything else. It must not be done in a haphazard fashion. The design will require not only discussion of what the lawsuit is about, what the factual and legal contentions may or may not be, but also how discovery will be conducted, how information will be collected, how this information is to be processed through the system, what will be done with this information, how the trial will be conducted, whether summaries will be utilized and how these summaries will be formatted, and the interrelationships among information.

At this stage hardware and software constraints may limit the freedom of systems design. The attorney may want to do X, but the programmer or systems analyst might tell him that it is not possible; or, if he decides to go that way it will be very expensive; or, perhaps an alternative systems design would provide the same information at less cost. Through this give and take process, the attorney and his computer assistants will complete the systems design. It is then up to the data processing personnel to program what the attorney wants to do and the manner in which it is to be done.

Out of this cooperative effort will evolve a systems design which will include:

1. General analysis of what the lawsuit is all about.
2. The initial framework for the factual and legal contentions involved.
3. The types of documents and other information that will be obtained.
4. The quantity of such information.
5. The manner in which the information will be obtained.
6. General categories of data that the attorney wants to be stored in his data processing system, such as factual contentions, areas of damage, and authors and recipients of correspondence.
7. The initial framework for the specific entries under each category of data, e.g., names of witnesses under witness category.
8. What the attorney wishes to do with each category of data; for example, if document date has been selected as a category of data, is a document date chronology required?
9. Any interrelationships among the categories of information. If the attorney asks the computer to retrieve a specific category, what other categories are to be automatically retrieved in conjunction therewith? If an inquiry seeks to retrieve all correspondence written by a specific company, will the system automatically retrieve all correspondence written by employees of that company by internally correlating companies and employees?
10. The types and formats of output required from the system; for example, does the attorney only want a narrative description

of each document stored, printed out by document number or does he want the computer to generate a pre-trial conference order?

11. The decisional and computational steps necessary to generate each desired output, based upon the variable data available to the computer. This step-by-step analysis of how the attorney would manually prepare his output will be the framework for programming the computer.

Once the systems design has been formulated, the next step is to add a systems flow. This will basically be the movement of paper, information, coded information and output reports through the systems design. All members of the litigation team, whether they be attorneys, legal assistants or computer personnel, must understand how the variable data is gathered, and then how this information is handled by clerical personnel or the attorneys themselves for evaluation, review and encoding into the computer. An overall design of the flow of information must be related to the systems design so that everyone who is a part of the litigation team will understand how the variable data is to be managed, how documents are to be numbered, stored, retrieved and encoded, and how the documents are to be maintained in numerical order for easy access based on the printouts from the system.

Program design

After the systems design and the systems flow have been established, the next step is a program design. This is the function of data processing personnel. However, the assistance of legal personnel is necessary to explain specific elements of the systems design. Program design refers to the preparation of the individual programs that will process the information to reach the results specified by the systems design. A given systems design may require as few as two or as many as 500 programs.

One product of the program design stage will be the definition of the form of input to go into each program and the form of output generated by each program. As an aside, many programs may in fact have no specific input or output that the attorney will ever see because the input to one program may be the output from another program, completely internal to the data processing system itself, carrying out different steps necessary to generate the final output which the attorney desires. The programming support personnel will constantly refer back to the attorney to discuss their design of input forms, e.g., coding sheets, to determine whether or not the information which they have included on the coding sheets is that which is necessary for the program to do what is required by the systems design. Further, report layouts, showing what the output of a given program will be, must be reviewed by the attorney.

This whole procedure, from the big thoughts department of the systems design to the nitty gritty of designing how many spaces will be allowed for a document number, is an interactive process; first among the litigation team to determine what they want from the system, based upon their evaluation of exactly how they are going to prove their lawsuit, and then between the litigation team and data processing support personnel to complete an appropriate, workable design and programming of the system. The result of this moderately arduous process should be a systems design manual. This will include not only the systems design and the scope of the job to be performed by data processing, but also a description of each significant program used, the format for the input and output for each such program and a scheme for the general flow of information through the system.

Change of design and a generalized system

One serious unknown in applying data processing to litigation is the inability of the attorney, at the beginning of a lawsuit, to project six months or a year down the road what the legal and factual contentions of his lawsuit will be, what facts will be at his disposal, how he intends to prove the lawsuit, and, ultimately, what output he wants from his data processing system. Further, because of the cost and time involved in designing a computer-based litigation support system, it is preferable not to reinvent the wheel every time a case comes into the office which might benefit from data processing. Therefore, the goal is to develop a generalized systems design which can be customized to fit the requirements of a particular case, and allow for maximum flexibility to absorb changes that will occur during the life of a lawsuit. This can be accomplished by the attorney, when he first applies data processing to a litigation case, by broadly designing his system so as to develop a generalized litigation system simultaneously with the development of the specific systems design for the immediate case.

In the application of data processing to litigation support, the similarities between lawsuits greatly outnumber the differences. The similarities include the storing and retrieving of documents, the providing of data summaries, the development of pre-trial conference orders, and the preparation of trial books. Therefore, a systems design should be flexible enough to be adapted to almost any litigation. An attorney can then customize a generalized litigation ystems design to handle the types of information peculiar to his lawsuit and add the specifics to predetermined categories of information. The end result will be a generalized systems design for the handling of litigation in general to be used again and again, at minimal cost. The only variable will be the degree of customizing that is necessary to make the generalized systems design useful in a particular case. Finally, if a generalized systems design can be used, allowing for customizing, at the onset of a case, all of the data categories and their interrelationships will be established, so that as change occurs during the process of discovery and trial the system will remain effective and useful.

Although a generalized systems design can be developed as a working tool for the attorney, there may be situations where a particular lawsuit is, in and of itself, unique to the point where the generalized systems design cannot be of use. If so, and the case is sufficiently large to warrant the design of a radically different system, then the attorney should repeat all of the development steps discussed in this article to formulate a new systems design. This should not occur often because the similarities between lawsuits and the arrangement of information usually exceed the differences, so that a generalized systems approach to the use of data processing can be formulated and can be of use.

Cost of change

Finally, the cost of data processing in litigation will, to a great extent, be determined by the frequency of substantive change. There is a basic cost floor for the use of data processing in litigation determined by the size of the data files and the frequency of inquiry. But once this floor is established, cost will be dependent upon the frequency of change. Change is expensive in data processing, because a change to program *A* may affect every other program in the system. If the facts change, i.e., the interrelationships between information and the types of output required, then so might the programs. The costs rise proportionally. If a change occurs, then it must be brought to the attention of data processing personnel as soon as possible so that current programming can be halted, the change evaluated, and the design of the program altered to avoid wasted effort and minimize the cost of change.

APPLICATION OF THE GENERALIZED SYSTEMS DESIGN

The economic justification for data processing is that once variable data is recorded in a machine-readable form, it need never be rerecorded. Information is permanently available to the computer system to be retrieved in any of a number of desired output formats using the select and sort capabilities of the computer. The clerical effort required to encode and arrange information is limited to the initial step of encoding. As discussed above, data is formatted into fields (the date of a letter), fields of information are assembled into a record (all information concerning a particular letter), and all records involved in a particular application are collected into a file (all of the letters and other documents involved in a given lawsuit). Once the record format has been designated and the fields within a record defined, the mass of variable data to be utilized in a given application can be recorded once, and then retrieved and rearranged as often as desired without any additional clerical steps.

However, before coding documents in a particular lawsuit can begin, the lawsuit itself must be understood in great detail. This understanding of the lawsuit will determine the significant items of information to be put into a computer system. This determination in turn will define the fields comprising the format of the computer record. Without such forethought, an attorney might include only the obvious information in the computer system. But the real utility of data processing is its ability to assist the attorney in arranging information according to legal and factual contentions, areas of damage, and other legal issues relevant to a particular lawsuit.

Once the lawsuit is sufficiently understood so that the relevant categories of information can be defined, the attorney can develop a coding scheme applicable to all documents in the lawsuit and allocate the information they contain to fixed fields and to a variable narrative field. This allocation will be structured to take advantage of the select and sort capabilities of the computer.

Information contained in, or derived from, a document (the computer record) can be conceptually categorized as either objective or subjective information. Objective information is that data which is readily observable from the face of the document. Such objective information would include exhibit numbers, the date of the document, the person sending the document, the person receiving it and the type of document.

On the other hand, subjective information is data pertaining to a specific document or record that is not readily observable from the face of the document. Rather, an analytical step is required between reading the document and drawing any conclusion as to its subjective significance. Subjective categories of information might include the various legal and factual contentions in the lawsuit, areas of damage and an assessment of the importance of a document to the lawsuit.

Having divided information into subjective and objective categories, the attorney must then relate this division to the capabilities of the computer. The computer has the capability of sorting, that is, rearranging records in a desired sequence, chronologically by date or in document number sequence. In order for the computer to sort, it must key upon a specific fixed field of information contained in a given record within the file. A fixed field is an area of information of predetermined length whose location within the record is always known to the computer. For example, a fixed field allocated to date would be comprised of six digits, two each for day, month and year. Its fixed location in the record, for example, positions ten through fifteen of a 100 position record, would be known to the computer.

The computer also has the capability of selecting a specific item of information contained in the variable field, a field of indeterminate length in which the position of individual items of information is not known to the computer. For example, a computer record might contain a narrative description of the contents of a document that will not be limited in length to avoid constraining the narrative. Particular dates, derived from the body of a document might be included in this variable narrative. The computer can scan an entire narrative and retrieve the whole or a portion of it, if a word within the narrative matches the item of information requested. For example, if the attorney desires to review any record that contains the date January 1, 1977, the computer can, at machine speeds, read all of the narratives and pull out those narratives that contain the date January 1, 1977.

The computer generally cannot sort out an item of information contained within a variable field, unless, after records are selected, they are rewritten as a new data file and the criteria for the sort rearranged as a fixed field. For example, those records selected because the date January 1, 1977 appears in the variable narrative field, could not, on that basis, be incorporated with the other records in the file for a chronological sort. Document date is a fixed field upon which the computer could sort, but the date derived from the narrative would not be in a fixed field. Therefore, in order to sort out the records retrieved by date within the narrative, the records would have to be rewritten and the date from the narrative formatted as a fixed field. This rewriting of files is expensive and requires specialized programming. It can be avoided by defining all fixed fields to be required in the lawsuit during the initial systems design stage.

In most litigation applications, the attorney will want to sort his records on objective data, such as document number or date. This will be the type of information assigned fixed fields in the computer record. Subjective information such as legal or factual contentions, will normally be assigned to a variable field, composed of a digest or narrative of the important points contained in a record. The attorney may want to select against specific items of information contained in the digest. This can be done through the select capability of the computer and the documents so retrieved can then be sorted by the objective information contained in the fixed fields. This becomes the generalized framework for the classification of information in the systems design.

One caveat must be mentioned as to the number of fixed fields. Because of the capabilities of standard programming packages provided by computer vendors, fixed fields must stand alone within the system in order to take advantage of the sort capabilities. Further, the standard computer printout is normally 132 characters in width and the more fixed fields that are used, the more compressed the area available on the printout for the digest or narrative field becomes. Figure 1[1] is a printout of computer records with three fixed fields, document number, date and a three-position alpha code signifying the type of document, for example DEP denoting deposition. By limiting the fixed fields in the record to three, most of the printout area is available to the narrative making it visually appealing and easy to use. Should a specific lawsuit require an extensive number of fixed fields that so compress the printout area available to the narrative as to make it unusable, customized programming can accommodate those requirements. Most computer vendors have standard program packages for the storing of information and selecting and sorting upon the records contained in the data base, and, because these packages are standard, they are relatively economical to use. Once specific programming is necessary to customize data storage and retrieval, however, the data processing expense of the lawsuit increases dramatically.

Consider a lawsuit for breach of contract and fraud involving the installation of a computer system. A customer sues the computer vendor for promising certain results if the customer would install a computer system, the customer alleging that the computer vendor failed to live up to his promises. The computer vendor first installed a card system, then upgraded the plaintiff to a disc system, making additional contractual promises in the process. According to the customer, neither computer system functioned as promised, and the plaintiff incurred loss of business revenue and expenses during the period that the defendant was trying to get the computer system to work as agreed. The customer further alleges that, when the vendor realized that the card system would not perform as promised and

[1]See figures at end of chapter.

warranted, he represented to the customer that a disc system was required because of work load, but that this was false and an attempt to cover up the problems with the card system.

As discussed above, the first step is to analyze the lawsuit and to determine the relevant and significant categories of information. Figure 2 is the abstract input form used for encoding the source data in this particular lawsuit for input into the data processing system. This abstract input form is a codified representation of what the attorney determined to be the significant categories of information in the lawsuit. It is directly derived from the mental process the attorney must go through in analyzing his lawsuit and defining those categories of information to be put into the system, and the manner in which he wants the information retrieved.

The first caption on the abstract input form, "control information," designates three fixed fields to be used for the computer record. Entry number is synonymous with document number, i.e., that number which is stamped on each document during discovery. The entry number has two major purposes: (1) the key to indicate to the computer that a distinct computer record follows, and (2) the link between the computer printouts and the original documents, which will probably be stored in file cabinets in document number sequence.

The next item on the abstract input form is the fixed field for a pertinent date, that date which is of significance in the document, but may or may not be the date of the document itself. The third fixed field designates the document type, a three-position alpha code such as LET for letter or DEP for deposition. Space is provided on the form for alternatives should the document not fall within the six predetermined types.

The reason for using predetermined document types on the form, as well as other predetermined codes, is to provide for ease of encoding by merely checking a block. The keypunch operator will keypunch the three-position alphanumeric code corresponding to the block checked.

On the abstract input form (Figure 2), after the control information is completed, all the remaining information required by the form is included in a variable-length narrative or digest field. Information included in the narrative field consists of both subjective and objective information. Objective information includes the author of the particular document and the recipient. Other objective information derived from the body of a document would be included in the area labeled "digest information," where the encoder would write, in ordinary English, a general description of the contents of the document. Subjective information would also be included in the narrative analysis of a document, but certain key categories of subjective information have been given specific codes. This subjective information comprises the legal and factual contentions in the lawsuit as determined by the attorney. In this particular case that information was broken down into four different categories: liability subjects, fraud subjects, damage subjects and general subjects.

When the abstract input form was initially prepared at the beginning of the lawsuit, space was provided on the form for increasing the specific codes under each of the above categories as knowledge of the lawsuit and its relevant facts increased. For example, under the liability subject category, only three specific entries were initially thought relevant to the lawsuit and designated L/1 through L/3, referring to disc system, card system and bill-of-material processor, respectively. However, space was provided on the form for up to nine liability subject codes. Because the digest is a variable-length field, additional entries could be added if necessary.

The next predetermined categories of information on the abstract input form consist of the author and recipient of a specific record of information. The "A/" and "R/" are codes whereby a given individual can be selected as an author only or recipient only or, by eliminating the "A" and the "R" during a select, by the name of the person only.

Following these predetermined categories of information, space is provided on the form for a narrative digest of the pertinent information contained in a given record. Again, the computer record is merely a predetermined composite of information distinct from all of the records. It need not be a physically distinct piece of paper. A line or paragraph of a deposition can be a distinct computer record if it is recorded with a unique document number.

The information contained in the last line of the form, above "abstracted by," indicates whether the document is a plaintiff's exhibit, defendant's exhibit, or other cross-reference. The code Pex/A/Com would indicate that the record is not only a plaintiff's exhibit, but it has also been attached to the answer and to the complaint. Coding schemes like this can be designed to suit the needs of the case.

Figure 3 is another example of a coding sheet, or abstract input form, that is somewhat more general in nature than is Figure 2. Conceptually, it is again derived from the same generalized systems design for storage and retrieval. Reading down the form, the control information includes document number, trial exhibit number, discovery exhibit number, and document date. In designing this form, it was determined that there would be no need, for sorting purposes, to assign a fixed field to document type, and that document date alone would be of significance rather than an alternative pertinent date. Trial exhibit and discovery exhibit numbers were added as fixed fields since the lawsuit involved numerous exhibits, and because, for trial purposes, sorting on the trial exhibit number, the discovery exhibit number, or both, after a select against a certain legal or factual contention, would be necessary, for example, in preparation of the pre-trial conference order. Further, in order to avoid reserving a separate record number for every page of a deposition, page and line were added to the control information as a continuation of document number in order to designate, if required, a given page or a given line of a deposition as a separate computer record.

The digest information follows the control information. The digest information is also a variable field containing all other relevant and pertinent information in a given record. The first code is an alpha code for document type. Following this code, space is provided for numerous legal and factual contentions. Because this coding sheet was designed for a very complex lawsuit, and because all of the legal and factual contentions were not determined as of the drafting of the coding sheet, the code is merely listed as LC/__ for legal contention. As the first legal contention was formulated, it was recorded in a systems manual and given the designation LC/1. This procedure was followed for all legal and factual contentions.

Following the legal and factual contentions on Figure 3, the coding sheet is divided into "I" for documents such as letters, and "II" for depositions and interrogatories. Under "I," the coding provides for author and recipient as to both person and company, and for those individuals who received courtesy copies of the document. "II" provides encoding for deponent by company and individual, and for listing individuals named by the deponent in his testimony. "I" and "II" could be combined using the document type code, (DEP for deposition), to differentiate a deposition from other types of documents. Following "II," space is provided which can be enlarged as necessary for the narrative digest of the document. This will contain the attorney's or paralegal's subjective evaluation of the document and its relevance to the lawsuit and interrelationships to other documents.

In the hypothetical lawsuit concerning fraud in the sale and installation of a computer system, consider a letter sent by J. Gray, the computer salesman, to B. Jones, the president of the customer. Gray wrote this letter to Jones to confirm their conversation wherein Jones requested that the computer vendor commit to a certain delivery schedule. In response to this request, Gray answered that there would be no particular conversion problem from the card system to the disc system so long as the preparation of the three major programs to be used by Jones was started prior to August 8, 1970. Let us assume that the date of the letter confirming the telephone conversation was July 31, 1969. Further, during discovery, this particular letter was stamped with the document identification number "18."

On the abstract input form (Figure 2), this document would be encoded as follows. For entry number, 000018 would be encoded, signifying document number 18. The date 07/31/69 would be encoded as the pertinent date. A check mark would be put next to the three position alpha code, "LET," designating the document as a letter. Because the letter concerns the disc system primarily, a check would be put next to the liability subject "L/1." Further, let us assume that additional fraud subject categories have been designated during the process of the lawsuit, and that "F/3" will be used to signify fraud concerning the development of programming support. There may or may not be relevant damage subject and general subject areas derived from this letter, but for the purpose of this example let us assume there are none.

The next items of information would concern the author and recipient of this letter. For author, we would encode under last name, "Gray," and for first initial, "J." For recipient, we would encode "Jones" for the last name and "B." as the first initial. Under digest information, we might encode the letter as follows: "Confirming telephone conversation, requested commitments of delivery schedule. No particular conversion problems on three major programs provided they are begun by 08/07/70." Finally, we may have additional coding as to whether or not this letter has been used for a plaintiff's exhibit or a defendant's exhibit, and whether it is attached to the complaint or to an interrogatory.

All documents in the lawsuit, whether they are letters, memoranda or depositions, would be similarly encoded for input into the system. Once all of the documents have been fed into the system, the attorney would have a "data base" consisting of all the relevant information in the lawsuit, which he can now proceed to sort and select against to obtain computer printouts useful in the conduct of discovery and trial. As an example, let us assume the attorney wants to retrieve all of the documents which involve Jones as either author or recipient. Further, the attorney wants these documents printed out by the computer in document number order, so that he can find the original copies. This printout may be useful in the preparation of an additional deposition of Jones, or in preparing for direct examination at trial.

Figure 1 shows the first page of a computer printout with all of the documents in the lawsuit which involve Jones, as either author or recipient. The documents are arranged in document number sequence. Reading from left to right across the printout, the first six positions of the computer record and the printout format show the document number. The next eight positions are the pertinent dates derived from the document. The next three positions are the alpha code for the type of document, such as DEP for deposition. Again, these three items of information alone comprise the fixed fields of the computer record. The remaining information contained in the computer record is the variable narrative field comprised of both objective and subjective information concerning a particular document/ record. Again, because it is a variable field, one normally could not sort on the information contained therein; but, one can select information from the variable field and, in turn, sort the records so selected by a fixed field. In this case, the documents were selected against "Jones," without the A/ or R/ so that Jones would be retrieved whether author or recipient, and the documents so selected, sorted by document number.

By looking down the document number column, sorted in document number sequence, one can see that certain document numbers do not appear. This is because not all documents in the data base involve Jones. Rather, this particular inquiry into the computer was a search of all records and a select against only those records that contain Jones in the narrative, regardless of whether Jones is qualified as an A for author or an R for recipient. After the select has been completed, the command to the computer was to arrange all the documents so selected in document number sequence. Therefore, documents numbered 000009, 000010 and 000011 contain no reference to Jones. Finally, document number 000018 is the document that was given as an example of the use of the abstract input form.

This is just one example of how information encoded into the system can be sorted, selected and retrieved in a desired order for use by the attorney. This same information, recorded once, can be selected again on the basis of criteria other than Jones, and then sorted out in either document number or chronological order. For example, the attorney may want to know every document that was authored by Gray, or every document where Smith is mentioned in the narrative, as in document number 000002. The computer would go into the narrative and retrieve, utilizing its select capability, all such documents. Further, the attorney may want to retrieve all documents pertinent to liability subject area 1 or damage subject area 2. The same approach would be used.

Effective combinations of sort and select as the basis for retrieval require the imagination of the attorney. The only limitation is the prior planning that determined the categories of information that were going to be encoded. The usefulness of the system is directly related to the coding scheme, and the coding scheme is a direct derivative of the attorney's understanding of his lawsuit and his ability to formulate the significant categories of information.

ALTERNATIVE HARDWARE AND SOFTWARE TO SUPPORT THE GENERALIZED SYSTEMS DESIGN

The generalized systems design discussed above can be adjusted to fit the hardware and software available. Computer vendors have a full product line and service bureaus have a full range of services. For both, cost and capabilities of hardware and software go hand in hand. How one approaches hardware will, to a great extent, depend upon two factors. The first factor is the potential recovery from the lawsuit. This will determine how sophisticated a use of data processing can be applied to the lawsuit because, as the system becomes more sophisticated, expense increases. Second, if a standardized systems approach is developed so that an established procedure can be set up to fit all lawsuits, allowing for a moderate amount of custom tailoring, high-priced data processing can be used for the small recovery lawsuit. Further, an understanding of available hardware and software will enable an attorney to moderate the sales efforts of the computer vendor and fit available hardware and software to his real needs.

The examples of the generalized systems design discussed above utilized moderately sophisticated data processing equipment which require that the data base be on-line to the CPU for select and sort capabilities. This approach is expensive because it requires a computer to do the information handling and retrieval. However, the concept of data processing, in that a record is recorded once, and equipment rather than clerical personnel is used for all successive rearrangements of information, can be applied without even using a computer.

The least expensive data processing system utilizes the eighty or ninety-six column punch card for storing information, but relies on only a card sorter and not a computer for retrieving information. The systems design, with fixed fields for document number and document date for sort capability, applies equally to this punch card scheme. However, it is practically impossible to select against a narrative field in a punch card-only application. The narrative can be used for the purpose of describing a document but the manner whereby records are retrieved from the data file can only be based on document number, document date or other fixed fields. This being the case, more fixed fields would be necessary in a punch card-only system in order to effectively retrieve information, using numeric codes to conserve space. For example, the first five columns of the punch card might be allocated to document number, the next eight columns to document date and three columns committed to a code indicating the witness referenced in a particular record. All the witnesses in a given lawsuit would be alphabetically arranged and then each assigned a three-digit code which would be punched into a card to signify that witness. The next four columns would be used for page number, and two columns would be assigned to allow for coding another witness numeric category. With an eighty column card, such fixed-field coding would take twenty-two columns. Columns 23 through 80 would be committed to digest information or commentary concerning the document. One or two columns must be set aside to provide for a sequence code, a 1 punch indicating the first card in a series of cards describing a given document, 2 for the second card, and so on. This sequence code permits a number of eighty column cards to be linked together in a numeric sequence so that the commentary or digest information can be of variable length extending from one to *n* cards providing sufficient space for a meaningful narrative. This sequence of cards, whether one or *n* describing a single document, constitutes a record.

In a card only system, the documents would be encoded and keypunched into cards, the first card of any given sequence containing the header or fixed field information of date, witness number, document number and so on, and including the beginning of the commentary. The second through *n* cards, containing the balance of the commentary, would simply repeat the document number and contain a sequence code. Once all variable data or documents are coded and keypunched, there is a data base in card form that can be rearranged in a desired sequence by sorting fixed fields. The file of records, contained in a box of cards, would be passed through a card sorter and rearranged in either chronological order or numerical order by witness number or document number. The cards would be kept in the sequence order within record so that the commentary would flow when printed out. This system does not allow for the retrieval of information from the commentary. The commentary is basically a fixed group of information that is associated with a date or document number without independent access. Once the cards have been rearranged by the card sorter in date or document number order, the cards can be taken either to a computer or to another piece of equipment that has the capability of reading cards and listing the information.

Because this simple card-oriented system does not allow for selects against the narrative, and because of the limited number of fixed fields available, it might be necessary in a particular lawsuit to create more than one data base. If additional fixed fields, such as legal contentions or factual contentions were needed, a separate set of cards could be encoded and punched replacing fixed fields in the first set with the additional required fields, and duplicating into the second set the balance of the first, such as document number and the commentary. This process would create a separate data base.

A card oriented approach would provide the attorney with a printout similar to that of Figure 1. If a simple printer is used, one that only reads and prints one card at a time, the width of the printout will be limited to eighty characters. However, the printout in Figure 1 was prepared on a computer capable of reading more than one card at the same time. Therefore, the printout covers a width of 132 characters. The basic difference between the card-only system and the computer system is the ability of the computer to access the narrative, seize upon a particular item of information and retrieve the entire record or a part thereof in document number or date sequence. All the card-only system can do is sort the records in number order, date order or based on another fixed field. The narrative is simply available to the attorney but not accessible by the system.

Finally, a card only system is limited not only by the physical space of the punch card and the inability to select, but also because sorting with a card sorter is a relatively slow process. The entire card file must be passed through a card sorter once for each column of numeric data to be arranged and twice for each column of alpha. If numerous columns are to be sequenced or the data file is large (over 500 records), sorting by means of a card sorter can be very time consuming.

The next level of sophistication above a card-only system is a card-oriented computer system. Basically, the data file is prepared as with the card-only system. However, a computer is used, rather than a card sorter, for rearranging the information in the desired sort sequence. Depending on file size relative to available core, entire card file can be read into the system and stored internally, rearranged by the system at machine speeds, and printed out in the desired sequence. The major drawback of most card-oriented computer systems is the lack of a capability to select against a variable narrative field because of insufficient software support or internal storage. The trade-off is between the cost of internal sorting and the time involved in sorting on the card sorter.

The next level of sophistication is to maintain the data file in a larger computer system with the hardware and software necessary for searching against data files. Larger systems allow for on-line storage of data files which permits the system to access the entire data file simultaneously and select against the variable length narrative fields. This provides the full capability of the generalized systems design discussed above. On-line storage during operation and the software support required are relatively expensive, but the usefulness of on-line data storage and retrieval, in a moderate- to large-size lawsuit, clearly warrants the costs involved.

One method of reducing the cost of the on-line storage computer system is to remove the data file off-line when not in use. Most service bureaus operate in this manner. The data file is kept on a disc pack or a tape until a request is received for information search and retrieval. The file is then mounted onto the system for access. The degree of on-line use will depend upon the frequency of inquiry against the system. The more a data file is on-line, the more costly the use of the system becomes because service bureaus charges are partially based on average monthly on-line storage. To keep costs at a minimum, inquires to the system can be batched and submitted in group to the service bureau. The data base is then mounted on the system and all inquiries processed at the same time. This may be inconvenient in that response to an inquiry is not immediate. The trade-off again is convenience and timeliness of response versus cost. At some point it becomes more economical to keep the data base on-line at all times to have the convenience of immediate response to an inquiry.

Once the data base in on-line continuously, teleprocessing terminals can be utilized. If the computer system is at a service bureau and frequency of inquiry against the system requires immediate turnaround, terminals can be installed in the law firm linked by telephone lines to the computer for immediate response upon inquiry. This is the most sophisticated approach that most law firms will use, and correspondingly the most expensive. It provides a typewriter terminal always available to the attorney for access to the data base. If the attorney is frequently requesting large printouts, a high-speed line printer can be used in place of the typewriter terminal to reduce the cost of connect time to the system.

The next variable in software selection is how the data file is to be fed into the computer. As discussed above, in a card-oriented system the data file is keypunched into cards and the cards, in turn, are fed into the computer. However, by using an on-line terminal to input variable data, one is not constrained to an eighty column or a ninety-six column format and the requirement of a sequence code. This permits use of the computer, and its text editing and data formatting capabilities, at the input stage.

When a data base is being created, the coding sheets, can be sent to the service bureau for encoding into the system by means of their terminal. Because the cost of connect time between the terminal and the CPU is normally a constant, if large data files are required, then it might be more economical for a law firm to acquire its own terminal, for access retrieval, and input. An employee at the law firm, trained in the use of data processing, can transcribe the coding forms directly into the computer utilizing a terminal. Again, there are trade-offs as to cost and efficiency that can only be analyzed in light of a specific case, size of file, availability of trained personnel, and the frequency with which a law firm uses data processing to assist in litigation

USING THE COMPUTER SYSTEM

How one uses the information stored in the computer, applying the generalized systems design considered in this article, is a function of the attorney's imagination. Once narrative information concerning each document/record is stored in the computer, it can be retrieved in any desired order within the limitations of the system. One can select against the narrative, rearrange the information in date or document number sequence and retrieve all or a designated portion of the narrative.

The first litigation stage where this information might be highly useful is during depositions. As documents are collected, they are encoded into the system to provide a chronological framework for the conduct of depositions. As each deposition is taken and documents are gathered on requests to produce, the data base is enlarged, providing an expanded base of information for the conduct of subsequent depositions. Further, if discovery exhibit numbers are used as an item of fixed field information, the printout can be sequenced to list all exhibits to date in exhibit number order for reference at deposition. In the preparation of the deposition, the attorney can go down the narrative and select documents relevant to the deposition and, if necessary, retrieve the original copy. If a deposition is to be conducted on the basis of chronological facts, the attorney can retrieve every document that involves the individual being deposed in date sequence. If the deposition is to be conducted on the basis of factual contentions, the same information for a deponent can be retrieved in factual contention order. The printout itself can be used as a chronological reference because the narrative description of each relevant document will be in date sequence. However, if warranted, a separate printout in document sequence can be called out for gathering the original documents to be taken to the deposition.

In addition to assistance at depositions, the computer data base can aid the attorney in the preparation of pre-trial conference orders. Depending upon the categories of information stored, the data base will have, at least in outline form, the information necessary for the preparation of a pretrial conference order. As discovery progresses, the data base will be continuously enlarged and updated and will presumably include admitted and uncontested facts, contentions of fact and law to be tried, exhibits, names of witnesses, and a narrative analysis of all documents considered to be significant and relevant arranged by any order sequence derivative from the data base. With a minimal amount of effort, the attorney can expand upon the computer printout as is required by the rules of court and, with a vastly reduced amount of effort, especially in a complex trial, prepare the pre-trial conference order.

The computer data base can also be applied to the preparation of a trial book. With this in mind, as the trial date approaches, the attorney can begin to refine his data base by designating those documents which are key to supporting his case and those that will be submitted in evidence. In this process, the attorney is basically creating a refined data base that will become the trial data base Sorts and selects can be made against this refined data base for the preparation of the trial book itself. For example, a command to the computer can create lists of exhibits that will be submitted into evidence. These can be arranged in document number or chronological order or by factual and legal contention to be proved. Similarly, a list can be called out of all significant documents authored by a given individual. These documents can be arranged in both chronological and document number sequence, and used to examine a witness by taking him chronologically through the documents that he prepared.

The system can also be of use during the conduct of the trial. If an event occurs during the progress of the trial which requires additional information for effective response, such as the impeachment of a witness, the attorney can immediately access his on-line data base and retrieve all relevant data. This information in turn can be rearranged by witness within legal or factual contention, and in document or chronological order, or any other arrangement that is required. This information then can be immediately available over terminals at the courthouse or even in the courtroom.

THE COMPUTER QUA EXPERT

The discussion concerning the use of data processing in litigation up to this point has involved the computer merely as the repository for masses of information, using the computer as a library. Although this is a highly important use of data processing, considering the capabilities of the technology available, it is remarkably mundane and does not take advantage of the computer as an analytical tool. Once the attorney gains an understanding of data processing, the outstanding capabilities of this technology can be available to him, with one's imagination being the only real constraint.

One way in which the computer can be of assistance, beyond the mere storage of document records and the printout of these records in a desired sequence, is to prepare summaries of masses of information. When we think of computer summaries, we often think of accounting summaries, payroll or accounts receivables, and additions of columns of numerical information portrayed in statistical or other tabular form. However, the computer can collate and analyze any information that can be numerically delineated and summarize it in tabular or graphical form.

Consider a lawsuit involving the building of an ocean liner. You represent one of the subcontractors suing the general contractor for breach of contract during the construction stage. Your argument is that the general contractor was required to keep all of the construction trades on time according to the construction schedule. Your client, the contractor responsible for painting the interior rooms of the ship, was delayed in construction and ran up sizable overtime costs in order to complete on schedule. You now sue the general contractor for this overage in excess of your bid on the ground that the general contractor breached his responsibility to pace the trades and keep them all on schedule. The defense is that your client mismanaged its own personnel, was unable to coordinate its work crews, and, therefore, the overage and overtime was its own fault. One key to proving your point might be an evaluation of where, chronologically during the construction of the ship, all of the construction trades whose work had to be completed before your client could paint, were working on the project. In other words, if steel decking or electrical or bulk head were late in completing their assigned tasks in a given area of the ship, it was impossible for your client to enter that area of the ship and complete its task. If you could show that the trades that paced your client did not complete on schedule and therefore the only way your client could complete its task on time was to use additional personnel or overtime, you may prevail in the lawsuit.

However, the problem of analyzing the construction of the ship, conceptually simple, becomes inordinately complex because of the mass of information available to the attorney. He may have five to ten thousand progress reports generated by all of the trades showing daily where they were in the ship during construction. There may be an additional ten to twenty thousand documents such as correspondence, inspection reports and minutes of construction meetings that date events during construction. The question then becomes how to collate and analyze all of this information to present to the court a clear visual expression of the delays which occurred during the construction of the ocean liner.

Here is where the computer, acting as an analytical tool, can assist the attorney. The dating of specific events can be encoded into the computer, broken down by area of the ship, by trade involved and by date. Once all of this information is assembled into a data base, the computer can be asked to portray, in graph form, where, within a given time frame, all, or one or a collection of trades were working in given areas of the ship. Graphs can be called out by week, by day, by all trades, by client against a particular other trade, within one or all or some of the areas of the ship, and compared with the construction schedule and payroll data.

Because it is possible to attach to the computer a cathode ray tube (CRT), a terminal device similar to a television screen, the attorney can sit down in front of the CRT and key in a request to the computer to display what construction events were occurring in a given area of the ship within a given time frame. This time frame will be displayed visually on the CRT. Another request to the computer can expand the time frame either backward or forward in time, and other pacing trades or factual events can be added or deleted from the graphical presentation. This information can be manipulated as it is displayed, and the attorney can begin to analyze the facts that are available to him, using the computer, in order to prove his lawsuit.

Further, payroll information can be fed into the system and displayed in conjunction with the graph of a given time frame of construction to show whether, at a particular point in time, your client was incurring overtime. Also, the construction schedule itself can be put into the system and overlaid against what was going on during construction to show where other trades were off the construction schedule and where their delay in turn caused your client to be delayed in its task.

After the attorney has determined what time frames and what events are significant to proving his position, he can then request that the computer provide him with graphical and statistical summaries of the information stored within it. This information can be summarized by bar charts, continuous line graphs, overlays of graphs or other forms. If the proper foundation were laid, these summaries, a composite of what occurred during the construction of the ship, could be submitted into evidence, to provide the court and jury with a manageable representation of what occurred in a complex factual situation.

This construction case is only one example of how the computer can be used to assist the attorney in analyzing the facts available and collating these facts in some organized fashion. What makes this example perhaps revolutionary is that the computer and the attorney interact in analyzing the data and evaluating its significance. The computer and attorney are basically in a conversational mode whereby the attorney bounces ideas off the computer and the computer, with its factual data base, tries to support those ideas. If the computer cannot, the attorney tries a new factual hypothesis. It is this give and take that moves this example beyond the mere storage and retrieval of information to the use of the computer to its real potential. The computer is no longer merely used in an accounting sense, storing and retrieving, but is now simulating events and evaluating hypotheses. The computer becomes a powerful analytical tool, not merely an organizational tool, providing the ability to grasp and analyze thousands of documents as though they were ten or fifteen. Without this capability, the attorney would have to guess as to what were significant documents, events and dates because of the impossibility of grappling with such a mass of information. Without the computer, there is a great probability that highly significant information would be unavailable merely because of the impossibility of understanding it.

CONCLUSION

This article has attempted to provide the reader with a threshold knowledge of data processing and a generalized conceptual framework for using the computer in litigation. It cannot be viewed as a how-to-do-it manual, but rather an attempt to provide that minimal amount of information which the attorney needs in order to ask intelligent questions of the experts in the computer industry. The attorney should not try to use data processing in litigation, or in any other application, without consulting systems engineers or other data processing specialists whose job it is to understand the capabilities of the computer. The world of data processing is as complex and sophisticated as any discipline. The attorney should approach the use of data processing on that basis. With a moderate amount of information, he can formulate what he hopes to accomplish and to address intelligent questions to computer experts. Further, he will be able to understand the answers of the computer experts as they try to design a system to assist in the conduct of his art.

With an understanding of data processing, the attorney will be able to provide better service to his clients at reduced cost as well as handle complex cases involving mass information. Using the technology available, he can effectively and efficiently marshal the mass of data at his disposal and correlate this data to his legal knowledge of the case. This combination should prove to be highly effective.

Figure 1

000001	05/10/70	DEP	D/1, A/Jones, B. Moved from 15 East 50th, Los Angeles to 17 Kenneth Blvd.,	4
			Glendale. Increased square footage. P/6-7.	5
				6
000002	01/00/68	DEP	L/3, D/2, A/Jones, B. M. Smith was office manager when EDP was introduced, had	8
			no prior EDP experience. P/9-10, P/11/18-24.	9
				10
000004	07/19/69	DEP	L/1, F/1, A/Jones, B. No recollection of anything said by defendant about comparison	12
			of defendant's computer to others. P/19/7-10.	13
				14
000006	01/00/69	DEP	D/2, D/11, A/Jones, B. Business was increasing while EDP was installed. Has progress	17
			charts in office to show 10-15-20% increase a year. Increased dock and office staff.	18
			Extra office manager because M. Smith devoted time to DPE. Released office manager	20
			since terminating EDP. P/24 to P/25/17.	20
				21
000007	01/00/70	DEP	D/11, A/Jones, B. Business decreased since 1970 because they had to impose higher	23
			costs. There was also a delay caused by the computer delaying the production of	24
			paperwork. Also decreased after computer removed in 1971, but doesn't know why.	25
			P/25/18 to P/26/22.	26
				27
000008	05/13/71	DEP	S/1, D/6, A/Jones, B. Paper cost went out of sight. Disc problems. 20-25 percent	30
			down time. No recollection of whether manual forms could be used. No change for disc.	32
			Increase caused by disc having to begin all over every time it went down. No recall of	33
			defendant recommending this procedure. Failure almost every night. Records kept that	34
			would enable mathematical computation of forms used. Keeps invoices for supplies for	35
			seven years. P/27/31.	35
				36

000012 07/19/69 DEP F/1, A/Jones, B. Defendant promised that EDP would cut cost, be faster, use less 38
people, a lot of peripheral information at no cost. Reason they went for data processing 39
was the promise of magic. P/34/4-18. 40

41

000013 01/00/68 DEP L/3, A/Jones, B. M. Jones has no knowledge of EDP. Neither did anyone else in the 43
office. P/34/3. 43

44

000014 02/12/71 DEP D/2, D/6, A/Jones, B. Was not involved in preparation. (Defex/N/MRD). P/36/22, 46
P/44/10. 46

47

000017 07/19/69 LET L/1, F/2, A/Gray, J., R/Jones, B. Demonstration of computer. Can deliver card 50
system and disc subsystem. Help you convert from present system. Pex/A/COM, 51
N1. Defex/A/INI. 52

000018 07/31/69 LET L/1, F/3, A/Gray, J., R/Jones, B. Confirming telephone conversation, requested 54
commitments of daily schedule. No particular conversion problem on three major 55
programs provided they are begun by 08/07/70. Pex/B/COM, Defex/B/INI. 56

57

000019 08/02/69 LET L/1, F/2, S/4, A/Gray, J., R/Jones, B. Delivery schedule. First step is direct conver- 58
sion. Defendant will convert two major programs, manifest and freight bill, and will 59
provide guidance to programmers in converting other programs. Step two is a program- 60
ming and operational system change from card to disc. Convert two programs, guide 61
others. Step three is equipment substitution. Any program changes made with guidance. 62
Description of proposed system and specification sheets attached. 63

ABSTRACT INPUT FORM

CONTROL INFORMATION:

Entry No.: 0 0 ___ ___ ___ ___ Pert. Date: ___ ___ / ___ ___ / ___ ___

Doc.
Type: ___ LET ___ DEP ___ INT ______ ___ ___ ___
___ MEM ___ FIN ___ TEC ______ ___ ___ ___

Liability Subjects: Fraud Subjects:

Mod Frt

Disk Sys ______ L/1 ______ ______ L/4 ______ ______ L/7 Fraud ______ F/1
Card Sys ______ L/2 ______ ______ L/5 ______ ______ L/8 ______ ______ F/2
Bill Prog ______ L/3 ______ ______ L/6 ______ ______ L/9 ______ ______ F/3

Damage Subjects:

Space ___ D/1 O/T-Dock ___ D/5 Perif rntl ___ D/9 ______ ___ D/13
Reg Time ___ D/2 Cptr forms ___ D/6 Constructn ___ D/10 ______ ___ D/14
O/T-Adm ___ D/3 Othr Suppl ___ D/7 Cust Loss ___ D/11 ______ ___ D/15
O/T-Cptr ___ D/4 Hrdw rntl ___ D/8 ________ ___ D/12 ______ ___ D/16

General Subjects:

Downtime _____S/1 ____________S/3 ____________S/5 ____________S/7
________ _____S/2 ____________S/4 ____________S/6 ____________S/8

Author: A/ ________________, ______ Recipient: R/ ________________, ______
Last F.I. Last F.I.

Digest Information:

____

____

____

____

____

____

Pex/__________ Defex __________ Pla/__________ Def/__________ P/__________
Page/line

Abstracted By: ______________________ Date: ___ ___ / ___ ___ / ___ ___
Entered By: ______________________ Date: ___ ___ / ___ ___ / ___ ___
Proofed By: ______________________ Date: ___ ___ / ___ ___ / ___ ___

Figure 2

Control Information
Document No. _ _ _ _ _ _ - _ _ P/_ _ _ L/_ _ _
Trial Exhibit No: _ _ _ Discovery Exhibit No: _ _ _
Document Date: _ _ / _ _ / _ _

Digest Information:
Document Type Cd: Let ______ Int ______ Prr ______
Dep ______ Mem ______ Drw ______
Legal Contention: LC/__, LC/__, LC/__, LC/__, LC/__,
Factual Contention: FC/__, FC/__, FC/__, FC/__, FC/__,

I.
[Author] [Person] AP/______________, ___, [Recipient] [Person RP/______________, ___,
Last F.I. Last F.I.
[Author] [Company] AC/______________, [Recipient] [Company] RC/______________
Courtesy copy: cc/______________, cc/______________
Last Last

II.
[Witness] [Person] WP/______________, ______, [Witness] WC/______________
Last F.I.
Parties Involved in Testimony
TW/______________; TW/______________.
Last Last
TW/______________; TW/______________.
Last Last

Narrative:

____

____

____

Figure 3

21

Computer-Generated Evidence Specially Prepared for Use at Trial

Martha M. Jenkins

Computers are not magic. Computers and their workings are not even—at least conceptually—all that complicated. Nevertheless, computers make it possible to consider, collate, manipulate, and analyze millions of discrete items of information, a task we humans have neither the time nor powers of concentration to perform effectively.

Though computer-generated evidence can do nothing which lawyers have not been doing via testimonial, documentary, real or demonstrative evidence for years, computers make it possible to present the same kinds of evidence on a much grander scale and to deal with larger volumes and more complex manipulations, often at less cost. This article will explore these latter possibilities. The uses of the computer as a substantive as well as a litigation management aid are mind boggling. It is hoped that this article will encourage lawyers to consider what the computer can do for them in a variety of cases and to constantly be on the lookout for new applications.

It is not the function of this article to be pessimistic. Nevertheless, it would be irresponsible not to issue a brief warning. While the computer may be used to generate, for use at trial, evidence that can aid in the "search for truth," it may also be used carelessly or in a biased fashion. Because the law on the admissibility of computer-generated evidence is still in the developmental stage, casual or greedy use of this tool may adversely affect its growth. Computer-generated evidence tends to mesmerize factseekers and relax their natural critical natures, yet there is great danger of it being erroneous, misleading or unreliable. The underlying data may be full of errors or discrepancies, or it may, for one reason or another, be irrelevant or improper as evidence. The data may have been fed into the computer inaccurately. The computer may have been improperly programmed or not programmed to detect errors. The assumptions on which the program was based may be wrong, illogical or simply irrelevant to the issues sought to be proved. Each one of these potential problem areas must be guarded against by proponents and assiduously investigated by counsel opposing the evidence.

While there are almost no reported decisions on the admissibility of computer-generated evidence that has been specially prepared for trial, the state of the art would lead one to believe that such evidence is frequently used in creative ways. If so, wise and skillful counsel and courts must have done so without the kind of evidentiary disputes which lead to published opinions.

THE RANGE OF POSSIBILITIES

Computers can perform a number of functions which may be very useful in the context of litigation.[1] In particular, the ability of the computer to rapidly summarize and manipulate a large volume of data has made it useful in executing the technical aspects of models.

One class of models commonly used and of great potential use to litigators deals with the simulation of physical events—simulation models. These models accept data which is representative of actual events, manipulate this data according to sets of rules which represent how the world works and present results which are an approximation of the actual results.

One potentially useful simulation model is based on what economists call "queuing theory." The queuing theory, as the name suggests, basically means to line things up. It is a model used to determine the optimum allocation of resources or to show how something runs. An example of a common use of queuing theory models is that of a bank which wants to determine the most efficient method of serving customers, e.g., how many teller windows it should have, whether it should have teller windows for all transactions or whether teller windows should be designated to handle specific kinds of transactions. The bank creates a model to process in the computer the information it has on the number of people who will want to be served, some random pattern of their coming in, what

[1]The author particularly appreciates the suggestions and aid of James A. Sprowl, Carol P. Eastin, Jerome J. Roberts and J. David DeHetre.

times of day demands for service are heaviest, how many and what kinds of transactions people will engage in and any other relevant data. The model, when executed utilizing the data described above, will tell the bank what use of tellers and windows will most efficiently serve its customers. Any case involving allocation or "best use" of resources might be ripe for construction of this type of model.

Other types of simulation models are designed to duplicate physical or mechanical motions. This kind of model is common in industry. It is most frequently used in the design of products, particularly products with moving parts such as machinery, automobiles and aircraft, to determine how they will stand up to the stresses to which they will be exposed. A model of this type would be useful, for example, in a product liability case to determine whether a particular failure was the result of a design defect and was predictable.

An interesting example of a model simulating physical or mechanical motions was given by R. Crawford Morris of Arter & Hadden, Cleveland, Ohio when he spoke on the use of computers in medical malpractice cases at the American Bar Association Litigation Section National Institute in New York in March, 1975. In the example he discussed, a patient had been treated and subsequently died, allegedly from radiation burns. The patient had a tumor in his head, and his doctors had prescribed a certain radiological treatment. The treatment was later reconstructed via computer. The precise measurement of the patient's skull, the location of the tumor and the direction, timing and strength of the radiological treatment was all fed into the computer. The parties were thus able to determine that the radiological treatment ordered was, in fact, not the appropriate one, that the burns were caused by the treatment, and that the patient died as a result of them.

Simulation models can also simulate particular environments such as the ecology of the entire world, the economy of the United States or the workings of a particular industry, business or organization. They may be used to predict what may happen in the model environment if a particular course of action is followed. For example, econometric models are commonly used to manipulate economic indicators to show what the economy is going to do. Similar models are used to simulate businesses to determine the effects of various courses of action. They are also used retroactively to determine what happened or whether a particular course of action was a reasonable one.[2] At least one large corporation has an executive game room where executives play with corporate models and are given prizes for having the most profitable business or the happiest employees.

[2]*See* accompanying symposium article by Carol P. Eastin.

Business schools have also developed models of the business environment for use as a teaching tool.

Environmental and ecological areas are appropriate for the use of simulation models for determining scientific facts such as what effect a particular substance might have on the environment. The purpose is to precipitate rational decisionmaking.[3] Environmental impact reports required by the National Environmental Policy Act of 1969 (NEPA) are frequently prepared with the aid of computer technology and mathematical modeling.[4]

An especially interesting project involving a simulation model of the environment is described in an article by Bruce Ackerman and James Sawyer.[5] The Delaware River Basin Commission consisting of representatives of the various riparian states and several federal agencies was formed to control the development of the Delaware River Basin and to alleviate water pollution. There were many problems in terms of comparative pollution, the unequal costs to each polluter of purifying its effluent and, in general, the allocation of the burdens of cleaning up the river. The Department of the Interior constructed a mathematical model simulating the impact of pollutants discharged by industries and cities along the river. This model was used to attempt to quantify the costs and benefits of a variety of proposed clean-up programs.

Another use of a simulation model might be in the area of zoning. A computer model could be constructed of a town. Elements relevant to the essentials of zoning decisions such as streets and traffic patterns, schools, utilities, necessity for open spaces and other variables would be programmed into the model. An application for a zoning variance could then be tested initially with this town model and its effects upon critical elements noted. If the model were not constructed until after litigation began, the decision could later be tested as to its reasonableness.

[3]*E.g.*, Pierce & Gutfreund, *Evidentiary Aspects of Air Dispersion Modeling and Air Quality Measurements in Environmental Litigation and Administrative Proceedings*, 25 Federation Ins. Coun. Q. 341 (1975); Ackerman & Sawyer, *The Uncertain Search for Environmental Policy; Scientific Factfinding and Rational Decisionmaking Along the Delaware River,* 120 U. Pa. L. Rev. 419 (1972). *See also* Crowther v. Seaborg, 315 F. Supp. 1205 (D. Colo. 1970) in which computers are not specifically mentioned, but the data accepted by the court was highly technical and the opinion is replete with words like "projected," "extrapolate," and "estimated." The case involved an attempt to enjoin detonation of nuclear devices as a means of obtaining natural gas from nonporous rock formations. The case turned on whether the court was satisfied with the Atomic Energy Commission's projection of the adequacy of their safety devices against projections of possible harmful radiation effects.

[4]Examples of environmental impact statements are frequently published in or reviewed in the Ecology Law Quarterly.

[5]Ackerman & Sawyer, *The Uncertain Search for Environmental Policy: Scientific Factfinding and Rational Decisionmaking Along the Delaware River,* 120 U. Pa. L. Rev. 419 (1972).

A model of a geographical area might also be used by businesses to select sites for stores, outlets or offices, or to uphold the business necessity or reasonableness of such selection at a later time in the face of an antitrust claim, shareholders' derivative claim or tort claim. Similar models could be used in an antitrust case to determine whether a merger or acquisition might lessen competition. They could also be used to help define a relevant market or to determine whether a particular anticompetitive practice would injure another's business or property.[6]

The use of computer models in construction cases is of growing benefit to litigators. In cases where delay damages or contract payments turn on what went wrong and whose fault it was, the "critical path" analysis of construction progress is of great use. The critical path method is not new, but its sophistication through the use of the computer is. A critical path analysis of how a construction project is to proceed typically is made prior to the beginning of construction. A similar analysis can be made at the end of a project to analyze what actually occurred and identify which events were the cause of delays. The critical path program can be written to consider when each contractor began working, the phases of the work in which he was engaged, the calendar days and employee man-days spent by the contractor, strikes, weather, delivery of materials and supplies, delivery of necessary equipment and other factors affecting the progress of the construction.[7] The program can recreate the status of the project at particular points in time, identify the effects of events on the progress of the project or demonstrate the timely completion of the project if a particular subcontractor had performed as promised or if some other event had not occurred.

A model might also be utilized simply to take a complex situation and put it into a more comprehensible form. Perhaps a particular

[6]*See* Lozowick, Steiner & Miller, *Law and Quantitative Multivariate Analysis: An Encounter*, 66 Mich. L. Rev. 1641 (1968), describing complex economic and statistical calculations to define the relevant market in a bank merger case. *See generally Bibliography on Economic and Scientific Proof*, ABA Section on Antitrust Law 1973; Bok, *Section 7 of the Clayton Act and the Merging of Law and Economics*, 74 Harv. L. Rev. 226 (1960). For a sometimes entertaining debate injecting some balance into the infusion of economics, computers and higher mathematics into the law, see the articles discussing Posner, *Economic Analysis of Law* (1973); Polinsky, *Economic Analysis as a Potentially Defective Product: A Buyer's Guide to Posner's Economic Analysis of Law*, 87 Harv. L. Rev 1655 (1974); Leff, *Economic Analysis of Law: Some Realism About Nominalism*, 60 Va. L. Rev. 451 (1974).

[7]Joseph E. Bennett Co., Board of Contract Appeals, G.S.A., 4 C.L.S.R. 1022, GSBCA-72-1, 2362 (1972), discussed a critical path method construction plan reduced to computer logic. In that case, however, the Board of Contract Appeals refused to accept the critical path construction plan as fully reliable because of mathematical errors, the degree to which the plan ignored apparently forseeable winter weather conditions, and changes made to the schedule when it was computerized for purposes of the litigation.

section of the Internal Revenue Code could be isolated and its rules programmed. Real data could then be fed into the computer to see the effect of the application of the rules. This would allow evaluation of whether the policies behind the rules are being served in situations where either the Code or the facts are too complex to conceptualize.

Statistical analysis is facilitated through the use of computer models. Statistical models consist of certain operating assumptions. Data is fed into the computer and manipulated according to the operating assumptions to test whether the statistical results are likely to have happened randomly or as the result of other causative factors. Employment discrimination is an area particularly susceptible to statistical analysis via the computer to show the probability that out of a given labor market a company intentionally discriminated in the hiring of particular groups of people or that the hiring ratios of the company could have occurred randomly.[8]

Computers are also increasingly used in cases where other kinds of statistical proofs are necessary. For example, in the antitrust area, in bid-rigging or price-fixing cases the computer can be useful in ascertaining patterns of behavior that previously would have been excruciatingly difficult to find.[9]

In addition to executing models, computers may be used in a complicated case merely to collate and summarize data into a form which can be understood by counsel, judges, and juries. Complex securities, antitrust or criminal fraud cases would be ideal for such treatment.

[8]A discussion of the use of models in employment discrimination situations may be found in Dawson, *Probabilities and Prejudice in Establishing Statistical Inferences,* 13 Jurimetrics J. 191 (1973); Ewald, *Discovery and the Computer,* 1 Litigation 27 (1975). *See also* Note, *Beyond the Prima Facie Case in Employment Discrimination Law: Statistical Proof and Rebuttal,* 89 Harv. L. Rev. 387 (1975).

[9]In terms of statistics, with or without computer technology, see the jury discrimination cases of the civil rights era. Alexander v. Louisiana, 405 U.S. 625 (1972); Whitus v. Georgia, 385 U.S. 545 (1967); Swain v. Alabama, 380 U.S. 202 (1965). *See also* Gairys, *Juror Selection: The Law & Mathematical Method of Analysis, and a Case Study,* 10 Am. Crim. L. Rev. 77 (1972); Finklestein, *The Application of Statistical Decision Theory to the Jury Discrimination Cases,* 80 Harv. L. Rev. 338 (1968). Also of interest are some of the cases applying statistical methods to the identification of defendants in criminal cases. They should at least make one think before playing too fast and loose with statistical proofs or models. State v. Coolidge, 109 N.H. 403, 260 A.2d 547 (1969); People v. Heard, 266 Cal. App. 2d 747, 72 Cal. Rptr. 374 (1968); Miller v. State, 240 Ark. 340, 399 S.W.2d 268 (1966); State v. Sneed, 76 N.M. 349, 414 P.2d 858 (1966); People v. Trujillo, 32 Cal. 2d 105, 194 P.2d 681 (1948); People v. Risley, 214 N.Y. 75, 108 N.E. 200 (1915); Kingston, *Application of Probability Theory in Criminalistics,* 60 J. of Am. Statistical Ass'n 1028 (1975); Kingston & Kirk, *The Use of Statistics in Criminalistics,* 55 J. of Crim. L.C. & P.S. 514 (1964); Finkelstein & Fairley, *A Bayesian Approach to Identification Evidence,* 73 Harv. L. Rev. 489 (1970); Tribe, *Trial by Mathematics: Precision and Retrial in the Legal Process,* 84 Harv. L. Rev. 1329 (1971); Finkelstein & Fairley, *The Continuing Debate over Mathematics in the Law of Evidence,* 84 Harv. L. Rev. 1801 (1971); Tribe, *A Further Critique of Mathematical Proof,* 84 Harv. L. Rev. 1810 (1971).

The possible uses of the computer to execute models, to facilitate statistical inference, to simulate environments or to aid in the decisionmaking process are endless. In addition to the uses already suggested, this technology could be used to determine the optimum management of investment portfolios, the impact of pornography or capital punishment or an optimum reapportionment plan. There is an infinite variety of possible uses.

While essentially extraneous to this article, the usefulness of computers can be turned around. Since the state of the art offers many analytical tools, perhaps a reasonably prudent person must use them. Thus, a person or business entity could be held liable for the failure to use computer models to determine the effects of a course of action, for the failure to control a potentially dangerous industrial process or for the failure to train personnel operating nuclear power stations or aircraft with simulated environments and simulated emergencies.

THE ADMISSIBILITY OF COMPUTER-GENERATED EVIDENCE SPECIALLY PREPARED FOR LITIGATION

Though the reported cases are few, some courts and administrative agencies have dealt with the question of the admissibility of computer-generated data developed specifically for use at trial. This question must be distinguished from the admissibility of computer-generated business records.[10]

In *United States v. Dioguardi,*[11] the defendants were charged with fraudulently transferring and concealing property of a bankrupt and fraudulently concealing assets from the trustee in bankruptcy. To prove its case, the prosecutor made a computer run of the inventory, daily sales and purchases to determine when items of inventory were or should have been exhausted on a specific basis and as a whole. The court had no trouble admitting the computer-generated evidence, but it did chastise the government for not turning the computer program over to the defense. It seems obvious that the defense should have been given the program since it was specifically developed for use at the trial. The question of the producibility of a program is more troublesome where the program is a regular business program of the

[10]*See generally* Younger, *Computer Print-Outs in Evidence: Ten Objections and How to Overcome Them,* 2 Litigation 28 (1975); Freed, Fenwick & McGonigal, *Mock Trial: Admissibility of Computerized Business Records,* 15 Jurimetrics J. 206 (1975); Roberts, *A Practitioner's Primer on Computer-Generated Evidence,* 41 U. Chi. L. Rev. 254 (1974); Freed, *Computers and Law—A Reference Work* (4th ed. 1974); Bigelow, *Researching Computer Law,* 20 Prac. Law. 71 (1974).

[11]448 F. 2d 1033 (2d Cir. 1970).

organization which was developed at great time and expense, the production of which could conceivably result in the loss of a competitive advantage. Protective orders may be readily fashioned, however, to protect against all such contingencies.

Computer studies are frequently reported in administrative proceedings, though the opinions are not particularly helpful here. For example, common carriers frequently computerize many of the studies they are required to file in pursuit of higher rates, different operating authorities or other changes they seek from the Interstate Commerce Commission.[12] As lawyers become more aware of the possible uses of the computer, the written authorities should increase rapidly.

General evidentiary considerations

Due to the dearth of reported cases on specially prepared computer-generated evidence, no firm evidentiary rules can be given for the admissibility of such documents. Nor can one do more than speculate because of the infinite variety of possible uses, underlying data sources, and factual and legal contexts. The authority for the admissibility of these programs will vary only with the imagination of the attorney seeking their admissibility and the type of computer-generated data which is sought to be admitted.

A highly respected jurist and scholar once told the author that one could get anything into evidence if one was open-minded and gave

[12]The main argument in those cases has not been so much the admissibility of the studies per se, as whether the carriers attempting to introduce those studies have supplied underlying data and other information to their adversaries. *See, e.g.*, Aggregate Weight Provisions on Paper, Mass. to N.Y. and N.J., 323 I.C.C. 525, 1 C.L.S.R. 327 (1974) (Unit cost study based on annual report not admitted because of failure to have a qualified witness available for cross-examination having knowledge of the preparation of the study and for failure to have any underlying data available); Glass Bottles, Muskogee, Okla. to Chicago Group, 323 I.C.C. 258, 1 C.L.S.R. 306 (1964) (Cost analysis study for 23 carriers would be admissible when a qualified person was made available to explain who selected the data input and the basis of the selection, the manner in which the data was processed, and that the procedure complied with that generally accepted); American Colloid Co. v. Akron, Canton & Youngstown R. Co., 321 I.C.C. 91, 1 C.L.S.R. 244 (1963) (Computer cost analysis offered to show railroad rates were too high was admitted over objection because underlying data and working papers were made available with any deficiencies going to its weight not its admissibility). The I.C.C. recognizes the usefulness of computers in making the complicated studies it requires. 49 C.F.R. §1104.3(d) requires, for example, that, when a computer is used in making a required cost study, a manual application of the costing procedure for one traffic and cost study carrier be submitted with the computer study to demonstrate the procedures by which the computer program distributes the annual report statistics and applies service unit-costs for each shipment. *See also* 49 C.F.R. §1104.10 (1974) which requires all underlying data to be made available. *See generally* Finklestein, *Regression Models*, 86 Harv. L. Rev. 1442 (1973) (Regression models purport to furnish estimates of the economic effect of changes in a factor subject to regulatory control on the assumption that other factors will remain constant or change according to a certain set of rules).

the matter enough thought and study. While the author has not tested this thesis—and would hate to have to do so for some of the more blatant examples of improper evidence that can be imagined—it is, nevertheless, an admonition not to let anything go too easily. In the computer area there are many possible avenues of approach beginning with business records, opinion evidence, scientific and demonstrative evidence, samples, polls, summaries or any combination of these or other rules of evidence.

Some computer-generated evidence will be admissible because it is based entirely on underlying business records and perhaps is merely a compilation or summary of those records even though it was prepared solely for use at trial and is organized differently from the originals. *Dioguardi* is an example of this type of evidence. The Federal Rules of Evidence sections 803(6) and 1006 read together permit such evidence. Bid-fixing information in an antitrust case may also fall into this category. The computer may be the only way to summarize all of the relevant dates, bidders, and prices into a comprehensible form.

Some computer-generated evidence, for example, models of a business environment, may be admissible as expert opinion evidence. The oral testimony of an expert could be based on a computer study or model which had processed the sort of evidence typically considered by the expert in his field,[13] or it could be typical for the expert in the particular field to rely on just such a model as happens to have been constructed. A good deal of support for this is lent by Federal Rules of Evidence section 703, which states:[14]

> The facts or data in the particular case upon which an expert bases an opinion or inference may be those perceived by or made known to him at or before the hearing. *If of a type reasonably relied upon by experts in the particular field in forming opinions or inferences upon the subject, the facts or data need not be admissible in evidence.*

Some types of computer-generated evidence, for example, the evaluation of radiological treatment described above, may be admissible as demonstrative or scientific evidence on much the same basis as a physical model of a railroad crossing or a laboratory test might be admitted.

In terms of the practicalities of admissibility, the attorney should disclose to opposing counsel and the court at the earliest possible point in litigation an intention to use computer-generated data.[15] This may have a number of advantages. First, if the case is presided over

[13]How much different from this was the evidence in Brown v. Board of Education, 347 U.S. 483 (1954) and its progeny or the "Brandeis Briefs"?

[14]Fed. R. Evid. 703 (emphasis added). *See also* Fed. R. Evid. 705, 402.

[15]*See* Manual for Complex Litigation §§2.70 *et seq.*

by a judge who still thinks computers are a newfangled invention, the judge will have a chance to become acclimated to the idea. Second, opposing counsel may well have objections to the manner in which the attorney offering the evidence wishes to proceed. To the extent the attorney is able to obviate an opponent's objections at this point or even to enlist his affirmative assistance, the opponent may well become, if not bound by the results of the attorney's program, at least estopped from making certain objections. Third, it is extremely important to give the opposing side the opportunity to conduct full discovery as to the validity of the underlying data; the selection of that data; the validity of the program and of the assumptions that the program makes; the reliability of the programming, the data input and the computer itself; and whether the end results of the program are appropriate to the original assumptions and techniques. As a caveat to those opposing admissibility, full advantage of discovery should be taken and objections noted prior to trial. No counsel should be permitted at trial to go on a fishing expedition or to suggest vague possibilities of problems with the computer-generated evidence. For example, the suggestion that on a ninety degree summer day the electricity load was so high that the transmission voltage was irregular and might have adversely affected the computer's functioning should be rejected out of hand unless counsel has proof that such a contingency did, in fact, have a deleterious effect on the computer.

Admissibility should depend on whether the computer-generated data is related to a material issue in the case; whether the data fits within a chain of inferences which would connect the data to an ultimate issue in the case; and whether the data can and will be presented in such a manner that it will not unduly confuse the issues or so confound and overawe the jury (if it is a jury trial) that it would be prejudicial to the opposing side.[16] In actuality, this analysis is no more than what counsel should do in every case. Counsel should have a clear idea prior to going to trial what the basic propositions are that must be proved. Evidence should be available to prove each of those propositions, and there should be a clear chain of proof from each element of proof through permissible inferences to the ultimate elements of the claim for relief.

Conclusion

Many companies now offer ready-made programs to assist attorneys in some or all of the areas suggested. Many universities and business

[16]*See* Fed. R. Evid. 401-03. A similar analysis is made with respect to criminal cases in Dawson, *supra* note 8, at 193.

schools have knowledgeable people who have already developed programs to do some or all of the things suggested in this article. Bar associations around the country are offering informative seminars relating to the use of computers. Law schools are beginning to offer courses in quantitative methods and the law or computers and the law. It should be an interesting though not very predictable future.

22

The Computer and the Practice of Law: Litigation Support

Robert S. Arthur

Some lawyers still need to be convinced of the functional inevitability of the computer in their work. Rather than taking a look at the distant future, let us consider the professional (r)evolution that will be largely complete by 1990. We are well on the way now, as a recent market survey showed that 83 per cent of law firms with more than fifty lawyers who responded stated that not only do they use electronic data processing but also that they have in-house computers.

Depending on which futurist one prefers, we are now in what is variously called the Post-Industrial Society, the Information Age or the Service Economy. In fact, the latter two are characteristics of the Post-Industrial Society and particularly describe what may be termed the "legal industry."

Computers are utilized in the legal industry in response to developments in the high technology, complex Post-Industrial Society, the demands of the Information Age and the economic reality of a services economy and service-oriented industry.

While the legal profession is old and perhaps relatively slow to change, its clientele operates in a rapidly changing, technology-dependent environment. Business enterprises and the organizations of society grow ever more complex. This has contributed to increasing specialization in all the professions. No longer can one professional gain mastery in both breadth and depth in order to serve clients in several industries, so breadth of practice is sacrificed in order to learn about and succeed in a client's special environment.

The Information Age is characterized by the proliferation of information, its ephemeral character, and the problem of dissemination. While one response has been to specialize ever more narrowly, a second is the development of rapid communication systems. One goal of the technological developments is to increase the speed of updating and dissemination of information and to make the necessary exchanging of information economically feasible. A second goal is to provide easy access on a reactive basis for the immediate need.

Because the information sector of the economy is so large, increasing attention is paid to servicing it. This results in rapidly evolving information processing and storage technologies.

The legal industry is only one of many in the information sector, but developments may be generalized across the sector as a whole: some new systems designed for education, for example, are easily and readily adapted to meet the demands of the law. Other systems, particularly in information processing, are so basic that their application requires no adaptation at all.

The legal profession, as part of the service sector of the economy, is subject to the same economic pressures that inflation imposes on all service industries. These pressures are more intense than in the goods-producing sector of the economy. While wages may account for only 30 per cent of the cost of a product, they can be as much as 70 per cent of the total cost of a service. A 10 per cent increase in wages (a cost-of-living increase to keep up with inflation) may add 3 per cent to the cost of goods (which can be partly offset by increasing productivity), but it adds a significant 7 per cent to the cost of a service.

Productivity in the service sector grows at an average of only 1.2 to 1.9 per cent a year. This intensifies the demand for automation—the substitution of equipment for people.

These elements in the national environment suggest why the computer is involved here and now.

THE HOW OF THE COMPUTER

The applications of the computer in the legal industry are varied and represented in a new vocabulary: the library becomes a "data base," the typewriter yields to the "word processing unit," the document archive becomes a "magnetic tape record," and the card catalogue is a "digital index." Lawyers and judges, moreover, have to deal with new specialists—"systems analysts" and "computer operators," for example—to apply the computer to the professional problems.

THE JUDICIAL SYSTEM: AUTOMATED COURT CALENDAR

While having minimum impact on lawyers, the computerization of court calendars has benefited the part of the legal industry that administers justice, primarily by eliminating the need for manpower for some tedious administrative tasks. The computer can select in a matter of minutes a random group to call for jury duty. By making economically feasible the integration of registered drivers with the traditional lists of voter registration, court administrators can attempt to balance the pool to reflect the community. For example, while the voter registration list includes roughly 65 per cent of the adult population in Hennepin County in Minnesota (including Minneapolis), the integration of licensed drivers in the pool increases that figure to 97 per cent of the adult population, which substantially increases the number of young adults and minorities available to be called.

When a court automates case scheduling, the data base becomes less the proprietary personal knowledge of the court clerk, who is subject to such human tendencies as illness, vacation and retirement, and more generally available to those who must rely on that information.

In Hennepin County, where the criminal court calendar is automated, the case data base contains a complete history, including information from the presentence investigation and actions by judges prior to disposition. It is available to the numerous agencies involved in a criminal case. It may be presumed that less imperfect information flow leads to better case management and perhaps less imperfect justice. In the long range, the court base will yield statistics enabling the court administrator to project staffing more accurately and all the adjunct agencies to analyze their own case management operations and efficiencies.

IN THE LAW OFFICE

Word processing and accounting

The use of computers for such tasks as document preparation and billing is a natural, and few lawyers raise objections to automating these activities. In view of the economic pressures on a service industry, it is clear why a segment of the legal business that is especially vulnerable to the demand to reduce the wages share of service costs is document preparation and accounting. Combine the pressure factor with the fact that word processing and accounting systems are panindustrial and highly cost efficient, and one can understand why this phase of the evolution is well on its way.

The side benefit of automation of the timekeeping and accounting system is the improvement of time management analysis and planning as needed by any small- or medium-sized business.

Legal research

With more litigation producing more case law, with a multifold increase in statutory law, and with increasing activity in administrative law, a major challenge is the integration, updating, dissemination and storage of the contents of the law library.

The computer is an invaluable research tool in other disciplines chiefly because the knowledge is collected and organized in a far less systematic and rigorous form than in law. When searching reference material in sociology or economics, for instance, one must be creative in identifying a multitude of classifications used to describe one topic. Legal research is unlike these disciplines, because it has specific conceptual and substantive classifications.

For this reason, lawyers have less need for features such as "keyword" text searches. Using traditional legal research techniques, the legal researcher is relatively sure of identifying pertinent references. The computer's benefits to the lawyer are the access to material not stored in one's own law library and the speed of identification and access. The saving in research time is measured in hours rather than in the days or months as realized by researchers in other disciplines.

Computerized legal research is available on a subscription basis from two major suppliers. Lexis is the product of Mead Data Central, and Westlaw is the system of the West Publishing Company. While the marketing of these services has focused on lawyers in large firms, their utility is filtering down into smaller practices as the economics of the computer industry change. This process of market maturation is being aided by the availability of computerized legal research services in law schools at preferential subscription rates, creating a computer-oriented generation among recent graduates of law school interested in these systems.

Litigation support

The most critical application of computers in law practice is in the management of documents for litigation. It is different from the two prior areas in several ways.

First, in the macro environment computerized litigation support is primarily a response to the complexity of the client's situation and—to a lesser degree—to the economic pressure of the service economy or the demands of the profession's own information explosion.

Second, while computerized word processing, text editing, timekeeping and legal research are applications whose benefits are shared throughout the firm computerized litigation support may be used by only a few in a large law firm.

Third, as a process it can result to a greater degree in the delegation of work to paraprofessionals, as well as creating greater reliance on computer professionals.

And fourth, from a technical standpoint, this type of data base management activity requires a greater amount of special work with and refinement of the computer's instructions than the other two applications.

Computerized litigation support has found a market in complex litigation that calls forth anywhere from twenty thousand to several hundred thousand document pages dealing with findings of fact. Users often are engaged in antitrust or major contract disputes that reflect complicated business arrangements or a set of activities giving even the most avid PERT-chart advocate pause.

By creating a computerized data base that describes documents and their contents, one gains critical advantages over the users of any manual classification system. First, more information about a document is recorded on the index. When searching for a piece of evidence, the lawyer identifies it by multiple categories—for example, by date, by topic(s), by author or recipient, or a combination of these. A computer easily cross-references these by as many as seven or eight specific criteria, well beyond the functional capability of any manual system.

Second, the search for information is at electronic speeds with time savings measured in days or weeks in any one evidence search.

Third, when storing information in a computer, professional turnover on a case has less impact on the continuity of research and case preparation. Manual systems frequently depend on the knowledge lawyers or paralegals acquire in the course of litigation, particularly as it relates to document usage. This information is carried on the computer, with far less risk of self-impeachment through inconsistent use of documents.

In my experience with civil litigation, information retrieval accounts for 60 per cent of the preparation effort and information development for about 40 per cent. Information development involves the analysis of the effects of a set of activities or events; information retrieval is the process of gathering the facts to demonstrate what the set of events or activities was. In litigation support, 90 per cent of the work usually involves information retrieval.

Essential to the use of the capability of the computer in information retrieval is an understanding of key computer concepts. There are fundamental differences between most manual information storage and retrieval systems and a computerized system.

With a manual system, the documents usually are organized in a fashion that relates to the process of retrieval—that is, chronologically, alphabetically, or by subject matter or some similar logical sequence. In applying computer concepts, the document organization logic is disengaged from the document retrieval logic. Documents are organized by a single criterion that is unrelated to the way information is retrieved. For example, all documents are identified by a unique identification number and stored sequentially. They are retrieved by other criteria (date, author, topic, etc.), based on a description of contents. The computer's memory and its sorting ability link the selection criteria and the identification criterion.

A lawyer who grasps the conceptual advantage of a computerized retrieval system then has only to learn how to communicate with the computer. During the planning phases one relies on computer professionals, who are responsible for making a computer resource responsive. After the computerized system is implemented, the responsibility for effective utilization shifts to the lawyer user. Efficient use depends on understanding, which enables the user to take full advantage of the data base management system.

FACTS, FUZZINESS, AND FICTION

Lawyers who have learned something about computerized litigation support are aware of a mini debate on the relative merits of "full-text" and "index" systems. Some feel that the direct access enabled by full-text storage is superior, because it resembles the way attorneys work, reading off the page. The basic consideration is the system's ability to retrieve accurately and completely the types of meaningful information contained in the documents. People who write do three things: they seek to communicate accurately, they muddle and obfuscate and they seek to conceal or deceive or both. How can a computer system deal with all three phenomena and a combination of the three in any number of documents?

The full-text storage system loads every word of every document onto the computer tape. The user who wants to locate documents relating to a certain activity enters a key word or phrase and the computer searches all documents. When it locates a document with that word or phrase, it identifies that fact for the user. This is fine for storing records of truthful and accurate information, because the words that describe the activity are the words used. Full-text storage is an excellent method for storing the contents of trial transcripts, depositions and legal documents.

But when a writer seeks to conceal—as is sometimes the case—accurate terminology usually is avoided. How, then, can meaningful information be retrieved? An unmodified, full-text system is ineffective. A system that identifies true meaning, along with actual words in context used is essential. A hybrid system requires paralegals trained in the case to read each document and assign values to those meanings not represented in the document's actual vocabulary.

IN-HOUSE COMPUTER V. COMPUTER UTILITY

A hybrid arrangement enabling the user to take advantage of both modes of accessing information requires an advanced computer software package, one that minimizes storage space for the full-text portion and maximizes retrieval capabilities for the system.

Many lawyers who never see a major case are interested in systems that represent appropriate technology for a small case. One man, whose firm handles some litigation support with its own small general-purpose computer, described the computer as his "reserve of five associates," which he can count on using if a large piece of litigation develops. With the additions of computer memory that doubled the computer's capacity and the creation of a simple base management system, the computer is useful for cases that require indexing of up to ten thousand documents.

Because of the limitations of a small general purpose computer, which are not just limitations of memory size but also of sophistication in instruction handling, the amount of information stored about any one document is limited. The trade-off is in the relatively low cost of using the extra time available from a paid-for resource.

Using a computer utility is probably not cost-efficient for many small cases for which a lawyer might use his own office computer. A common practice in larger cases, which demand a greater technological resource, is to use the high-powered big computer of the computer utility or the large general purpose computer of the lawyer's client. A data base management systems software package adapted for use in litigation support often is purchased outright by the lawyer's client.

The purchase option has merit. The production side of the document handling task is a nuisance for a law firm to manage. If the client is responsible for the production work, the client can manage the needed resources. In some cases both attorneys and clients prefer not to have employees involved directly in the case, either handling evidence or being part of a litigation strategy.

Some large law firms prefer the turnkey utility approach. The prefer not to have responsibility for the management headaches but to have the role of end user.

The computer utility has some merits for both the client and the law firm. Using a computer utility enables the lawyers to concentrate on using the resource without having responsibility for development, implementation and production.

SEE HOW YOU LIKE IT FIRST

If lawyers admit that the computer is here and that its role will be much larger in the immediate future, then the question is how to prepare for this brave new world.

Preparation for survival in the face of radical societal change is an expensive investment for an individual because it involves more than input from a didactic source. Seminars and instruction may contribute some understanding of basic concepts, and exposure to war stories—true and false—may inform, but they are no substitute for hands-on experimentation with the new technology.

The course of wisdom and caution is a limited experiment on a trial basis with other people's equipment, with loaned resources or through computer utilities. Take an individual instance of litigation as a test base and set a specific period of time for experimentation and evaluation. The important thing is to conduct a real-time experiment.

The lawyer's Catch-22 takes two forms: the consultant and the paralegal. Hiring a consultant can alleviate an immediate problem; it does not prepare you for the necessarily pervasive changes in your thought and discipline. Delegation to a paralegal may be a necessity, but again it is not a satisfactory long-term substitute for your own knowledge and understanding of computer concepts. The fact is that you and you alone have to understand how the computer meets your needs and is subject to your control and direction. Nobody else can ride the tiger.

While there is really no question that the consultant and others can help you set out on this journey, its completion is part of your responsibility.

23

Litigation Support: Beyond Data Retrieval

James I. Keane

For over a decade computers have been penetrating the courtroom. They are not simply a new form of evidence or the basis upon which an expert witness draws his conclusions. They are, rather, a new tool in organizing complex and massive litigation. For all the experimenting, tinkering and cost overruns, they have worked. From volumes of indexes and directories to pinpoint searches on video terminals, huge document collections have been brought under control by careful planning and sensible utilization of the computer's organizational and retrieval power. This has been Phase I: the computer experts and information scientists have worked with the legal profession to tackle the most unruly and ephemeral of libraries—a litigation file. Hundreds of thousands of documents—several million pages—have been the order of magnitude for cases involving IBM or FTC's suit against the oil companies. What will happen next?

Two trends are discernible. On one hand, these developed systems will apply legal information technology to smaller and smaller cases; on the other, experienced, innovative users will take more and more advantage of the analytical and not just the organizational power of the computer. It will take only a short while—a few years, at the most—for these trends to mature. They will be an outgrowth of the past phase of legal data processing, which has been constrained by hardware, software and the emergence of information science.

Computerized litigation support has historically been limited by the effort, skill and money required to create a structured, machine-readable record or data base of the trial documents. Elaborate procedures have been devised for screening, coding, indexing and abstracting countless memos, statements, letters, depositions, transcripts and pleadings so that an essentially stupid machine can sort and retrieve useful information on request. Information scientists have grown from automated librarians into real explorers of the structure and meaning of language and logic in a legal environment. Human beings can sort out the difference between homographs by contextual intuition. But steel mills, soft drinks and illicit drugs are meaningless dimensions to a computer looking for c-o-k-e. Precise coding techniques and sophisticated development in the art of query formulation have made it possible to harness the computer's inexorable power despite the subleties of language.

Similarly, software development has constrained legal document retrieval capabilities. After 20 years, we are now seeing several tested programs extract concepts from a witness statement and match them against 50,000 other documents for impeachment or surrebuttal. The ability to scan the file for an unexpected eleventh hour issue in a ten-month trial is a present and available technique of computer technology. A demonstration of full-text legal document retrieval was given to the American Bar Association in 1959 by the Health Law Center of the University of Pittsburgh. The refinement of those techniques since that time has been very encouraging. Retrieval data can be sorted by author, subject, article, or other combinations with relative ease, and most systems allow the user to browse and sample qualifying documents. Natural language queries on simple points and highly structured searches on more complex ones can give a proficient Scrabble or crossword player a clear edge in the battle of automated legal data bases. Trained as a questioner, the lawyer can quickly adapt to the rigors of query formulation necessitated by full text retrieval software.

Another retardant factor has been hardware. The early debates were over the lawyer as a direct user, keyboarding his own searches, or as a subscriber who called an expert to run a search. Then, batch processing (key in query and wait for a printout) maintained an aesthetic distance between man and machine. Response time was slow, it was clumsy to correct mistakes; costs for storage and processing were too high. The proliferation of office terminals now permits an attorney to type his query directly onto a videoscreen in his office and to have the computer guide his search by immediately responding whether his query is in error, or that a particular word does not exist in the file. This takes a reasonable amount of training and practice, but it provides the flexibility of a live sparring partner. Memory costs have dropped also; mini-computers will aid this trend considerably. With a terminal in his office, a lawyer can not only query his own litigation file, he can also access other available data bases, both of decisional and statutory law and of large general library type files from the New York Times Data Bank to chemical abstracts.

It is still expensive to build and access a legal data base. $5 to $10 per document, higher for more complex processing, is a fair charge. This includes the manual study time it takes a para-legal or coder to fill in all the blanks on a pre-coded control form, assign all appropriate index terms and compose an abstract. It also covers the cost of keyboarding, computer time and certain printout lists, but not search time, which can be charged hourly and on the basis of output volume. The base figure can also include the system design for the whole litigation project—where lawyers, lexicographers, computer specialists, and information scientists put together an overall system that will do justice to the complexities and fine detail of a large case.

Once the expense is met and the demanding standards of high-stakes litigation are satisfied, the computer can provide very useful tabletop directories of witnesses, authors, titles, events or organizations as well as subject indexes (excellent tools to keep computer time low). The data base itself can also be searched word by word to identify comparable documents. The lawyer is freed from organizing his file; now he can study it. He can scan back over it for the elusive details; he can begin to marshall evidence. But this only lays the foundation for the application of information technology to litigation. To build an expensive total recall library is only the beginning—for trial document collections as well as decisional law data bases.

The longest list or the finest search do not fully tap resources of the computer. Far beyond saving labor on large routine chores, it can add whole new dimensions to our assessment of the facts in a case. Indeed, our professional colleagues in the sciences are relying more and more on computer technology not simply to speed up their processes but to add qualitative dimensions to them. Mixing and matching coded maps of real estate values, water service, and electrical hookup service is a direction which urban planning is taking with computer technology. New dimensions in astrophysics and molecular biology have been similarly opened with the application of computer science. These disciplines deal with what has traditionally been regarded as "hard data." The data assembled for trial is not of that nature, but tools are presently being built to deal with natural language and text files which will aid in the analysis of this equally complex information.

Econometric modeling is already a technique that has been adapted to litigation requirements. Anti-trust, rate regulation and restraint of trade actions lend themselves very efficiently to the computer's ability to analyze data statistically. Long-term patterns arising from vast and divergent financial data can and have been matched against machine-readable information regarding corporate policy. Economic experts regularly forecast energy consumption trends, for example. Such opinions, based on computer models, are admissible in evidence. During the investigative and strategy phases of trial the attorney and computer expert can explore alternatives or analyze groups of data to test hypotheses against evidence. The use of such techniques can be applied with equal force in tax, insurance and security fraud, or substantial white collar economic crimes, not to mention regulatory actions over an industry whose operations are becoming more and more computerized.

Confronting data that is already in machine-readable form will become an increasing requirement in even simple litigation. The ability to organize and code nonelectronic data and convert incompatible tapes so that the several groups may be interpreted together will test the mettle of a litigation systems designer. Medicaid/Medicare abuse is a ready example of such mixed evidence; yet the vast number of suspect cases will perhaps only be reachable when payment records are simultaneously searchable with physician and nursing notes. Creating profiles by which the computer can screen out reasonable from unreasonable payment record patterns and generate statistical patterns of fraud is a ready example of catching a thief who has left transactional fingerprints on computer records.

Even more sophisticated computer techniques are available but not yet applied to the litigation or investigation environment. The intelligence agencies have been quietly perfecting analysis systems that can link disparate data into meaningful patterns. The social scientists have also developed statistical and survey techniques which effectively harness the computer for the evaluation of field interview responses and social problems of multitudinous proportions. The scientific community has perfected techniques such as signal processing, by which limited data from a particular point in time can be projected into substantial conclusions regarding a future point. This is done now with hard structured data. Think of the expanded horizons of a lawyer who has just processed his first wave of discovery and now wants to focus on the best litigation scenario.

Another wholly different development lies in the area of computer graphics. If an astronomer can rotate a three-dimensional display and modify the motion of an orbiting binary star system on a videoscreen, what could an inventive attorney do with a car crash scenario, or other demonstrable evidence. Viewing an event from different perspectives can provide both analytical leads during pretrial activities as well as marvelous courtroom displays when even the judge nods during an expert's testimony.

The application of existing information technology to the evidence-marshalling process is the next challenge for the Bar, aided by information science and computer experts. To go beyond indexes and searches to analytical evaluations of the file for discovery and pretrial strategy is the next phase. To take the plotline of a large-scale conspiracy, manipulate it, test alternative case theories, match statements against events even as the transcript develops, will open up new avenues for trial advocacy. For now, the Bar must grapple with this new tool and develop it according to the needs of the law and to the expanding horizons of mastering large documentary litigation files.

24

The Computer as an Aid to the Litigator

Steven E. Rosen and Robert S. McCormick

Modern life confronts knowledge workers, whether lawyers, scientists, businessmen or bureaucrats, with a massive overload of data. This has led to the dominance of the digital electronic computer among contemporary technological developments. Unaided, the human brain must ignore most of the data presented to it, or else be paralyzed by the onslaught. As a tool which extends human data processing capability, the computer reduces the inhibiting effects of massive information. Just as modern transportation technology dramatically increases man's capacity for travel through physical space, so the computer has magnified man's ability to function in his unique inner space—the mental processes required to extract information from random data. As a knowledge worker experiencing keenly the demands of the information explosion, the lawyer—who no longer travels by stagecoach—may be expected to place increasing reliance on modern technology to manipulate data.

Early computer usage centered around numerical calculation and quantitative record keeping, thus offering only tangential assistance to most litigants. In recent years, however, the computer has become useful to store, retrieve and manipulate large amounts of documentary information, primarily due to the development of faster, large capacity memory devices. In addition, the development of user-oriented computer systems has enabled lawyers to interact dynamically with their data and thereby obtain continuous feedback as an adjunct to the thought process. English language retrieval applications have brought the computer across the threshold of the legal profession, where needed information is customarily nonnumerical in nature.

In the last decade, the computer has begun to assist the lawyer in tasks central to his profession. In both law research (access to statutes, regulations and opinions) and fact research (access to private confidential files specific to a particular controversy), computer assistance has expanded greatly the lawyer's ability to acquire, manipulate and present both precedent and evidence. The freedom from investigative drudgery which the computer now offers will enable attorneys to concentrate on the discretionary and judgmental tasks constituting the essence and value of lawyering.

In this article, we discuss the use of the computer to organize and recall the factual material needed to develop and execute litigation strategy. The goal in using the computer to support modern complex litigation is to remove the impediments of scale, thereby permitting Counsel to apply effectively his skills of advocacy, despite a large or complex body of evidence. These impediments of scale are challenges which, if unresolved, will impede effective advocacy, regardless of the amount of legal talent which is brought to bear.

CHALLENGES OF VOLUMINOUS OR COMPLEX EVIDENTIARY DATA

Very often, files relating to complex litigation may run to tens or hundreds of thousands of pages which need to be readily accessible by many individuals engaged in the litigation process. Procedures must be developed which provide for:

A controlled chain of custody for evidentiary documents

Access to a complete document collection at all times for authorized research

Avoidance of misfilings, misappropriations or losses which make documents inaccessible, in the face of heavy use over a long period

Security against unauthorized research or file alteration

Access to the documents, or a copy of the documents, at more than one geographical site (for multi-district and multi-case litigations)

Organization of the data into reports and sequences as required to analyze patterns and trends

Access to the data in timely fashion to meet deadlines imposed by the court or procedural rules

Maintenance of file currency by adding new information and disseminating it to those who might otherwise rely upon incomplete, inaccurate or obsolete information

Document indexing to permit rapid identification of documents based upon relevance to diverse and multifarious search criteria

The resistance of these conceptually simple tasks to facile implementation is learned through concrete experience in establishing document control and indexing systems. These requirements are most fully appreciated by attorneys who have had prior responsibility for managing large evidentiary collections, thereby learning firsthand the degree of commitment to precision and diligence required.

The duration of most complex litigation makes it likely that substantial turnover of staff will occur, including key employees of the law firm and its client. Even where there is no turnover, one cannot rely upon the frailties of human memory to provide the continuity of procedure necessary to protect the consistency and reliability of litigation files. Thus, a central goal of all preparation in the litigation must be documentation and transmittal of acquired knowledge and procedures developed to ensure consistency in the files, the data and the indexing strategy.

The outcome of major litigation frequently depends upon nonlegal tasks aimed at gaining and keeping control over the information in the case. Attorneys typically receive little or no training in management or information science. It is not surprising that they increasingly seek assistance in imposing a systematic approach on large evidentiary collections. Although any litigation requires an information flow, the potential for mis-step in large-scale litigations can easily jeopardize the outcome. Judicious use of available management tools can ensure that evidentiary complexity has no undesirable repercussions. The well-planned computer system is a useful tool to enhance the litigant's chances that the result will be at least as good as the theory and facts warrant.

HOW THE COMPUTER ENTERS THE LITIGATION

Consider the following idealized scenario for the introduction and utilization of technology in the litigation effort. Near the outset of the litigation, Counsel analyzes the information requirements of the case. These include the nature and extent of the document population, expected growth of the population, ways in which the evidence will be searched, scheduling constraints and requirements for information dissemination, special reports and statistical analysis. From the outset, and at various stages thereafter, he inquires whether a manual information system will suffice, or whether his information needs can be met best by automation. Counsel will be sensitive to the following factors which point in the direction of automation:

Sizable evidentiary collection, including documents, transcripts and derived materials

Factual complexity which requires the examination of the case from many perspectives

Dependence of litigation strategy on the contents of documents which have not been or cannot be fully read or recalled in all pertinent particulars by Counsel

Complex deposition or trial situation involving many witnesses or exhibits

Dependence of the case on the detection of trends or patterns in primary materials

Probable involvement of several attorneys or firms

Multiple geographical litigation sites

Probable protracted duration of the litigation

Relatively inflexible litigation schedule

Anticipated reuse of the same document collection for many cases

Unless the law firm or litigant has sufficient expertise in the analysis of information system requirements, it will need to acquire outside resources to evaluate whether automation is feasible and warranted. The primary goal of such a study is to define the benefits and costs of establishing a computerized information system. It must also consider alternative combinations of automated and manual procedures. If, in the early stages of litigation, it is thought that computerization is not yet warranted, initial manual procedures should be flexible and compatible with later automation. Planning the manual system in this way is essential if unpleasant surprises and unnecessary costs are to be avoided. The design of such procedures should include provisions for document security; document control; information flow; compilation, control and growth of indexes; file organization; a methodology for use of the system; and the documentation of all system procedures.

Unfortunately, systematic planning of these items often occurs only when a lawsuit is automated, although it is needed for a complex manual system as well. In one sense, planning is more crucial for a manual system than for a computerized system. The compilation of manual indexes to a large body of data may normally not be accomplished within the scheduling constraints of trial, whereas a new index to computerized files may be rapidly generated (by some vendors). Thus, a poorly planned manual system will likely be nonresponsive to many questions which arise later in the litigation. Of course, not all questions may be anticipated. But proper planning can go far toward minimizing this natural drawback of manual systems. This is why it is wise to seek assistance from experienced information systems professionals, whether or not computerization is intended.

WHAT SHOULD BE INCLUDED IN THE COMPUTER DATA BASE?

This broad inquiry is really two questions: First, what types of documents require organization and searching by computer? Second, for each qualifying document type, which items of information need be obtained from each document? These questions ultimately depend on the information retrieval needs of Counsel. Retrieval is the act of locating portions of the document collection related to logical criteria such as one or more personal or organizational names, subjects, locations or dates, or combinations thereof. This retrieval may be accomplished by the aid of a computer; it can search its memory for relevant documents, organize, sort, display, print and condense them in a useful format. These activities are performed in response to specific needs of Counsel to locate references to a given person, firm, date, place, thing or concept, to identify patterns of activity reflected in the evidence, or to organize the information in preparation of briefs and other materials. The following sections of this article explore the fulfillment of information retrieval needs typically encountered in a litigation, assuming that those needs are recognized, planned for and addressed in a timely fashion.

The criteria for computerization to satisfy the needs at each stage of the case should reflect certain general principles. First, the goal of a computer system is to facilitate retrieval; it is not best used primarily to provide a vehicle for reading documents or transcripts. It is much more efficient and less costly to use the computer system to select only relevant portions of text and provide the researcher with locating information such as microfilm or file number. The full text may be obtained easily from a document archive on paper or microfilm. Second, only those portions of each document which are of probable value in discovery, deposition or trial should be included. Irrelevant portions should be screened out of the computer system.*

*An exception to this guideline exists for some computer systems which do not have the ability to add new information to the data base quickly and inexpensively. In such cases—which include some very well known systems—the lawyer should err liberally on the side of inclusion, despite correspondingly higher costs.

Third, different approaches are normally required for different types of documents, depending on the uses to which they will be put. For example, in a given litigation some documents may need only be inventoried by date, author, recipient, and persons and organizations mentioned, with a pointer to the file location. Other documents may require subjective analysis such as subject terms, index codes, attorney comments or informative abstracts. A final group may require the extraction of key words, or even inclusion of part or all of the actual language used. The precise complement of techniques used will vary with each case. It is important that the attorney select a computer system capable of handling all methods deemed potentially desirable.

Fourth, the list of data elements to be obtained from each document class should correspond to the retrieval requirements for the class. These should be determined in advance. The elements may be numeric quantities upon which statistical operations are required; nonnumeric elements identifying subject matter, persons, locations, organizations or dates referenced; bibliographic data such as document date, author, recipient, deponent or witness; marginal notations; textual abstracts; or any combination of these or other elements.

Fifth, whatever types of data are deemed important to capture must be controlled and verified. No matter which approach is used, there are several ways in which errors may be introduced. In the process of converting the information on paper to a form readable by the computer, typographical errors are generated. Material prepared by a paralegal, indexer or coder, may have been erroneously conceived or written down. In the event that the material is taken directly from the document or transcript (full text), it may have been originally misspoken or transcribed in error.

If these errors remain uncorrected, the use of the computer system may be substantially less beneficial, because the computer will not be able to find all references of concern to counsel. In addition, some references identified by the computer will lead down blind alleys. For example, if the date 1978 is mistakenly typed as 1973, an inquiry for all documents with a date of 1978 will miss the document in error; an inquiry for 1973 documents, on the other hand, will mistakenly obtain the error document. This principle extends to errors of varying degrees of complexity, subtlety and harmful effect.*

*Some types of data are more susceptible to error correction than others. Detection of some types of errors may be accomplished automatically by the computer system as the data are processed; other errors must be manually identified. Corrections are made to the data base after its creation through an update procedure if the computer system has such capability. If no such capability exists, the entire data base will need to be recreated, at substantial cost.

The error correction process depends not only on the computer system but also on

These guidelines and principles should be considered by Counsel in determining which data to include from documents obtained at various stages of the litigation. Other rules and procedures may be recommended by litigation support professionals, depending on the nature of the litigation, the data and the needs of Counsel. However, the question of which documents to include in the computer system in preparation for each strategic point is a matter largely for determination by Counsel. The decision for inclusion is based on the anticipated use and value of each type of document and whether it can be managed effectively without computer assistance. The following discussion outlines such uses and the potential applicability of computerization to the strategic points in a lawsuit.

INITIAL ASSESSMENT OF THE CASE

Normally, at the outset of litigation, client personnel and other friendly sources of information are interviewed, under conditions of varying formality. Documents and other information believed relevant are collected from the client. The transcript or notes of such interviews and the voluntarily produced files are among the first items which may be included in the information system, if voluminous. They will provide an initial assessment of the merits, unfolding promising directions for both offensive and defensive strategy.

Client discovery

Based upon examination of this information, the first round of discovery may be planned to fill in the document collection with material from the opposing side. The data received may be entered into the system, after being screened for relevance and duplication. A minimal level of information may be entered from all documents, to assist in document management as well as in the identification of duplicate or missing documents. More detailed commentary and analysis, such as abstracting or subject coding, may be applied to significant documents at this time by Counsel, paralegal assistants or trained analysts, or it may be added at a later time.

The rapid absorption of all relevant discovered material will assist in eliminating duplicate documents. More importantly, it will permit

the structure of the data. For example, verifications are not performed well on full-text documents. The computer systems currently available cannot detect nonsense words, or examine the contextual validity of language. As a further example, words in full text may not be validated automatically. In addition, the computer currently has no way of knowing whether a number in text is representative of a date or some other numeric quantity such as tons, miles or dollars. In the case of full text then, error detection and correction is largely a manual process.

the effective use of a second round of discovery as a meaningful supplementary effort aimed at areas of inadequate or evasive response, or claims of privilege. This is particularly true with respect to interrogatories, where answers are often casual or superficial in the first instance. A clear signal that responses have been carefully scrutinized for accuracy and completeness may result in greater cooperation on a second round of interrogatories.

Response to opponent's discovery and production orders

When planning a response to discovery demands and interrogatories, Counsel faces a key decision concerning revealment of the use of automation. From the outset, the decision may be made to project to opposing counsel one of a variety of images:

Absolute control over the litigation and the intention to make things difficult, and "by the book." This approach is particularly useful with respect to legitimate claims of privilege.

The desire and ability to cooperate due to confidence that quick evaluation of the evidence by opposing counsel will lead to abandoning excessive claims or unmeritorious contentions.

Lack of control over the evidentiary material, or lack of desire to assist in its evaluation, forcing opposing counsel to perform all screening and analysis. This so-called "truckload" approach has one significant drawback—prudence dictates that every document turned over to opposing counsel be controlled. Otherwise, Counsel either will be unaware of exactly which documents have been produced and what they say, or must expend extra effort and funds on every document turned over.

Although establishing early control over the document collection represents a substantial initial investment in the litigation, whether the investment is justified must be judged in the context of the entire course of the proceeding. Avoidance of redundant document processing by Counsel is a significant cost savings. Such redundant efforts are the hallmark of most manual systems. Additionally, early document control can signal a serious intention to press a claim or defense, which may lead to a favorable settlement. By enabling a focused rather than "shotgun" approach to discovery, it increases the readiness with which the attorney can approach the deposition stage. In fact, the ultimate expense of early computerization may be far less than the cumulative cost of an early manual approach followed by belated automation. This is due to the ability to plan a cohesive system which will not require redoing or undoing previous efforts. Frequently, Counsel have expended large sums in an attempt to support an inadequate manual system prior to ultimate establishment of a computerized system.

DEPOSITION STAGE

Although movement toward early control increases the chance of early settlement, it does not guarantee a settlement, of course. With the advent of depositions, the overall cost of litigation typically escalates. As a result, the use of the computer to manage the litigation efficiently takes on increased importance. As each deposition approaches, the documents deemed relevant to the examination may be coded with fact or issue information, as well as the names of individuals responsible for the authorship or receipt of the documents or having knowledge of their contents. It is normally useful for the computer to produce witness kits or subject packets, which are used by Counsel to plan deposition efforts. Such planning will lead to a more informative deposition with effective scheduling and lower cost. As the depositions proceed, the deposition transcripts may be entered into the system, including subject coding, digests, full text, or a combination of these. Each exhibit used during the deposition stage should be added to the data base if not previously entered. Exhibits and depositions should be linked together so that exhibits and the depositions in which they are discussed will be cross-referenced.

The pretrial brief

The information entered during the discovery stage can be reorganized with ease by the computer to assist in the preparation of the pretrial brief. The computerized data may be obtained in sequence by issue, date, witness, or any other criterion provided for in the design of the system. This use of the computer permits compelling arguments to be discovered and patterns of activity over time to be discerned. It also shows the lack of supporting facts for a particular thread of an argument. The computer file may be tested for hundreds of alternative approaches, and may display many alternate arrangements of the evidence. The attorney may avoid time-consuming and costly xerographic duplication and manual sorting of the physical file. Unlike a manual system, exploration of this type creates no risk of document misfiling. Information can be obtained in minutes at a desk-top terminal. Records of productive arrangements may be saved; unproductive arrangements may be easily recognized and discarded. The end result of this process will be a stronger pretrial brief. All exhibits, deposition testimony, and other material may be cross-referenced to the appropriate paragraphs of the pretrial brief, providing all of the evidence to support any contention. Effective requests for admission may also be formulated, based upon early knowledge of the structure of the trial presentation.

Opponent's pretrial brief

A similar process of matching available documents and deposition testimony against the opponent's pretrial brief can lead to a realistic assessment of the strengths and weaknesses of his case. Such a comprehensive analysis of both briefs may lead to key settlement discussions. The degree to which the detailed knowledge developed through the computer should be shared with opposing counsel will vary on a case-by-case basis, depending both on the image counsel wishes to project, discussed herein, and on counsel's assessment of the impact on opposing counsel of laying out the probable presentation structure for both sides. Whether or not settlement is pursued, the examination of opponent's brief will be quite helpful in the preparation of contravening arguments for trial.

SCHEDULING AND PLANNING FOR TRIAL

Once the trial preparation shifts into its final stages, the data base may be used to assist in drafting subpoenas and to prepare arrangements of the evidence most useful for witness preparation and examination. The computer system may be used to print lists for each witness of the exhibits and other documents to be used to lay foundation, present affirmative or rebuttal evidence and impeach by prior inconsistent statement or otherwise.

A potential application of the computer not yet fully exploited for trial preparation involves trial strategy planning through the use of mathematical optimization techniques. If provided with certain information about witnesses and evidence, it would be possible for the computer to assist in this effort. For example, the computer could be given:

Credibility ratings for witnesses

Information about witness availability

Logical order of foundation and evidence

Witness utility for laying foundation or introducing evidence

Through ranking and tabulating algorithms drawn from statistics, alternate presentation strategies could be tested by the computer to determine the degree to which logical flow or persuasiveness is improved by a change in strategy. Fallback scenarios could be developed to cope with witness unavailability or other unforeseen circumstances. The attorney's ability to respond rapidly and effectively to scheduling changes could well have a demoralizing effect on the opponent. It should be emphasized that the development of such an application would involve creation of refined algorithms based on modeling of the process of litigation strategy. To the authors' knowledge, no operational system presently provides such assistance, although computer modeling is currently being used by some litigants for other purposes such as developing econometric analyses to support expert testimony.

COMPUTER-GENERATED EVIDENCE

The uses of the computer for litigation support discussed herein primarily contemplate computerization as a method for organizing, maintaining, controlling and accessing evidence which already exists and which is obtained through traditional means. The attorney may use the computer system to build his case, but in court the presentation is made from the documents and testimony itself.

In addition to their use for organizing the presentation of primary evidence, computer products may themselves be used as evidence. For example, computerized business records of a corporation may be directly introduced.* The computer may also be used to derive new evidence through simple or sophisticated analysis of information in the case using standard quantitative techniques. With appropriate foundation by expert witnesses, establishing the methods and theory underlying preparation of the material, computer-generated products may be used in trial to support or refute factual contentions. Although the utility of any particular method of presentation depends upon the nature of the litigation, computers have been used to produce maps, statistical reports, graphs, simulations, correlations and many other types of information display. If prepared carefully, these products are normally well received by the finder of fact.

*If useful to compare with other documentary evidence, such files may be incorporated in the litigation support data base. This is frequently a relatively inexpensive way to build a litigation file, since the incorporated records are already in magnetic form. Of course, expert analysis is required to assess the significance of the data obtained, the coding structure and conventions used in their development, and the standardization and controls required to incorporate the new data into the litigation data base.

THE TRIAL

During trial, a "war room" is normally established near the trial site. It provides on-line computer access to the data base and a full set of the documents and transcripts either in hardcopy form or on microform. After each day of trial, the transcript can be keyed for inclusion in the data base, or an abstracted or coded summary of the trial proceedings may be entered. Each section of transcript may be cross-referenced to pretrial brief sentence numbers, exhibit numbers or other key materials. Creation of these links allows verification that each exhibit has a sound chain of introduction, and that each issue is adequately developed. The presentation of evidence by both sides should be analyzed. Necessary motions and closing statements can be planned and assimilated into the litigation strategy.

In addition to these routine uses, the computer may assist in reacting to unforeseen events of the trial. The authors' experience has shown that computer system usage during trial is likely to be heavy, despite the most thorough advance preparation. Examples of such unexpected usage reflect reliance on the computer system to:

Find unexpected contradictions in past testimony

Find documents in the data base not previously thought to be material

Cope with reorientation in trial strategy caused by unavailability of a key witness, or readjustment of schedules due to unexpected events

Produce information desired by the Court either in an *ad hoc* fashion, or in the form of trial briefs. The computer can provide all the raw material for such a brief, and even display such information in a selected sequence. The actual synthesis into a brief will require human analysis and intervention, but this is greatly facilitated by the computer printout.

Research issues brought to the fore by the trial judge

The ability of Counsel to react quickly to judicial requests may lead to the formation of a bond of reliance and trust between Counsel and the Court.

CLOSING THE TRIAL: THE APPEAL

At the end of testimony, the closing arguments and the more formal post-trial brief may be prepared. With the assistance of the computer, the orderly flow of proof promised in the pretrial brief may be confirmed and documented in the post-trial brief. Errors in laying foundation may be similarly cataloged. A properly prepared and compelling post-trial brief may be adopted by the Court in its opinion, in whole or in part. Should the conclusion of the legal action be less than satisfactory, Counsel may need to marshal factual information in support of an appeal. Computerized selection and organization of material from the trial to frame and document appeal issues is of great assistance in analysis and preparation of the appellate brief and arguments.

VISIBILITY OF THE COMPUTER

To decide the appropriate level of visibility for the computer system, the effect of computers on jury, judge and opposing counsel should be carefully evaluated.

The effect in general of computer usage on a jury may not be easily predicted, and depends on the circumstances of the case. In a consumer or products liability suit, an argument might be made that its profile should be low, lest it arouse an image of wealth or unfair advantage and thereby create an unsympathetic jury reaction. On the other hand, the opposite conclusion may be reached on the ground that knowledge of computer use may instill confidence in the contentions of counsel. This is especially true in cases involving large institutional entities and complex subject matter.

The effect of computer use on the Court is also dependent on circumstances. The favorable bond of reliance which may be formed by quick and accurate response to information needs of the Court has already been mentioned. Some court analysts have asserted, in other contexts, that jurists may be subject to a subtle (and subconscious) inclination toward a legal ruling which would end a difficult factual battle, and extended encumbrance of the trial calendar. If that were true, then a party desiring an early end to the proceeding might not wish to indicate that computer usage could facilitate the trial.

As to the visibility of the computer to opposing counsel, secrecy seems to be the rule rather than the exception in present uses. Since the data base should be privileged as attorney work product, if it is properly prepared and maintained, this secrecy may represent excessive caution. However, the privilege has not yet been definitively established, and caution has been exercised to date.

Given the security precautions which are normally taken in limiting access to litigation data bases, it should even be possible for both parties to share the same data base; access to certain classes of information can be strictly limited to the authorized users. Although the writers know of only one instance of cooperation between opposing parties, there are increasing tendencies toward this phenomenon among partially adverse co-parties. This is particularly sensible when the litigation is expected to center upon a legal issue to be resolved on appeal, and for which both parties desire resolution. In these instances it is often in the parties' interest to cooperate in data base generation and maintenance. Substantial cost savings could result, since the alternative is independent preparation by both parties. A data base can easily protect access to portions of each document for private materials such as attorney comments, relevance codes, and privileged components (although not all systems provide such a capability).

FAIRNESS AND THE COMPUTER

If only one party has access to sufficient resources, the computer can serve to widen the gap of power. Because of the tremendous advantage it gives the litigant—independent of legal merit—computerization can sharply distort bargaining positions. Obviously, it is not the only means by which money can alter litigation prospects. Consider, for example, a litigation in which twenty attorneys from a prominent law firm were pitted against two government attorneys with less than ten years' total experience. In this instance political restrictions on hiring new personnel made the computer system the only way of redressing the balance without increasing the staff of attorneys. Thus in some cases a litigation support system can help to equalize the strength of adversaries.

It is technologically feasible for a jurisdiction to offer the advice and facilities for computerization of cases to be tried in its courts, at cost. Although this would require a substantial initial investment, it could improve the administration of justice. Many cases which require litigation support involve matters of widespread importance. Antitrust and trade regulation matters, construction suits, class actions and major product liability cases exemplify litigations which can clog courts for a decade. Enactment of legislation, or judicial announcement of a legal doctrine, when there are not adequate means to try controversies arising from that law or doctrine, may lead to disparities between public law and practice. An investment in resolving these claims, which often affect interests of thousands of stockholders, executives, taxpayers, injured parties, and the development of entire industries or communities could well serve the needs of private, public and institutional interests.

At the present time, however, litigation support rarely raises the issue of fairness. Currently, computerization of evidence occurs most frequently in cases in which power is nearly evenly distributed among the litigants. Such litigation normally involves large corporate interests, engaged in disputes with other large corporations, institutions or the Federal government. Usually, there is adequate wealth at hand on both sides to commit to litigation support. This is not to say that an imbalance of power may not result. For example, governments have made notably weak commitments to certain antitrust litigations in recent history. The authors are also familiar with cases in which powerful institutions failed to apply their resources to litigation support, and were outmatched by corporate general counsel or law firms more aware of technological tools. Perhaps the greatest "unfairness" in these cases is in the greater willingness of Counsel for one litigant to institute needed procedures, combined with the resistance of other counsel to new methods. In some cases, litigants have attempted to support their own cases internally and failed; in a few others, vendors have produced systems of poor quality. Thus, in most cases the question is not one of wealth and power, but rather one of good judgment.

ASSUMPTIONS REVISITED

Against the backdrop of our assumption that the support system is available early in the litigation stands a contravening reality. The decision to develop a computer system, or even an upward compatible manual system, is frequently deferred until the crisis of impending deposition or trial. Usually thousands of dollars have been spent on *ad hoc* manual processing of documents. In these instances, systems frequently must be created under crisis conditions. Attempts are made to salvage the prior manual work regardless of quality, and heavy premiums in cost are incurred. Yet a system implemented at the eleventh hour may be used only during the twelfth, and by personnel who may not have adequate time to fully benefit from the availability of information provided by the computer system.

At the very least, in major litigations, litigating attorneys should: (1) ensure that a system study is conducted near the outset; (2) ensure that all manual document processing is compatible with later conversion to more powerful methods; (3) keep the client fully informed as to the availability and potential need for computerization; and (4) periodically forecast future support needs. Given evolving doctrines on legal responsibility, it is probable that in some situations failure to use such tools or at least to propose them to a client for his evaluation, could invite action against counsel by a client dissatisfied with litigation results. Despite these negative inducements, however, the focus of general counsel and law firm alike should be primarily on the positive results of litigation support: better, more professional service; clearer, more certain determination of the facts underlying the controversy; the potential for more favorable settlements; greater confidence on the part of the finder of fact; greater client satisfaction; and greater leverage of the legal staff to larger case loads and higher levels of productivity.

25

Information Management in Complex Litigation

Palmer Brown Madden

Many articles have been written about the use of computers to manage information in a complex case. But the literature pays little attention to the management of the team of people needed to go through all the documents, depositions, and trial material so that the information can be put onto the computer. This article addresses that management task.

There are two major facets to the management problem posed by the volumes of information in a complex case. The first concerns cost control. It has been publicly reported that in the *Bay Area Rapid Transit v. Parsons Brinkerhoff Tudor and Bechtel, Westinghouse* and *Rohr* litigation BART had over 150 people working on the documents and that more than $1.5 million was spent over two years to create the data base. Expenses of this magnitude are common in complex litigation. To control the costs on an undertaking of this scale, the lawyer must implement a sensitive monitor of the cost-effectiveness of the project.

The second facet concerns the hiring, training and quality control necessary to ensure that the work product of those working with the information will be useful to the trial lawyer. No matter how sophisticated the computer system used to organize the information, if the material has not been carefully selected and prepared, errors and gaps in the underlying information will destroy the utility of the data base.

In considering the issue of cost control, one myth should be dispelled immediately. I often hear lawyers who have not worked on a

Reprinted from *Litigation*, Vol. 4, No. 3; Copyright 1978, American Bar Association.

complex case discussing whether a new case will "justify the cost" of a computer. They believe that using a computer greatly increases the cost of the document work. Nothing could be further from the truth. Ninety percent of the cost of an information system will be identical whether or not a computer is used.

By far the largest expense of any large document project is the cost of the people needed to screen documents, to identify the relevant ones, and then to prepare them for access either by putting them into a filing system or by preparing coded indices. If one were to rely solely on people to manage the information in a complex case, one would have constant problems of keeping enough of them who are knowledgeable about the case and intelligent enough to be of help. Large clerical projects using skilled personnel often have high turnover because of poor pay and the dull nature of the work. One advantage of computers is that they do not have morale problems. The use of the computer adds a small cost at the start of the litigation that will be recouped over time by decreasing the cost of retrieving information.

BIG CASES NEED COMPUTERS

A computerized document retrieval system is essential in a complex case. In medium-sized cases one must conduct a cost-benefit analysis to determine whether a computer will be beneficial. An article by Ron Rust and John Rome, "The Combination of a Manual and an Automated Approach to Trial Preparation," 11 *The Forum* 810 (1976), outlines some of the considerations about using a computer in a medium-sized case. But for the complex case one can no longer gather a marginal advantage over one's opponent by surprising him or her with a computerized retrieval system. The only surprise will be yours if you do not have an automated data base, because your opponent surely will.

Where, then, can one look to save money in a large document case? The primary area should be the strict limitation of the volume of information entered into the system. Every piece of information put into the system is costly. By controlling not only the number of documents, depositions and the like, but also the amount of information entered from each document, one can control costs. The trial lawyer must thus identify what information will be needed during pretrial and trial and ensure that the lure of the computer does not lead to loading into the retrieval system volumes of at best marginally useful material.

The goal is not to take every piece of information that can be found relevant to the litigation and put it into a computer. For example, if the case is likely to be settled very early, it is inappropriate to establish an information management system that is going to take many months to get under way and will not produce useful output for the first four or five months.

Many lawyers believe a computerized data base will be most useful at trial. They envision a computer being used in the middle of trial to produce mysteriously the key document that will impeach a witness. The reality of complex cases if far more mundane. The greatest use for an information system in a complex case is during the pretrial phases of litigation.

It is in taking depositions and answering interrogatories that the information management system will be most useful. Documents are often the key to successful depositions, since they never say "I don't remember." By the time of trial, the trial counsel will have organized the documents. The information management system, while it will be useful, will not be nearly so critical as it was during the pretrial phases. So the sooner one can establish a working system, the greater will be the benefit.

One step that may be taken early in the litigation is to identify by document type the classes of information that will be available and how each class will be used. For example, in a criminal tax fraud case, there may be thousands and thousands of invoices, but it may be quite sufficient for them to be arranged chronologically. Then, when the key transactions are identified, the relevant invoices can be easily located. This simple system is effective, inexpensive, and all that is needed. Loading all of this information into a computer would waste the client's money. On the other hand, in this same tax fraud litigation it may be necessary extensively to cross-reference and cross-index letters and memoranda. A computer will probably be necessary to do this if the matter involves tens of thousands of such documents.

After it has been established how different types of documents will be used during the litigation, you should consider whether it is possible to refine some of the classes to identify certain subclasses by subject matter that can be handled in a less complex and less expensive manner than other documents in the same general category. Thus, you may believe that letters and memoranda within a company should be extensively cross-indexed, but that letters between the company and third parties need only be filed by date under the name of each of the third parties. Again, since indexing is expensive, you should strive to avoid over-indexing. If you can manage a given subgroup of letters by merely putting them in chronological order or filing them by subject without the need to establish a complex indexing structure, you will save considerable expense. You should also be alert to identify classes of documents that are sufficiently well-organized by the client's filing system. Diverting documents to the least costly technique for management is the largest way in which time and money may be saved.

Only the trial lawyer is in a position to make these decisions. It is his responsibility to use the documents at the end of the case. Inexperienced junior associates cannot forecast how documents will be used and, therefore, will tend either to underestimate the importance of certain documents and therefore weaken the usefulness of the system or, more commonly, to overestimate how certain documents are going to be used and overload the system. Moreover, only the trial counsel has the judgment to appreciate how much is at stake in litigation, how much the client can afford to devote to a management information system. When, because of time or cost, certain things that could be done are not going to be done, only the trial counsel can determine which are most important.

At the same time the lawyers are beginning to formulate the goals for the information management system, legal assistants should begin an information survey. Its purpose is to identify the location and volume of the information that must be managed. The legal assistants should determine by type, number, and location all the relevant documents. They should also make their best estimate of the types of documents that will be produced by their opponents. Trial counsel should aid them by estimating the number and extent of depositions to be taken and by forecasting the extent of pleadings to be filed and the extent of internal correspondence of the law firm.

It may seem unusual that one would want to put the lawyer's own correspondence into an information management system, but it is not unusual in a complex case for fifty or more letters or memoranda to be generated every day, and over time it often will be important to be able to go quickly back into these files. A daily index of this material should be prepared and circulated to all lawyers on the team to keep them informed on what is occurring in areas outside of their primary responsibility.

As one begins to implement the system, one is faced with the choice of where to find the people to do all of the necessary tasks. It is generally not preferable to have the client undertake the job of screening and coding documents. One of the most important reasons for this is that one wants to protect from discovery the attorney's work product. If the client's personnel do the work, one runs the risk of a court finding that it is the client's work, not the attorney's. Moreover, if the people who do the document work are to be deposed it will be difficult to limit their testimony to avoid matters they learned while working on the documents. Perhaps as important, the client's personnel can probably be employed most effectively in the client's main business and not diverted to the short-term project of the litigation.

If the law firm has an established group of people familiar with complex cases, they can be called upon to manage the litigation project. This does not mean a silver-haired senior partner who has managed a complex case should call upon several junior associates and put them in charge of the data base. This is an invitation to disaster. A large management job should be undertaken by people experienced in this kind of work. If the law firm does not have experienced people it should look to the various vendors of litigation support services to supply administrative personnel and possibly the screeners and coders as well.

A lawyer who had hired a vendor of litigation support services to screen, code and load into a computer many thousands of documents in a complex construction case called me recently. He had some questions about systems design that we discussed at length. During the conversation, he spoke of "turning this problem over to the vendor." I immediately said he was headed for trouble if he approached the document work with the idea that he could delegate it to somebody else. This work demands the most of the lawyer's legal and analytic skills. It cannot be "turned over" to a vendor of litigation support services, a legal assistant, or a junior associate.

Fortunately, there are several persons in this developing area who are available to provide consulting services to law firms. You may wish to retain one of these consultants to help you decide how best to implement the project. They can be of great assistance in selecting a vendor to best suit your needs.

In my experience, while various vendors of litigation support services will try to talk about the features of their own computer systems and the like, the key element for the success of the project is the quality of the people. In picking a vendor of litigation support services, one wants to know who one is going to be dealing with and who is actually going to be doing the work. You must get to know these people and find out what their credentials are.

You should enquire into both the experience and the financial stability of the vendor. You want to be sure that your vendor will be here today and here tomorrow. I know of litigation in which a vendor went bankrupt and shut its doors just before trial.

Vendors are quite sensitive about disclosing their clients, but if pressed they can usually find one who will permit them to give you its name for a reference. (You also should bear in mind that, if the theories of your litigation raise the possibility of an award of attorneys' fees, the cost of the legal assistant team may possibly be included. *Pacific Coast Agricultural Export Assn. v. Sunkist Growers, Inc.*, 1973 TRADE CASES, ¶74,523 (N.D. Cal. 1973); but see *Trans World Airlines, Inc. v. Hughes,* 321 F. Supp. 478 (S.D.N.Y. 1970).

As you are deciding who will do the work, you will also begin to design the system for managing the information. A variety of systems is available to manage the documents in a complex case—for example, filing systems, edge-notched cards, and computers. For lawyers who have not worked on a large case, the idea of "system design" may imply merely an exercise in computer programming. It is true that system design in a large case may well require the lawyer to become familiar with computers. When a data base will be managed using a computer, someone on the litigation team inevitably must learn about bytes, disk packs, inverted files and the like. However, over the years computers have come to be designed so that they may be used quite easily by lay people. Less technical knowledge is required than in the past. The mechanical issues once debated at length are no longer of great moment. You will find that with some background reading you can become knowledgeable enough to make sound judgments.

In the past there has been substantial debate over whether documents should be coded or entered in full text, whether the data should be available "on line" or in "batches," and whether computers are necessary at all. In my opinion we have moved beyond this debate. The fourth generation of computer systems now on the market is as flexible as any user could demand. One no longer picks between opposing systems with distinct features; one is able to select from a variety of vendors who offer a full array of alternatives. The issue today is not whether to use coded or full-text entries but when, within one system, to use coded entries and when to use full-text entries. The flexibility that the new generation of litigation support software offers makes it possible now to focus on the interesting problem of designing the system of document management within a full range of options.

No one technique will meet all the needs in a case. In a complex case, the appropriate technique should be used for each type of information that must be managed. Consider, for example, defending against a four-count complaint where only one count has any merit and the other three are likely to be dismissed early by summary judgment. The most appropriate way to handle the documents that relate to the insubstantial counts may be to gather up the files on which one can easily lay one's hands, put them all together in a box and stick them somewhere out of the way. If it ever becomes necessary to put one's hands on the documents quickly, they are all in one box. To put all these documents into a sophisticated computer system would be a dreadful waste of the client's money.

Moreover, some classes of documents may already be organized and stored in a form that permits satisfactory access. In every large case there are classes of documents in which a large number need not be cross-indexed. One needs to use these documents only because of one type of reference. Consider, for example, invoices needed in an antitrust case to describe a certain market practice. It may not be necessary to know who prepared the invoice or who bought the goods. The only question will be whether there were in fact sales at a certain time. The client probably has these invoices already filed chronologically, and one need only ask for a compilation from the appropriate period.

CROSS-INDEX FOR SOME

For certain documents, it will be necessary to develop a cross-index. This will typically be true of letters and memoranda about which the lawyer will want to know who the author and the recipients were and the subjects discussed within the text. When there are not very many of these types of documents it is possible to make photocopies and place one copy in an author file, one in a recipient file and as many as necessary in the reference subject files. However, when there are thousands of documents, this system becomes prohibitively expensive and it is better to prepare a surrogate that can be indexed.

One type of surrogate is the edge-notched card. This is a card, typically 4-by-5 inches or 8-by-10 inches, of a heavy paper that has numbered holes around its perimeter. Each document is given an identification number, which is typed on the edge-notched card, along with other useful information such as the names of the author and recipient and a short summary of the contents. A coding structure is developed that corresponds to the numbered holes that surround the card. The hole that corresponds to each relevant code is then clipped. The cards are stored so that when a long needle is passed through a deck of them, the needle lifts the deck and the cards that have been clipped at that hole fall out. In this fashion, all of the edge-notched cards that relate to a given code fall out of the deck and the relevant documents may be selected. This system has been used successfully on cases where there were thousands of documents and where something under 200 coding categories provided an adequate index.

In a complex case certainly some documents (usually letters, memoranda and depositions) will be so voluminous and will have to be so extensively indexed that a computer must be used for them. It is critical to understand, however, that many documents should not go on the computer at all but should be left in the filing system where they were found, that other documents should be copied and reorganized into new subject files, and that still other categories might be managed using the edge-notched cards.

Once trial counsel has firmly in mind the use that will be made of the information, the size of the information universe and the technique of management that should be used for each type of information, he should have a planning memorandum prepared. This memorandum summarizes all of the decisions, makes an estimate of the number of people and the time necessary to accomplish the goal, and the total cost.

The cost may come as something of a shock to the lawyer; it will certainly shock the client. The client should be involved in all the preliminary stages so that when the time comes for the lawyer to tell him the cost of the management system, it will not come as too great a surprise. One fact that has to be brought home to the client is that the computer, if used, is only a small part of the cost of the management system. Probably the most accurate description I have heard of the computer cost is that it represents no more than the equivalent of a sales tax on the rest of the system. All the other costs for screening and coding documents are going to be incurred whether one uses filing cards, edge-notched cards or a computer.

The next step is the design of the screening process for reviewing the documents. This is the stage at which the greatest cost savings can be realized. The more documents that can be diverted into a filing system or screened out as irrelevant, the greater the savings. It costs only a few cents a document to screen documents but can cost several dollars to code a document.

Every reasonable effort should be made during the screening to weed out unnecessary duplicates. In my experience, if a document is important in a large organization, it has been copied at least twenty times. If it is also confidential, it has been copied at least fifty times. If it was an "eyes only" document you can count on finding hundreds of copies! It may be important to index all the copies, to know who had one. But if this is not crucial, a filing system should be set up for often-reproduced documents. The screeners can divert all copies into this file, and once the screening is complete, a single copy can be pulled out for coding.

ORIGINAL STATE

A good argument can be made for leaving a client's files in the state in which they are found. First, one may be obliged to produce documents in the state in which they were found and if the lawyer has reorganized the files, he may have to go through the tedious process of putting them back in their original condition. Second, by setting up a separate filing system, one makes all the more clear that this is the lawyer's work, not the client's. If the lawyer wants a hard copy of the documents with which to work, he or she should make one and put it into the information management system established for the litigation.

One should go back to the information survey to determine how many of what types of documents will have to be screened and write a manual to tell persons who will do the screening what documents should be diverted into which system. Documentation is a mandatory part of every task for a management system. If a record is not made of how one went about each task, the litigation team will find itself relying on folklore about what tasks were undertaken.

A critical trade-off must be made in the screening criteria. If one chooses very simple criteria, such as, "All letters and memoranda are to be sent to be coded," one will screen many documents per hour, but since it is impossible to make fine distinctions with broad criteria, one will wind up coding a large number of documents. On the other hand, if one uses detailed screening criteria, the screening itself will move slowly but one may save money in the coding process, since fewer documents will have to be coded. If screeners select documents on the basis of document type, they can go through a thousand pages an hour. But if they are going to read documents and determine from the content how they should be classified, screeners cannot handle documents at a rate much in excess of 200 pages an hour.

Inherent in any screening process is the problem of the unanticipated or new issue. In any complex case there will be unanticipated issues. One wants to avoid having to go back and rescreen all the millions of pages to find documents relating to these issues.

There is no complete solution to this problem, but two steps can minimize the risk of having to rescreen the documents. The first is to ensure that the screening criteria are reviewed at the outset by as many people as possible on the litigation team and on the client's staff, to minimize the chance of missing an issue. The second is to have the screeners prepare an index of every file that is reviewed, listing the types of material in the file by name of key persons mentioned, dates mentioned and subject matters. Then, when a new issue arises, one can go back through this index and locate the files most likely to contain material related to it.

Yet another difficult problem is how to ensure that privileged documents are not produced inadvertently. While some courts have held that inadvertent production of documents entitles one to their return, *Connecticut Mutual Life Insurance Co. v. Shields,* 18 F.R.D. 448 (S.D.N.Y. 1955), one cannot be sure of achieving this result, *see United States v. Kelsey Hayes Wheel Co.,* 15 F.R.D. 461 (E.D. Mich. 1954). What's more, often the harm is done once the document is produced. If possible, one should obtain a stipulation and court order that provides for the return of inadvertently produced documents. However, even with such an order, one will want to take certain steps to reduce the risk of inadvertent production without running up a prohibitively expensive bill for the client.

One can minimize the risk that a privileged document will be inadvertently produced by having a lawyer or the most experienced legal assistants screen the files most likely to contain privileged documents. However, because a privileged document may turn up in the most out-of-the-way files (a circumstance unfortunately all too common), all of the legal assistants screening documents must be trained about the importance of the privilege and given some understanding of why documents are privileged.

The best procedure is to give the screeners a brief course about the privilege and a list of all the lawyers and law firms that have ever worked for the client. The screeners should be asked to bring to the attention of the lawyer supervising the screening operation any document that has one of these names on it.

The lawyer can then determine if the document is privileged. If so, or if further review is needed the lawyer can remove the document from the file, leaving a record there of its removal and attaching to the removed document a note of the file from which it was removed. Since screeners will improve over time, counsel should initially give them files that are most easily screened and least likely to contain a privileged document. As their skills increase they can move into more sensitive files.

As the screening gets under way, one must design a coding structure to permit indexing the documents. Some lawyers would like to believe that a full-text loading of documents into a computer is a panacea that obviates the need to go through both the discipline of developing a coding structure and the cost of coding documents.

In my discussions with people who work in this area, a general consensus is that, while loading the full text of the document into a computer may be appropriate for certain depositions and trial transcripts, there is no better way to handle letters, memoranda and the like, than to index them. You may add a full-text computer system to the index, if the client can afford this cost, but a full-text system cannot substitute for a coded system. (However, a full-text system for depositions is one of the more useful services a computer can provide to litigators.)

LAWYERS AS DESIGNERS

The lawyers will have to design the coding structure for indexing the documents, as only the lawyers can appreciate which documents must be coded and which facts are the relevant ones. In designing the index system the lawyers must recognize that documents do not speak in terms of legal issues. Documents do not record persons discussing the possibility of committing a violation of Section 2 of the Sherman Act. Instead, one finds a competitor writing to another, discussing the instability of prices in the marketplace and suggesting that they get together and talk about it. Therefore, the coding structure must be designed so that a non-lawyer reading the document can extract from it the information appropriate for coding.

Codes are broken down into two categories: objective codes that require merely the recognition of certain fields of information such as author, date, addressee and the like, and subjective codes that require reading and understanding the text of the document. If only objective information is being removed from the document, letters or memoranda can be coded at a rate of about sixteen pages an hour. This rate may be cut in half, however, if a substantial subjective coding structure is established.

This is another area where major cost savings may be accomplished. The vast capability of a computer to handle a large coding structure with ease can lure the litigator to establish page upon page of codes. Coding manuals six inches thick are not uncommon in a complex case. While a computer can quickly and cheaply handle all of this information, it is very time-consuming and costly to have the coders work with such a complex structure. Keeping the coding structure as simple as possible will reduce costs. But if the coding structure is too simple, too much extraneous material will be mixed in with each retrieval.

In my experience the best way to design a coding structure is for the lawyer in charge of the design project to lock his or her door, get out a stack of 3-by-5 inch cards and start writing down the names of everyone who is important in the case and all of the important issues. After completing this task, put the cards aside. Then come back a day later, review the cards, see if there are any additions to be made, and arrange the cards into a logical outline structure.

It is important to arrange the coding structure logically so that the coders will not spend a long time looking to find relevant codes. During the coding operation the greatest cost saving can be made by minimizing the "look up" time needed by the coders. Good, logical organization of the codes will help the coders memorize the codes and reduce the time searching for the appropriate code.

Once a first draft of the coding structure has been prepared, it should be circulated to everyone familiar with the case to see whether all of the subject matters are listed. Moreover, the coding structure should be checked against the complaint, answer, and all counterclaims to be sure all relevant issues have been noted and that there are coding categories for all facts needed in the litigation.

After the coding structure is in final form, the lawyer in charge of the project should spend a week coding documents himself. This task cannot be delegated to a legal assistant since only by coding the documents can the lawyer appreciate the strengths and weaknesses of the coding structure.

After the final coding structure has been prepared, the person in charge of the coding should write a dictionary explaining the relevance of each code and give examples of the type of information that should be coded under each category. As the coders use the coding structure over time, they should update and amend this dictionary. This is an area where a person skilled in library science can be of great help.

When document coding begins, the coding structure should be as complete as possible. If changes have to be made during coding, one faces the task of having to recode documents. Every effort should be made to avoid changing codes once coding has started. But if you must add or change a code, you must keep a record of the day the change was made. Then, if you enter into the computer the date the coding was done, you will know whether certain codes were in use for certain documents.

The coding structure should be arranged in various formats for the benefit of the coders. Coders generally find that an outline form, with short pithy sentences explaining each code, is the most easily understood form to learn the coding structure. But an alphabetical cross-index is also very helpful, as is the full dictionary that explains the various codes and, where two codes are closely related, differentiates between them. Counsel should constantly solicit suggestions from the screeners and coders on steps to improve the system. They are an invaluable source of information.

Consistency is the key to a successful information system. You should run tests on both the screening manual and the coding manual to determine whether the people doing the work share a common understanding of the instructions. You can give all of the screeners or coders a test group of identical documents to determine if they are screening or coding in a consistent manner. Then you can review any errors with them.

A side benefit from these tests will be obtained if you keep a log of common mistakes. Then, when you assemble the manual at the end of the project to explain how to use the system, you can include samples of common mistakes so that the users will know the most likely places to look for documents that were improperly screened or coded.

As you implement the information management system you must consider problems of security. Security has a number of aspects. First, the lawyer should be concerned about the possibility of fire or theft. If a large document depository is established, the lawyer should investigate the available fire detection equipment and ensure that every precaution is taken to prevent a fire.

Fire is one of those things people think will never happen, but does, under Murphy's Law, at the least-expected time. In one case with which I am familiar, a fire broke out in a document depository and was quickly extinguished by the fire department. The fire fighters managed to soak all the documents that were not burned. A lawyer had to spend four months in a large aircraft hangar, hanging up documents with clothespins to dry them out.

Counsel should also be concerned about the possibility of theft of documents and take steps to ensure a tight control over people who go in and out of the document depository so that no document is removed. Any person who has access to the documents should be required to sign a confidentiality agreement.

One must also be alert to the possibility that one's opponent might be able to use discovery to take advantage of one's document data base. An article by Haley Fromholz that summarizes the existing law on this subject is in *Computer Framework for Complex Litigation,* 1977 WASH. U.L.Q., No. 3, p. 445. To date, few cases have addressed the issue of the discoverability of a data base. However, a lawyer can take steps to maximize the chances of preventing one's opponent from reaping the fruits of all the labor of putting together the management information system.

First, you should do everything possible to keep the data base and its operation under a lawyer's control and out of the client's control. This will forestall an argument that it is the client's data base. Second, every effort should be made to protect confidentiality of the data base and to make a good record of these attempts. This will provide substance to support an affidavit setting forth the steps taken to ensure confidentiality. Third, one should make a record of the fact that the lawyers, not the client, designed the data base, and that it was designed for use on the litigation.

Choose very carefully the people hired to work on the information system. Make every effort to determine if they will keep the confidences entrusted to them. I know of one large multidistrict antitrust case where a legal assistant quit in the middle of the case and held a press conference to denounce her employers. Obviously, this is something to avoid.

One also wants to avoid the problems of attrition that seems so often to occur when people are called upon to do the very routine tasks of screening and coding documents. I know of several large document cases where attrition rates of 30 percent or more every six months were routine. I know of other cases where this has been avoided through a combination of good pay, good management, reasonable working conditions, continuing contact with the lawyers, and a considerable effort on the part of the lawyers to keep morale high among the people working on the case. A businessman I know who was in charge of a multi-billion dollar antitrust case often said that the most cost-effective persons on the project were the legal assistants. They must be treated well to keep their skills on the project. The longer they work, the more they will know and the more valuable they will be. This should be reflected in their paychecks.

In my experience the people who make the best screeners and coders are those who have a long-term commitment to the project. Either they are offered the opportunity of continuing employment with the law firm after the case is over, or if the case is of sufficient duration, they can see the possibilities for long-term employment within that case itself.

A key person for the project should be the archive librarian. A librarian and supporting staff should work full time on the litigation so that they may assist counsel in finding information. You will want all of your search requests to be indexed to avoid frequently duplicated searches. Only persons who maintain a day-to-day relationship to the data base will be able to tell the trial counsel the confidence level that can be attributed to the search requests.

Training for the screeners and coders is obviously critical. In the BART litigation a one-week training course was given to the screeners and coders. Portions of it were videotaped so that people being trained outside the Bay Area could familiarize themselves with the technical and factual issues. Additionally, a weekly continuing education course for the legal assistants was presented by a lawyer and an engineer, who would go over in depth some part of the case or some technical area the assistants might have been having some problem with.

Quality control is critical during the screening and coding of documents to ensure that like documents are being handled in like fashion. In the initial stages of screening one should review every evening the work done by every screener and provide immediate feedback about mistakes to the screeners the next morning. One should also keep a record on the quality of every screener's work.

After a week or so of screening it may be possible to spot-check the screeners' work to ensure that they maintain the standards set during the first week of screening. For the coders it will probably be necessary to check-code every document that is coded to catch clerical errors made in the coding. The check-coders should keep a record of errors made by the coders so that a process similar to that for the screeners can be maintained. (It is a good idea to capture the coders' initials as part of the information entered into the computer. Then, if you find a coder doing a consistently poor job, you can retrieve all the documents handled by the coder and review his or her work.)

When the initial management plan for the litigation support project was established, cost estimates were given to the client. On a large document project, it is possible to run up costs extremely quickly. Unless good control is kept over the costs week-to-week and these are compared with the planned costs, one will find that one overshoots the budget quickly and will be in the difficult position of explaining to the client why the system is going to cost twice the budget.

To create successfully an information management system the trial lawyer himself must oversee the project and make sure that the material that will be needed at the time of trial—and not extraneous material—is entered into the system. The key to good quality control is planning, plus sensitive monitoring of every step so that problems are identified and corrected before they weaken the system.

26

Bibliography on the Uses of Computers in the Management of Trial Evidence

Robert P. Bigelow

Freed, Roy N., "Machine Data Processing Systems for the Trial Lawyer" in 6 *Practical Lawyer* (April 1960) p. 73.

Cohen, Sheldon S., "Current Developments in the Chief Counsel's Office," 42 *Taxes* (October 1964) p. 663.

Lyons, John, "Automation and the Administrative Process," 64 *M.U.L.L.* (March 1964) p. 37.

Lyons, John, "Uses of Computers in Large Trials," in *Quo Vadimus*, 58 *Law Library Journal* (November 1965) pp. 408, 419.

Freed, Roy N., "Improved Information Processing in the Conduct of Large Trials" in Bigelow, Robert P., *Computers and the Law* (1966) pp. 72-75.

Freed, Roy N., "Records Managers and Computer Records" in *Records Management Journal* (September 1966) p. 2.

Bigelow, Robert P., "Computer Aids for the Law Office" in *Partnership Problems and New Developments in Law Office Equipment* (1967) pp. 207, 210.

"Law Case Speeded by Simple Program," *Computerworld* (January 17, 1968) p. 4.

"Documentary Evidence for Court Case Organized by Computer at Information Engineering," 17 *Computers and Automation* (February 1968) p. 42.

Fensterwald, Bernard, "Report of the National Committee to Investigate Assassination" in 20 *Computers and Automation* (February 1971) p. 48.

Shuman, L. K. and Bagley, P. R., "Electronic Data Processing as an Aid to Trial Lawyers" in *Computers and the Law,* pp. 66-74: reprinted in 3 *Computer Law Service,* 2nd ed., 1969, Section 5-4.3, Article 2.

Berul, L., "Computerized Litigation Research," 3 *Computer Law Service,* Section 5-4.3, Article 1, Callaghan and Company, Chicago, Illinois (1972).

Bigelow, Robert P., "The Use of Computers in the Law," 24 *Hastings Law Journal* pp. 707, 724.

Walsh, "Computer for Watergate Probe," 180 *Science* (June 15, 1973) p. 1153.

Index